THE FAMILY

Other Books by Jack O. Balswick and Judith K. Balswick

A Model for Marriage: Covenant, Grace, Empowering, and Intimacy

Relationship Empowerment Parenting: Building Formative and Fulfilling Relationships with Your Children

Authentic Human Sexuality: An Integrated Christian Approach

The Dual-Earner Marriage: The Elaborate Balancing Act

Families in Pain: Working through the Hurts

The Gift of Gender (with Allen Corben and Margery Corben)

Raging Hormones: What to Do When You Suspect Your Teen Might Be Sexually Active

Other Books by Jack O. Balswick

The Reciprocating Self: Human Development in Theological Perspective (with Pam Ebstyne King and Kevin S. Reimer)

The Inexpressive Male

Life in a Glass House: The Minister's Family in Its Unique Social Context (with Cameron Lee)

Men at the Crossroads: Beyond Traditional Roles and Modern Options

Social Problems: A Christian Understanding and Response (with Kenneth Morland)

Other Books by Judith K. Balswick

Life Ties: Cultivating Relationships That Make Life Worth Living (with Boni Piper)

Mothers and Daughters Making Peace: The Most Intimate, Tangled, Beautiful, and Frustrating Relationship Shared by Women

Then They Leave Home: Parenting after the Kids Grow Up (with Boni Piper)

THE FAMILY

A CHRISTIAN PERSPECTIVE
ON THE CONTEMPORARY HOME

3RD EDITION

Jack O. Balswick
and Judith K. Balswick

Baker Academic
Grand Rapids, Michigan

Published by Baker Academic
a division of Baker Publishing Group
P.O. Box 6287, Grand Rapids, MI 49516-6287
www.bakeracademic.com

Printed in the United States of America

Library of Congress Cataloging-in-Publication Data
Balswick, Jack O.
    The family : a Christian perspective on the contemporary home / Jack O.
Balswick and Judith K. Balswick. — 3rd ed.
        p.   cm.
    Includes bibliographical references and index.
    ISBN 10: 0-8010-3249-0 (pbk.)
    ISBN 978-0-8010-3249-3 (pbk.)
    1. Family—Religious life. 2. Marriage—Religious aspects—Christianity.
    3. Parenting—Religious aspects—Christianity. I. Balswick, Judith K. II. Title.
    lBV4526.2.B357 2007
    261.8'3585—dc22   2007000200

A copy of *Strengthening Your Family Life*, the study guide to this book, can be obtained by sending a check for $5.00 to:

Jack Balswick
Fuller Theological Seminary
182 Oakland Avenue
Pasadena, CA 91182

    11   12   13   14   15   16   9   8   7   6   5

With Our Love and Appreciation to Our Parents,
Agnes and Arvid Nelson
Frances and Orville Balswick

CONTENTS

ILLUSTRATIONS

Figures

Tables

PREFACE

WE INITIALLY WROTE *The Family: A Christian Perspective on the Contemporary Home* to present an integrated view of contemporary family life based on current social-science research, clinical insights, and biblical truth. The biblical integration reflects broad theological truths woven throughout the Scriptures rather than specific proof texts. We chose to present the social-scientific knowledge in an easy-to-read style rather than one that was academic but more cumbersome. The positive response to the previous two editions of our book has warranted this updated third edition. Building on the previous material, this new edition incorporates the most current research to date and includes two new chapters: "Family Spirituality" and "Complex Families in Contemporary Society." We also include a new focus on trinitarian theology of relationship to enhance the biblical themes in the earlier editions of covenant, grace, empowerment, and intimacy. This is the essence of our integrated model of family relationships.

Our book is divided into seven parts. In part 1, "Theological and Social Perspectives on Family Life," we put forward a basic theology of relationships and theoretical perspectives on the family as a developing system. Part 2, "Marriage: The Foundation of Family Life," is devoted to the topics of mate selection and the establishment of a strong Christian marriage. In part 3, "The Expansion of Family Life: Parenting and Beyond," we focus on the development and rearing of young children, the particular challenges of midlife parents and their adolescent children, and the joys and challenges of the later-life family. In part 4, "Gender and Sexuality: Identity in Family Life," we consider the changing definitions of masculinity and femininity and the implications they have on family relationships, and discuss the complex dimensions of becoming an authentic sexual self as part of God's design and intention. Part 5, "Communication: The Heart of Family Life," describes the expression of love and intimacy as well as the expression of anger and normal conflicts that inevitably occur between family members. In part 6, "The Social Dynamics of Family Life," we attend to the critical aspects of family life such as power, life stressors, divorce, single parenthood, remarriage, and building new family forms. Part 7, "Family Life in Postmodern Society," deals with the effects that modern industrialized society and postmodern thinking have had on family life. Suggestions are made for changing social structures to create a more family-friendly environment.

Rather than taking a piecemeal approach, devoting each chapter to a specific topic, we have attempted to make every chapter an integral part of the overarching theme of the book. Therefore, we have aspired to weave into the content of each chapter our theological basis for family relationships from the perspective of the family as a developing system.

Coauthorship and teamwork make this book a collaborative project. A marriage and family therapist for over forty years, Judy is senior professor at Fuller Theological Seminary in the Marriage and Family Therapy Department. Jack, a professional sociologist with forty years of teaching, research, and writing experience at the university and seminary level, is also a senior professor at Fuller. We have had postdoctoral seminary training in theology and biblical studies and speak throughout the United States and abroad on marriage and family life.

Although we have attempted to blend an academic, clinical, and theological understanding of the family, our interest in family life is not merely as scholars. The core of our lives has been experienced in the context of family, and our joint calling is to minister to families. We both feel most fortunate to have been reared and nurtured in loving Christian homes. Our parents modeled an unconditional love and grace that provided a secure foundation and brought a profound spiritual meaning to our lives.

Being married for over forty-five years has taught us much about what it takes to live out the principles we propose in this book. Our adult children, Jacque and Joel, have challenged and continue to challenge us to grow throughout every life stage. We have tried to maintain balance through the joys and pains, ups and downs, ebb and flow, stress and elation of family living. Thirty years ago our beloved ten-year-old son, Jeff, died of bone cancer. Working through that loss as well as remembering the delight of his life has changed us all. We spent three years living in an extended-family arrangement with Jacque, her husband, and our two- and three-year-old grandsons, Curtis and Jacob, who are now in college. We are now grandparents of four grandsons in our daughter's reconstituted marriage to Dana, which also includes their two young sons, Taylor and Liam, ages seven and six. Our son Joel is married to Uyen Mai, a Chinese Vietnamese woman, which has enriched our multicultural perspective. In addition they have gifted us with our first granddaughter, Elizabeth Binh. We've been through the agonizing illness and deaths of all four parents and had the privilege and challenge of having Judy's aging mother live with us for nine months prior to her death at age ninety-two.

All in all, we have learned a lot and continue to learn as we encounter the blessings and struggles of each unique stage of family life. Having preached on the fragility of the isolated nuclear family, we are constantly reminded of our need for God as our strength as well as for those who have walked alongside us on the journey. Our couples group, Judy's small women's support group, our dear friends, and community of faith add a wealth of wisdom and perspective. Jeff Wittung and his staff at Baker Academic, through their attention to detail and helpful suggestions, have greatly improved this third edition. We trust that what we have learned will benefit our readers.

PART 1

Theological and Social Perspectives on Family Life

W E BEGIN OUR book with biblical, theological, and sociological perspectives on family life. In chapter 1 we present a theology of family relationships based on what the Bible says about relationality through the Holy Trinity: God as parent in relationship to the children of Israel, Christ as groom in relationship to the church as bride, and the Holy Spirit in relationship to all believers who are empowered to live in rightful relationships with others. The emergent theology of family relationships highlights the elements of covenant, grace, empowering, and intimacy as family members strive to maintain their unique individuality within family unity.

In chapter 2 we introduce two sociological perspectives. The systemic perspective, which views the family as a unit of interrelated parts, concentrates on the relationships between family members. The developmental perspective focuses on the various stages of individual and family life. By integrating these two sociological perspectives we will discover some of the basic marks of a resilient family.

1

A THEOLOGICAL FOUNDATION FOR FAMILY RELATIONSHIPS

The Use of Scripture in Developing a Theology of the Family

Hﾠow CAN WE best use Scripture to learn God's intention for family life during the new millennium? A common approach is to pick out the key verses from the various scriptural passages dealing with the family. These verses are then arranged as one would arrange a variety of flowers to form a pleasing bouquet. However, such a use of Scripture presents problems when Christians come up with different bouquets of verses and then disagree as to what the Bible says about family life. This method of selecting certain verses about the family can be compared to strip mining. Ignoring the historical and cultural context, the strip miner tears into the veins of Scripture, throws the unwanted elements aside, and emerges with selected golden nuggets of truth. Too often, searching for God's truth about the family ends up with a truth that conforms to the preconceived ideas of the miner doing the stripping.

Prominent among the golden nuggets that are typically mined are New Testament regulations regarding family and household relationships (e.g., Eph. 5:22–6:9; Col. 3:18–4:1; 1 Tim. 2:8–15; 6:1–2; Titus 2:1–10; and 1 Pet. 2:18–3:7). These passages indicate early Christianity's concern for order in three basic household relationships: between husband and wife, between parent and child, and between master and slave. New Testament scholar

James Dunn (1996), however, emphasizes the importance of considering the total context of scriptural passages about family life. Dunn notes the problem when scriptural texts are read without considering the social, historical, and cultural context of the time of writing. Although the motive of discovering hard-and-fast rules for household life is understandable, a "problem arises here when we try to make the household codes into timeless rules which can be simply transposed across time to the present day without addition or subtraction" (p. 62). Doing so means that we accept slaves as part of God's intention for family households. Dunn concludes that such an approach is an abuse of Scripture.

In contrast to this approach, we believe it is important to consider relevant biblical references and a theology that offer deeper meaning and concrete principles of living in our complex, postmodern world. Stephen Post (1994) speaks of an "analogical-familial theology." This is the approach we have taken. By way of analogy we base our theology of family relationships on *relationality within the Holy Trinity* and throughout the Old and New Testament descriptions of *God in relationship*.

Trinitarian Relationality

The process whereby a man and a woman marry and become one yet maintain their individual distinctiveness is a major aspect of marriage. Likewise, the process of children developing into their own unique selves within the context of family unity is an ongoing part of family life. Family scientists and practitioners refer to this as *differentiation*—the process of maintaining a separate identity while simultaneously remaining connected in relationship, belonging, and unity. Interdependency is another way to describe this universal experience that all family members learn to navigate throughout the various stages of life.

We believe human beings are created by a relational Triune God to be in significant and fulfilling relationships. The good news is that Scripture presents a model in the Trinity—God being one, yet composed of three distinct persons. Stanley Grenz (2001, 48) puts it this way: "The same principle of mutuality that forms the genius for the human social dynamic is present in a prior way in the divine being." Building on this truth, our starting point in developing a theology of family relationships is to recognize that, by way of analogy, relationships between family members are to reflect the relationality within the Holy Trinity.

Relationality is the primary way human beings reflect God's image. Genesis 1:26–27 states, "Then God said, 'Let *us* make humankind in our image, according to our likeness . . . So God created humankind in his image, in the image of God he created them; male and female he created them." The *us* connotes the Triune Godhead (Father, Son, and Holy Spirit), who in unity created humankind in the image of God (*imago Dei*). Throughout the Bible, *unity* and *uniqueness* are simultaneously described as the relational aspects of the Godhead.

Gary Deddo (1999) has built a strong case for applying trinitarian theology to family relationships. Drawing on Karl Barth, Deddo states that "the nature of the covenantal relationship between God and humanity revealed and actualized in Jesus Christ . . . [is] grounded in the Trinitarian relations of Father, Son, and Spirit" (p. 2). As distinction and unity coexist in the Godhead, so is it to exist among family members. Deddo states, "In the revelation by the Son of the Father through the Spirit we come to recognize the activity of the one God apportioned to each person of the Trinity. The Father is the Creator, the Lord of life; the Son is the Reconciler, the renewer of life; the Spirit is the Redeemer, the giver, the conveyor of this life which is given, sustained and renewed" (p. 36). Family relationships are analogous in human form to this divine model. As the three distinct persons—Father, Son, and Holy Spirit—mutually indwell in a trinitarian fellowship, so are family members to mutually indwell in similar ways.

Miroslav Volf expands on this concept by examining the use of the New Testament Greek word *perichoresis*, which "connotes mutual interpenetration without any coalescence or commixture" (1998, 208–13). For example, in John 10:38 we read, "so that you may know and understand that the Father is in me and I am in the Father." While distinct, they mutually indwell in complete unity in the Godhead.

The trinitarian model reflects the nature of relationality (distinction and unity) and becomes a core ideal and a central theme of understanding family relationships. However, we acknowledge that, unlike God, we are not perfect, and therefore in applying these principles, we will have to struggle with our human imperfections. We must look to God for grace and strength to attain personal distinction in relationships. The relational process, be it the initial forming of the marital relationship, nurturing and guiding in the child-rearing years, building new family structures, or dealing with the end of life, involves the fundamental issues of forming unity while embracing each person's distinctiveness. We use the biblical analogy in terms of how the members of the Godhead act in unity through distinctiveness through the themes of covenant, grace, empowerment, and intimacy.

God in Relationship

Examples of familial descriptive language used in the Old and the New Testaments are the relationship between the Creator God and the created ones; God as parent relating to the children of Israel; Christ as groom in relation to the church as bride; and the Holy Spirit, who indwells and empowers believers as brothers and sisters in the Lord. God's actions toward Israel are characterized by compassionate loving, disciplining, guiding, pursuing, giving, nurturing, respecting, knowing, and forgiving. Jesus welcomes little children, women, the disenfranchised, and his disciples into close, intimate connection. The Spirit prays in and through us when we cannot find the words to speak.

The establishment of a covenant between God and the nation of Israel has become the foundational focus in developing a theology of the family. Ray Anderson (1982) uses the concept of co-humanity to build a theological anthropology. Beginning with the theological truth that "humanity is determined as existence in covenant relation with God" (p. 37), Anderson applies the concept of covenant to all human relationships. He considers covenantal relationships in the family as a "secondary order, made possible by the primary order of differentiation as male or female" (p. 52). Differentiation achieves the godly purpose of interdependence and cooperative interaction between people.

In applying covenant as a paradigm for the family, Anderson and D. Guernsey (1985) highlight the unconditional quality of covenant: "It is covenant love that provides the basis for family. For this reason, family means much more than consanguinity, where blood ties provide the only basis for belonging. Family is where you are loved unconditionally, and where you can count on that love even when you least deserve it" (p. 40).

Similarly, Stuart McLean (1984) suggests the following ways that covenant can be used as a metaphor for marriage and family relationships: (1) people are social and live in community; (2) the basic unit of family and of covenant is the dyad; (3) people living in community experience struggle and conflict as well as harmony; (4) people living in covenant must be willing to forgive and be forgiven by one another; (5) people living in covenant must accept their bondedness to one another; (6) people living in covenant accept law in the form of patterns and order in relationships; and (7) people living in covenant have a temporal awareness as they carry a memory of the past, live in the present, and anticipate the future (pp. 4–32).

Elements in a Theology of Family Relationships

We build on the concept of covenant and propose a theology of family relationships that involves four sequential but nonlinear stages: covenant, grace, empowering, and intimacy. We further suggest that family relation-

Figure 1 **A Theological Basis of Family Relationships**

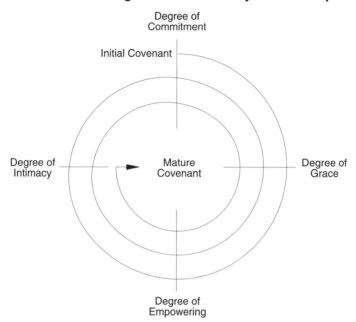

ships will be either dynamic and maturing or stagnant and dying. A model of this process of family relationships is presented in figure 1. The logical beginning point of any family relationship is a covenant commitment, which has unconditional love at its core. Out of the security provided by this covenant love, grace develops. In this atmosphere of grace, family members have the freedom to empower one another. Empowerment leads to the possibility of intimacy among family members. Intimacy then leads back to a deeper level of covenant commitment.

The sequential change in figure 1 is depicted by an inward spiral representing the potential for family relationships to grow into ever-deepening levels of mutual commitment, grace, empowering, and intimacy. For example, the relationship between a parent and an infant child begins as a unilateral (one-way) love commitment, but as the parent lives out that commitment, the relationship grows into a bilateral (mutual) love commitment.

For such growth to take place in any relationship, there must be mutual involvement. Growth in family relationships can be blocked or retarded when one person in the relationship is unable or unwilling to reciprocate covenant love, grace, empowering, or intimacy. Thus, growth in a relationship can come to a standstill at any point in this cycle.

Because relationships are dynamic and ever changing, if a relationship does not spiral to deeper levels of commitment, grace, empowering, and intimacy, it will stagnate and fixate on contract rather than covenant, law rather than grace, possessive power rather than empowering, and distance rather than intimacy.

This model is not exclusive to family dynamics but extends to nonfamilial relationships as well. The bonding in familial relationships expands a family member's capacity to be involved in meaningful relationships outside the immediate- and the extended-family system.

The four elements of growth relationships are considered as separate sequential stages for analytic purposes only. In practice, covenant, grace, empowering, and intimacy often overlap in family and community life. Thus, it is futile to press the suggested logical sequence into a strict linear model. However, considering each separate dimension in depth provides a better understanding of how these four principles interact in human relationships.

These relationship principles are derived from an examination of biblical writings that show how God enters into and sustains relationships with humanity. The Bible teaches that God desires to be in relationship with humankind and also longs for humans to be in relationship with the Godhead and others. We recognize, however, that although we are created in the image of God, we are fallen creatures who will fail in all aspects of relationship with God and others. In a sense, no person can ever make a covenant commitment in the way that God covenants with us, nor can anyone foster an atmosphere of grace in the same way God gives grace. Our empowering attempts often resemble possessive power, and our attempts at intimacy pale into insignificance when compared to God's knowing and caring. Yet we are hopeful, because God has been revealed perfectly in Jesus Christ. He is our model and enabler as we live out our lives and relationships according to God's purpose.

Covenant: To Love and Be Loved

The central point of covenant is that it is an unconditional commitment, demonstrated supremely by God to the creation. Although the concept of covenant has a rich heritage in Christian theology, the biblical meaning has been eroded by the modern notion that commitment is no more than a contract. The first biblical mention of a covenant is found in Genesis 6:18, where God says to Noah, "But I will establish my covenant with you; and you shall come into the ark." God tells Noah to take his wife and sons and daughters-in-law, along with all living creatures, and Noah does everything that God has commanded. In Genesis 9:9–10,

God repeats this promise of covenant: "As for me, I am establishing my covenant with you and with your descendants after you, and with every living creature that is with you." The covenant was even extended to nonhuman creatures. Next, God makes a covenant with Abram: "I am God Almighty; walk before me, and be blameless. And I will make my covenant between me and you, and will make you exceedingly numerous" (Gen. 17:1–2). Upon hearing this, Abram threw himself down on his face. God continues in verse 7, "I will establish my covenant between me and you, and your offspring after you throughout their generations, for an everlasting covenant, to be God to you and to your offspring after you." Then in verse 9, Abram's role in the covenant is specified: "God said to Abraham, 'As for you, you shall keep my covenant, you and your offspring after you throughout their generations.'"

What can we learn from these two accounts of God's establishing a covenant with Noah and Abraham? First, we see that God is not offering either of them any choice in the matter. That is, God is by no means saying, "Now I am going to commit myself to you if this is your desire." Instead, the establishment of the covenant was based entirely on God's action. Second, God's offer is in no way contractual; that is, it is not based on Noah or Abram keeping their end of the bargain. God's commitment stands sure, no matter what their response. However, God desires and even commands a response. Does this make God's covenantal offer conditional? Is God free to retract the offer if it is not reciprocated? The answer is a resounding no! The covenant God offers is steadfast and true, "an everlasting covenant," regardless of the response to it. Third, although the covenant itself is not conditional, the benefits or blessings are determined by the response. Both Noah and Abraham are given a choice to respond. If they are to benefit from the covenant, they need to make a freely determined response of obedience. Although the continuation of God's love is not conditioned on their response, the blessings of the covenant are conditional. Now that they receive and respond to God's covenant, they also receive the fulfillment of the promise. Fourth, we notice that God extends the covenant to their families from generation to generation. Neither Noah nor Abram can anticipate obedience on the part of their descendants, further evidence of the unconditional nature of the covenant. In the same way, the blessings of the covenant are conditional, depending on whether the descendants decide to respond to and follow God.

Indeed, the Old Testament account in the book of Hosea conveys the central theme of the covenant relationship between God and the children of Israel. The cycle is as follows: The children of Israel turn away from God and get into all kinds of difficulty. God pursues them with a love that will not let them go, offering reconciliation and restitution when they respond. Then comes the incredible blessing of being in relationship with the Almighty God, who mothers like a hen and leads with cords of human kindness. The children of Israel reap the satisfaction of basking in the intimate presence and profound connection with their loving God.

The life of Jesus is the supreme expression of unconditional love. It is noteworthy that Jesus tells the story of the prodigal son (Luke 15) in response to the Pharisees' and scribes' criticism of his sitting with sinners. Just as the father in the story welcomes his wayward son home with open arms, Jesus demonstrates unconditional love to a people who have rejected his Father. The unconditional nature of God's love is perhaps most clearly expressed in 1 John 4:19, "We love because he first loved us," and 1 John 4:10–13, "In this is love, not that we loved God but that he loved us and sent his Son to be the atoning sacrifice for our sins. Beloved, since God loved us so much, we also ought to love one another. No one has ever seen God; if we love one another, God lives in us, and his love is perfected in us. By this we know that we abide in him and he in us, because he has given us of his Spirit." Here is the promise of the mutual indwelling of God's unconditional love in us as we dwell in God's love through the sacrifice of Christ and the presence of the Spirit. And as we have received that unconditional love represented in the unity of the Godhead, we offer that unconditional love to others.

Having discussed the unconditional quality of God's covenant commitments, we now turn to a related consideration—the issue of reciprocity. Whereas the unconditional nature of covenant love is unquestionable, in a familial context the concept of covenant can be used to refer to both unilateral and bilateral relationships. Figure 2 depicts the different types of commitment found in family relationships.

Any covenantal relationship is based on an unconditional commitment. However, covenantal relationships can be either unilateral (one-way) or bilateral (two-way). We have labeled a unilateral unconditional relationship an initial covenant and a bilateral unconditional relationship a mature covenant. All biblical references to the covenant God initiates are examples of initial covenants. It would be erroneous to think of an unconditional unilateral relationship as partial, dependent, or even immature, because from the individual's perspective a personal covenant without restrictions is given. From a relational perspective, unilateral unconditional commitment entails the attractive possibility of someday becoming a two-way street. The desire of God in each initiated covenant is that the unconditional commitment will eventually be reciprocal and mutual.

When a child is born, the parents make an unconditional commitment of love to that child. The infant or young child is unable to make such a

Figure 2 **Types of Commitment in Family Relationships**

	Conditional	Unconditional
Unilateral	Modern Open Arrangement	Initial Covenant
Bilateral	Contract	Mature Covenant

commitment in return. However, as the child matures, the relationship that began as an initial (unilateral) covenant can develop into a mature (bilateral) relationship. True reciprocity occurs when parents themselves age and become socially, emotionally, and physically more dependent on their adult child. Here, in a mature bilateral commitment, reciprocal and unconditional love is especially rewarding.

Our ideal for marital and mature parent/child relationships is an unconditional bilateral commitment. As shown in figure 2, there are two types of conditional family relationships. An emerging type, which we call the modern open arrangement, is symptomatic of a society in which people are hesitant to make commitments. A typical example is a person who begins a marriage with the unspoken understanding that as long as his or her needs are being met, all is well, but as soon as those needs are no longer met, the relationship will end. When both spouses adopt this conditional stance, the marriage amounts to a contract, a quid-pro-quo arrangement. The couple believes they have fulfilled the marital contract when they get about as much as they give in the relationship.

In reality, much of the daily routine in family life is carried out according to informal contractual agreements. When we advocate relationships based on covenant, we must recognize the importance of mutuality, fairness, and reciprocal processes that lead to interdependence. Yet there are extraordinary dimensions of loving unconditionally, such as sacrificing one's self for the other and going the second mile even when things aren't equal. It is a matter of being willing to be *unselfish* rather than thinking only of self (*selfish*) or only of others (*selfless*), as Stephen Post (1994) defines the terms. Any mature relationship based on contract alone will forgo the incredible acts of love that far exceed any contract made by two individuals.

Grace: To Forgive and Be Forgiven

We indicated previously that we have separated the four elements of our theology of family relationships for analytical purposes only. It is especially difficult to distinguish between covenant and grace. By its very nature, covenant is grace. From a human perspective the unconditional love of God makes no sense except as it is offered in grace. Grace is truly a relational word. One is called to share in a gracious relationship with God. Grace means unmerited favor.

John Rogerson (1996) applies to family life the understanding of grace as a natural extension of covenant love. He cites Old Testament texts suggesting that God desires the establishment of structures of grace to strengthen family life. These structures of grace are defined as "social arrangement[s] designed to mitigate hardship and misfortune, and grounded in God's mercy." The following example is from Exodus 22:25–27: "If you lend money to my people, to the poor among you, you shall not deal with them as a creditor; you shall not exact interest from them. If you take your neighbor's cloak in pawn, you shall restore it before the sun goes down; for it may be your neighbor's only clothing to use as cover; in what else shall that person sleep? And if your neighbor cries out to me, I will listen, for I am compassionate." From his analysis of Old Testament teachings about the family, Rogerson concludes, "What is really important is that theologically-driven efforts were made to counteract the forces that undermined the family" (p. 41).

Family relationships, as designed by God, are meant to be lived out in an atmosphere of grace, not law. Family life based on contract leads to an atmosphere of law and is a discredit to Christianity. On the contrary, family life based on covenant leads to an atmosphere of grace and forgiveness. There must be a willingness to forgive if right relationships are going to develop in family life, according to Borrowdale (1996). Just as the meaning and joy of being a Christian would be deadened if we conceived of our relationship with God in terms of law and not grace, so would meaning and joy be constrained in family relationships. On both the individual and the family level, law leads to legalism, whereas grace offers freedom. In an atmosphere of grace, family members learn to act responsibly out of love and consideration for one another.

The incarnation is the supreme act of God's grace to humankind. Christ came in human form to reconcile the world to God. This act of divine love and forgiveness is the basis for human love and forgiveness. We can forgive others as we have been forgiven, and the love of God within makes it possible for us to love others in the same unconditional way.

One may ask if there is any place for law in family relationships. Are we to believe that when grace is present in the family there is no need for law at all? Our answer must be the same as that given by the apostle Paul, who writes, "For Christ is the end of the law so that there may be righteousness for everyone who believes" (Rom. 10:4). It is not that the law itself is bad, for it points the way to God. But because humans are limited and fallen, we can never fulfill the law. Christ is the end of the law because he is the perfect fulfillment of the law. We are righteous by faith alone! No one can keep the law perfectly. We are free from the law because of Christ's perfection and righteousness, which leads to our salvation.

The same can be said concerning family relationships. Through Scripture we can know something of God's ideal for family relationships, but none of us can expect to measure up perfectly to that ideal. In a family based on law, the members demand perfection of one another. Rules and regulations are rigidly set to govern relationships. This kind of pressure for flawlessness adds guilt to the failure that is inevitable in such a situation.

Although the covenant of grace rules out law as a basis for family relationships, family members living in grace accept structure, forms, patterns, order, and responsibility in relationships. In reality, much of the daily routine of family life must be performed according to agreed-upon rules, regularity, and order. The application of the concept of grace in family relationships is a challenge when we are working out family structures, roles, and rules. Grace means that order and regularity are present so that family members' needs are met and their lives enhanced, not as a means of repressing their needs and limiting their lives.

Empowerment: To Serve and Be Served

The most common and conventional definition of power is the ability to influence another person. In such a definition, the emphasis is placed on one's ability to influence and not the actual exercising of the authority. Most research on the use of power in the family has focused on a person's attempt to influence or control the behavior of another (Szinovacz 1987). An underlying assumption in such analyses is that people using power try to decrease rather than increase the power of those they are trying to influence. They tend to use power in a way that assures the maintenance of their own more powerful position.

Empowerment is a biblical model for the use of power that is completely contrary to its common use in the family or in society at large. Empowerment can be defined as the attempt to establish power in another person. Empowerment does not necessarily involve yielding to the wishes of another person or ceding one's own power to someone else. Rather, empowerment is the active, intentional process of helping another person to become empowered. The person who is empowered has been equipped, strengthened, built up, matured, and has gained skill because of the encouraging support of the other.

In a nutshell, empowerment is the process of helping another person recognize his or her potential and then reach that potential through one's encouragement and/or guidance. It involves coming alongside a person to affirm her gifts and building her confidence to become all that she can be. In other words, it is helping a person achieve his or her full potential. Sometimes the empowerer must be willing to step back and allow the one being empowered to learn through experience and not by being overly dependent. An empowerer respects the uniqueness of each person and equips that person according to his or her individual ways of learning. Empowerment never involves control, coercion, or force. Rather, it is a respectful, reciprocal process that takes place between people in mutually enhancing ways.

If covenant is the love commitment and grace is the underlying atmosphere of acceptance, then empowerment is the action of God in people's lives. We see it supremely in the work of Jesus Christ. The celebrated message of Jesus is that he has come to empower—"I came that they may have life, and have it abundantly" (John 10:10b). The apostle John puts it this way: "But to all who received him, who believed in his name, he gave power to become children of God, who were born, not of blood or of the will of the flesh or of the will of man, but of God" (John 1:12–13). Ray Anderson (1985b) insightfully exegetes this text by noting that power "of blood" is power in the natural order, and "the will of the flesh" refers to tradition, duty, honor, obedience, and everything that is part of conventional power. In this passage, then, it is clear that the power is given by God and not by either physical or conventional means.

The power given by Jesus is power of a personal order—power that is mediated to the powerless. To us in our sinful and powerless condition God gives the ability to become children of God. This is the supreme example of human empowerment. Jesus redefined power by his teaching and by his relating to others as a servant. Jesus rejected the use of power to control others and instead affirmed the use of power to serve others, to lift up the fallen, to forgive the guilty, to encourage responsibility and maturity in the weak, and to enable the unable. His empowerment was directed to those who occupied a marginal status.

In a very real sense, empowerment is love in action. It is the mark of Jesus Christ that family members need to emulate most. The practice of empowerment in families will revolutionize the view of authority in Christian homes. Sadly, authority in marriage continues to be a controversial issue today largely because of a widely accepted secular view that power is a commodity in limited supply; therefore, a person must grab as much power as possible in relationships. Whether through coercion or manipulation, striving for power leads to antagonizing competition rather than to the cooperative building up of people. Power becomes a distortion that distances, in contrast to mutual empowerment, which leads to unity.

But the good news for Christians is that the power of God is available to all persons in *unlimited supply*! Ephesians 4 reminds us that unique spiritual gifts are given to everyone for the building up of the body of Christ, "until all of us come to the unity of the faith and of the knowledge of the Son of God, to maturity, to the measure of the full stature of Christ" (v. 13). In a similar vein, Galatians 5:22–23 contrasts the works of the flesh against the fruit of the Spirit, which is freely given and defined as love, joy, peace, patience, kindness, generosity, faithfulness, gentleness, and self-control. In verses 25 and 26, we are encouraged and admonished: "If we live by the Spirit, let us also be guided by the Spirit. Let us not become conceited, competing against one another, envying one another." This is the character of God, and it is available to all family members who draw on the inexhaustible resources in Christ Jesus!

Empowerment is born out of God's covenant love and the incredible grace we find in Christ Jesus. The Spirit of God empowers us to empower others. And when mutual empowerment occurs among family members, each will be stretched in the extraordinary ways of servant love and humility. Family members will grow in the stature of Christ as they mature into the character of Christ in their daily interactions. When they use their areas of strength to build up one another, they are placing unity and interdependency at the heart of their relationships. It has nothing to do with having power over others but rather involves taking great delight in building up one another to become all God wants us to be. This is the essence of what we read in 1 Corinthians 8:1b: "Knowledge puffs up, but loves builds up."

Traditional thinking about parent/child relationships is also based on the false assumption that power is in limited supply. Thus, parents often fear that as children grow older and gain more power, their parental power will automatically be reduced. In contrast, a relationship-empowering approach to parenting begins by reconsidering the nature of power and authority. In the biblical sense, parental authority is an ascribed power. The Greek word for authority, *exousia*, literally means "out of being." It refers to a type of influence that is not dependent on any personal strength, achievement, or skill, but that comes forth "out of the being" of a person. The Greek word for power, *dynamis*, is the word from which *dynamo* is derived. The authority of Jesus flowed from his personhood. It was dynamic.

Parents too have authority over their children that flows from their personhood as they earnestly and responsibly care for their children's physical, social, psychological, and spiritual development. The process of empowering children certainly does not mean giving up a position of authority, nor does it mean that parents will be depleted or drained of power as they parent. Rather, parents and children will both achieve a sense of personal power, self-esteem, and wholeness. Successful parenting involves building a relationship in which children gain personal power and parents retain personal power throughout the process.

Once again, human fears and personal or cultural needs may stand in the way of parental empowerment of children and adolescents. In the frailty of human insecurity, parents may be tempted to keep their offspring dependent on them. In the attempt to use their power over their children, they may inadvertently have a false sense of security in their parental position. When children obey out of fear and under coercion, it is likely to backfire. An emotional barrier develops when children are loyal out of obligation rather than by choice. The parental demand for unreasonable obedience and loyalty may be culturally motivated, but it is often related to selfish needs as well. In contrast, covenant love and empowerment leads to a mature interdependency in which there is both freedom and a continued sense of belonging for adult children. This kind of love remains faithful, honorable, and predictable even when differences threaten to endanger the relationship.

All parents have experienced the temptation to keep a child dependent, which is often rationalized as something we do for the child's own good. Many times, however, the child is kept in a dependent position for the parents' own convenience. Empowering is the ultimate goal, where parents release the child to self-control. Of course, mistakes will be made, and failure will be the occasional consequence of trying out new wings. Parents have a hard time letting their children make mistakes (especially the same mistakes they themselves made when young), so this transition to self-reliance is difficult for parents and children alike. It is important for parents to remember that the key to their authority lies not in external control but in internal control that their children can integrate into their own personhood. When this integration occurs, it is a rewarding and mutually satisfying achievement.

On the community level as well, Christians are called to live according to extraordinary social patterns. Even though we are sinners, God provides us with the ability to follow the empowering principle in our relationships. He empowers us, by the Holy Spirit, to empower others. The biblical ideal for all our relationships, then, is that we be Christian realists in regard to our own sinfulness and tendency to fail, but Christian optimists in light of the grace and power available to live according to God's intended purposes.

Intimacy: To Know and Be Known

Human beings are unique among living creatures in their ability to communicate through language, a capacity that makes it possible for them to know one another intimately. Our Christian faith is distinct from Eastern religions in its teaching that God has broken into human history to be personally related to us. A major theme that runs through the Bible is that God wants to know us and to be known by us. We are encouraged to share our deepest thoughts and feelings through prayer. We are told that the Holy Spirit dwells within us and that God understands the very groanings within that cannot be uttered (Rom. 8:26–27).

Adam and Eve stood completely open and transparent before God. Only after their disobedience did they try to hide from God out of a feeling of nakedness and shame. In their perfect creatureliness, Adam and Eve had been naked before each other and had felt no shame (Gen. 2:25). The intimacy that Adam and Eve felt enabled them to be themselves without any pretense. They had no need to play deceptive games. Shame is often born out of a fear of unworthiness or rejection. When shame is present, family members put on masks and begin to play deceptive roles before one another. By contrast, as we examine the nature of the pre-fall human family (which is the only social institution that belongs to the order of creation), we find an emphasis on intimacy—on knowing and being known. This is what it means to be a servant, to empty oneself as Jesus did when he took the form of a servant. This is how one is to be submissive and loving in relationships. It is also true that to have any union or partnership or interdependence with another person, one must always be willing to give up some of one's own needs and desires. When family members come to one another with this kind of attitude and perspective, they will find a common ground of joy, satisfaction, and mutual benefit.

When family members experience covenant love, grace, and empowering, they will be able to communicate confidently and express themselves freely without fear. Family members will want what is best for one another. They will make a concerted effort to listen, understand, accept differences, value, and confirm uniqueness.

The capacity for family members to communicate feelings freely and openly with one another is contingent upon trust and commitment. They are not afraid to share and be intimate with one another. John gives us insight into this: "God is love" (1 John 4:16); "There is no fear in love,

COVENANT LOVE MEANS ACCEPTING THE DIFFERENCES
AND UNIQUENESS OF EACH FAMILY MEMBER.

but perfect love casts out fear" (v. 18). God expresses perfect love, and we can respond in love because God loved us first (1 John 4:19).

This brings us back to the unconditional covenant love that is the cornerstone for family communication and honest sharing without the threat of rejection. As family members offer their love unconditionally to one another, the security that is established will lead to deeper levels of intimacy.

The unconditional love modeled by Jesus gives a picture of the type of communicative intimacy desirable in family relationships. Recall how Jesus, at the end of his earthly ministry, asked Peter not once but three times, "Do you love me?" (John 21). Peter had earlier denied Jesus three times; Jesus was giving Peter the opportunity to assert what he had previously denied and to reaffirm his love three times. Perhaps the relationship between Jesus and Peter had not been the same since Peter's triple denial. Likewise, family relationships become strained as we disappoint, fail, and even betray those whom we love the most.

Forgiving and being forgiven is an important part of renewal. There is a need to confess as well as to receive confession. This is a two-way street that can resolve the unfinished issues between family members. Being willing to admit mistakes and acknowledge being offended by another person opens intimacy between two people. One need not be ashamed to admit failure and seek reconciliation. Family members should communicate their affection toward one another. Intimacy will bring the relationships to full maturity.

Applying the Theological Model: From Hurting to Healing Behaviors

In examining biblical themes that have a bearing on the nature of family relationships, we have suggested that (1) commitment should be based on a mature (i.e., unconditional and bilateral) covenant love; (2) family life should be established and maintained within an atmosphere of grace, which embraces acceptance and forgiveness; (3) the resources of family members should be used to empower rather than to control one another; and (4) intimacy is based on a knowing that leads to caring, understanding, communication, and communion with others. These four elements of Christian family relationships are part of a continual process: intimacy can lead to deeper covenant love, commitment fortifies the atmosphere of freely offered grace, the climate of acceptance and forgiveness encourages serving and empowering others, and the resultant sense of self-esteem leads to the ability to be intimate without fear.

Table 1, which represents a summary of our theological model, illustrates how a family that places its allegiance in Jesus Christ can move toward God's paradigm for relationships. Although believers experience different levels of maturity in Christ, each one has a capacity to follow God's way because of the spiritual power within. Inasmuch as all family members are imperfect, with their own individual temperaments and experiences, they progress at different rates in the process of realizing God's ideals of unconditional love, grace, empowering, and intimacy. That is to say, all family members fall on a continuum between hurting and healing behaviors. As long as they move in the direction of healing, they will grow and the family will benefit. When they choose hurting behaviors and move away from God's way, however, the entire family will be negatively affected.

Among the hurting behaviors in a family environment are conditional love, self-centeredness, perfectionism, faultfinding, efforts to control others, unreliability, denial of feelings, and lack of communication. With such behaviors, the focus is on self rather than on the best interests of the other family members. In hurting families, each individual is affected on the personal level. For example, one may not feel loved or worthy of being loved by the other family members. Such individuals are limited

Table 1

From Hurting to Healing Behavior

Hurting Behavior	Problem at the Personal Level	Obstacle to Interpersonal Relationships	Behavior Perpetuating the Problem	Healing Behavior: The Cure
From Conditional Love to Unconditional Love				
Conditional love	Feeling unloved	Fear of not being loved	Loving others in order to be loved in return	Unconditional love
Self-centeredness	Feeling unworthy of love	Fear of being thought worthless	Focus on self	Christ-centeredness
From Shame to Grace				
Perfectionism	Fear of making a mistake	Fear of not being accepted	Trying harder	Acceptance
Fault finding	Expectation of perfection in self and others	Fear of being criticized	Blaming others	Forgiveness
From Control to Empowering				
Efforts to control	Lack of confidence in one's ability to influence	Fear of losing others	Overcontrol	Building others up
Unreliability	Lack of control of oneself	Fear of disappointing others	Being out of control	Reliability
From Lack of Feeling to Intimacy				
Denial of feelings	Fear of feelings	Fear of rejection	Avoidance of feelings	Experience of feelings
Lack of communication	Distrust of others	Fear of being hurt by others	Superficial conversation	Open and honest communication

in their ability to love others unconditionally. A vicious circular pattern results. Such problems at the personal level cause the individual to view interpersonal relationships as potential threats. The result is behavior that perpetuates the root problem. For example, an individual who does not know what it is to be loved unconditionally is prone to approach others defensively.

Hurting families tend to withhold grace, often demanding unreasonable perfection and blaming those members who don't measure up. Individuals in these families fear they will make a mistake and be rejected because of their failure to meet the standards. So they try harder to be perfect. What they need is acceptance for who they are and forgiveness when they fail.

Hurting families also tend to control rather than empower their members. Individuals in these families lack the confidence that they can influence others; they fear they will be discredited because of their inadequacies. The result is a desperate attempt to get power by coercing and controlling less powerful family members. What is needed instead is affirmation and validation by the family. Empowerment will build confidence so that all the family members can reach their greatest potential.

Hurting families are characterized at the individual level by their members not being in touch with their feelings. Their fear of rejection keeps them in denial of their emotions. What they need most is a safe atmosphere in which they can express their feelings, thoughts, wants, and desires and be heard and understood by the other family members. Open communication helps each person share more honestly rather than hide his or her feelings and thoughts from others. In turn, this experience increases one's capacity to be known by others and to know oneself at deeper levels.

A cure is needed to break the perpetual cycle found in hurting families. An individual who has been loved only conditionally needs to experience unconditional love in order to feel lovable enough to give love and to support others. The breakthrough comes when one receives God's unconditional love. Being cherished by God gives a sense of self-worth and a new self-perception ("I am lovable"). Drawing on the Holy Spirit and maturing in the faith, the individual now has reason to follow God's paradigm and to adopt healing behaviors.

We have seen that living in covenant love is a dynamic process. God has designed family relationships to grow from hurting to healing behavior, that is, to a maturity analogous to that of individual believers who attain the full measure of perfection found in Christ (Eph. 4:13). This maturing of relationships eventually enables family members to reach out to people beyond the boundaries of the family.

2

THE FAMILY AS A DEVELOPING SYSTEM

EXPERIENCE SHOWS THAT it is possible to observe family life, or even to be a part of family life, and yet to be limited in understanding it because our vision is limited. In fact, active involvement in family life may be the very reason we fail to understand it from a wider perspective.

In this chapter we introduce two theoretical perspectives that family clinicians and sociologists have found helpful in gaining a wide-angle view of family life. The first one is called family-systems theory because it views family life not merely as the sum total of the actions of all the individual members but rather as the interactions of all family members operating as a unit of interrelated parts. It considers individuals in the context of their relationships. The other is family-development theory, which views the family as developing over time through natural life-cycle stages. In this chapter we explain these two family perspectives, which will serve as a basis for focusing attention on family life as a whole.

Family-Systems Theory

A major cultural theme in modern society is individualism. Individualism has caused us to focus on the individual's needs and perspective rather than on relationships and groups. When analyzing contemporary society, we see that the delicate balance between individual rights and family rights has been skewed in favor of individual rights. Currently,

FIGURE 3 **Family-Systems Theory**

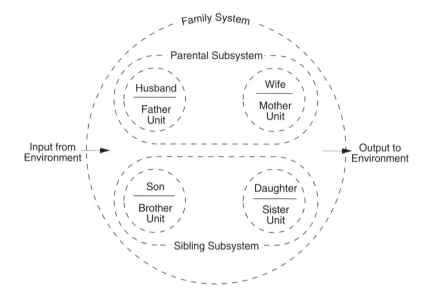

however, a revolution in the clinical profession is shifting the focus from the individual to the broader family system and beyond, to include multileveled systems. Both family therapists and sociologists now view family life from a broader systems perspective.

What is a family-systems perspective? Basically it is a holistic approach that understands every part of family life in terms of the family as a whole. A system is by definition any identifiable whole composed of interrelated individual parts. To understand any system one must begin by identifying the various levels within that system. Think of a series of circles reverberating from the center. The level at the core is the individual (bio-psycho-social dimensions); the next level includes the nuclear family (the family one lives within); then comes the extended family (grandparents, relatives, significant others); the next level includes school, work, friends, neighbors, and faith communities; and the final multicultural level includes socioeconomic, cultural, ethnic, racial, geographical, religious, and historical context. All these systems are interrelated. They influence and are influenced by one another simultaneously. The boundary around each of these multileveled systems involves belonging and membership. In Western societies the boundary of the family system is usually defined as a husband, a wife, and their children. In many other societies the extended family is defined as the basic family system.

The fundamental concepts of systems theory are illustrated in figure 3. Anything within the boundary is considered part of the system, and anything that falls outside the boundary is identified as part of the environment. Input includes any message or stimulus that enters the system from the environment. Output includes any message or response from the system to the environment. Boundaries around a system can be relatively open or closed. In an open family system, boundaries are said to be permeable, allowing for significant input from and output to the environment. In a closed family system, boundaries serve as barriers to limit such interaction.

Once a boundary has been established, objects within the system are identified as units of the system. In the newly established family, there are two units (individuals), the husband and the wife, each with identifiable positions and roles within the family. As children enter the family, the system becomes more complex since each new member (whether biological, adopted, or fostered) occupies a given position in the system and is assigned a role to play within it and subsystems are created.

In a family that includes children, there are at least two subsystems: the parental subsystem, composed of the mother and the father, and the sibling subsystem, composed of the children (or, in the case of an only child, the child subsystem). Each sibling is also identified as an individual unit with unique traits, qualities, and biological makeup. An extended-family system includes grandparents, relatives, and nonrelatives who are considered part of that system. For example, when a divorced father of two children unites with a widowed mother of three, a broad definition of this family system includes relatives and/or friends from all sides of that family. In most systems, rules of hierarchy exist between the subsystems. The major rule is that the adult subsystem (parents/adult members or nonfamily members) is considered to have authority and responsibility over the children in the home.

Theoretically, it is possible to regard any integrated whole as a system and to identify the smaller units within it as subsystems. In a broader sense, a church could be identified as a system, with each family or group within it a subsystem. Figure 4 illustrates the levels at which social systems can be analyzed. Keep in mind that the environment and the units are relative to the system one is analyzing. For example, if one is studying the world social system, which includes all the peoples of the world, the environment is all nonhuman phenomena and the units are specific societies or cultures.

The notion of multilevel systems theory is in large part a reflection of the inadequacies of a mechanistic cause-and-effect model of social behavior. The difference between a process model such as ecological

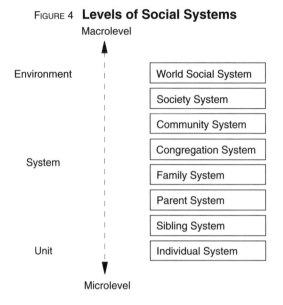

FIGURE 4 **Levels of Social Systems**

systems theory and a mechanistic model can best be seen in the various ways in which behavior can be controlled, balanced, or changed through a feedback process. There are four major levels of feedback operating within a mechanistic system: simple feedback, cybernetic control, morphogenesis, and reorientation.

Simple feedback is identical with a cause-and-effect model. For example, to assist parents in toilet training a child, a behavior-modification therapist focuses on the behavior itself. Giving the child candy intermittently when the task is accomplished reinforces the desired behavior. By contrast, withholding the reward (candy) conditions the child to relinquish undesired behavior. Family members frequently use simple feedback as a stimulus for change. It is a simple exchange between the system and the environment.

Cybernetic control is somewhat more complex. Here an output from the system feeds back to a monitoring unit within the system, which sets in motion a systemic adjustment to the original output. Perhaps the best example of cybernetic control is the self-monitoring action of a thermostat. On a cold winter day, we may set the thermostat at 70 degrees. When the room temperature gets below a certain point (say 68 degrees), the needle in the thermostat makes electrical contact and the heater is turned on. The heater will stay on until the needle rises to the point (say 72 degrees) where it loses electrical contact; then the heater turns off. This is cybernetic control because the heating system has a built-in mechanism to control itself.

Family life can be understood in much the same way. Families have rules or norms that define expected behavior for each family member. Each of these rules has a tolerance limit beyond which one cannot go without the family as a system taking some counteraction. In our thermostat analogy, the tolerance limits were 68 and 72 degrees. The family will need some flexibility in setting its tolerance limits, for if they are set too rigidly, there will be a constant need to correct, and normal family living will be impossible. For example, imagine what would happen to the heater if the tolerance limits were set at 69.999 and 70.001 degrees. The heater would be turning on and shutting off constantly, and all the energy would be exerted in that endeavor.

Consider a family that has a rigid rule that everyone must be home and be seated at the table at exactly 6:00 p.m. for the evening meal. The family may be willing to wait for about thirty seconds for Maria to get off the phone so they can begin, but they most certainly will not tolerate a five-minute delay. The system will draw on its storehouse of memories and choose an action to correct the undesirable behavior. It may be that Maria's siblings will put pressure on her to hang up, or that her parents will warn her that she won't get anything to eat unless she hangs up immediately. In either case, the system works as a whole to shape her behavior.

All families have rules that each member obeys for the good of the whole. Deviance from these rules is monitored by the system. Cybernetic control is the action the system takes to maintain the rules or status quo. This is referred to as homeostasis in systems-theory language.

Families often go beyond cybernetic control, however, for they are continually redefining and changing their rules, regulations, and procedures. Expanding our illustration, let's suppose that the family is determined not to begin eating without Maria, and that none of their tried and proven techniques succeed in getting her off the phone. A system that functions only at a cybernetic level can do absolutely nothing. It must either resort to a past response or do nothing. However, a system that operates on a morphogenetic level is capable of generating or creating new ways of responding to the situation. New responses are created whenever tested methods no longer work or the system is facing a situation for the first time.

One advantage that effective family systems have over ineffective family systems is the ability to operate at this higher level. The family that is overly rigid is usually incapable of morphogenetic responses because it lacks flexibility. However, families that are chaotically structured with few rules or boundaries have similar difficulty because they do not possess the cohesiveness to act in a united way.

The family is usually required to generate new response patterns whenever predictable or unexpected changes in its life cycle occur. For example, when a member of the family loses a job, gets sick, or dies, new response patterns are demanded. This is also true for positive life-cycle changes that occur, such as the birth or adoption of a child into the family, a wedding or anniversary celebration, or an unexpected inheritance of money. The family will be challenged to form new response patterns to these events as well.

Another important aspect of an ecological model is that people bring meaning to their behavior. We must do more than understand a person's actions; we must pay attention to the beliefs (perspectives) of that person in relation to his or her behavior. So Maria may have a very good reason to ask the family to make an exception for her lateness because she is working hard on an important project for school and needs them to be flexible. If family togetherness is the mother's priority, however, she and Maria will have to negotiate change according to the meaning each one brings to the issue. In general, there is no right or wrong way for a family to be organized, but the family must determine how their system will function by considering the best interest of each family member in addition to what is in the best interest of the family system itself. This is how the many levels of a system are embedded within and build on each other.

The tendency in most families is to respond in old, familiar ways to new situations (homeostasis). These old ways will likely be inadequate, and the family will become stuck in them rather than be motivated to

BOY, I'M SURE GLAD THAT OURS IS A FAMILY OF GRACE WHICH FORGIVES ONE ANOTHER ON EVERY OCCASION!

operate on the morphogenetic level. It is also true that families do not stagnate simply because changes are always occurring in the family, whether it be at an individual, a relational, or a family level. In other words, the family members constantly need to be in tune with the complex changes that are happening at all levels as they make adjustments in their daily living. The effective family understands that flexibility in structure as well as relational connection between family members is needed to operate on the morphogenetic level. Members of these families are alert and responsive to one another in the realm of individual differentiation and in keeping family togetherness a priority.

The fourth and highest level is reorientation; here the family changes its entire goal. In morphogenesis new ways of responding are generated, whereas in reorientation the goals themselves are changed. Reorientation involves a dramatic change in family life in which the entire system is converted to new ways of thinking and behaving. For example, reorientation may occur when the family of an alcoholic comes to grips with an understanding of how every member contributes to the problem. Treatment affects not only the alcoholic but also each and every family member, so change occurs at all levels. Another example is a radical change in an entire family's belief system, when an individual religious conversion spreads to all members, resulting in an entirely new pattern of family living.

Major systemic change is fairly rare, and most families operate out of morphogenesis or homeostasis. Reorientation is most needed when a family's existing patterns of behavior prove to be totally unworkable and damaging to its members.

Family-Development Theory

Imagine that we had access to a time machine and could view the Lee family at different points in its development. Let us suppose that we could view Mr. and Mrs. Lee during their first month of marriage, the year their first child was born, the year their youngest child was born, the year their youngest child became a teenager, the last year that child lived at home, and the year their youngest grandchild was born. Altogether we would have six slices from the life of this family. They would look quite different at each of those points, but there would also be certain elements of continuity: the basic organization of the family, the siblings' birth order (family constellation), family history and traditions, the presence of extended family, and so on. It should be noted that each stage of family life has predictable times of tension, and certain stages require more family structure than do others.

The developmental perspective allows us to view the typical family's progression through various stages of life. The family is dynamic rather than static. Within each stage the family must accomplish certain key developmental tasks. Likewise, there are developmental tasks to be mastered by each individual family member at a particular stage. A degree of variation and oscillation is normal in this process, since both the family as a unit and individual family members must accomplish their respective tasks before the family can move on to the next stage of development. To the extent that the developmental tasks are not accomplished, the family will be less prepared to move on. It is helpful to think about developmental tasks in terms of age appropriateness for each unique family member and determine when an individual is over- or underdeveloped in a particular area. While one is working toward a balance in many areas of development, it is always important to recognize the natural ebb and flow that occurs as an individual family member proceeds through the life stages.

Some developmental tasks are stage specific, while other tasks are accomplished throughout the phases of family life. For example, in the first year of marriage it is important for a couple to make joint decisions about finances and household chores, while interpersonal communication is a skill that will be important throughout their married life.

Table 2 lists the basic developmental stages, the major task associated with each stage, and the event that initiates it. It should be noted that all families are unique and that these stages are not as precisely laid out as the chart would indicate.

In general, a family can be said to have moved from one stage to the next when a major transition takes place. We begin our list with the premarital stage because of the importance of differentiation from one's family of origin (the family into which a person was born). The goal of differentiation is to develop a clear sense of self that enables one to relate to and interact with others in interdependent ways. Such a capacity for self-sufficiency leads to deeper levels of connection. Note that differentiation does not negate intimacy in favor of autonomy. It allows for intimacy and autonomy, for both are intriguingly dependent on each other. The process of differentiation begins in childhood but intensifies during late adolescence and continues throughout the life stages. Success in differentiation gives one the best chances for achieving mature marital intimacy and forming an interdependent union.

The most obvious and important transition in the life cycle is marriage. When two people marry, a new family begins in the form of a dyad. The major developmental task involves the husband's and the wife's adjustment to each other in their new roles as married rather than single people.

Table 2

Family Development

Stage	Major Task	Initiating Event
Premarital	Differentiating from family of origin	Engagement
Marital dyad	Adjusting to marital roles (establishing a household)	Marriage
Triad	Adjusting to new child	Birth/adoption of first child
Completed family	Adjusting to new family members	Birth/adoption of youngest child
Family with adolescents	Increasing flexibility in family system	Children's differentiating from the family
Launching	Accepting departure of family members	Children's choosing career and marriage partner
Postlaunching	Establishing new patterns and embracing new members	Departure of last child from home
Retirement	Accepting aging process Regenerative meaning	End of employment

There is an incredible agenda to be accomplished during this stage: setting up a new household, dividing up household chores, creating a budget, establishing work and career roles, meshing together sexually, developing friendships and planning social events, making decisions about church involvement and spiritual growth, and so on. This is an important time of establishing a sound foundation for future stages. The couple will be faced with questions about whether or when to have children, and some will face infertility questions and decisions.

In view of the amount of energy and cooperation needed to accomplish the items on this agenda, it is vital that the newly formed couple follow the biblical mandate to "leave and cleave." If they are to make these many decisions, the couple must clearly define their united relationship. They need encouragement and support from their respective families in this process, but if the families interfere, the foundation will be weakened.

The third family stage, the triad, begins with the birth, adoption, or fostering of the first child. Research indicates that the optimal length of time to be married before the arrival of the first child is two to five years. Many couples benefit from having at least a few years together to form the spousal union and accomplish the tasks required of newlyweds. The early arrival of a child can prematurely shift the focus of attention from the tasks of the marriage relationship to those of the parent/child relationship.

When a child is born, adopted, or fostered into a family, the existing system must make necessary changes to welcome the new member. New boundaries will need to be defined and established between members and subsystems; physical space must be made to accommodate the new member, since relating to her or him will be a new challenge.

When children reach adolescence, increased pressure is placed on the family system to accommodate itself to greater demands for flexibility. At this time, differentiation is especially pronounced because of the emotional and physical separation taking place. It is also the time when parents approach midlife, which often involves stress. Many challenges arise when the stressful stages of adolescence and midlife occur simultaneously. This may also be the time when a person is building a new family made up of a new spouse and his or her children and/or one's own.

The launching stage begins when children are hankering to make it on their own. The parents must allow their children to leave the family of origin while supporting this rather shaky interim period. It is crucial for parents to be open to their adult child's decisions, such as finding a place to live, entering the military, choosing a college or training for a career, entering the workforce, choosing a mate, taking a trip, and so on. In some cases, the adult children are not ready to launch, and new rules for household living must be instituted.

The postlaunch stage brings new challenges, depending on one's life circumstances. Given the expanded life expectancy in our society, the postlaunch stage accounts for nearly half the lifespan of the typical family system. This can be a period of renewed closeness and/or struggle between husband and wife as they refocus their spousal relationship and develop meaning without children in the home. It may be an exciting time of searching for a job or pursuing a new career. Perhaps one is grappling with life after a divorce or the death of a spouse, or life as a single parent. If children were previously the major focus, it can be a period of disillusionment and loneliness (the empty-nest syndrome). Another complication involves caring for elderly parents and working through their deaths. Often there is time for sibling relationship connection and/or reconciliation. Then, just when it looks as if there is plenty of freedom to progress, spousal illness or financial responsibilities pose a problem. Dealing with boomerang kids who return home for one reason or another can become an unexpected focus. It is also a time to plan retirement, make decisions about where to live and/or travel, and prepare for a fixed-income lifestyle. An unusually delightful aspect of this stage is developing relationships with grandchildren.

An Integration of Systems and Development Theory

In this book we use both the developmental and the systems perspective in discussing family life. The family is a developing system that embraces

Table 3

The Characteristics of Strong and Weak Families

	Strong Families	Weak Families
Cohesion	Individuation	Enmeshment
	Mutuality	Disengagement
Adaptability	Flexibility	Rigidity
	Stability	Chaos
Communication	Clear perception	Unclear perception
	Clear communication	Unclear communication
Role Structure	Agreement on roles	Conflict over roles
	Clear generational boundaries	Diffuse boundaries

the arrival of new members and then releases them when they depart. It must be able to tolerate and respond to the changing needs of its individual members while providing a sense of belonging. It must maintain a stability that can provide a firm foundation yet is flexible enough to adapt to changing circumstances. This is not an easy feat, especially with the enormous demands made on the family in our postmodern urban society. A multitude of extrafamilial systems (the work world, the educational system, the church, clubs, and organizations) all contend with the family for the time and devotion of family members. Only strong families can survive the intrusiveness of our contemporary society.

To understand how to build strong families, we must begin with a definition of what it takes to be an effective family. Table 3, which is based on clinical and sociological literature, presents a summary of various characteristics of strong and weak families. There are four major areas of analysis: cohesion, adaptability, communication, and role structure. In each area two characteristics mark the resilient family.

Cohesion

Cohesion refers to the degree of emotional closeness existing in a family. In resilient families the members are differentiated (have a healthy degree of separateness) and have a strong sense of belonging (connection and interdependence). There is mutual respect for the unique qualities and personalities of the other family members. At the same time, there is a family togetherness in which members belong to one another and realize they are interdependent in their family unity. When family members are overly cohesive (enmeshment), family members lack a sense of separate identity or individuality, and each member is overly dependent on the family or other members for identity. An example of enmeshment is when an entire family is devastated by one member's problem. The family members are so overly involved and concerned that they lose perspective. In the process the problem worsens, and the chance of finding a solution lessens as they are pulled down together as a group.

The opposite extreme is a very low level of cohesion, which can be described as disengagement. In the disengaged family, the life of each member rarely touches the other members in a meaningful way. The members lack involvement, and they do not contribute to or cooperate with one another. In times of personal crisis, the members of a disengaged family are likely to be indifferent and uninvolved. In fact, they may not even be aware of the problem because it hasn't been shared. Here the system cannot provide help or support for the hurting member. Each individual is too busy or is uninterested in what is happening with the others.

Strong families, by contrast, have a degree of mutuality and involvement that is supportive but not intrusive. This quality is lacking in both enmeshed and disengaged families, which are at the opposite ends of a continuum. In the middle of this continuum are resilient families, which display an appropriate degree of cohesion and engagement.

For analytical purposes mutuality and individuation can be discussed separately, but in actuality they overlap in what we refer to as differentiation. Disengagement, differentiation, and enmeshment are illustrated in figure 5. The bold lines in the figure represent the boundaries around the family, and the light lines indicate the boundaries around each individual family member. In the disengaged family (A), the lives of the individual members very rarely touch one another. Cohesion is so low that each person lives in psychological isolation from the others.

In the differentiated family (B), daily lives overlap, but each individual is also involved in activities outside the family. Each member has a separate life and identity and is therefore actively and meaningfully engaged with others. Although a vital part of each member's identity and support is found within the family, much is also found beyond the family boundary.

In the enmeshed family (C), the lives of all members are hopelessly entwined. Each family member has little identity beyond the boundary of the family. Even within the family, there is little space for a given member to be independent of the others. A member of an enmeshed family who tries to separate is likely to be labeled disloyal and to experience pressure from the others to remain enmeshed.

Needless to say, the amount of cohesion varies from family to family and from one life stage to another. For example, the degree of cohesion is higher with young children when the emotional bonding between parent and child is a primary focus. When children become teenagers and are working toward self-identity, it is fitting that they separate emotionally in

FIGURE 5 **Disengagement, Differentiation, and Enmeshment**

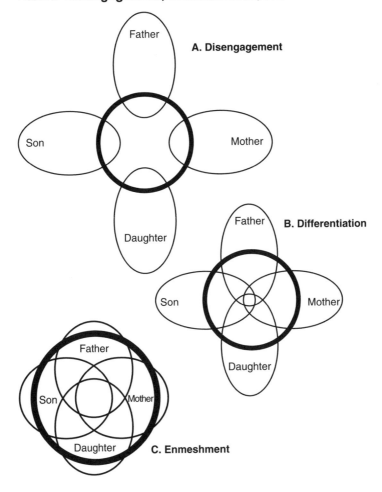

preparation for the independence necessary to eventually leave home. But even when suitable autonomy has been achieved, they view themselves as part of and keep close ties with the family throughout life.

Adaptability

A second important criterion for judging family life is adaptability. Families that have too high a level of adaptability tend to be chaotic. They lack the needed structure and predictability that provide stability and security. At the opposite extreme, inflexible families have a very low degree of adaptability and can be equally unbalanced. These families

Figure 6 **Adaptability and Cohesion within Families**

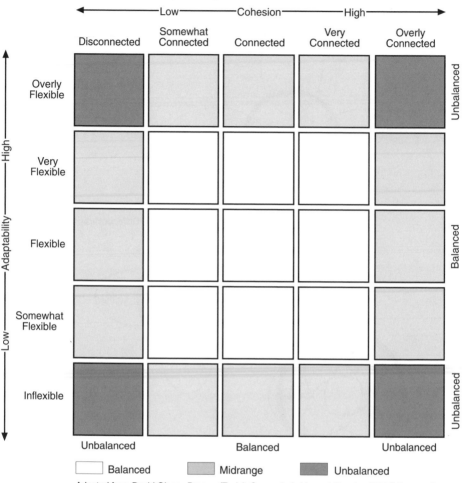

Adapted from David Olson, *Prepare/Enrich Counselor's Manual, Version 2000* (Minneapolis: Life Innovations, 1998), 81.

have created such a tight, unbending system that they have no give or grace, a strength that is especially needed during periods of change and transition in the family life cycle.

A balanced level of adaptability characterizes strong family life. The two dimensions of flexibility and stability mark the orderly family. In resilient families there is a sense of orderliness that entails both flexibility and structure. The difference between families in this particular area can be observed in the dinner patterns. In the chaotic family, dinner is at no set time, and family members come and go from the dining table whenever it is convenient. In the inflexible family, it is understood that dinner is at 6:00 p.m. sharp and that time will never be altered. In the stable yet flexible family, dinner is scheduled for a certain time because the members value family togetherness, but exceptions are made when needed and determined by the family as a whole.

David Olson (1998) has combined cohesion and adaptability in the Circumplex Model in which he describes balanced and unbalanced family systems. The families at the center of figure 6 are balanced. They experience satisfying degrees of adaptability and cohesion. The four corners represent four types of unbalanced or extreme family systems, combinations of disconnectedness or inordinate connectedness with either inflexibility or excessive flexibility. Families that experience life in these extremes need a better balance and more appropriate levels of cohesion and adaptability in their relationships. It is important to note that the balanced category includes a broad range of family styles. There is room for a variety of styles. The family needs to determine what is good for itself according to cultural values, input from all family members, age appropriateness, and what is best for the unique family members as well as the unique family system. Families at the extremes have the most difficulty satisfying both individual and family needs.

Communication

There are probably more self-help books on family communication than on any other topic. Because communication contributes in such an important way to effective family life, this is probably as it should be. The dynamics of good communication boil down to clarity of perception and clarity of expression. Clarity of perception pertains especially to the receiver of communication. It involves good listening skills, the ability to pick up on the sender's intonations and body language, and the willingness to ask for clarification when needed. In effective families, members have empathic skills, which include the ability to put oneself in the other's shoes and to understand what it feels like to be in that person's situation. This enables the communication to be on target so the receiver can make a response that helps the communicator feel understood and keeps them connected.

The more obvious dimension of good communication—clarity of expression—pertains to the sender. In resilient families, members are able to communicate feelings, opinions, wishes, and desires in a forthright and unambiguous manner. Clarity in sending messages is often a result of congruency between the person's words and body language. Care in this area goes far to ensure effective communication.

Role Structure

Shakespeare's suggestion that the world is a stage and we are merely actors and actresses provides dramatic insight into family relationships. Each family member has a role to play in the family. The family as a whole usually defines this role. In a family with two parents and two children, every member has at least two roles: the adults take the roles of spouse and parent, while the children take the roles of child and sibling. And, of course, each person has roles outside the family (student, employee, etc.).

Conflict over roles is a common characteristic in less effective families. When the role of one member is in conflict with the role of another member, contention results. For example, husband and wife may both want to work outside the home and have the other spouse be responsible for the housekeeping and child care. Highly effective families in contrast are characterized by agreement on respective roles. The husband and the wife agree on what each spouse's role will be. It may be, in the case cited for instance, that they will decide to share responsibility in the home so they can both work outside the home. Note that the issue here is not who plays a particular role, but whether there is mutual agreement about the roles.

A second dimension in regard to role structure concerns the generational boundaries in the family. Strong families are characterized by clear boundaries around the parental subsystem and clear boundaries around the sibling subsystem. However, the boundaries are obviously too diffuse when one sibling begins to play the role of parent to a brother or sister. Of course, in the single-parent home or when Mom and Dad are away, the oldest child may be put in charge. However, this role is readily relinquished when a parent returns home. When the oldest child is saddled with this role and continues to parent the younger siblings when the adults are present, it becomes a problem. This is a blurring of generational boundaries.

Boundaries in effectual families are clear but permeable. This means that family members have the freedom to take on different roles. For example, a parent can become playful and childish at times, while children may sometimes act as nurturers to their parents. For a parent or a child to occasionally break out of a fixed role is a sign of flexibility. A mother may playfully stand on the coffee table and perform for her children, or a child may comfort the parent who comes home discouraged and needs consideration and support. Though these are not their dominant roles, family members have the freedom to take them on occasionally.

Flexibility in roles and permeable boundaries are important, but a problem arises when generational boundaries are crossed. For example, it is confusing when one of the marriage partners assumes the role of parent to the other or when a child becomes a parent to the parent. In a single-parent home, it is quite natural for the oldest child to take on extra responsibility to provide the support needed. However, the single parent must be careful not to over-burden the child with adult responsibilities because taking on inappropriate responsibility infringes on the child's sibling relationship. Another example is siblings who jump out of their age-appropriate roles and either regress to a younger role or assume an unsuitably older role in their sibling relationships. In another scenario, grandparents may attempt to parent grandchildren, thereby taking over the role that rightfully belongs to the parents. This may occur because the grandparents desire control or because their own adult child has abdicated responsibility. But whatever the case, it can disrupt the relationships among family members.

In the first part of this chapter, we described the systemic and developmental approaches to understanding the family. A resilient family is effective in the context of their unique cultural values.

The biblical basis for family relationships presented in chapter 1 together with this social-scientific developmental systems approach provides the overarching framework for this integrated view of marriage and family relationships. The initial task of integration is delicate. Our Christian presuppositions include values and biases that influence our response to the social-science literature. Likewise, our social-science presuppositions will be present as we attempt to understand how Scripture applies to the contemporary family. We encourage the reader to join with us in the demanding task of integrating biblical and social-science knowledge about the family.

PART 2

MARRIAGE

The Foundation of Family Life

FAMILY LIFE COMES after marriage, yet everyone has already experienced family life prior to marriage. When two people marry, they bring with them recollections and experiences from their families of origin. The comment that there are "six in the marriage bed" is a way of alerting young spouses that each brings a set of parents into this new union.

Chapter 3 focuses on the coming together of two individuals and their respective families. The marriage ceremony proclaims to family, friends, and members of the community that a new union has been formed. The reception provides an opportunity for these groups of people to become introduced to one another so that new relationships may develop among them. The wedding day can be a stressful time for the new couple, full of the emotions related to separation, endings, and beginnings. If both families approve of the marriage, there will be accompanying support to help the couple establish a firm foundation for their union. If the new couple lacks support, however, they are likely to start out on shaky ground, and they will need to make a concerted effort to achieve a stable marriage.

Chapter 4 is devoted to the process of establishing a firm marriage. Family therapist Virginia Satir (1983, 2) has referred to the marital partners as the architects of the family. They are also the foundation on which the family will be established. The essential supports in a solid foundation include the strengths of the two families of origin, the character strengths that each spouse brings into the marriage, the strength of the relationship itself, and the strength that comes from friends and community. These sources of support are all crucial in establishing a well-functioning foundation. And in Christian homes, of course, the cornerstone is Christ.

Although the foundation is established early in marriage, it is important to recognize that the marital dyad is a dynamic and growing relationship. There is no such thing as a static marriage because, like any living organism, marriage is in either a state of growth or a state of decline. Chapter 5 presents the constituent elements of a marriage relationship that is based on and grows in accordance with biblical principles.

3

MATE SELECTION

Romance and Reality

IN ALL SOCIETIES there is a process whereby unmarried people come to be married. This process is called mate selection. While the beginning phase of marriage is technically the first stage of family life, mate selection is a necessary preliminary. Understanding mate selection is an important starting point for understanding all other stages in the life cycle of the family.

Mate Selection in Traditional Cultures

In the United States selecting a mate is usually an individual matter. Unmarried people court and then choose for themselves the person they will marry. Contrary to popular opinion, this approach is actually a fairly recent development. In most societies throughout history, selecting a mate was a decision made solely by the parents, whose age, experience, and cultural heritage brought the wisdom to make this important decision.

In societies that practice parental arrangement, mate selection is more a link between two extended families than a uniting of two individuals. There is great variability across cultures in the mate-selection process, extending along a continuum from parent-arranged marriage at one end to total free choice at the other. In societies where marriages are arranged by parents, the two dominant approaches are the bride-price system and the dowry system. The bride-price system is the norm in subsistence economies where the labor performed by women is greatly valued. In exchange for the bride, the groom's family gives her family various material goods. The dowry system is the norm in agricultural societies, where organized family units live on and work their own property. A dowry consists of goods that parents give to their unmarried daughter to make her an attractive commodity on the marriage market. In such a system, the wife brings the dowry with her into the marriage.

In this postmodern world, the modernization process has challenged the tradition of parent-arranged marriages. In the effort to accelerate technological advancements, many countries are influenced by individualistic values. A by-product of accepting these modern trends has been the gradual erosion of parent-arranged marriages and the emergence of romantic love as the basis for marriage.

Young people in traditional societies are increasingly exposed to a Western view of romantic love through the mass media. Many of these youth are quite familiar with American and Western European movies, popular music, and magazines that glorify romantic love. When youth in traditional societies begin to embrace the concept of romantic love, they do not immediately challenge the time-honored mate-selection procedure, but on an unconscious level these new ideas begin to undermine the old ways. Acceptance of these new ideas occurs in a sequential order: (1) two people should be romantically in love before they marry; (2) only the two people directly involved can determine if romantic love is present in their relationship; and (3) romantic love is most effectively cultivated within a social environment where unmarried youth can become acquainted with members of the opposite sex through dating.

In response to these modern notions of mate selection, parents may be willing to consider the opinion of their children and even seek their approval of a selected mate. They may even allow a courtship time for the young people to become acquainted and fall in love. However, most often these young people gradually assert themselves regarding their future mate and demand a say in the matter. This changes the entire process. The Western notion that compatibility of personality should be a factor in mate selection is adopted. Thus, unmarried youth want the freedom to become acquainted with potential partners for the purpose of determining whether they are in love and compatible. It is at this stage that dating enters the picture. Dating is often a major point of contention between parents and children, because it signals that control of the mate-selection process is passing from the hands of the parents to the hands of the unmarried youth. When two unmarried young people believe that they are in love and want to marry, the parental arrangement will be only a formality. In time, perhaps over several generations, the formality of parent-arranged marriages will most likely cease to exist.

Mate Selection and the Role of Romantic Love

Having first considered mate selection in a traditional context, we will now focus on mate selection as a prerogative of the two people directly involved. In our postmodern era many people believe finding a mate is primarily about personal attraction and romantic love (Fisher 1996). The popular Internet matchmaking business also emphasizes compatibility as a factor. Taking personality tests, indicating preferences, writing biographies, and viewing photographs are all part of the mate-finding process.

Although some would argue that romantic love is not unique to Western cultures (Grunebaum 1997, 296), the concept of romantic love is generally thought to have had its beginnings in European societies during the eleventh century, when "courtly love" became fashionable among the privileged class. Courtly love usually involved a romantic relationship between a married aristocratic lady and an unmarried knight or troubadour. As portrayed in literature, stereotypical courtly love involved

MOM, DAD, THIS IS THE WONDERFUL, SUPERORDINARY, STUPENDOUS GUY I'VE BEEN TELLING YOU ABOUT.

a knight going forth into battle, motivated by the love of his lady, or a troubadour serenading a young lady on a moonlit night. According to this early version of romantic love, true love was often unrequited love that didn't culminate in either a sexual relationship or marriage.

The concept of courtly love introduced the element of affection into male/female relationships. Affection was uncommon in most marriages of the day because they were primarily economic arrangements. By the sixteenth century, courtly love had changed to include sexual involvement between the lady of nobility and her paramour. The emerging middle class of European society during the sixteenth and seventeenth centuries came to value romantic love yet held to faithfulness as a value in marriage. This dilemma was solved when the love object changed from a married person to a single person. Thus, during the seventeenth and eighteenth centuries, parent-arranged marriage and romantic love existed side by side. By the twentieth century, it became proper and somewhat of a formality for a man to ask for parental permission to marry the daughter.

During the first half of the twentieth century, the irrational head-over-heels concept of romantic love reached its zenith. Confusion over the exact meaning of romantic love made it difficult for people to know if true romantic love was present in their relationship. Psychiatrist Erich Fromm recognized this fact when he wrote his famous book *The Art of Loving* (1956). Fromm observes that most people see love primarily in terms of being loved rather than in terms of loving. He argues that we need to learn how to love in the same way we learn how to play a musical instrument. Love is an art to be practiced, requiring discipline, concentration, patience, and supreme concern. Fromm asserts that when people start working at love (giving, caring, taking responsibility, respecting), knowledge will characterize their relationship. Family therapist Frank Pittman (1997, 312) continues this thought: "People who want to feel loving should start by acting loving—at home." Pittman criticizes the notion of romantic love by comparing it to a dangerous drug that puts one into "a state of temporary insanity, akin to a manic episode. It is a narcissistic intoxication that has no relationship to loving but is rather a response to crisis that triggers a bigger crisis" (p. 309).

On the basis of clinical evidence, Henry Grunebaum (1997, 296) links romantic love to erotic love, which he construes as having three identifiable features. First are feelings of longing for the other person and the desire to be sexually and psychologically intimate; second, the beloved is idealized and regarded as necessary for one's happiness; and finally, preoccupation with the relationship results in an overestimation of the other person.

In fact, romantic love leads to rather dramatic changes in one's character. New studies suggest that an area of the brain known as the caudate is associated with romantic passion. Neuroscientists have produced brain scan images of this fevered activity prior to long-term commitment. Brain imaging reveals that only pictures or thoughts of the object of one's desire can "light up" certain areas of the brain. Based on these findings, Helen Fisher and her colleagues (2002) suggest that what we call romantic love develops over three sequential stages, beginning with *lust* (sexual drive), then *attraction*, and finally *emotional attachment*. Such "falling in love" is a romantic attachment that differs from one's relationship with family or friends and changes one physiologically as the body increases the production of hormones and chemical substances known as peptides, vasopressin, and oxytocin (Fisher et al. 2002). Romantic love is similar to drives such as hunger, thirst, or drug craving rather than to emotional states such as excitement or affection. During this intense time, emotions may shift from euphoria to anger to anxiety and become even more intense when love is withdrawn or one is rejected. As a relationship deepens, the neural activity associated with romantic love alters to long-term attachment.

The moral of the story should be obvious. People in romantic love should be cautious, for real love is much more about faithful behaviors than about mushy feelings. A person easily gets caught up with the "being in love" emotions and fails to use reason. The initial romantic phase in which two people are overly intrigued with each other leaves little time for anyone else. While this is a wonderful aspect of initial attraction, loving demands much more than being absorbed in oneself or the object of one's romantic love. Both partners must move beyond this to the demands of relationship building before they can plan a future life together.

During the 1950s, the mate-selection process in Western societies moved to a new stage called rational-romantic love. This type of love incorporates rational consideration of compatibility with one's true love. Although few people would marry someone they do not love, it is now true that few people marry only on the basis of love. Rational-romantic love is especially common among people who are college-educated. Marriage is seen as being a rational decision as much as it is a head-over-heels response to one's partner.

Roger Sternberg (1986) has attempted to sort out the complexity of what our society calls romantic love. He believes that love includes three dimensions: commitment, the cognitive component; intimacy, the friendship factor and emotional component; and passion, the motivational component. These three dimensions of love are quite similar to the three types of love known from ancient Greek culture, *agapē*, *philia*,

FIGURE 7 **Four Types of Love Relationships**

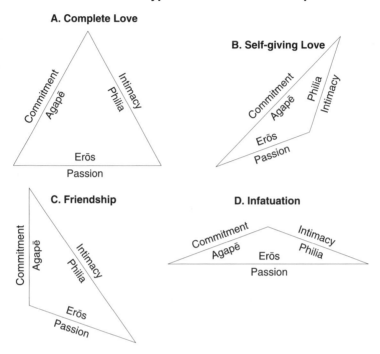

and *erōs*. C. S. Lewis has written eloquently about these loves in *The Four Loves* (1960a). The self-giving *agapē* corresponds to commitment; *philia*, brotherly friendship, corresponds to intimacy; and *erōs*, physical desire for one's beloved, corresponds to passion.

Utilizing these dimensions, figure 7 depicts four types of love relationships. Complete love (A) embraces an equal portion of all three loves: commitment/*agapē*, intimacy/*philia*, and passion/*erōs*. In most cases, passion is likely to dominate at the beginning of courtship, followed by a surge in emotional and friendship intimacy and, last, commitment. While all three dimensions of love are important for a Christian marriage, it is a commitment to the other person that provides an environment in which intimacy and passion can grow to full maturity. The ideal relationship exhibits equal amounts of commitment, intimacy, and passion prior to marriage.

In self-giving love (B), commitment is dominant. In many societies (including those with parent-arranged marriages), the resolution of a couple to be faithful and self-giving in their love is the most desired prerequisite for marriage. It is noteworthy that marriages based on faithful commitment end in divorce far less frequently than those based solely on romantic love. However, this fact should not imply that parent-arranged marriages are more likely than love-based marriages to achieve the Christian ideal. For while intimacy and passion may develop in arranged marriages, the familial structure and cultural values promoted in traditional societies may also hinder such development. The commitment that keeps these marriages together may be less a self-giving commitment to one's spouse than a commitment to the extended family and community. When marriages lack a personal covenant, it is unlikely that the spouses will achieve true intimacy.

In friendship (C), emotional intimacy is dominant. Although few relationships move into marriage on the basis of friendship alone, it is an essential factor in a good marital relationship. Many people describe their spouse as their best friend, an indication of being an emotional companion to one's mate. Others complain that the friendship is so strong they find it difficult to feel passionate with their partner, and this compromises the sexual passion.

In infatuation (D), passion is dominant. Some relationships get off to a passionate start: two people connect on the basis of immediate attraction and sexual response, which may lead to an impulsive marriage. Such relationships do not ordinarily have the emotional core and stability of commitment to sustain the marriage. But since passion by itself cannot carry a relationship over time, infatuation often burns itself out before a couple decides to marry.

Theories of Mate Selection

In view of the flexibility and complexity of the modern courtship system, family researchers have been challenged to explain the mate-selection process. One of the most studied aspects of present-day mate selection is the degree to which people choose mates who are similar or different from them. If we believe both clichés, "like marries like" and "opposites attract," there will be similarities and differences in the couple.

The theory that like marries like. Studies have shown that endogamous factors, or similar social backgrounds, are key components in mate selection. These factors include race, ethnicity, religion, education, occupation, and geographical proximity. It should be noted that some of these factors directly relate to the opportunity to get to know another person. Close contact in the workplace, for example, affords the opportunity to view someone as a potential marriage partner. For this reason, it is fairly common for people in the same occupation to marry. It has also been shown that homogamous factors, or similar personal characteristics and interests, are of importance. Included here are religious and political beliefs, moral values, hobbies, intelligence, height, weight, and physical appearance. Another important finding is that most people seem to marry partners with a similar amount of ego strength. A person with low self-esteem tends to marry a person with low self-esteem, and a person with high self-esteem will marry another person with high self-esteem. Thus Internet matchmaking sites that take these important factors into account are more likely to yield good matches than those that rely on more superficial indicators, such as photos or bios.

The theory that opposites attract. Evidence that opposites attract is not as clear-cut as is the evidence that like marries like. Studies do suggest, however, that when opposites attract, personality factors are usually involved. Dominant people tend to marry submissive people, and nurturing people tend to marry people who need nurturing. It appears that people have an unconscious desire to complete a perceived personal deficiency by choosing someone who can make up for what is lacking.

Filter theory. Alan Kerckhoff and Keith Davis (1962) have suggested that endogamy, homogamy, and complementary needs are three different filters through which a potential mate must pass (see figure 8). The first and broadest filter in the mate-selection process is endogamy, as most people date and establish relationships with individuals from similar backgrounds. The second filter is homogamy, which is narrower and more selective. Only those people who have similar interests and characteristics pass through this filter. Casual dating allows individuals to discover which potential partners have compatible interests and characteristics. The last filter, complementary needs, is the narrowest. Whereas a number of potential mates may pass through the endogamous and homogamous filters, only a few will have the exact personality traits to meet one's most pressing needs.

Stimulus-value-role theory. The stimulus-value-role theory of mate selection is similar to the filter theory, except it conceives of mate selection as an open market in which individuals try to find the best mate they can, given what they have to offer. At the stimulus stage, factors such as physical attractiveness, social competence, and status draw two people to each other on the basis of "equity of the weighted amalgam of stimulus attributes" (Murstein 1980, 785). In other words, the more equal the mixture of these different stimulus factors, the greater the likelihood that two people will be initially attracted to each other. Some will then move on to the value stage, where they assess the compatibility of their respective standards and beliefs. A few relationships will move on to the role stage, where each person will assess whether his or her expectations of a mate can be fulfilled by the potential partner. A relationship that passes through all three stages has the possibility of culminating in marriage. Some couples, however, launch into marriage after their

FIGURE 8 **A Filter Theory of Mate Selection**

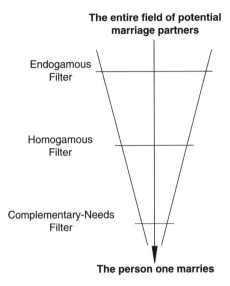

**The entire field of potential
marriage partners**

Endogamous
Filter

Homogamous
Filter

Complementary-Needs
Filter

The person one marries

relationship has passed through only stage one or two. When this happens, there is a greater possibility that divorce will occur.

Dyadic-formation theory. Robert Lewis (1972) created a most elaborate mate-selection theory. His dyadic-formation theory conceives of a dating relationship as developing through six stages of increasing seriousness: (1) perception of similarities in each other's background, values, interests, and personality; (2) establishment of rapport as evidenced by ease of communication, positive evaluations of each other, satisfaction with the relationship, and validation of self by the other; (3) openness through mutual self-disclosure; (4) anticipation of the role each would play as a marriage partner; (5) adjustment of these roles to fit each other's needs; and (6) dyadic crystallization as evidenced by progressive involvement together, the establishment of boundaries around the relationship, commitment to each other, and emerging identity as a couple.

The wheel and clock-spring theories. Ira Reiss (1960) proposed the wheel theory of love in his explanation of mate selection in Western society. According to this theory, heterosexual love is a primary relationship that our society has singled out for special attention. The typical relationship between a man and a woman moves through four phases: (1) rapport—coming to feel comfortable with each other; (2) self-revelation—being open and sharing oneself with the other; (3) mutual dependency—the realization that one needs the other person as a confidant or a listener;

and (4) intimacy-need fulfillment—the awareness that one's needs for sympathetic understanding are being met by the other person.

Dolores Borland (1975) expanded on the wheel theory by describing heterosexual love as a process of cycling through the four phases of courtship at increasingly deeper levels. She likened this process by which a couple comes to know each other's real self to tightening a clock spring. Borland warned that a love relationship will fail to grow if one of the partners is unable to move on to a deeper level of rapport, self-revelation, mutual dependency, and intimacy-need fulfillment.

A Christian Perspective

Taken together, the various sociological theories of mate selection comport well with the theological model of family relationships that we presented in chapter 1. This will become clear as we describe what mate selection would be like if it developed according to the principles suggested in our theological model.

At the beginning of courtship there is a minimal degree of commitment between the partners. With an increased degree of commitment comes an increased sense of trust and security. And as mutual commitment increases, grace can be expected to grow proportionately. Grace is experienced through acceptance and appreciation by the partner. The presence of grace promotes a feeling of security because differences are respected, and because there is an atmosphere of forgiveness whenever failure occurs. The partners are valued and accepted for who they are and not for what they might be or do for the other.

Out of grace emerges a mutual empowering process. In the early stages of courtship, the couple may operate on a quid-pro-quo basis (something for something), with each attempting to have personal needs met through the relationship. Where there is a minimal degree of commitment and acceptance, partners are likely to think more in terms of what they can get from a relationship rather than what they can contribute to it. The empowering model is hopeful in that it shows that love can be elevated above self-centered exchange. A depth of commitment and grace can imbue each partner with a genuine desire to empower by both giving to and receiving from the other. This involves being interested in the growth of the other person and finding ways to encourage the partner to reach his or her greatest potential and thus to be all that God created him or her to be.

Some courting relationships are not empowering but rather are based on mutual dependency. When couples are overly dependent on each other, they tend to demand that the partner meet their every need. They fail to develop their own resources as they look to each other to meet all their needs. The expectations and disappointments are extreme when partners are focused solely on each other. The tendency then is to be possessive and demanding rather than empowering. Such a desperate need for the other puts great pressure on the relationship and often results in turmoil, jealousy, and chaos.

Codependency is the exact opposite of differentiation as noted in trinitarian theology, where distinctiveness and unity are intermingled. Differentiated partners are responsible to God for their lives and therefore bring unique gifts to the couple relationship. They are for each other out of strength rather than deficit. They are able to ask for what they would like without demanding the partner provide it. Being centered in Christ gives them confidence that God is the best resource to guide, empower, nurture, inspire, and soothe. They look to God for personal growth but also openly share and offer themselves to each other in that process. When spouses cling to each other for dear life in a raging river, they perpetuate an enabling system in which they both are likely to drown together. But when sufficiently differentiated, they are a strong resource for each other so that when one is struggling, the partner is standing on solid ground to extend a helping hand.

Ecclesiastes 4:9–12 refers to this idea that two sufficient persons are better than one alone. Because they bring their unique strengths to the union, they can be there for each other rather than be dragged down in an overly dependent relationship. "Two are better than one, because they have a good reward for their toil. For if they fall, one will lift up the other; but woe to one who is alone and falls and does not have another to help. Again, if two lie together, they keep warm; but how can one keep warm alone? And though one might prevail against another, two will withstand one. A threefold cord is not quickly broken." Being united in unique strengths and making God the center of their relationship (a threefold cord) presents a wonderful image of marital partnership and union.

We live in a society that encourages people to think that they can have instant gratification. This mentality carries over into the dating relationship, where people look for instant intimacy. Much of the behavior in singles' bars centers on the search for the instant intimacy of the one-night stand, which is free of long-term commitment.

In our theological model, intimacy entails a deep level of knowing and being known through understanding, listening, caring, and sharing in vulnerable ways. It is not simply a physical or sexual encounter but a deeply felt process of becoming known. Accordingly, intimacy builds on commitment, grace, and empowerment. Using these foundational biblical concepts, people who trust the commitment, experience acceptance and forgiveness during courtship, and find their partner interested in and actively affirming empowerment during the courting process will feel safe enough to reveal more about themselves. They are willing to take off their masks and resist the temptation to put on pretenses. They share with a desire to truly know each other. The couple is more interested in a relationship with the other person than in the mere pleasure that person can give in a superficial sexual encounter. Intimacy of this nature leads to deeper levels of commitment, grace, and empowering.

Certain beliefs about mate selection, such as "love is enough" or "there is a one and only for me," may be a serious hindrance in discerning God's will. A research study has identified seven such *constraining beliefs* that limit, inhibit, hinder, or perpetuate exaggerated or false expectations about mate selection (Cobb, Larson, and Watson 2003). The beliefs that "there is a one and only, that love is enough, that cohabiting before marriage will improve chances of being happily married, that I will have complete assurance, that the match will make a perfect relationship, that choosing should be easy and effortless, and that one should choose someone to marry whose personal characteristics are the opposite of their own" seem to adversely affect mate selection. These myths blur the clarity of vision needed when choosing a mate. The study discovered that "men and women were found to be equally susceptible to constraining beliefs about mate selection, with the exception of the One and Only belief, the Idealization belief, and the Complete Assurance belief, all of which women appear to endorse to a slightly greater degree" (p. 229). An additional finding worth noting is that Mormons had significantly fewer constraining beliefs, which along with their strong emphasis on marriage preparation may partially account for their lower divorce rates when compared to non-Mormons.

Discerning God's Will

Marriage is an important, sacred event in most societies. Marriage is pivotal because it is necessary to the psychological well-being of the individuals involved, the social well-being of the married couple and family, the economic well-being of communities, and the survival of society itself. One advantage of parent-arranged marriage is that it protects young people from the pressure, confusion, and agony of having to make such a major decision on their own. The obvious disadvantage is the impact of their being excluded from this critical process, which has enormous implications for the rest of their lives. This leads us to the question of how Christians are to approach the mate-selection process.

To answer this question, we must begin by considering how one comes to discern God's will in the matter of choosing a mate. First, a couple contemplating marriage will want to view their relationship through the theological and biblical relationship lenses we have presented in this chapter. As they look at their relationship history in light of these values, they will begin to answer that question through their experiences with each other. Many couples already recognize trouble in their relationship during courtship but deny the seriousness of the problems. For this reason, long engagements are predictive of successful marriage. When the couple gets beyond the romantic stage during the months and years prior to marriage in a long engagement, they gain a more realistic idea about managing their relationship. They will have experienced conflicts and struggles during this time and have a good understanding of how they deal with each other in the process. They will have had time to see each other in all sorts of situations and been willing to discuss their expectations about roles and future plans.

We strongly suggest that a couple intentionally learn all they can about their relationship through a premarital inventory identifying strengths and weaknesses in their relationship. David Olson's *Prepare/Enrich* (1998) is a 125-item questionnaire used by clergy and counselors to assess a couple's chances for a successful marriage. The inventory matches each person's responses to questions in major areas such as personality, friendships, conflict, communication, finance, sex, views on children, and family of origin. It has proven to be quite accurate in predicting whether a couple will be successful or eventually divorce (Fowers, Montel, and Olson 1996). Another helpful inventory is the "Preparation for Marriage Questionnaire" (Holman, Larson, and Harmer 1994). It consists of 178 items that evaluate the following five areas that are predictive of marital satisfaction and stability: (1) degree of unity in values, attitudes, and beliefs; (2) personal readiness for marriage (the indicators include emotional health and maturity, self-esteem, and independence from one's family of origin); (3) partner readiness (communicating ability and skills, self-disclosure, and empathic behavior); (4) couple readiness (agreement on basic issues, stability of the relationship, approval of each other's friends and relatives, and realistic expectations); and (5) background and home environment (satisfaction with the home environment, the quality of the home environment, the quality of the parent-child relationship, and absence of physical and sexual abuse). If there are deficiencies in one or several of these areas, the couple must determine whether they can overcome the obstacle.

We definitely believe these assessment tools can provide concrete information that will help a couple determine the potential success of their future together. Spend time discussing these relationship dynam-

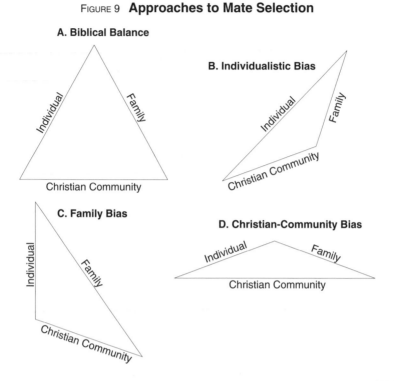

FIGURE 9 **Approaches to Mate Selection**

ics and process the results of the inventories with a trusted counselor or minister; grapple honestly with family of origin and multicultural challenges; take time to work out a financial budget, attend workshops on relationship skill development; be aware of your personality differences, and consider how it affects your relationship; deal openly with your sexual relationship with a counselor and read and discuss an informative book on the subject. Take advantage of reading a book such as *Saving Your Marriage before It Starts* (Parrott and Parrott 1996) to prepare for marriage.

No one particular way of finding God's will is best for everyone, but in most cases a combination of activities is advisable. Here are four specific guidelines to consider when seeking God's direction about marriage. First, look to God directly through prayer, Bible study, and meditation. Second, seek wisdom and input from parents, significant family members, and good friends. Trusted people who know and are willing to be honest about each partner's individual strengths and weaknesses will prove invaluable. Third, as mentioned earlier, go through a premarital counseling process in which you honestly examine all aspects of your relationship and spend time clarifying expectations with an objective professional or pastor. Fourth, seek wisdom from trustworthy Christians in your community of faith. Those in the body of Christ provide a communal perspective that will help you affirm or disaffirm your decision.

Figure 9 depicts four possible approaches to mate selection. We advise you to discern God's will through a biblically balanced approach (A). Input from three sources—the individuals directly concerned, family and close friends, and the Christian community—serve as a check against an incorrect decision. When decisions are made without input from all three sources, there is a greater probability of error. Given the power of passion and today's emphasis on intimacy in romantic relationships, the individualistic bias (B) is the most likely to have fatal consequences. Family bias (C) is typical of parental arrangements. When parents are discerning Christians, they can be an invaluable source of wisdom, though they may have a limited perspective because of personal and/or cultural biases. Christian-community bias (D) is probably the most difficult to detect since it is generally felt that a corporate body is less prone to bias. However, an obvious danger is the power one particular leader or leaders may wield. Leaders also have human limitations and are therefore capable of using their influence in misguided ways. Particularly troubling are communities in which congregants are required to submit to an authoritative leader out of loyalty.

Even if one concedes the wisdom of this model, there is always the possibility of disagreement. Consequently, the individuals, family, and Christian community should work together to bring about a congruous decision that will enhance the probability of a lasting covenant.

4

Establishing a Strong Marriage

A Differentiated Unity

Each spouse's experiences growing up in his or her particular family of origin are major preparations for marriage. Accordingly, marriage involves more than a uniting of two individuals; it is also a uniting of two extended families. Bringing aspects of two culturally diverse families into a new unit is a process of affirming the best of both cultures (sense of belonging) and discovering the spouses' own sense of identity as a couple. In the process, they may choose to discard some of their heritage, expand aspects of it, and create a unique union that exceeds what either of them would be on their own. Forming a new relationship as a couple distinguishes each of them from their family of origin (family each grew up in) and at the same time keeps each of them connected with it. We begin this chapter by recognizing the impact of family of origin as well as other important factors that contribute to marital quality.

Factors That Predict Marital Quality

Researchers have identified three categories of factors that are predictive of marital quality—background and contextual factors, individual traits and behavior, and a couple's interactions with each other (Larson and Holman 1994; Larson and Hickman 2004).

Sociocultural contextual factors that affect the quality of marriage include age at time of marriage, level of education and income, and occupational stability. Being similar (homogamy) in race, socioeconomic status, religion, intelligence, and age are factors that affect a new marriage in a positive way. Individual characteristics such as physical and emotional health, lack of neurotic traits, conventionality, and level of self-esteem contribute to the quality a couple can achieve in their new union. Also, having similar values, attitudes, and beliefs seems to bring out the best in both spouses.

When it comes to interpersonal dynamics, it's good communication and conflict-resolution skills that bring strength and quality to the marriage. Not having cohabited and low participation in premarital sexual intercourse also contribute to a couple's quality of marriage (Holman et al. 2001; Larson and Hickman 2004; Larson et al. 2002).

There are a number of background factors relating to family of origin that are predictive of marital quality. When parents have had a high-quality marital relationship, the couple has a better chance of developing quality in their own marriage. When both sets of parents have achieved a long-lasting marriage (no divorce) and are free of mental illness, chances for high quality in the newly formed marriage increase. Also, when families are supportive and refrain from pressuring the couple, marital quality is more likely. The new couple needs time and space to develop their relationship. In the next section we will consider in more detail the family of origin dynamics.

Resolving Issues Related to the Family of Origin

Parents as Role Models

Parents are powerful role models. They teach through verbal communication, but their nonverbal behavior is probably even more influential. Children learn important lessons about marriage by observing how their parents communicate with each other—how they express their feelings of love, affection, and anger. Everything that parents do in their role as marriage partners will profoundly influence their children's behaviors and attitudes as marriage partners. A study found that experiences in the family of origin affect the patterns of marital adjustment (Sabatelli and Bartle-Haring 2003). Although true for both husbands and wives, there was a stronger relation between wives' positive experience in their family of origin and reported marital adjustment.

No matter how good the parents' marital relationship, there are always a few things that an adult child vows to do differently. Fulfilling this vow, however, takes a conscious effort. Since modeled behavior is such a strong conditioner, most people are not aware of how often they simply imitate their parents' actions.

Research indicates that regardless of whether we agree with the way our parents handled their marriage or parenting responsibilities, when a similar situation arises in our own family, our spontaneous reaction will be to behave exactly as our parents did. The young wife who witnessed her mother's temper whenever her father was running late may be determined to give her husband the benefit of the doubt rather than lash out in anger. However, when a similar situation arises, she finds herself scolding her husband before he has a chance to explain his tardiness. The husband, who remembers that his father was less than considerate in not calling home about being detained, nevertheless forgets to call his wife.

Spouses must make an effort to recognize and correct faulty attitudes and behaviors they unthinkingly bring into their marriage. It is imperative to avoid the fatalistic attitude that denies responsibility for one's own behavior by saying, "My parents have been such a strong influence on my behavior that there is nothing I can do about it!" To make excuses of this nature is tempting. A husband may say, "My wife wants me to be more open in communicating my feelings to her; she just doesn't realize that we didn't do that in my family." A wife may say, "I can't help worrying about you when you go on a trip; my mother always worried about my father." These defeatist attitudes do not facilitate needed change.

Equally detrimental is the naive belief that one's family of origin does not have an effect on one's own marital life. Such thinking leads to a denial of behavioral patterns that have similar negative outcomes in one's own marriage. Without personal awareness of these patterns, change is unlikely to occur.

Parental Support

As noted at the beginning of this chapter, research indicates that social, emotional, and financial support from parents and other relatives are very important factors in helping a newly married couple establish a solid marriage. In an ideal situation, children have the freedom to move some distance from home for schooling or employment, and their parents remain available to them for emotional and even financial support. This involves both appropriate differentiation (no strings attached) and support (we want to empower you). Some parents make their support conditional on the new couple reciprocating in some way. For support (financial or emotional) to be empowering, it must be unconditional and freely given. For example, financial arrangements should be clearly negotiated in an attitude of mutual respect and agreement. If there are expectations such as paying back a loan at a later time, these conditions must be specified up front so that responsibility becomes part of the empowerment.

Some parents are threatened by their children's independence and want to keep control. The demands they make can undermine the newly established unit, forcing the couple to concentrate on meeting the expectations of the family of origin rather than on building the newly formed marital dyad. The couple that continually needs parental financial or emotional help has failed to accomplish the important task of establishing autonomy, which includes the ability to manage financially and to become functionally independent of parents. The manner in which supportive arrangements are made and the accompanying attitude and expectations of both parents and married children determine whether such help will have positive or negative effects.

The principle of empowerment can be demonstrated by asking the following question: Does the support lead to responsible action and mutual respect, or to indebtedness, dependency, and obligation? If parents use their resources to control, the result is emotional distance and resentment. If parents use their resources to empower, they help the couple establish a strong marital bond along with a desire to maintain solid ties and connection with extended family.

Differentiation

A person's identity is formed in the family of origin. In fact, until puberty it is hard to think of ourselves apart from our family. In our family we acquire the majority of our attitudes, beliefs, and values. Our self-concept is shaped by what we believe our parents think of us.

At puberty, however, differentiation begins to intensify. By this process teenagers establish an identity separate from their family. Differentiated individuals are both connected to their family and at the same time sufficiently separated socially and psychologically. It takes a great deal of emotional, intellectual, and spiritual energy to accomplish this extremely important task of sorting out and determining one's own values and beliefs rather than indiscriminately taking on the values and beliefs of one's parents. We describe the process of adolescent differentiation in greater detail in chapter 9. At this point, it is sufficient to say that people are not ready for marriage until they have clearly differentiated themselves from their parents.

There are two types of undifferentiated individuals: those who are overly close and dependent on their family of origin and those who are disengaged or emotionally severed from it. In overly close (enmeshed) relationships, people are so tightly involved with their family that there is

HOW AM I EVER GOING TO DEVELOP A DIFFERENTIATED SELF-STRUCTURE IN A FAMILY AS ENMESHED AS THIS?

no healthy separateness. Disengaged people, however, are so emotionally removed from their family that there is no healthy connectedness.

Differentiation for the marital couple is described in Genesis 2:24: "Therefore a man leaves his father and his mother and clings to his wife, and they become one flesh." A person cannot leave mother and father if he or she clings to them. People who are overly connected with their parents have difficulty creating a new marital dyad. Yet, leaving mother and father is equally impossible if there has never been a sufficient connectedness with them. In disengaged families, children lack the skills to make close emotional connection with others, even a new spouse. In both extremes, it is highly difficult to establish a meaningful "one flesh" union. The concepts of enmeshment and disengagement are illustrated in the parable of the prodigal son (Luke 15:11–32). The prodigal son disengages from his family. He demands his full inheritance and severs all connections with his family. In the process, he cuts off all social, economic, and psychological ties by moving to a far country. On the surface it may appear to be a sign of independence, but it proves to be premature.

One might also wonder if the elder son who stays home is somehow enmeshed with his family. As the story unfolds, he appears to be undifferentiated. His reaction to his father's acceptance of his lost brother is indicative of enmeshment. A differentiated son would have established a solid connection with a clearly defined self and thus would have celebrated his brother's return. Instead, his jealous and angry reaction suggests that he is threatened by his erroneous belief that his father has only so much love to give and that giving love to the younger brother means that the father loves him less. He is not sufficiently separated from his family of origin, and his dependency leads to possessiveness and jealousy.

Empowerment would convey to both brothers in this parable that they are each unique and of equal worth in their distinctiveness. There would be an assurance that the father's love is abundant and more than enough for both of them. The security that comes from empowerment leads to differentiation: the feeling that one belongs and is connected as well as separate and responsible for one's self.

The way God parented the children of Israel afforded them the possibility of achieving differentiation. God offered covenantal love. On the one hand, when the children of Israel went their own way (disengaged/cut off), he held them accountable and responsible for their actions. On the other hand, God continually offered grace in the form of reconciliation and restoration. This balance of both offering emotional support and affirming differentiation leads to interdependence in relationships.

We have seen that a very important factor in establishing a solid foundation in marriage is the differentiation of both spouses from their families of origin. There can be no cleaving without leaving. When two individuals are differentiated and secure in their own identities, they can give themselves to each other and make room in their selves for the distinct other that contributes toward forming a differentiated unity. Their close and stable relationships with their families of origin promote a loyalty to the old while creating a new and distinct system.

Adaptability

In general, people need order in their lives. Scripture teaches that a human community should be an orderly one. Effective families function well with a certain amount of routine and structure. Yet the desired degree of order varies greatly among families and cultures. Some families demand an excessive amount of order; others have almost no structure at all. For example, children's bedtimes may be observed so precisely in some families that if the youngsters are not in bed with the lights out at the prescribed minute, punishment is sure to follow. Other families have such little regard for order that bedtimes are not even prescribed, let alone enforced. These two extremes are examples of very low and very high degrees of adaptability. Degree of adaptability is an important dimension that marriage partners bring with them from their family of origin (see chapter 2).

Most often, effective families have a healthy degree of structure and flexibility (i.e., they are neither overly rigid nor chaotic). Marriages with a capacity for adaptability endure well over time because they are more open to and can adapt better to the changes that continually occur in family life. This ability is especially important because change is inevitable whether it occurs in the development of individual members, in relationship dynamics, throughout the family life stages, or because of an unexpected internal or external stressor.

But what happens when a person from a rigid home marries a person from a chaotic home? Both spouses will naturally attempt to implement their own family style, and this presents interesting clashes, to say the least. Spouses who come from more balanced and similar backgrounds will undoubtedly have an easier time of it. All couples need to work out a system that works best for them. Even such matters as how to celebrate particular holidays or to implement daily family routines such as eating, sleeping, and playing, or rituals such as manners or prayers at the table or reading stories at bedtime will need to be negotiated. The couple will begin to establish their own routines, household rules, roles, and rituals. Once again, they may take certain things from each of their family traditions to enrich their homes and to mutually create new ways of organizing their family life.

The Dilemma of Modern Marriage

The notion that it is difficult to establish a strong marriage in a postmodern society is supported by the high rate of divorce in most Western cultures. Although a variety of explanations can be proposed, such as urbanization, industrialization, changing gender roles, and high social and geographical mobility, high expectations that marriage will fulfill personal needs is surely a key factor. Up to one hundred years ago, marriage was primarily a social institution designed to meet economic needs and provide a place for rearing children. This view of marriage as an institution has been replaced by the concept that marriage is a *companionship* grounded on romantic attraction, self-fulfillment, and ego-need gratification (Cootz 2004). As the marriage expectation bar continues to be raised, fewer marriages are capable of delivering what they promise in the way of personal fulfillment and satisfaction.

The tremendous expectations placed on marriage today are further exacerbated by the notion that each spouse must compete for power and a separate identity while in the marriage. In the past, wives simply yielded their individual identity and rights to their husbands. As late as the mid-1800s, ownership of any property contributed by the bride's family was transferred to the husband. In the traditional marriage, the goal of two becoming one was met by the bride giving up her own identity and taking on the identity of the husband's wife. While few would want to return to this kind of arrangement, the "challenge in modern marriage is to build a relationship that is mutual, reciprocal, and balanced by equal regard for each spouse and mutual sacrifice for the good of the relationship" (Balswick and Balswick 2006).

One response to the contemporary marriage crisis is to abandon the ideal that marriage is a lifelong commitment. Family sociologists have documented this response in the literature as the "deinstitutionalization of marriage" (Cherlin 2004), the "retreat from marriage" (Smock 2004), and the view that lifelong marriage is "something of an aberration that existed" in the past (Gillis 2004). Ellen Lewin (2004) discusses the question these writers pose. The concept of marriage as the only legitimate conjugal arrangement is being challenged. John Gillis (2004) welcomes the new trend of a wide range of formal and informal marriage arrangements and asserts that "seen in the larger historical and global perspective, there is nothing particularly alarming in the tendency. In fact, there is much to recommend it" (p. 991). A careful observer might note that these comments are based on naturalistic assumptions that society should accept what is happening as normative and not make value judgments about what marriage should be. Contrary to a biblical view, much contemporary writing views marriage as a relationship of convenience, formed according to what the two people decide to make of it.

Adrian Thatcher (1999) suggests that Western societies are now exhibiting the common features of a *post-Christian marital system*. Elements of this ethic include the marginalization of marriage itself, the rejection of marriage as a lifelong covenant commitment, an emphasis on individualistic satisfaction and self-fulfillment, and the idolatry of romantic love that makes falling in love a "surrogate religion." Thatcher concludes that the postmodern marital ethic fails to take into account marital commitment or the place of children in marriage, but focuses exclusively on the satisfaction derived from the relationship itself.

The contemporary crisis in marriage is real. But rather than cave in to postmodern marital ethics, we believe the dilemma of modern marriage can be solved by recapturing a biblical view of marriage. Whereas God intends for marriage to constitute a *unity* as in "two become one," it is not God's intent for either the husband or the wife to lose his or her own identity in the process of forming that union. God intends for marriage to reflect the unique type of relationality found in the Holy Trinity. This truth is a core derivative of Genesis 1:26–27: "Then God said, 'Let *us* make humankind in our image, according to our likeness'; . . . So God created humankind in his image, in the image of God he created them; male and female he created them." The *relationality* between the distinct human beings (male and female) reflects the *imago Dei*—the image of God.

Stanley Grenz (2001) developed his theological anthropology by focusing on relationality as the key aspect of being human. Likewise, F. LeRon Shults (2003) points out that social scientists, philosophers, and theologians see *relationality*, not *rationality*, as the fundamental quality of being human.

We bring this emphasis on relationality into our model for marriage. The relational nature in marriage is analogous in human form to the divine Trinity. As the Father, the Son, and the Holy Spirit (three distinct persons) mutually indwell in a trinitarian fellowship, so do spouses (two distinct selves) mutually indwell in the marriage union. Ever mindful of our human limitations, we believe this model offers great promise. It is in their distinctiveness that spouses mutually permeate each other when they form their union. Unity and distinction coexist. Reciprocal and mutual interdependency is what God had in mind for marriage. A differentiated unity brings great satisfaction to both spouses and their relationship. To be human is to be a particular spouse in a relationship, distinct and unique and yet inextricably intertwined and interdependent with the other. Mutual indwelling never negates but rather enhances the particularity of each spouse. As Gary Deddo asserts, "The unity and the distinction are each unimpaired by the other" (1999, 23).

In other words, both spouses are more than they can ever be by themselves because they have become something bigger in their union. In marriage, spouses are both distinct (male and female differentiation) and equal (directed to be fruitful and have dominion) in their created purpose. They find ultimate meaning in and through their relationship with God and each other. The supreme meaning of being created in the image of God is that spouses reflect a relationship of *unity* without absorbing one into the other. Marital mutuality is reached through a reciprocating relationship in which spouses encounter their own uniqueness in relation to God and the other.

Differentiated Unity: Becoming One While Maintaining Uniqueness

In this section we address specific aspects of this process of becoming one while maintaining individual uniqueness. Anytime two people come together in a relationship as intense and demanding as marriage, one of four types of interaction is set in motion: competition, conflict, accommodation, or assimilation. Although some marriages are characterized by competition or conflict, these qualities are not conducive to establishing a firm marital foundation.

Assimilation is a process in which two separate entities become one, while accommodation is an agreement by two separate entities to be different. The biblical concept of one flesh might appear to be assimilation. However, the Bible also describes the relationship of the believer with Christ as becoming one with him. Does this mean that we lose our identity and personhood when we become Christians? Of course not! In fact, this is the difference between the various Eastern religions and Christianity. Salvation, according to the Eastern religions, is to acknowledge the self as an illusion and then to recognize oneness with the eternal force in the universe. In Christianity, however, salvation is relational. It comes when the person is rightly related to God, the Creator and provider of eternal life.

Assimilation in marriage, where the personhood of one spouse is given up, is not what God intended. Christian marriage is more like accommodation, where two separate people each maintain a distinct personhood but choose to come together in a unity and oneness of commitment, meaning, and service. It is noteworthy that the key verses in Ephesians 5 that speak about the marriage relationship are introduced by the directive, "Be subject to one another out of reverence to Christ" (v. 21). Ideally, in Christian marriage each spouse is subject to the other, that is, each makes room for the other to love and be loved, to forgive and be forgiven, to serve and be served, and to know and be known. A marriage in which one partner, the husband or the wife, is asked to give up his or her personhood for the sake of the other denies God's expression in and through that unique member of the creation. The relationship is remarkably more fulfilling when both people are equally expressed in their union, providing others an opportunity to know two distinct people as well as to relate to the couple as a unit.

Just because a couple forms a union does not mean there are no differences between the spouses. Quite the contrary. Precisely because they bring unique perspectives to the union, they will need to navigate through their differences. In doing so they need to be open and responsive to each other in an attitude of humble respect. Conflict is to be expected when two distinct and unique individuals express themselves equally. Marriage without conflict signifies that one spouse has given up personhood. In a vital relationship, conflicts are viewed with an eye to finding a solution that is in the best interest of each spouse and the relationship as a whole. Agreement is never at the expense of one spouse over the other. Being subject to one's spouse does not mean giving in for the sake of avoiding conflict or maintaining harmony. In fact, giving in for the sake of avoiding conflict may be a way of letting a spouse down.

Commitment involves a willingness to express your desires and opinions, to confront a partner in love, to listen with openness to your spouse's desires and opinions, to have compassion, and to affirm the other's ideas. Differentiated unity assures a mutual love that works out differences for the good of the relationship.

Learning New Roles in the Marital Dance

Perichoresis is the Greek word used in the New Testament to describe the relationality between members of the Trinity. Eugene Peterson (2005, 44–45) points out that in the original language *perichoresis* literally means "a round dance." Like a round dance, marriage can be described as two people moving rhythmically together as they repeatedly embrace, release, hold on, and then let go of each other. Partners will dance in unity when they share an understanding of their roles in relation to each other as they perform their particular dance. It may be an ever-changing dance with new moves as circumstances alter, but when spouses are in step there is great joy in observing the graceful movements. We find it helpful to think of spouses being in tune with each other as they anticipate, construct, change, and live out their roles throughout their marriage.

Prior to marriage, most spouses have already formulated in their minds a role for themselves and a role for the person they are to marry. This subjective anticipation of new roles before entering marriage is known as *role taking*. A rat running a maze is limited to learning by trial and error. It must randomly follow each corridor in search of food until it either reaches a dead end or finds the reward. Humans use their rich vocabulary and elaborate thinking ability to run a maze in their minds. In fact, before two people decide to marry, they both probably run through an elaborate symbolic maze by imagining what it would be like to be married to the other person for the rest of their lives. We constantly engage in role taking when anticipating the new roles we eventually assume.

An important ingredient in the achievement of marital adjustment is the ability to take on the role of another person. This requires empathy—the ability to view the world from someone else's perspective and to stand in that person's place. Research shows that people with role-taking ability score high on marital-adjustment tests. It is extremely important that partners be able to see things from the viewpoint of their spouse. This is what understanding the other is all about.

After marriage, spouses engage in *role playing*. Role playing is the process of actually assuming the role of spouse and dancing out the part that has been only imagined up to this point. The first part of role playing can be thought of as *playing at a role*. Spouses play at a role to the extent that they are self-conscious and unsure of themselves in marriage. We can engage in role taking hundreds of times. However, when we actually assume the role, we find it to be somewhat different from what we imagined. A newly married couple will experience some awkwardness in playing at their new roles as spouses. Even though they are acutely aware that they are newlyweds, they are not yet accustomed to their new role as married people. It takes time to become comfortable with the role so that it feels natural.

People who begin marriage by playing at a role will eventually become comfortable with it and spontaneously engage in playing the role of marital partner. Meanwhile, because of the expectations formed prior to role taking, the early stages of marriage often bring *role conflict*. Both people enter marriage with their personal and/or family of origin definition of what their role and their spouse's role should be. This can lead to confusion and difficulty.

Much emotion is invested in one's new role as husband or wife, and consequently there is also great potential for conflict. A husband and wife may disagree about the definition of the spouse's role. He may enter marriage thinking that husbands do not do dishes, while the wife may consider this to be his role. Similarly, a wife may view her role as including responsibility for the budget, but the husband may see this as his territory. As the couple begins to clarify these messages, tension is likely to occur. If they resort to pulling or pushing while learning this dance, they will appear uncoordinated and will likely step on each other's toes. Finding the mutual rhythm and coordinating the right steps is worth every effort it takes to create a harmonious pattern of movement.

Role conflict arises naturally and not necessarily because a person is immature or unprepared for role skirmishes. Role conflicts need to be worked out in an atmosphere of grace, acceptance, and dialogue. Spouses who have good skills in problem solving and conflict resolution will have a head start. Resolving role conflicts throughout marriage gives the couple a solid base of operation. Those who cannot achieve solutions are likely to struggle with these same role conflicts, and the marriage will resemble a wrestling match more than a dance.

The marital-role dance is an ever-changing dynamic that must evolve as new patterns emerge. Role definitions appropriate in the beginning stages of marriage may become outmoded two or three years later. In the daily acts of being husband and wife, new ways of playing out roles are constantly attempted. Role taking does not stop when a couple marries but continues throughout the life cycle. A couple may have decided early in the marriage that one spouse would stay home with the children when they are young. But when that spouse begins to imagine what a full-time job outside the home would be like (role taking), a role conflict is evident. When any new course of action is taken, the couple must carefully consider its impact on household chores and responsibilities, cooking, child care, socializing, and so on. A step in time will make a huge difference in the final outcome.

The most troublesome adjustments in marriages are those that are not clearly worked out ahead of time. In such situations, each spouse may have unspoken expectations of which the other is unaware. Assuming that spouses can read each other's mind is a recipe for relationship breakdown. A typical example is the wife who assumes that her husband's agreement that she be employed outside the home means that he will take on household responsibilities. When he fails to do so, she finds herself doing double duty, a common complaint in marriage that understandably leads to resentment. Many women who imagine they are entering an egalitarian marriage have been disillusioned to find that they are expected to be the superwoman who does it all.

A spousal role can be defined objectively by spouses, family, culture, church, community, and society at large, but the one who performs the role defines it subjectively. And there is rarely a one-to-one correlation between how a role is generally defined and how that spouse actually defines it. Because each individual person is unique, role playing is always *role making*.

Each person plays the role of husband or wife according to one's own distinctive taste and style—a person embellishes the marital dance with his or her unique flair. Marriages in which either partner has a highly rigid definition of what the other's role should be will most likely encounter trouble. In happy marriages each spouse is willing to let the other create and develop a uniquely personal role. When the individual is enhanced, the relationship is enhanced.

Let us give an example from our own marriage. During our early years together, we occasionally argued over issues that we now believe were the result of overly rigid definitions of marital roles. The most conspicuous example was Jack's complaining that Judy was too much like her mother. Judy's mother was a very spontaneous and expressive person who would freely wave to her grandchildren from the choir loft during a church service. Such behavior would invariably embarrass Jack. Judy tended to express herself in very spontaneous ways as well. For example, when she would meet a friend in a public place, she would wave delightedly and yell out a greeting that would embarrass Jack, who was more reserved in public. He would then reprimand Judy for her behavior, since it caused him discomfort. He now looks back on his own behavior with equal embarrassment, for he recognizes that the rigidity of his role expectation for Judy resulted in his dampening her free spirit. When Judy confronted him and he took an honest look at himself, he understood what role rigidity can do. This realization led to an acceptance and appreciation of Judy as a unique person and became a significant stepping-stone to growth in the relationship. Judy also took more effort to consider his feelings in these situations.

Adjustment in the Marital Dance

Throughout the marriage, role adjustments must be made for the sake of the relationship. Whatever the reason, both partners must recognize the continual need for flexibility. On occasion a marriage is adjusted at the expense of one or the other. Although this may occur from time to time out of particular circumstances and by mutual decision, when one spouse is always giving in to the demands and needs of the other, it is a one-sided proposition. This is contrary to *perichoresis*, which involves two people agreeing to make room in themselves for the needs and desires of the other. Each learns to honor and not compromise the unique contribution of the other. Reaching mutual satisfaction through assuming marital roles is the goal. This occurs when both spouses derive fulfillment and pleasure from the marriage union. Their commitment to each other, the relationship, and the marriage permits flexibility and creative openness to change that is in the best interest of both spouses and the relationship.

5

CHRISTIAN MARRIAGE

A Model for Postmodern Society

WHILE THE PREVIOUS chapter dealt with some of the social and psychological issues involved in marriage, this chapter applies our theological basis for family relationships, as presented in chapter 1, to marriage in postmodern society. Marriage today has been influenced by both modern and postmodern ideology. For the sake of simplicity, we use the term *modern marriage* to refer to contemporary marriages that have been affected by both, in contrast to the traditional marriage preceding these influences.

It is a common mistake for Christians to defend a cultural version of marriage as the biblical ideal. They fall into this trap by reading the customs of their own culture into biblical passages or by regarding the biblical accounts of specific historical marriages as normative instead of descriptive. Records of marriages during biblical times do not necessarily reflect God's intention for today.

One mistake is to assume that what our society regards as traditional marriage is biblical. Another mistake is to uncritically endorse secular humanistic ideals and automatically embrace modern/postmodern ideas about marriage. Somewhere between these two extremes is what we believe to be the biblical model. Table 4 summarizes the major characteristics of traditional marriage, modern/postmodern marriage, and

Table 4

Traditional, Biblical, and Modern Marriages

Traditional	Biblical	Modern
Commitment		
Commitment (to the institution)	**Covenant** (between partners)	Contract (self-fulfilment)
Coercive	Cohesive	Disengaged
Dutiful sex (male pleasure)	Affectionate sex (mutual pleasure)	Self-centered sex (personal pleasure)
Adaptability		
Law	**Grace**	Anarchy
Predetermined (segregated roles)	Creative (interchangeable roles)	Undetermined (undifferentiated roles)
Rigid/Stilted	Adaptable/Flexible	Chaotic
Authority		
Ascribed Power	**Empowering**	Possessive Power
Authoritarianism (dependence)	Mutual submissiveness (interdependence)	Absence of authority (independence)
Male-centered	Relationship-centered	Self-centered
Communication		
Inexpressiveness	**Intimacy**	Pseudointimacy
Pronouncement (legislation)	Discussion (negotiation)	Demand (stalemate)
Nonassertive/Aggressive	Assertive	Aggressive

biblical marriage, comparing them in terms of the four aspects of our theological model: covenant (commitment), grace (adaptability), empowering (authority), and intimacy (communication). Close examination will show that the traditional and the postmodern relationships fall short of the ideal.

Commitment

Because Western laws have come to treat marriage as a contract rather than as a covenant, the common statement "Marriage is a commitment!" is often misunderstood. Is it really true, as is generally believed, that marriages are less stable today because people are not as committed as they were in the past? The answer is both yes and no. In the past the emphasis was on a commitment to marriage as an institution. The notion that a couple should stay married for life involved a view of marriage as a sacred institution that must be upheld at all costs. There was also a collective emphasis on loyalty to the group (family or community) rather than to the individual. Over the years this collective emphasis has given way to an individualistic, "me-oriented" theme. The focus has shifted to the individual's right to personal happiness. Thus commitment to marriage as an institution is rejected when it interferes with the individual's self-fulfillment.

Divorce was rare under the traditional system because of an intrinsic commitment to marriage as an institution. Divorce was unthinkable because it transgressed a strongly held belief that violating the institution was morally wrong. The youth counterculture movement of the 1960s challenged these traditional ideas and asserted that commitment to the institution was an invalid reason to stay married. It was argued that too many people were committed to institutional norms rather than to personal happiness. The self-fulfillment movement continued in the 1970s in the form of various sensitivity and encounter groups in which people sought to find and assert the self. This self-absorption continues to be strongly emphasized in our postmodern culture.

Accordingly, in the early 1970s the divorce rate began to rise dramatically and continued to do so for nearly ten years. Social scientists now believe that one of the major reasons for this phenomenon was that people who were unhappy increasingly turned to divorce as a way to remove themselves from their past and to find happiness. Since they believed they had a right to personal happiness, this value took precedence over commitment to the sanctity of marriage as an institution.

In the postmodern marriage, continued commitment is contingent on self-fulfillment. Indeed, one of the main criteria that sociologists now use to measure marital success is happiness. A marriage is considered successful if the partners describe themselves as happy. In many contemporary marriages, however, it seems as though the baby has been thrown out with the bathwater. Realizing that something is missing in the concept of commitment to marriage as an institution, many people have discarded the whole concept of commitment in favor of individual happiness. This is a tragedy because commitment is the cornerstone of the marriage relationship. The problem lies with too narrow a definition of marriage: in the past it was solely a commitment to the institution; in the contemporary secular view it is solely for self-fulfillment.

The solution is found in the biblical perspective that God created humans in the context of relationship. Genesis 2 recounts that God saw it was not good for the man to be alone, so he created the woman. The man recognized her as equal and complementary, bone of his bones and flesh of his flesh; they became one flesh and were naked and not ashamed (vv. 23–25). This is a beautiful picture of interdependency.

Marriage is not only a commitment to the institution but also a commitment to the relationship. The relationship is vital in and of itself and needs to be nourished in order to be all God intended it to be. The commitment of Yahweh to Israel as depicted in the book of Hosea provides a profound example of a commitment that endures, renews, forgives, and restores. Marriages are strong when both partners are committed to the institution, to the relationship, and to each other as persons. Commitment only to the institution results in legalism; commitment only to the other person results in humanism. A commitment to all three (person, institution, and relationship) brings the right balance. This biblical model takes into account the importance of caring for the needs of the individual, the relationship, and the social system.

A balanced commitment is reflected in the view of marital sexuality. In traditional marriage, sex is viewed as a right to pleasure for the man but as a duty to be endured by the woman. In postmodern marriage, sex tends to be self-centered, with the emphasis placed on the individual's right to personal pleasure. There is much to be said for the idea that married people are to be fulfilled sexually, but when this becomes the dominant emphasis, the relationship suffers and thus the real meaning of sexuality is lost.

The biblical response emphasizes person-centered affectionate sex in marriage. Scripture advocates mutual pleasure and mutual benefit. This involves a mutual decision to give and receive in love. First Corinthians 7:3–4 clearly states that our bodies are for each other as the ultimate expression of ourselves to each other.

The security that stems from a commitment to the marriage relationship provides an atmosphere of freedom and willingness to learn together through the sexual expression of love. Spouses learn to mesh their lives as sexual persons in the security of relationship commitment. The biblical ideal, then, is much more than personal sexual pleasure or one spouse submitting to the other out of commitment to the institution of marriage. It is relating to each other on all levels: physical, mental, and spiritual. The scriptural concept of one flesh entails a mutual commitment to one's mate, the relationship, and the institution.

Adaptability

In traditional marriage the roles are segregated. The husband usually assumes the role of working outside the home, and the wife assumes the role of homemaking and caring for the children. Most people who argue for separation in marital roles are not aware of how recent this phenomenon is. Until the Industrial Revolution, 90 percent of all families lived on farms, and even as late as one hundred years ago two-thirds of all families in the United States did so. That the marital roles there were far from segregated will be no surprise to anyone who has lived on a farm. Whereas some kinds of work were designated as the man's or the woman's province, both husbands and wives performed manual labor on the farm, and both shared the responsibility in raising their children.

Segregation in marital roles developed only with the emergence of the urban family, where home life and work life are divided. In this type of family, the husband works outside the home, leaving child care to the wife. One would be hard pressed to argue, on the basis of either historical or biblical evidence, that woman's place is in the home and man's place is in the business world outside the home.

The postmodern view that spouses can take on roles in marriage in many ways is refreshing, yet at the same time undifferentiated roles may result in chaos or conflict about what will get done and who will assume a given responsibility. In the modern world, who does what is often worked out according to a system of social exchange. This system is based on the simple assumption that all relationships involve costs and rewards. That which one gives to a relationship is experienced as a cost, and that which one receives is experienced as a reward. Marriages thrive when the rewards outweigh the costs for each partner. As long as one gets more than or as much as one gives, there is reason to stay married. The concept of social exchange can be stated as a formula: *Rewards* minus *Costs* equals *Profit*.

Let's imagine a couple trying to decide who will cook the evening meal. The conversation may begin with the husband suggesting that his wife cook, pointing out that he has had a hard day at the office and also because he cooked the previous night. The wife may respond that she has had an equally hard day at work and that she cooked dinner three out of the last four evenings. The husband may then agree that he will cook if she cleans up, washes the dishes, and takes out the garbage. The point here is that this arrangement demands constant bargaining and negotiating skills. Disaster looms around the corner when roles are not agreed upon beforehand.

We suggest that roles be clearly defined but subject to change and interchangeable in terms of gender. In the case of segregated roles, tasks are predetermined according to gender with no room for interchange. In modern marriages, roles are often undetermined. Determining roles through mutual agreement opens up creative possibilities for husbands and wives to serve each other through their roles. They are committed together in cooperative efforts to take on certain tasks of daily living. They agree to periodically review how things are going so that they can make changes when necessary.

Although no Bible verses deal explicitly with marital roles, Scripture does teach that everything ought to be done with a sense of order and harmony. Assigning tasks on the basis of a person's interests, skills, and availability is a loving way to work out marital roles. It also respects differences and recognizes the unique talents of each spouse and his or her special contribution to the marriage.

Of the various tasks to be performed, parenting is without question one of the most crucial. In the traditional family, the mother automatically does most parenting. Unfortunately, this leads to the neglect of fathering, a major problem in our society today. In modern marriages, parenting roles and responsibilities may be shirked because of overinvolvement in work and/or extracurricular roles, to the detriment of parenting. These parents fail to prioritize the needs of children over and against their personal goals. Single- and dual-earner parents rely on excellent child-care facilities to fill in for them while they are bringing in the income.

In a balanced marriage, both the mother and the father are actively involved in the parenting process. There is no biblical evidence that would lead one to believe that a mother's involvement with children is more important than a father's involvement. Scripture refers to the responsibility of both parents, as in Ephesians 6:1–4: "Children, obey your parents in the Lord, for this is right. 'Honor your father and mother.' . . . And, fathers, do not provoke your children to anger, but bring them up in the discipline and instruction of the Lord." Coparenting seems especially critical in our day and age, when breakdown in the family system is often related to the lack of effective fathering (Lindsey, Caldera, and Colwell 2005).

In the traditional marriage, roles are stilted and rigidly defined. There is very little flexibility as to how they may be performed. In the modern marriage, expectations are so loose that marital roles can be truly lacking. Without any set procedures to bring stability to these roles, the marriage relationship lacks integrity. The balanced marriage has flexible and interchangeable roles as each occasion calls forth what is needed.

Since change can be expected throughout the cycles of family life, it is vital that spouses be flexible and adaptable. Married life and family life are at their best when they are neither predetermined nor undetermined but provide structured security. This structured security allows spouses and family members to experience the exciting process of each member working for the good of the whole. Family members are empowered to serve others in collaborative efforts.

Authority

Authority in marriage is currently a controversial issue among Christians. Until very recent times, authority in marriage exclusively meant male headship. Christians and non-Christians alike have adhered to the idea that the husband is to be the head of the home, whereas the wife is expected to submit to her husband. Recently in Christian circles, a renewed philosophy of authority has emerged involving mutual submission. The husband is challenged to love, serve, and submit to his wife, just as Christ gave his life for the church. Modern marriages are opposed to the traditional male headship arrangement and emphasize individual spousal power in marriage. While this may present power dilemmas for spouses, it enhances equality, freedom, and personal power. In particular, the postmodern perspective recognizes that there are a variety of authority styles, determined mainly by cultural values, and, therefore, not just "one" way to define authority in marriage. Each couple, taking into account their generational and culture values, will determine authority issues accordingly.

The system of social exchange plays an integral part in dealing with personal power struggles in modern/postmodern marriage. The focus is on the quid-pro-quo notion of getting something for something—"if you scratch my back, I'll scratch yours." Spouses are satisfied as long as everything comes out equal and neither partner perceives things as unfair. However, it is hard to define equal, and therefore authority and decision-making power may cause conflict.

Under a system of social exchange, negotiation is the best way to deal with conflict. Each partner tries to maximize the returns on his or her investments in the marriage. Accordingly, research shows that in this system wives who work outside the home have greater power in the marriage relationship than do wives who do not. The money earned can be converted into power, thus elevating the authority of the wife in the marriage.

It should be noted that the system of social exchange is built on an assumption about human beings that is consistent with Christian thought, namely, that people are basically self-centered by nature. In reality, social exchange is a fairly good model to describe how many marriages operate. We would, however, question the assumption that fighting for your own rights without regard for a partner is ideal. The Christian worldview, by contrast, values unselfish giving, mutual exchange, and even going beyond what is expected. The goal is not to maintain power over one's partner but to empower and be empowered through the relationship.

Authority in Christian marriage includes dual submission to the lordship of Jesus Christ and to each other. The chain-of-command view that a wife should submit to her husband, who in turn should submit to God, is popular in some Christian circles. This faulty authoritarian persuasion fails to take into account the great news of the New Testament promotion of mutual love, joyful service, and reciprocal submission.

Ephesians 5:21, "Be subject to one another out of reverence for Christ," is crucial in this connection. It sets the foundation for the verses that follow. "Husbands, love your wives, just as Christ loved the church and gave himself up for her" (v. 25). From this it is clear that headship is to be understood not in the hierarchical sense of the husband's lording it over his wife but rather as taking the role of a suffering servant who gives himself out of his love. Christ's example as a compassionate servant who gave his life for his bride, the church, is the model of how the husband is to be a *source* for his marriage. Wives too are called to this same self-giving, suffering-servant role. Mutual submissiveness, then, is the overriding message of Ephesians 5.

Feminist ideology has reacted strongly against conceptualizing the marital relationship in terms of submissiveness. This is partly due to the way in which the concept has been unequally applied in the past, but it also stems from the fear that legitimizing self-sacrifice will open the door to personal abuse. In place of mutual submissiveness, Don Browning proposes that Christian marriage be based on the concept of "equal regard" (Browning et al. 1997). That is to say, the biblical view is for marital love to be mutual, which means regarding the other's self-hood as one would want to be regarded. Although Browning is open to the concept of self-sacrifice in love, he sees it as "derived from equal regard" (pp. 283–84).

We agree with Browning in substance but recognize that the concept of partnership is also helpful for understanding mutual submission (Garland, Richmond, and Garland 1986). At times one partner may be required to give much more than an equal share to the marriage. God calls both spouses to give generously of themselves for the sake of the other when sickness or some other circumstance makes it difficult for one to give much at that time. Putting the interests of the spouse first out of regard for his or her needs is the extraordinary way of the cross.

Communication

In the traditional marriage, there is little need for verbal communication. What communication there is tends to take the form of pronouncements, talking at, rather than with, one's spouse. The husband as head of the marriage legislates without consulting his wife. When conflicts or delicate matters arise, they are often dealt with by sidestepping the issue. Verbal communication is de-emphasized because meeting socio-emotional and companionship needs is not considered a major part of marriage. Marriage is regarded more as an institutional arrangement that provides for economic needs and social status.

Communication in the modern marriage can be characterized as a series of declarations and demands that each spouse makes to the other. When conflicts arise, confrontation is the way to get one's needs and disappointments out on the table. The motto is "Openly express what you need from your mate." While such openness can be refreshing when compared to the traditional pattern, a combative posture and insistence on satisfying personal needs will obviously obstruct a sensitive caring for the other. Making aggressive demands, such as "I want my needs met regardless of how you are affected," results in counterdemands that ultimately lead to stalemate.

In a balanced marriage, the partners communicate by expressing themselves in an open manner. When one talks, the other listens. They care about what is best for their partner. Differences are dealt with by respecting each other's needs and desires. They make an effort to understand each other's point of view and to respond accordingly. There is an attitude of submission and a willingness to consider giving up one's own needs and desires for the sake of the other and the relationship. Both spouses work together to seek solutions through mutual and reciprocal decision making.

Dual-Earner Marriage

Discussions of marriage can no longer be considered complete without tackling the topic of dual-earner marriages. The U.S. Bureau of Labor Statistics (2001) reports that 56 percent of all married couples with children under the age of six and 63 percent with children under the age of eighteen are dual earners. It should also be noted that evidence generated from a sample of 2,093 women found that "throughout early parenthood, women exhibit significant movement into and out of the labor force" (Hynes and Clarkberg 2005, 222).

Economic necessity leaves many families little choice but for both parents to work outside the home. They must decide the question of whether the husband and the wife should both be employed as they consider what is in the best interest of everyone concerned. If a couple decides that they will both work outside the home, then the question is how to accomplish this in the most satisfactory way. The key to doing it well is learning how to balance work and family so that neither impinges on the other in disruptive ways (Balswick and Balswick 1995).

We believe the working couple must proactively establish and maintain a rightful balance between work and family. The couple will be most successful in coming up with a suitable arrangement if they (1) mutually contribute unconditional love, grace, empowering, and intimacy to their relationship; (2) have an extra dose of cohesion and adaptability; (3) agree on priorities, recognizing what is essential and what is nonessential in their family and work roles; and (4) identify resources within themselves, their marriage, the family, and the wider community to help them meet the demands of their dual roles.

In seeking to fulfill their commitment to work and family life, dual-earner couples can be characterized as adversaries, acrobats, allies, or accommodators (Hall and Hall 1980). Adversaries have a higher commitment to work than to family life. Each spouse may claim to value home life as much as work but expects the partner to be the one who puts family before work. As a result, the couple has an adversarial relationship that may result in serious conflict and neglect of parenting roles.

Marriage partners who have equally high commitments to work and family can be described as acrobats. To meet the demands of both the work and the home arena, they need the agility of an acrobat. Wanting to do it all, the couple sooner or later discovers that something has to give, whether it is their work, marriage, parenting, or emotional and physical health.

Allies have similar degrees of commitment to their jobs and their home, but they distinguish essentials from nonessentials. They are allies in the sense that neither expects the other to carry more of the load in the home. While they share responsibility for family life, they also strive to be equal in their commitment to their careers. As allies they work together to carry the load of earning a living, managing a home, and establishing a good relationship with the children.

Accommodators agree to differ. In an accommodating marriage, one spouse gives priority to career, the other to the home. Accommodators choose to balance work and home life through complementary roles. While allies emphasize equality in contributing to work and home life, accommodators find that complementary roles accomplish the same purposes but in a different way. Accommodators benefit from the individual strengths of each spouse. Over time, as the demand of one's job changes, accommodators may switch the balance. One spouse may pull back from work commitments to increase the time given to family life and vice versa. Accommodators usually function as allies in that they respect and honor each other's commitments to work and the home.

A comparison of dual-earner couples from 1970 to 2001 indicates that the proportion of income contributed by wives relative to husbands has steadily increased (Raley, Mattingly, and Bianchi 2006). It is a legitimate question whether a husband's contribution to housework and parenting tasks has correspondingly increased. Some research notes a startling imbalance in dual-earner marriages as wives continue to do the majority of housework, according to Arlie Hochschild (1989) in what she terms the *second shift*. Those husbands who do contribute describe themselves as "helping out." Such research points out the dire need for dual-earning husbands not only to increase their contribution to home and parenting tasks but also to change their idea of being a helper to taking an active leadership role in parenting.

There are major benefits for both men and women in a dual-earner marriage in which responsibilities are equally shared. John Gottman (1994, 1995) found that men who do housework are emotionally and physically healthier as well as more responsive to their wives. The incorporation of relational skills with household tasks further endears men to their families. An important aspect for the man is knowing that his intentional choice to be involved as a father leads to validation and appreciation. Also, when the wife relaxes her household standards and parenting expectations, it is much more inviting for the husband to willingly join in. Through the sharing of roles, the wife is not only validated in her work role but more fulfilled in her marriage and her parenting role.

Research indicates that when work-home conflict occurs among wives in dual-earning couples, they immediately want to decrease the number of hours they are employed, whether the conflict originates at home or at work. Men want to decrease their hours at work only when work-home conflict originates at work. However, some men respond to conflict by *increasing* their hours at work (Reynolds 2005).

A hard lesson for all dual-earner couples to learn is that they can't do everything! In prioritizing what needs to be done, they must learn to do a "good enough" job. Venturing into previously uncharted territories, dual-earner couples represent a type of frontier marriage. They need all the support they can get as they work toward a satisfying and meaningful family life. Recent findings indicate that dual earners perceive themselves to be part of a family-friendly community when that community includes a sufficient number of other couples in their same marital life stage (Swisher, Sweet, and Moen 2004). A significant part of those family-friendly environments involves the provision of high-quality child-care centers. Many churches are offering such service to their community.

Many dual-earner parents rely on day care for their children, and an increasing number of young children spend some of their time in day care. It is important to ask questions about the effectiveness of substitute care. Responses to this question range all the way from it *turns kids into bullies* (Reeves 2001) to the view that substitute care *rescues children from overly invested parents* (Warner 2005).

In a landmark study, over thirty scholars investigated 1,364 randomly selected families during an eighteen-month period to help answer this question (*Child Care and Child Development: Results from the NICHD Study of Early Child Care and Youth Development* 2005). The findings were sobering: many infants typically spend long hours at two or more mediocre-quality child-care facilities during their first year of life. The parent/child attachment during the first fifteen months of an infant's life remained intact, but prolonged nonmaternal care before the age of three years seemed to adversely affect the mother's sensitivity to her child's needs. The conclusion was that parents must make every effort to secure high-quality day care and also be alert to the unique needs of the child. If the experts don't speak out, children who spend an inordinate time in these mediocre centers will be shortchanged. Sharon Lanesman states, "The culture of silence among scientists and professionals is . . . [that we] dare not inflict even more guilt upon parents, or ask that they consider forgoing much needed outside income or spending more of their little economic resources to obtain better quality care. As a result, many people become paralyzed by the magnitude of reforming our nation's standards for care" (2005, 435). Every effort must be made to ensure that children receive the highest quality care at these centers, and parents must be dedicated to staying highly involved in their children's lives.

The Heart of Christian Marriage

When we asked our friends Gene and Virginia the secret of their fifty-year marriage, Gene teased, "You have to be willing to give up!" We laughed a little about the way his answer could be interpreted, but after thinking about what he had said, it seemed rather profound. At the very heart of marriage is the willingness of spouses to let go of their personal agenda so that they can truly listen to what their partner is saying. Philippians 2 describes Christ as emptying himself and taking on the form of a servant.

It is really a matter of the heart, an attitude of grace and empowerment to take on the form of a servant and to keep the best interest of others and relationships as a precious priority. It means we have to give up our selves at that moment. Yet when this is a mutual practice and both spouses are practicing this principle, it will automatically be a mutual and reciprocal process. Michael Vasey points out that "the Jewish and Eastern tradition understands [stable] marriage as a gift. . . . Marriage is seen as an aspect of human life, with its own inherent potentialities and responsibilities, that comes to us from the hand of the creator." Furthermore, "marriage is then seen simultaneously as a gift to the couple and to the community in that it carries blessings and responsibilities for both" (1996, 181).

We should not overlook the Jewish and Eastern tradition that marriage is a gift for the community as well as for the couple. It is wise to move beyond our individualistic bias and affirm that the bond of marriage is strengthened when a couple invites a supportive group of people to share in their commitment to their marriage and family life.

In this chapter we have sought to apply biblical principles of relationality to marriage. A review of the religion and marriage literature reveals a positive correlation between a couple's religiosity and marital satisfaction (Dollahite, Marks, and Goodman 2004). Given the biblical bases for most religious beliefs in the United States, this can be viewed as confirming evidence for the benefits of practicing unconditional love, gracing, empowering, and intimacy in marriage.

PART 3

THE EXPANSION OF FAMILY LIFE

Parenting and Beyond

I N THIS SECTION we move beyond the marriage relationship to parent/ child relationships. A strong marital relationship serves as the secure foundation, while children are the building blocks through which the family structure changes during each life stage. It is a universal truth that the couple experiences a dramatic change when children enter as well as when they exit the family. In fact, marital adjustment has been found to be at its highest just before the birth of the first child and continues to decline until the last child leaves home (Twenge, Campbell, and Foster 2003).

Making the necessary adjustments from the dyad to the triad can be relatively smooth for some couples, whereas the transition to parenthood is a trying time for others. Recent research also indicates that *"cohabiting women experience remarkable declines in social and psychological well-being"* when they become mothers (Woo and Raley 2005, 218). Having children becomes even more of a stressor when parenthood takes place outside marriage (Nomaguchi and Milkie 2003). Although the strain of becoming new fathers is greater for men in cohabiting relationships than for those in marriages, it is greatest on single men, who experience greater depression associated with not living with their child (Woo and Raley 2005). Parenting is more difficult than most of us ever imagined it to be, and we find ourselves looking to the experts for help.

A major adjustment also occurs during the later stages of family life when adult children leave home and/or boomerang back or when the care of elderly parents brings other kinds of stressors to the couple. Like any sound group, the family must have not only a well-organized structure to function effectively but also one flexible enough to survive the twists and turns of life. The following chapters present some blueprints for successful family living.

Chapter 6 introduces a model of Christian parenting that empowers children to become competent, mature, responsible adults. We look at the pros and cons of some common parenting styles and then offer a biblical model that we believe incorporates the best of these styles. We propose that as children mature, parents must also grow so that there is mutual empowerment and transformation.

In chapter 7 we examine the life of the child from the perspective of several developmental theories. We evaluate how these theories comport with the Christian view of human personhood and indicate important aspects in parenting young children. A primary concern in this discussion is the matter of empowerment. The topic of chapter 8 is family spirituality, an umbrella term we use to represent the role of the family in inculcating values, morals, beliefs, and religious faith within children.

Chapter 9 deals with the stresses and strains that can develop when adolescence and midlife occur simultaneously. Important to this discussion is the origin and impact of adolescence in modern/postmodern society. These life stages of adolescence and midlife often are accompanied by crisis, resulting in a serious clash between the generations. Finally, in chapter 10 we discuss the dynamics of the family in later life. This begins with the launching of adolescent children, an ambivalent time of life for both parents and children. Parents struggle to let go, while children seek freedom and yet fear leaving the security of their home. Following this is the postlaunching stage, when parents move into the so-called sandwich generation. At this time, parents feel the squeeze of dealing with both adult children and elderly family members who are physically, emotionally, and/or financially dependent on them. This period of family life involves losses of many kinds as well as gains reaped from meeting the challenges of changing relationships.

6

PARENTING

The Process of Relationship Empowerment

STEVEN MINTZ (2004) identifies three overlapping phases in the conceptualization of childhood. During the colonial era, the *premodern childhood* phase, children were perceived as adults in training. During the *modern* phase (late 1800s to mid-1900s), childhood came to be viewed as a prolonged and protected period of dependency. Finally, in the *postmodern* phase (beginning in the later 1900s), childhood has been redefined by an increasingly intrusive consumer culture and changing gender roles, family life values, and sexual mores. It should come as no surprise that parenting children is often experienced as a bewildering struggle over how to do it well.

On any topic, from growing flowers to creating scrumptious gourmet dishes to raising children, we can find 101 "how-to" formulas promising that the right technique will produce beautiful flowers, succulent meals, and perfect children. This may work for flowers and gourmet dishes, but parenting children is much more complex.

In most societies parents simply expect their children to grow up to be normal, healthy adults—no special techniques are deemed necessary. In our modern/postmodern society, however, parents are conditioned to believe just the opposite—we presume we need the help of experts to tell us how to be successful. Parents are sometimes reduced to a state of fear that they may do something that will have a lasting harmful effect on their children. As a result of this insecurity, parents increasingly turn to the experts for advice on how to raise children. In this psychologically sophisticated world, we have developed a cult of the expert by keeping our eyes keen on seeking authoritative opinion and our ears attuned for the latest wisdom on parenting. Living as we do in a child-oriented society, we are extremely sensitive and concerned about the parenting role. Even TV shows have developed around the theme of hiring a nanny expert to teach parents how to discipline their children.

It is certainly helpful for parents to gain solid understanding of the biological, psychological, and social development of children so that they have realistic "age-appropriate" expectations. In the long run, they need to feel confident in themselves as they nurture, discipline, guide, and relate to their own children. Together, husband and wife must be coleaders in deciding what is in the best interest of their unique children. This develops as they integrate expert knowledge with the personal knowledge that comes from building a secure relationship with their children and empowering them to be all they can be.

As contributors to the growing body of expert opinion, we would hasten to point out that our quarrel is not with expert opinion but rather with the dogmatism under which some advice is given. Parents begin to feel their own judgments are not to be trusted. We advocate informing parents about child development and parenting methods and also encouraging them to critically analyze the information and compare it with biblical principles. Effective parenting must always take into account the particular needs of the family and incorporate or discard ideas accordingly.

The Christian life is described in various New Testament passages as growth from spiritual infancy to maturity. The new believer starts as an infant and eventually grows up in Christ. One moves from a state of dependency, in which others model, teach, and disciple, to a mature walk with God. As this growth occurs, the believer begins to disciple others. Although the believer is always dependent on God and the Holy Spirit in that growth process, there is also a natural progression in maturity leading the believer to be used by God to serve and minister to others.

The human developmental process encompasses a similar progression from dependency and infancy toward maturity and adulthood. Maturity is often defined as self-sufficiency and independence from one's parents. Most developmental theorists, however, hold that maturity involves more than independence; it entails the capacity to contribute in a positive and constructive way to the good of others.

The notion of empowerment is described in the New Testament as a building up of one another in the Christian faith. It involves loving and serving others and helping them mature spiritually. This description is consistent with the social-science literature regarding the type of parenting that helps children mature. The parenting model we present in this chapter focuses on the parent/child relationship. Each parent and each child is developing and maturing throughout the entire process. We believe that our model, which emphasizes empowering children to maturity, is a needed alternative to models that emphasize control and coercive power. Our model is based on engendering hope and growth in parents and children as they journey together toward maturity.

Speaking for a moment from our personal experience as parents and grandparents rather than as experts, we would challenge parents to concentrate less on the technique of good parenting and more on the process of being a parent. Good parenting is a matter of interacting with our children day in and day out. It is these day-to-day experiences that build our relationship with them. The best advice we can give to parents is to throw away their how-to-parent books and simply become real persons to their children. Even though these materials offer useful guidelines that contribute to an understanding of the child-rearing process, parents can function more freely and openly in their role if they are simply willing to be more genuine with their children.

The Basic Components of Parenting Styles

Now that we have dispelled the notion that there is one correct way to parent children, let's investigate what the social-science literature says about various parenting styles. Parents and other primary caretakers have a significant impact on children's emotional, social, cognitive, and spiritual development. While some parenting styles encourage growth and empowerment, many others hinder or block growth either by fostering dependency or by expecting premature self-reliance. Before we analyze these various styles, it will be helpful to examine some of the components that go into them, namely, approaches to discipline and types of leadership.

Approaches to Discipline

Early research into parent/child relationships distinguished between permissive and restrictive parenting. Proponents of permissive parenting, while not denying the need for discipline, stressed that a child's greatest need is for warmth and security. The restrictive school of thought, while not rejecting parental affection, emphasized that a child's greatest need is for discipline, responsibility, and self-control.

More-recent studies have taken the same approach, but use the terms *control* and *support* instead of *restrictive* and *permissive parenting*. Support is defined as making the child feel comfortable in the presence of the parent and giving the child a sense of being accepted and approved as a person. Control is defined as directing the child to behave in a manner desirable to the parents. Examples of control include giving guidelines and setting limits.

Based on the parental support and control dimensions, Diana Baumrind (1996, 2005) identifies three types of parents—authoritative, authoritarian, and permissive—each of which differs in effectiveness in eliciting obedience and responsibility in a child's moral/character development. A number of studies have found that a combination of high levels of control and support—authoritative parenting—is most conducive to developing competency in children (Aunola and Jari-Erik 2005; Barber, Stolz, and Olsen 2005; Hart, Newell, and Olsen 2003; Pellerin 2005). Authoritarian style (low support and high control) produces children who respect authority but who show little independence and only moderate social competence. Permissive parenting (high support and low control) tends to produce children who lack both social competence and interdependence.

Underlying the controversy between the permissive and the restrictive school of parenting is the question of whether to use physical punishment to obtain compliance from a child. Would the authoritative parenting style allow the use of spanking as a means of control? Although experts differ on this matter, many understandably discourage spanking because of the high incidence of physical abuse suffered by many children.

Unfortunately, the terms *discipline* and *punishment* are often confused in our society. Physical punishment is defended by some Christians on the basis of verses like Proverbs 13:24, "Those who spare the rod hate their children." However, in applying that verse, it is important to consider how the rod was used in the pastoral culture of Old Testament times. It was an instrument to *guide* ignorant sheep, not a means of beating them into submission. Note how the verse concludes: "but those who love them are diligent to discipline them."

On the basis of her twenty-five-year longitudinal study, Baumrind (1996) concludes that "it is not the specific disciplinary practice but *how it is administered* and in what cultural context that determine its efficacy and long-term effects" (p. 405). More specifically, she reports that "authoritative parents endorse the judicious use of aversive consequences, which may include spanking, but in the context of a warm, engaged and rational parent-child relationship" (p. 412). She also notes that child-rearing patterns considered authoritarian in Western culture might be viewed differently in other cultures. For example, Asian families frequently exert coercive control because of the demands for high achievement and conformity in the culture. Children in these homes tend to adopt their parents' family and societal values.

In her review of research on the effect of corporal punishment on child outcome, Elizabeth Gershoff (2002) warns that although corporal punishment is associated with immediate compliance, it is also associated with higher levels of aggression and lower levels of moral internalization and mental health. In their response to Gershoff's article, Baumrind, Larzelere, and Cowan (2005) suggest that undesirable child outcomes are caused not by corporal punishment but by inept, harsh parenting. They conclude that "a blanket injunction against spanking is not justified by the evidence presented by Gershoff" (p. 580). The literature suggests that spanking is not the most effective means of discipline and when resorted to is most effective when combined with other means of discipline, especially when dealing with young children. The number of qualifications given in studies should make us extremely cautious to keep physical punishment to an absolute minimum. A parent also needs to consider that punitive measures may lead to unwanted and unexpected results, such as children hitting back or coercing younger children in a similar way (Sim and Ong 2005). There are almost always sounder ways to deal with disciplinary problems.

Disciplining children takes time, patience, and wisdom. Parents who employ corporal punishment as the primary method of discipline are, by their very behavior, admitting bankruptcy in disciplinary approaches. They are demonstrating an inability to be creative and effective in their discipline of children.

Rudolf Dreikurs (1991) points out that physical punishment leads to disempowerment, whereas natural and logical consequences lead to empowerment. Having children face the consequences of their behavior in a consistent, firm, and loving manner is the best way to empower them. Recognition of the consequences of one's behavior leads to internal control, whereas punishment focuses on external means. Although coercive punishment does work when parents are attempting to eliminate certain behaviors, it also teaches children that force is what counts. Imposing power in this way may lead children to retaliate or try to get even.

In an atmosphere of mutual respect, there will be firmness without domination. An effective parent wins a child's cooperation by leading rather than coercing. Logical and natural consequences also serve to stimulate children's creative responses. Parents who fail to honor and respect their children will find that their children fail to honor and respect them. The traits of an effective parent include wisdom, vision, a sense of humor, patience, encouragement, and good judgment, not the exercise of superior power. Using everyday situations to teach consequences promotes the child's self-confidence, the ability to take others into account, and responsibility for one's own behavior (Dreikurs 1991).

Types of Leadership

Building on research on leadership and small groups, we suggest that parenting involves two different types of leadership skills: instrumental and socioemotional (J. K. Balswick et al. 2003). Instrumental leadership is task oriented, focusing on the things that need to be accomplished in the group. Such leadership organizes activities, sets goals, and generally keeps the group focused on accomplishing those goals. Socioemotional leadership, by contrast, is person oriented and concentrates on maintaining a healthy relationship among group members. Research indicates that both types of leadership skills are necessary if small groups are to function well. Interestingly enough, it has also been discovered that the two types of skills are rarely found in the same individual.

The studies on instrumental and socioemotional leadership in small groups apply to the family as well. Instrumental parenting aims at inculcating beliefs, values, and attitudes, It involves teaching children what they must know and how they must behave to be in good standing within the family. Socioemotional parenting attends to the emotional nature of the relationship between parents and children. Whereas instrumental parenting focuses on tasks and content, socioemotional parenting focuses on the affective bonding between parent and child (Baumrind 1996).

Alternative Parenting Styles

Having briefly defined parental support and control as well as the instrumental and socioemotional aspects of parenting, we are ready to combine these two areas of concern to discuss alternative styles of parenting and their effects on children. We will consider various instrumental styles and then several socioemotional approaches.

Instrumental Parenting

Figure 10 represents the four styles of instrumental parenting. Two dimensions are involved: action and content. Parenting styles can be classified as either high or low in action. That is, some parents actually engage in and thus demonstrate the type of behavior they want their children to adopt; other parents make no such effort. Parenting styles can also be either high or low in content. Some parents verbally com-

FIGURE 10 **Styles of Instrumental Parenting**

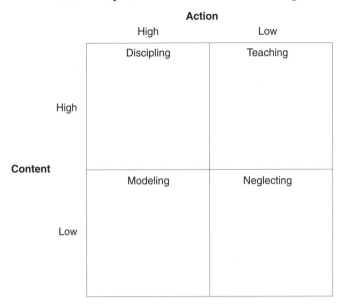

municate through a rich elaboration of rules, norms, values, beliefs, and ideology; others simply do not bother to teach their children.

Neglecting. Parenting that is low in both action and content is the neglecting style. Proper behavior is neither displayed nor taught. Because the parents give no direction verbally or otherwise, the children are on their own to latch on to any social norm or form of behavior. The parent who is neglectful in instrumental parenting is also likely to be neglectful in socioemotional parenting. This style leaves much to be desired, since the children lack good supportive care and must learn by trial and error to fend for themselves.

Teaching. Parenting that is low in action and high in content is the teaching style. The parent in effect says to the child, "Do as I say but don't look to my behavior as a model." Children in such a situation feel that they are being preached at. Though this style may be effective in bringing about the desired behavior in children, it may also breed disrespect for the parents, whose words do not match their lives. As children mature, they become increasingly sensitive to any form of contradictory behavior in their parents. The typical teenager is quick to point out such inconsistency.

In spite of its shortcomings, the teaching style is better than the neglecting style. The teaching style becomes a problem for children, however, when the parents' teaching is inconsistent with their behavior. It may be that the parents do not intentionally cause this confusion if they truly believe in and desire to live up to the standards they enunciate but fail to do so.

Modeling. Parenting that is high in action and low in content is the modeling style. It also is only partially effective in that a child must rely entirely on observing the behavior of parents to gain a system of values, norms, and beliefs. Modeling does have some advantage over the teaching style, however. While the teaching style lacks behavior to back it up, the modeling style offers the behavior (but with little or no explanation of the values behind it). The old adage that what children learn is caught rather than taught applies here, and parents will find that modeling is an effective way to inculcate values and desired behavior in their children. Recent research has verified the effectiveness of modeling.

In *Christian Nurture*, the nineteenth-century American scholar Horace Bushnell advises parents of his day that they should do a little more modeling and a little less teaching. He believed that Christian nurture is best achieved when the spirit of the parents' Christian life flows into their children to develop their character. Emphasizing a nonverbal, nonexplicit approach, Bushnell cautions, "We preach too much, and live Christ too little" (cited in Astley 1996, 187).

Discipling. Parenting that is high in both action and content is discipling. This style is complete in that parents teach their children by word and by deed. It is curious, however, that while the concept of discipling is popular in the contemporary church, it is rarely used to refer to parental training. The term *discipline*, it should be remembered, is related to the word *disciple*, which refers to one who accepts certain ideas or values and leads or guides others to accept them as well. Discipling, then, is a system of giving positive guidance to children.

Socioemotional Parenting

Figure 11 represents the four styles of socioemotional parenting. Here again there are two dimensions, support and control, each of which can be classified as high or low. The four styles depicted should be thought of as hypothetical rather than precisely representative of the way any one person engages in parenting.

Neglectful. The easiest style to criticize is neglectful parenting because of its obvious shortcomings. With low levels of support and control, very little bonding develops between parents and children. In many homes, particularly those where economic factors play a devastating role, children are indeed neglected. This parenting style can also be found in homes where our modern individualistic society leaves little time to meet the demands of caring for and providing sufficient structure for

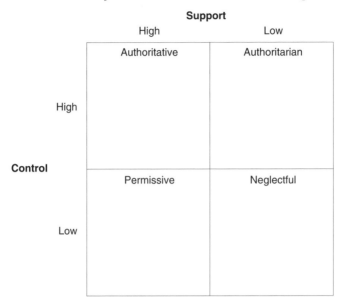

FIGURE 11 **Styles of Socioemotional Parenting**

the children. The latchkey child may be a victim of this system. Single parents have little choice and agonize over their lack of time for providing support and exercising control because so many other demands are made on them.

There are those who advocate this very free lifestyle for children. They see no need to teach morals; rather, children should experiment and come to their own conclusions about personal values. This philosophy emphasizes the child's right to discover his or her own beliefs and lifestyle and suggests that character is built by allowing children to make their own way in the world.

This low-control, low-support style of parenting is characteristic of disengaged families in which each member's life rarely touches the others in any meaningful way. It also characterizes many urban families in which both parents work outside the home or in which there is only one parent. The tentativeness of many people in making a commitment to another person may be a result of being reared in a neglectful home.

We believe that a home without parental leadership is lacking a great deal. Children who grow up without adequate guidance become fertile ground for authoritarian leaders or cults that prey on neglected young people. Indeed, recent literature suggests that most recruits to authoritarian cults come from neglectful homes. These individuals hunger for a strong, strict leader to follow and obey without question. Such people are most susceptible to the dictates of an authoritarian figure, because they have never experienced bonding with any authority figure. Such people lack a developed superego (internalized societal rules) to serve as a guide and rule for their behavior. Lacking a value base, they often yield themselves to an authoritarian cult leader, who in essence becomes their superego. Needless to say, there is no biblical support for the neglectful home.

Authoritarian. When support is low and control high, we have what is called authoritarian parenting. A partial bonding between parents and children takes place in such homes. The children are likely to be respectful and obedient to their parents. What is missing, because of a deficiency in the bonding process, is a sense of warmth, openness, and intimacy between parents and children.

In a variation of the authoritarian style, the father is cast in the role of the instrumental leader who expects obedience from his children and teaches them what they need to know, while the mother assumes a socioemotional role. Thus there is high emotional support in the home, but only on the part of one parent—the one who is not seen as the ultimate authority figure.

This pattern is found in many Far Eastern cultures. In Korea it is believed that a warm, intimate relationship between parent and child automatically forfeits the child's respect for the authority of the parent. For this reason Korean fathers tend to avoid becoming emotionally close to their children. This parenting style was also prevalent among European immigrant families of the nineteenth century. It is also common in most patriarchal agrarian societies. While it seems unproductive to dichotomize the parenting roles, this may be the most widespread style of our day, a result of the industrialized society. Dad was taken out of the home and assigned most of the instrumental tasks, while Mom was left at home and assigned the relational ones.

Permissive. Where control is low and support high, we have permissive parenting. It is based on the assumption that a newborn is like a rosebud, needing only tender love and support to blossom slowly into a beautiful flower. Present-day permissive parenting can be traced back to the ideals of the counterculture movement of the 1960s, which can in turn be traced back to the bohemian morality of a century earlier. The thinking here is that every child has special potentialities at birth that are destroyed by societal rules and standards. Therefore, children need to be allowed to find their own purpose through free expression. During the 1960s, this philosophy was epitomized in the slogan "Do your own thing."

Noticeably absent from the permissive style is any idea that children tend to be self-centered and need parental guidance in learning values and interpersonal skills. Consequently, children raised in permissive homes tend to lack a sense of social responsibility; they also fail to develop interdependence.

Authoritative. Authoritative parents combine the best qualities found in the authoritarian and permissive styles. Authoritative parents attempt to direct the child in a rational, issue-oriented manner; encourage verbal give-and-take; explain the reasons behind demands and discipline but also use power when necessary; expect the child to conform to adult requirements but also to be independent and self-directing; recognize the rights of both adults and children; and set standards and enforce them firmly. These parents do not regard themselves as infallible, but they also do not base decisions primarily on the child's desires.

It has been well documented that socially competent children are products of homes in which the parenting style is authoritative. Social competence results when parents attend to their children's self-esteem, academic achievement, cognitive development, creativity, moral behavior, and instrumental abilities. Children thrive in such an environment of high support and high control (Buehler 2006; Galambos, Barker, and Almeida 2003).

Note, however, that certain kinds of parental control are more effective and produce better results. For example, a coercive approach that forces a child to act against his or her will usually results in low levels of social competence in that child. Withdrawing one's love to obtain compliance is also ineffective. Inductive control—giving explanations, using reasoning, and encouraging a child's voluntary compliance by avoiding direct conflict of wills—proves to be the most effective approach. Coupling this type of control with strong emotional support produces competent children (Buehler 2006; Peterson and Rollins 1987). The conclusion that coercion has an adverse effect on the development of social competence in children supports the type of empowerment we have suggested (McLoyd and Smith 2002).

A Biblical Model of Parenting

Having summarized the social-science literature on the effects of various parenting styles, we will now present a biblical model, with the goal of eventually integrating these various materials into a model of Christian parenting.

We believe that a biblical model of parenting can be derived from the scriptural depiction of God as parent. Myron Chartier (1978) has marshaled the biblical evidence to show that God displays parental love in seven ways. (1) God cares for people. Although this is preeminently demonstrated in the incarnation, death, and resurrection of Christ, numerous other biblical passages stress the caring nature of God (Luke 15:11–32; 1 Pet. 5:7). (2) God is responsive to human needs. This can be seen in the covenant that was established after the flood (Gen. 9:8–17), in the rescue of Israel from Egypt, and in the free offer of mercy and restoration (John 3:16; Titus 3:3–7). (3) God bestows the richest gifts on us—the only begotten Son and the Holy Spirit as Comforter. (4) God shows respect for, values, and cherishes us; there is no attempt to dominate, and we are given the freedom to be ourselves. (5) God knows us, for Jesus came in human likeness (John 1:14; Phil. 2:5–8; Heb. 2:17–18; 4:15); this knowledge penetrates to the core of our existence (Ps. 44:21; John 2:25). (6) God forgives (Matt. 26:28; John 3:16–17; Eph. 1:7). (7) God disciplines us (Prov. 3:11–12; Heb. 12:5–8; Rev. 3:19). The discipline of Israel can be seen as an attempt to create a faithful and obedient people.

Taken as a whole, the Bible clearly emphasizes the love and grace that God freely gives. However, this unconditional love is not free of expectations and demands. God's love includes disciplinary action for our good. His love as parent bears a striking similarity to the parenting style advocated in the social-science literature: a high degree of support and of inductive (rather than coercive) control.

The actions of God as parent clearly point to a model in which parental love (support) and discipline (control) intertwine to help children develop toward maturity. This model comports well with the theological basis for family relationships that we introduced in chapter 1—covenant, grace, empowering, and intimacy. Parent/child relationships begin when the parents make an initial covenant (a one-way unconditional commitment) of love with their child. Although the infant cannot return this commitment, as the child matures, the initial covenant should grow into a mature covenant (a two-way unconditional commitment). This maturing of the parent/child relationship is possible because the covenant commitment establishes an environment of grace and forgiveness in which parents empower their children and reach new levels of intimacy with them. Intimacy is defined as a mutual knowing and caring free of embarrassment or shame.

In an ideal situation, the four elements of the parent/child relationship are in a continual process of maturing: intimacy leads to deeper covenant love, which enhances the atmosphere of grace, which strengthens the empowering process, which leads to deepened intimacy, and so on. This cycle is relational and requires reciprocity. The foundation consists of a faithful commitment and accepting environment where children and parents can be vulnerable and open with each other. This relationship connection promotes the empowerment process in which parents and children learn to serve and to give to each other.

Empowerment is the central element in our biblical model of parenting. Exactly what is involved here? We know, of course, that differences in status and resources place parents in a position of leadership over their children, and that power is defined in the conventional social-science literature as the ability to influence others (Szinovacz 1987). Good parenting is the wise exercise of that position and ability. Empowering is the process of instilling confidence, of strengthening and building up children to become more powerful and competent. Parents who have been empowered by the unconditional love of God and the Holy Spirit are best able to empower their children.

Jesus came to empower others to have abundant life. His model for human relationships shows that empowering entails serving others. Witness his radical reply to the disciples who wanted to sit in powerful positions with him in glory: "But it is not so among you; but whoever wishes to become great among you must be your servant, and whoever wishes to be first among you must be slave of all. For the Son of Man came not to be served but to serve, and to give his life a ransom for many" (Mark 10:43–45). Jesus redefined power by his teaching and by his action in relating to others as a servant. He rejected the use of power to control others and instead affirmed it to serve others, to lift up the fallen, to forgive the guilty, to encourage responsibility and maturity in the weak, and to enable the unable.

The capacity to be a servant-leader to others requires a high level of maturity and unconditional love. It demands that a person achieve a maturity going beyond self-sufficiency to interdependency. Abundant life is more than a narcissistic euphoria in which all one's personal needs and desires are met. It involves having a meaning beyond oneself. The admonitions in the New Testament to submit to one another, to love, forgive, serve, and value all of God's people, are actually a call to mature living.

The most striking example of mature servanthood is the way Jesus honored children. His example is vital to developing a proper theology of power. James Francis (1996) observes that in the teaching of Jesus we see a

startling reappraisal . . . about the powerless and the Kingdom of God. . . . As it imprints itself upon patterns of discipleship, [it] shows the church occasionally seeking to transcend, and not merely to reflect, the culture of its day. Since power is part of all human relationships it is also an inherent part of relationships within the family. The literal and metaphorical understanding of children and childhood in the New Testament has much to tell us of the role of power in this particular context where so much of who we are is shaped and fashioned, and where our imaging of the divine is also formed. (p. 85)

Like his approach to children, Jesus's relationship to his disciples should be understood in terms of empowerment. He even provided for a continuation of the process after his departure: "But the Advocate, the Holy Spirit, whom the Father will send in my name, will teach you everything, and remind you of all that I have said to you" (John 14:26). He wanted them to have the capacity and confidence to carry on the message. They had been prepared by his teaching ministry to be independent and by his example to be servants.

Parents who empower help their children become competent and capable people who will in turn empower others. Empowering parents are actively and intentionally engaged in various pursuits—teaching, guiding, caring, modeling—that equip their children to become confident individuals able to relate to others. Parents who empower help their children recognize their inner strengths and potentials and find ways to enhance these qualities. Parental empowering is the affirmation of the child's ability to learn, grow, and become all that one is meant to be as part of God's image and creative plan.

AND JUST WHY DO YOU FEEL I'M KEEPING
YOU FROM GROWING UP?

Empowerment, from a biblical perspective, does not entail the child's gaining power at the expense of the parent. The view that the supply of power is limited is purely secular. When empowering the children of Israel, God did not give up power but offered it in unlimited supply. Jesus's authority (*exousia*) flowed from his personhood; it was in no way diminished when he empowered his disciples. Similarly, the authority of parents, which flows from their personhood, is not diminished when they exercise the responsibility to nurture their children to maturity. The process of empowering them does not mean relinquishing parental authority, nor are parents depleted or drained of power when they empower their children. Rather, when empowering takes place, authority and ascribed power are retained as children develop, grow, and achieve a sense of personal power, self-esteem, and wholeness. Successful parenting results in the children's gaining as much personal power as the parents themselves have. In the Christian context, children are empowered to love God and their neighbors as themselves. They are capable of going beyond themselves to reach out to others.

Christian Parenting: Empowering to Maturity

Figure 12 is a visual representation of the process by which Christian parenting empowers children to reach maturity. The empowering curve represents the levels of parental control and socioemotional support. Note that these levels vary with the different styles of parenting (telling, teaching, modeling, delegating). At the extreme left, there is very little empowerment. Here we find parents who perpetuate dependency in their children. At the extreme right, the children have reached the goal of empowerment, the opposite of dependence.

The first parenting style is *telling*, which is characterized by one-way communication—parents tell their children what to do. This parenting style is needed when children are young and unable to do things on their own. During their early years, children need the clear directions and close supervision that telling provides. Exercising a high level of control, the parents clearly define the tasks to be performed, telling their children what is to be done, as well as where, when, and how. Socioemotional support is minimal but is offered as a reward for compliance. It must be stressed that in this connection low socioemotional support has reference only to the tasks that the parents are trying to get the child to master. At this stage they will, of course, need to give much unconditional socioemotional support. In fact, young children probably need more unconditional (non-task-related) socioemotional support from their parents than will be required at any subsequent stage of development.

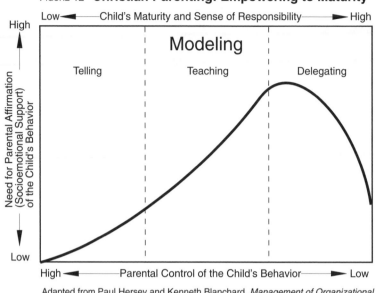

FIGURE 12 **Christian Parenting: Empowering to Maturity**

Adapted from Paul Hersey and Kenneth Blanchard, *Management of Organizational Behavior*, 4th ed. (Englewood Cliffs, NJ: Prentice Hall, 1988), 287.

The second parental style, *teaching,* is best for children who are low to moderate in maturity. As children move into latency, they may be willing to take responsibility for specific tasks or functions but do not always know how to do them. Teaching involves moderately high levels of both control (guidance) and socioemotional support. Teaching differs from telling in that communication can be two-way. Children at this age ask many questions and are able to learn through dialogue and discussion; in time they can be encouraged to attempt to find their own answers. Most of the communication, however, is still done by the parents, who must decide when to reduce the amount of direct instruction and increase the level of task-related socioemotional support.

Note that *modeling* or *participating* is a parenting style that extends across the empowering curve. It encompasses every stage of parenting. Participating parents become, so to speak, player-coaches who directly engage in activities with their children. Instruction is still taking place, but proper behavior is modeled in addition to being taught. This parenting style is particularly important for children who are moderately to highly mature, the level of a typical preteenager. Although preteenagers may have the ability to perform certain tasks and carry out fairly important responsibilities, they typically lack the confidence to do so. Modeling parents encourage their children to begin doing things on their own; in that process the amount of parental control is reduced.

Participating parents encourage their children to be their own persons, allowing them to learn through trial and error and offering support and consolation when needed.

The *delegating* style is for highly mature children who are both able and willing to take responsibility and perform tasks on their own. In delegating responsibility, parents do not need to exercise a high level of control (guidance) or give a substantial amount of socioemotional support. While a continued high level of socioemotional support may on the surface appear to be desirable, an overabundance of it could be interpreted as a lack of confidence in the child.

Parents whose children mature to the point where the delegating style is in order are often simultaneously empowered by them. Parenthetically, we might observe that willingness to learn from and be empowered by one's children is a sign of parental maturity. Reciprocal giving and receiving is an indication of a mature relationship. Parents who can let go and give increasing amounts of freedom to their children at appropriate stages are showing respect for and belief in them. This is an empowering experience for the child, especially if the letting go is done with a genuine blessing and not with reluctance and conditional love. With the added measure of freedom, the teenager will often make independent choices and express opinions different from those held by the parents. This is the beginning of an adult relationship of mutual respect that empowers children to become their own persons. Through reciprocal giving and receiving, parents and children become close friends at this point. When parents allow themselves to be served and empowered by their own children, intimacy deepens. This kind of reciprocity is good preparation for the relationships that the children will eventually experience as adults.

The four parenting styles—telling, teaching, modeling, and delegating—develop along a continuum reflecting the child's increasing maturity. There is also a sense in which the parents must be able to grow with their maturing children. Parents who cannot change their styles to meet the progressing needs of their children will retard the growth of everyone involved. Maturation of the parental style is an essential factor in the mutual empowering process. Parents must have both the insight and the skill to employ the parenting style most appropriate to each situation.

As suggested earlier, the combination of high parental support and high inductive control produces the most competent children. The empowering curve in our model does not contradict this view, but it does present a refinement. It suggests that with increased maturity children need less support and control. We are suggesting not that parents need to hold back their unconditional support as their children mature but only that the children will be decreasingly dependent on their parents' support. God's ideal is that children mature to the point where they and their parents empower each other.

Social-science literature suggests that the combination of high parental support and high inductive control produces the most competent children. A comprehensive study of African American, European American, and Hispanic children examined the relationship between physical discipline, emotional support, and behavior problems in children. It was found that parental spanking increased the level of problem behavior in the child over time but only when maternal emotional support was low. When maternal emotional support was high, spanking did not result in an increase in a child's behavioral problems (McLoyd and Smith 2002). Parental support is a key factor in how children respond to spanking.

A majority of studies have failed to take into account the developing maturity of children when looking at these two factors. The empowering curve in our model suggests that with increased maturity children need less support and control.

Wendy Grolnick (2003) makes a helpful distinction between parents being *in control* and parents who are *controlling*. While the former style is facilitative, the latter is inhibiting. What is most beneficial to children is facilitative parental behavior, which Grolnick refers to as "autonomy support." Her model of parenting children is called Self-Determination Theory, which emphasizes agency (children being free to make choices) and inherent competence. This view comports well with the empowerment model presented in this chapter.

A more detailed account of our model is found in the book *Relationship-Empowerment Parenting: Building Formative and Fulfilling Relationships with Your Children* (J. K. Balswick et al. 2003). Also helpful is Lev Vygotsky's (1986) concept of the *zone of proximal development*, which refers to that zone containing a range of tasks a child cannot yet accomplish without the active assistance of parents and others with greater knowledge and capabilities. Borrowing a concept from the construction industry, Vygotsky suggests that parents/caretakers must provide a scaffold of development that optimally extends just slightly beyond the child's abilities but never so far beyond as to create unreasonable expectations that end in certain failure.

The Case for Coparenting

It should be noted here that the relationship-empowering ideal is most efficiently achieved if both parents bring their respective strengths to the process in a complementary way. There are two types of complementarity. In the case of *longitudinal complementarity*, parents complement each other over time. One parent may be better at dealing with infants or young children, while the skills of the other emerge once the children have developed greater cognitive ability. In the case of *situational complementarity*, parents complement each other on a day-to-day basis throughout their parenting years. Here the situation determines which parental skills are most needed. Thus at times the parent who is more capable of helping a child with homework is needed; at other times the parent who is more able to provide encouragement when the child is lacking in self-esteem is needed. Complementary parenting offers an advantage in that one parent does not have to meet all the child's needs. The main point is that both parents—mother and father—have an essential role in the empowerment of children. As a cautionary aside, it should be noted that children are most directly negatively affected by marital disagreements about parenting issues (Stright and Bales 2003). Thus while children benefit from having both parents involved, it is imperative that parents agree on the parenting process.

Parenting that empowers children to maturity is conceptually similar to the New Testament depiction of discipleship. Jesus gathered and trained disciples, empowering them in turn to "go therefore and make disciples of all nations, baptizing them in the name of the Father and of the Son and of the Holy Spirit, and teaching them to obey everything that I have commanded you. And remember, I am with you always, to the end of the age" (Matt. 28:19–20). Parenting follows a similar course. The ultimate reward for parents and children is a relationship that grows into maturity so that when the children have been empowered, they will in turn empower others.

7

DEVELOPING A MATURE
RECIPROCATING SELF

I T HAS BEEN said that every society except ours expects its children to grow up into normal adults. Part of the reason for the insecurity of many American parents is a fear that they may be doing something contrary to expert opinion. There are two types of experts on child rearing. One is the scientific investigator who systematically studies child development. The other is the popularizer of this knowledge who offers advice on how to be the perfect parent who raises the perfect child.

As we mentioned in the preceding chapter, we believe that parents need to resist bowing uncritically before expert opinion and simple formulas that guarantee parenting success. It is more important to develop a parenting philosophy that takes into account cultural beliefs, family of origin heritages, personal strengths and limitations (both one's own and those of one's children), knowledge derived from firsthand experience, and common sense. Confidence in one's ability as a parent comes from integrating these elements with the clear findings of child-development professionals and solid biblical principles. Parents who wait with bated breath for the next gem of wisdom from the so-called experts are setting themselves up for disillusionment when their offspring do not automatically develop into the ideal children they were promised. Child rearing is a much more complex process than most people realize.

In chapter 2 we introduced the *family developmental systems perspective*, and in this chapter we use developmental systems theory (DST) to understand child development (Ford and Lerner 1992; Lerner 2002). Consistent with biblical assumptions about human nature, DST provides an integrative approach to child development.

Many child development theories are limited in that they split explanations of development into oppositional camps—nature versus nurture, individual versus the group or family, mechanistic versus organismic, continuous versus discontinuous (stage) development, and so on. In its emphasis on *relationalism*, DST emphasizes the interaction between all factors that contribute to human development.

Rather than focusing exclusively on the unique contributions of nature or nurture, DST emphasizes how the interaction between them play a significant role. A proper understanding of child development must consider an *interactive* rather than an additive process. It's not enough to simply add together the influence of the mother, plus the father, plus other family members, plus peers, plus school and church; we must consider the overall impact of all these factors interacting together on the development of a child.

Some key assumptions in DST (Lerner 2002, 184) are that (1) child development includes a multiplicity of biological, cultural, social, and psychological influences; (2) influences are reciprocal in that parents not only affect their child but also are affected by the child at the same time; (3) each child is a unique human being; (4) the development of each child is uniquely different; (5) children are active choosing agents, participating in their own development; and (6) children are created for community. At the end of this chapter, we revisit these basic assumptions as we critique child development theories in light of biblical assumptions about being human.

Jack Balswick, Pamela King, and Kevin Reimer (2005) seek to understand human development from a Christian theological viewpoint. In doing so, they note that developmental theories lack a guiding *teleology*, an understanding of the *goal* of development. They cite this as a *developmental dilemma* resulting from the lack of a theologically informed understanding of development completeness (p. 17). The naturalistic assumption underlying most developmental theories alludes to *survivalistic* inclinations (humans evolve based on characteristics that best contribute to the survival of the human species) but lacks theological explanation.

In response to the developmental dilemma, we begin with the assumption that human beings are created to reflect the image of God. While part of that image includes rationality (mind), the *relationality* of God, as exemplified in the relationship between the three persons of the Holy

Trinity, is also a core part of that image. Being created in the image of God encompasses a relationality that simultaneously includes differentiation *and* unity. From a theological perspective, the goal or purpose (teleology) is for people to develop a mature, *reciprocating self*—a self that in all its uniqueness and fullness of being, engages others in relationship (Balswick, King, and Reimer 2005, 21). Therefore, our understanding of child development theories centers on how each child develops into a reciprocating, relational self with respect to God and others.

Theories of Child Development

Theories of child development consist of systematically organized knowledge accumulated through empirical observation of children. A good theory is like a pair of glasses in that it allows one to focus more sharply on that which is being observed. We draw attention to the major child-development theories so that we aren't blinded by one theory and ignore the others.

To illustrate this point, let us suppose that representatives of the major theories of child development are watching a child playing in the family living room. Although the observers will be exposed to the same behavior, they will not see it through the same set of lenses. Each observer will perceive the child's activity through the lens of predetermined notions about human behavior. The cognitive-development theorist will be especially aware of the particular stage of development; the psychoanalytic theorist will look for unconscious motivations in overt behavior; the symbolic interactionist will concentrate on the child's self-concept; the social learning theorist will pay special attention to what the child has learned from observing others. Although it is not a conscious process, all theorists engage in selective perception, viewing the child's actions in accordance with their own general conceptualization of human behavior.

Table 5 compares these major theories of child development. A good strategy is to consider how these theories are complementary, and not just contradictory, in yielding insights into the child-development process. After presenting brief summaries of each theory, we will compare and contrast the strengths and limitations of each based on biblical assumptions about being human.

Psychoanalytic Theory: Internal Focus

The father of psychoanalytic theory, Sigmund Freud, began by describing the newborn baby as all *id*—a bundle of unrestrained instinctive energy seeking gratification. Although he posited that the id contained both a

Table 5

Major Theories of Child Development

	Psycho-analytic	Erikson (Neopsy-choanalytic)	Symbolic Interaction	Cognitive Development		
				Piaget	Kohlberg (Moral)	Fowler (Faith)
(0–1½) Infancy	Oral	Trust	Preparatory	Sensorimotor		Undifferentiated
(1½–3) Toddler Stage	Anal	Autonomy	Play	Preoperational	Punishment and obedience	Intuitive-projective
(4–6) Early Childhood	Genital	Initiative	Game			
(7–12) Childhood		Industry		Concrete operations	Self-interested exchanges	Mythic-literal
(13–21) Adolescence		Identity		Formal operations	Maintenance of good interpersonal relationships	Synthetic-conventional
(21–) Adulthood		Intimacy			Maintenance of law and order	Individuative Reflective
(30–45)		Generativity			Social contract and individual rights	Conjunctive Universalizing
(46–)		Ego Integration			Universal ethical principles	

positive instinct (Eros, or life) and a negative instinct (Thanatos, or death), Freud described the id as amoral, impulsive, and ruled by unconscious and irrational demands for immediate gratification. Freud saw parents as attempting to impose their own wishes on the child, which when internalized by the child formed the *superego*. You can imagine the internal struggle between the id wanting immediate gratification and the superego (the internalization of parental wishes) seeking to deny the impulses of the id. The superego operates as a moral police officer attempting to contain the id. The third part of the mind, the *ego*, develops out of the struggle between the id and the superego. The ego functions as a type of internal diplomat (self) attempting to calm the wishes of the id and the superego by finding acceptable ways of rewarding each. The superego rewards the ego by building up self-esteem, but punishes the ego with guilt when it does not comply (Freud 1949, 1954).

Parenting from a psychoanalytic perspective can be thought of as a journey through a minefield of potential dangers. If parents are overly rigid and moralistic, they risk suppressing positive aspects of the life force residing in the id. If they are too permissive and fail to provide adequate boundaries for the child, they risk allowing the formation of a child with an inadequate superego, resulting in the unchecked id running wild. Effective parenting is a balance of allowing a child's expression of innate creativity while at the same time taming the child through societal behavioral norms.

According to the psychoanalytic theory of the mind, healthy development is characterized by a strong ego, which can monitor the extreme demands of the id and the superego. During their first six years of life, children move through three developmental stages—*oral, anal,* and *genital*—in which they must negotiate their need for gratification with parental and societal approval. Secure gender identity and self-esteem develop during the *latency* stage (age seven to twelve) if a firm foundation is established during the first six years of life. If earlier conditions were less than ideal, the child may have difficulty relating to others and experience increasing self-doubt and lack of self-esteem. The internal conflicts (id, ego, and superego) are experienced through each stage of the relationship with parents. When relationships with both parents are strong and unwavering, the child will feel a sense of well-being and worth.

Erikson's Neopsychoanalytic Theory: Infancy through Adulthood

In traditional psychoanalytic theory, the basic personality is thought to be formed by puberty, with minimal change likely thereafter. A correction to this notion is found in the development theory of Erik Erikson (1968, 1985), who argues that development continues into adulthood. Erikson suggests eight developmental stages, the last emerging at approximately age forty-five. Erikson focuses on how parents and wider psychohistorical factors affect a person's learning each stage-specific developmental task. Mastery of the developmental tasks at each stage is vital to successful achievement of the tasks at the next stage.

The degree of mastery determines the strengths and deficits with which an individual develops. To arrive at maturity, the last stage of development, with a sufficient sense of ego integrity, one must have achieved trust, autonomy, initiative, industry, identity, intimacy, and generativity during the previous seven sequential stages. At the opposite extreme are those individuals who end up in a state of despair because they have experienced mistrust, shame and doubt, guilt, a sense of inferiority, role confusion, isolation, and stagnation sequentially during the developmental stages.

A major strength of Erikson's theory is its recognition of the importance of both familial and extrafamilial influences on human development. Recognizing the cumulative effects of experience throughout the life span, the theory also suggests interventions to help those who have been socially or psychologically deprived at a specific stage of development.

Object Relations Theory: The Child as an Object Needing Love

Even though object relations theory is rooted in psychoanalytic theory, it is useful in understanding the child's development of self within the context of parent/child relationships. Object relations theory emphasizes the development of the self or personality within the context of an infant-caregiver relationship. Object relations theories contend that personality is shaped and formed by the early interactions of an infant (to young child) and its most intimate caregiver, usually the mother.

In object relations theory, there is a shift from *biological* to *interpersonal determinism* and a corresponding change from an internal to a *relational* structural model. Melanie Klein (1932) replaced biological drives with *psychological and relational drives*. Her work brought about a major paradigmatic shift from biological determinism to a perspective that took into consideration the significance of interpersonal interaction.

The core element in Klein's theory consists of the internalization by the child of its relationship with the primary caregiver(s). Once internalized, the internal object can bring the child comfort or pain. No matter how well the caregiver interacts with the infant, the infant most likely will internalize an object with some negativity. The internalized object then becomes an organizing principle for future interactions. If the child internalizes a good or safe object, he or she will feel secure and will be able to form positive relationships. If the child internalizes an anxious or hateful object, he or she will anticipate having negative experiences in other relationships.

Donald Winnicott's (1971) version of object relations theory strongly emphasizes that the mother or the caregiver is almost solely responsible for influencing the development of the self. He refers to the "holding environment," since a mother provides a physical and psychological space where the baby experiences a sense of well-being. In this secure holding environment, the infant begins to gain a sense of self and other. The mother as an internal object provides a sense of security and safety. If the holding environment is adequate (good enough), the infant's needs are satisfied. Parents who are attuned to the baby's physical and emotional needs provide the foundation for trust and security. The good-enough mother can also find a balance between empathetic gratification of the infant's needs and satisfying her own needs. Parents who are attuned to the child's needs *mirror* the child's behavior and feelings. Rather than ignoring or overwhelming the child, an appropriate response provides an authentication and validation of a child's sense of self.

Transitional space (psychological space) emerges through the process of internalizing the presence of an emotionally attuned but nondemanding parent. The child who has *internalized* the parent as a *good object* has the capacity to be alone. Sometimes a *transitional object* (a special blanket or stuffed animal) can help the child internalize the mother. By symbolizing the calming presence of the caregiver, transitional objects allow toddlers to feel secure even when they are alone.

Transitional space allows for the expression of the true self. The true self is the authentic, spontaneous self, aware and comfortable with his or her uniqueness. The false self results from a lack of transitional space. The major contributors to the false self can be seen in the extremes: *absent* parents or *impinging* parents.

In summary, a good holding environment includes a present, mirroring, nonimpinging mother, transitional space, and a fostering of the ability to be alone. Transitional space is created by the nondemanding, good-enough mother in a holding environment where she mirrors the child in a nonimpinging way.

Social Learning Theory: The Child as Learner

During the past half century, behaviorism has been shaped by the creative research and writing of B. F. Skinner. Skinner (1953) developed what is known as operant conditioning, which is a modification of classical conditioning. Rather than using a stimulus to bring about a desired response, Skinner's model emphasizes reinforcement, that is, a system of rewards for desired behavior and punishments for unacceptable actions. The basic principle here is that behavior is shaped and maintained by its consequences. Operant conditioning has proven useful in bringing about changes in behavior.

Social learning theory emphasizes learning by observation rather than through direct reinforcement (Bandura 1977). Children learn how to behave by observing the consequences of the behavior of other people. For example, children learn not to hit other children on the playground primarily by observing that children who do hit others experience negative consequences, such as getting hurt themselves or being reprimanded by a teacher.

Social learning theory also observes that children learn from the modeling of parents and important others in their lives. As role models, parents influence their children in both positive and negative ways. Comparison of direct learning (reinforcement) and indirect learning (observation and imitation of modeled behavior) reveals that modeling is more effective. The application is obvious: effective parents are those who model the behaviors they want their children to implement.

The idea that learning comes through the child's observation and interpretation of behavior implies a self-consciousness and self-determination within the child. Change, then, can be activated both by environmental stimuli and by the child, a discovery that has enhanced learning theory.

In Albert Bandura's concept of *reciprocal determinism*, *behavior*, the *person* (i.e., one's cognitive makeup), and the *environment* reciprocally influence one another. Children not only change their environment but are being changed by it. Children do not simply react to their parents but act upon them and influence how they parent. The colicky baby elicits a different parenting response than the easy baby does, just as the way the parent deals with the baby affects the baby's response. Although social learning theory doesn't stress innate or biological factors, it views children as actively involved in the construction of their environment and thus in their own developmental process.

Symbolic Interaction Theory: The Child as a Developing Self

Symbolic interaction theory views the child as a *self* that develops through relationships. Some symbolic interaction theorists go as far as to suggest that infants are not born human but become human through social interaction. The symbolic (language) interaction with one's parents/caretakers humanizes the infant in a social sense. Human beings are unique because of the vast amount of culture (learned and shared) they possess. The accumulation of culture is possible because humans have elaborate language systems, which distinguish them from other living creatures. The infant is born without language, without culture, and without a sense of self or of others. All these develop through communication. George Herbert Mead, the father of symbolic interaction theory, explains that child development takes place in three stages (1934). First comes the *preparatory stage*. During this period the infant is being prepared to use language. Communication can be thought of as occurring on two different levels. A gesture is any part of a social act that is a sign for something else. Gestures have meaning, but the meaning is not precise enough to build an elaborate language system. A language system can develop only when oral gestures have shared meaning, thus becoming significant symbols. A significant symbol is a gesture that has the same meaning for the creature giving it as for the creature receiving it.

Parents begin to communicate with their children through gestures—a smile, a soft pat on the hand, a warning glance, or a wave of the finger. Words accompany the gesture, and children learn the meaning of a word in the context of specific situations. For example, once the word *no* is understood in relation to a behavior, even when that action has never been forbidden, the child has learned its general meaning.

Children develop a self-concept by seeing themselves from their parents' point of view. Not only do children see themselves as they think their parents see them, but they define themselves with their parents' very words. Words such as *smart* and *gifted* become part of a child's self-concept, just as words such as *stupid* and *clumsy* are internalized.

When children can communicate through significant symbols, they have entered the second stage of development. This *play stage* begins between the ages of one and two and continues for several years. Children begin to imagine themselves in the roles of a number of other people through play. Casting themselves in the role of another, they assume that person's attitude toward them as well. A child can easily switch back and forth as follows: In Daddy's chair, little Kara turns toward the chair she usually occupies and asks in a deep voice, "Did you have fun today, Kara?" She proceeds to the chair where her big brother sits and says, "You are such a crybaby!" In each instance her self-concept is defined by taking on what she imagines to be that person's attitude toward her.

Increasingly, the child's sense of self sharpens as distinguishable and separate from others. At age four or five, children reach the *game stage*, at which time they are able to assume the roles of several others simultaneously. Before reaching this stage, children cannot play certain games because they are unable to take on the role of more than one person at a time. To play hide-and-seek, a child must be able to take on the perspective of both the hider and the seeker. To play a game such as baseball is even more complex; now the child must be able to take on the perspective of each team member at the same time. When a ballplayer strikes out with the bases loaded, she imagines the team's collective attitude toward her. The cumulative effect of relationships with other individuals and groups is that children continue to take on new and changing attitudes toward themselves.

We acquire a general view of ourselves from the groups to which we belong (and even from groups we wish to join). These relationships help us define ourselves. Even our identity as male or female is anchored in gender categories that have defined us in the early years of life. New experiences, such as entering school for the first time, continue to expand (student identification) and alter our (Christian) identity. In the end, human personality is the sum total of self-concepts gained as a result of our relationships.

Perhaps the most important idea in symbolic interaction theory is that our self-concept reflects what we believe others think of us, and we behave according to these definitions. This contention is supported elsewhere in child-development literature. For example, children who fail in school begin to have low opinions of their learning abilities and therefore live them out, whereas children who excel develop a positive view of themselves as learners from their experiences. Labeling a child has harmful outcomes. When juvenile delinquents are constantly told that they are no good, worthless, and destructive, they proceed to behave in accordance with the stereotypes others place on them.

Cognitive Development Theory: The Child as a Developing Scientist

As the name implies, cognitive development (CD) theory singles out the cognitive aspects of human development. Swiss psychologist Jean Piaget starts with the assumption that children are not merely passive objects but active agents in constructing their personal reality, that is, they turn all life experiences into action. In a rational fashion, the child continually attempts to make sense of the world. Piaget observed how babies make use of their natural reflexes as they make contact with an object or a person. The child is a little scientist, learning by acting upon the world. Children are actually discovering the scheme into which a thing fits so they can act toward it consistently. A ball is to be bounced, but a dog will bark, growl, move away, or bite. Therefore, the child learns to act accordingly by picking up on these cues. The acquisition of language brings a wide variety of new possibilities. With time, the child learns to discriminate between and distinguish parents as "Mommy" or "Daddy" and strangers as "man" or "woman" (or "boy" or "girl"). In analyzing this process, Piaget uses the terms *assimilation, accommodation,* and *equilibration*. Assimilation is taking information in and construing it in terms of one's established way of thinking. Whatever is perceived is made to fit into existing schemes. The more refined a scheme, the less likely it is that new pieces of information will be misplaced (Piaget 1932).

However, if children could only assimilate experiences into existing categories, no new scheme would emerge. And because many things do not fit into existing schemes, new schemes must be formed. This is the process of accommodation: altering the existing cognitive structures to allow for new objects experienced. Children continually engage in assimilation and accommodation. The balance between the two is equilibration. People with mature cognitive structures engage in both assimilation and accommodation. People with immature cognitive structures fail to engage in one or the other and thus do not achieve equilibration (cognitive balance).

According to Piaget, cognitive development in a child takes place in four major stages. The first is the *sensorimotor* stage, which covers the period from birth until about two years of age. During this stage, children are primarily focused on basic motor skills and learning to adapt their behavior to their external environment. The child classifies objects by acting upon them. In the process, the child begins to grasp the idea of *object permanence*, that is, to realize that objects that are out of sight have not ceased to exist.

Children also learn to coordinate the different parts of the body during the sensorimotor stage. For example, when trying to reach for an object, they will stand on their tiptoes and stretch their arms as high as they can. Toward the end of the sensorimotor stage, children intentionally engage in goal-directed behavior, that is, they push a chair up to the table and then climb on the chair to get the cookie on the table, all in an orderly sequence.

Mastery of linguistic skills is primary during the *preoperational* stage, in which children are able to name objects, to place words together into meaningful sentences, and to begin to construct a view of reality.

Because the acquisition of language skills is so complex, the thinking and behavior of a child are characterized by unsettledness, fear, and confusion, precisely why this stage is referred to as *pre*operational. For example, the child may conclude that firefighters, since they always appear at the scene of a fire, set fires, or that police initiate trouble. Parents must be mindful that children need help in logically explaining the events they experience. It is natural at this stage for children to think everyone else experiences the world as they do. If they are happy, they project happiness onto everyone else; when they are sad, then everyone else must be sad.

Eventually children are able to move beyond self-focused thinking. At about seven years of age, they reach the stage of *concrete* operations, when thought processes become more stable and consistent. Children at the concrete-operations stage can understand the principle of invariance (certain matters of space and weight are in some sense unchangeable) regardless of the shape. For example, children at the concrete-operations stage understand that the water's volume does not change, no matter the shape or size of the container it is poured into. Children at this stage are also avid collectors since they love to classify and arrange their priceless objects on the basis of color, size, shape, and every other aspect imaginable. This is a reflection of an expanded reasoning ability.

At the *formal-operations* stage, children understand causality and can perform scientific experiments. By using deductive reasoning, they formulate hypotheses, carry out experiments, and reach conclusions on the basis of evidence. At this time in children's lives there is an increased concern for basic values and truths.

Vygotsky's Sociocultural Theory: Parenting as Scaffolding

In forming a *sociocultural* theory of child development in the 1930s, the Russian theorist Lev Vygotsky concentrated on the relational influences on children as they live in a sociocultural context. Along with George Herbert Mead, Vygotsky paved the way for understanding how *culture* affects development and how language serves as the primary vehicle for the transmission of cultural information. Vygotsky's concept of the *zone of proximal development* is especially helpful in understanding how a child masters a task. The zone contains the range of tasks that a child cannot yet accomplish without the active assistance of parents and others (Vygotsky 1986). The expansion of the child's skill comes through interpersonal relationships since children's immediate potential cannot be magically realized on their own. The child learns new skills each step of the way in the context of relationship support until he or she masters a specific task.

The child is a collaborator, learning new skills through interactions with more cognitively advanced people. Parents must create what Vygotsky refers to as appropriate *scaffolding*. Those who provide an adequate scaffold (not too much or too little support and control) provide an optimal learning environment. The scaffold extends just slightly beyond the child's abilities, but never so far beyond as to create unreasonable expectations that end in failure. The concept of scaffolding is similar to the empowering principle, according to which guidance, assistance, and support are given so the child reaches his or her full potential and mastery. When parents do too much or "take over," the child is disempowered and feels inadequate and dependent. As one can see, when children accomplish a task on their own, the parent wisely removes the scaffolding. The child is now competent and confident and has no need to be dependent on the parents.

Children require a high level of interpersonal commitment as they develop. It follows that abused or neglected children often develop negative representations of the self. They have not had sufficient support or scaffolding to reach full maturity. In fact, they need to develop protective strategies for self-survival. Susan Harter (1999) notes that abuse frequently results in the child internalizing the social influences of shame, violence, or emotional abuse that lead to negativity toward others, such as bullying, delinquency, or violence.

Social Ecology: Child Development in the Village

The African proverb "It takes a village to raise a child" is verified in a social ecological theory of child development. Urie Bronfenbrenner (1979) suggests that child development is best understood within four increasingly encompassing ecological systems. At the smallest, most specific level is the *microsystem*, the parent/child relationship. Beyond the microsystem is the *mesosystem*, consisting of social environments such as a child's kindergarten, Sunday school class, neighborhood playgroup, and so on. Each of these settings in and of itself is a microsystem, but the collection of all these microsystems and the relationships between them constitute the mesosystem for the toddler.

Children are also influenced by what occurs in the social environment beyond the settings in which they directly participate. This constitutes their *exosystem*. When both parents are employed outside the home, the child is affected because of their involvement in these work environments. The child's exosystem consists of all those environments, even though he or she is not a direct participant, because even from a distance they affect the parents or the siblings in them.

Encompassing all three of these systems is the *macrosystem*, best understood as the wider cultural level. Macrosystemic influences are such things as popular culture, the mass media, the government, and moral and religious beliefs and practices in a culture.

According to Bronfenbrenner, "The ecology of human development involves the scientific study of the progressive, mutual accommodation between an active, growing human being and the changing properties of the immediate settings in which the growing person lives, as this process is affected by relations between these settings, and by the larger contexts in which the settings are embedded" (1979, 21).

A social ecological understanding of child development complements the child development approaches that have a more limited focus. Parenting is best understood as part of a web of social relationships that affect the development of a child. As children mature they become increasingly involved in a variety of settings as they learn to adapt to new environments, roles, and relationships in the process of developmental growth.

A Critique of Child-Development Theories in Light of Biblical Assumptions

Although it is beyond the scope of this chapter to present a complete synthesis of the child-development theories discussed, it will be helpful to briefly critique them on the basis of how well they comport with biblical teachings on being human. We shall build our critique around three biblical doctrines: (1) humans are in a state of constant internal tension: though created in God's image, they have fallen into sin; (2) humans are active agents who have the capacity to make choices; and (3) humans are created for community.

Internal Tension

None of the theories adequately takes into account the biblical view that human beings are distinct from all other living creatures because they carry the image of God within them. Granted, the human condition is marked by sin, and therefore we are a broken image. The biblical view acknowledges that the human condition is marked by internal tension. As Paul states in Romans 7:21–24: "So I find it to be a law that when I want to do what is good, evil lies close at hand. For I delight in the law of God in my inmost self, but I see in my members another law at war with the law of my mind, making me captive to the law of sin that dwells in my members. Wretched man that I am! Who will rescue me from this body of death?"

Perhaps psychoanalytic theory comes closest to the view that human beings are trapped in a state of internal tension between good and evil. Freud (1949) believed that a child is born with both constructive (Eros) and destructive (Thanatos) instincts. This tension, which arises between id, ego, and superego, corresponds with the biblical view, which sees internal tension as a natural human condition.

Symbolic interaction theory looks at the self as caught in a state of internal conflict between the impulsiveness of the *I* and the conformist orientation of the *Me*. However, it explains this tension as the result of inconsistent internalization of the external norms of behavior. The core part of the self (*I*) was internalized in the distant past, whereas the more exterior part of the self (*Me*) was internalized by current social norms. In the individual's subjective experience, the *I* is what one really wants to do and the *Me* is what one thinks others want one to do.

In viewing human behavior as part of the natural order, developmental theories refer to internal tension but stop short of using the concept of sin. If the ultimate meaning and purpose of human development is to be understood, we need to know what it means to fall short or miss the mark in human development. In Ray Anderson's theological anthropology, sin is understood in a relational context. He defines sin as "defiance of God's gracious relation to those who bear his image . . . [resulting] in separating persons from the gracious life of God" (1990, 234). In like manner, Shults states that at the "heart of the doctrine of original sin . . . is that each and every person is bound by relations to self, others, and God that inhibit the goodness of loving fellowship" (2003, 309). Sin is the condition of failing to be in proper relationship with self, others, and God. Brokenness in relationship is the heart of human sin. Thus the goals of child development from a Christian point of view are realized in capturing a sense of the relationality in the divine Trinity, as exemplified in covenant love, grace, empowerment, and intimacy modeled by God for us in the Old and New Testaments.

The Capacity to Make Choices

In developmental theories, the capacity to make choices is generally couched in terms of *human agency*. From a theological perspective, human agency is understood in terms of people struggling to live as broken images of God yet being responsible to God and others for their behavior. Child-development theorists differ significantly in the degree to which they conceptualize humans as choice-making creatures.

Classic learning theory assumes that children are born as clean slates upon which social conditioning imprints the cultural script. In this mechanistic view, people operate on much the same principles as do machines.

Social learning theory leans toward the conviction that children are active organisms who continually act upon and construct their own environments.

The contemporary theories maintain that children are unable to take any action apart from the options presented by their environment. While we can use the wisdom of child-development theories to understand human freedom, we must not allow this knowledge to deter us from accepting the scriptural view of free will.

Created for Community

Whereas child-development theories have only recently leaned toward the view that children are active organisms, they have been in continuous agreement that human input is necessary if children are to take on human characteristics. Deprived of a human social environment, very little in the biological structure of children would induce them to embrace norms, values, or attitudes. When children are part of a human social environment, however, they take on the attitudes and behaviors of that community.

Human beings were created by God to live in community. This is the message we learn from Genesis 2:18: "Then the Lord God said, 'It is not good that the man should be alone; I will make him a helper as his partner.'" This core theme of living in community is woven throughout the Old and New Testaments and is central to our theological model of relations. Humans require an empowering community of grace, based on covenant commitment, to provide the security and emotional intimacy all humans need.

In summary, children not only need a family; they also need a family of families. This is essentially the New Testament model of what the church is to be to the family—a place where family members are nurtured, empowered, and developed in a faithing community. The covenant is to care for members as well as to help them mature spiritually.

Parenting Young Children

The major theories of child development provide a basis for discussing important dimensions of parenting young children. In this section we address the matter of how parents can best facilitate the social, psychological, and spiritual growth of their children. In keeping with our theological basis for family relationships, we believe that parents need to provide unilateral unconditional love. This is the indispensable component in the empowering process. The fundamental qualities of loving, accepting, knowing, and communicating with our children kindle in them the capacity for mature bilateral commitments. The question of how to empower children comes down to a twofold concern: (1) how to build self-esteem and (2) how to discipline.

Unconditional Love and Self-Esteem

Children need to be valued for who they are and their unique contribution to their family. Parents who have high self-esteem and model mutual regard and cooperation in their marital relationship establish a climate in which self-esteem is nourished in their children.

Unconditional love should be shown not only in the parents' commitment to be responsible and faithful in their child-rearing tasks but also in verbal and behavioral demonstrations of affection for their children. The children will then begin to recognize that they are loved not only for what they do but also for who they are. This gives them a sense of security and increases the incentive to be cooperative and helpful family members.

Acceptance of Differences Inherent in the Family Constellation

The order in which siblings enter into a family is referred to as the family constellation. Each position in the family is important, and every child needs to feel secure in his or her place. Particular characteristics accompany each position. For example, the oldest child is usually an achiever since parents tend to give first children special attention and expect them to take responsibility early. Middle children often try to compete with the older sibling(s), but since they cannot catch up, they often achieve in areas untried by the older sibling(s). Sometimes middle children feel squeezed or lost. The youngest children are usually catered to by the rest of the family and therefore tend to be more easygoing and relaxed. The terms *babied* and *spoiled* are usually affectionate labels, but there can also be resentment toward the youngest children. An only child is similar to the oldest child but tends to be more adult in attitudes and actions. Children who come from large families tend to separate themselves into smaller sibling groups.

Every position in the family has certain advantages and disadvantages. The only girl in a family of boys or the only boy in a family of girls has special privileges and problems. Siblings who are more than five years apart tend to feel separated into different subsystems. And of course there is also great variability in how each unique family reacts to each individual child.

It is important that every position be respected and that age-appropriate behavior be expected of every child. Parents who exert too much pressure or expect too much burden a child unnecessarily; however, parents with low expectations or who show little faith in a child's abilities provide insufficient stimulation. Neither of these extreme approaches empowers the child.

Older siblings need assurance that their position in the family is special and secure. Knowing that younger children are not more loved or more valued encourages them to be helpful with their younger siblings rather than jealous or competitive. If middle children are noticed and perceive that they are cherished as special and capable, they will not feel the need to outdo the older children. If the youngest children are given adequate attention and encouraged to accomplish appropriate tasks, they will be able to contribute to the family system without feeling overindulged or coddled. Parents give their children a strong message by believing in them and in their ability to contribute to the well-being of others.

Communication

Parents use verbal and nonverbal communication to show that they respect and value their children. Critical to effective communication is the ability to be genuine. Most children can sense an inauthentic remark because the verbal claim is incongruent with the body language. It behooves parents to be congruent, that is, that words, body language, and tone of voice convey a consistent message. Expressing one's feelings honestly gives children clear and direct messages to which they can accurately respond.

When there is a discrepancy between verbal and nonverbal messages, a child will be confused and frustrated. This is sometimes called the double bind: the child cannot respond to both messages at the same time without being contradictory. The major problem is that neither the parent nor the child talks openly about the confusion, which further obscures the truth. Such distorted communication disrupts family functioning.

Communication will be enhanced if parents use encouraging statements such as, "Mike, you did a fine job of cleaning out the sink," or "Barb, I know it's difficult for you to do those math problems, but you're getting better at it." These messages are very different from negative appraisals, which tend to become self-fulfilling prophecies, for example, "What's wrong with you; don't you know any better?" Such remarks lead to discouragement and uncooperative attitudes.

The most important element of communication is listening. When we are listened to, we feel validated and cared for. Our children also need to be heard and understood. Considering their ideas and caring about their feelings are ways in which parents show they accept their children's perspective. Taking the time to know how they think and feel leads to deeper understanding. This is the very essence of how children gain the confidence that culminates in self-esteem and good decision making.

The following illustration demonstrates the supreme importance of listening. When eight-year-old Juan comes home because he has been hurt by his friend Reed, it is important for him to process his feelings with a parent who will listen and try to understand what he feels. This is not a time for the parent to question, scold, or insinuate that Juan was at fault, nor should the parent march to Reed's house to solve the dispute. Listening is especially helpful because it gives Juan a chance to express and deal with his feelings safely with someone who truly cares about him. Doing so provides a perspective that most likely will enable him to decide for himself how to handle the situation. Knowing that parents accept, understand, and support them gives children confidence in themselves. Given such assurance, they will be empowered to act appropriately.

Forgiveness

Forgiveness is a two-way process. Parents are not perfect and need forgiving when they make mistakes. Children are not perfect, and they also need forgiveness for the mistakes they make. Everyday we need to admit when we've offended or disappointed someone. Saying we forgive each other is living out grace and acceptance, which is rooted in unconditional loving.

Love You Forever, a wonderful children's book by Robert Munsch (1986), illustrates this kind of love. The boy in this story makes many mistakes throughout his growing years, infancy through adolescence. However, he is assured each night by his mother that he is loved unconditionally: "I'll love you forever; I'll like you for always!" This guarantee of always being accepted, no matter what he has done, gives him the confidence and incentive to love others in the same unconditional way. Such is the love we experience as God's children and ought to extend to our children.

Serving

Empowering helps children sense that their contribution to the family is valuable. The perspective that each family member serves and supports the others imparts a feeling of worth and esteem to children and adults alike. When children are expected and encouraged to participate in the functioning of the family, both emotionally and physically, they sense that the family is more than a group of separate individuals. They begin to see themselves as part of a larger system that is greater than all the individual members put together.

When children sense that they are an integral part of the family and that their input is esteemed, they are glad to cooperate and serve. Their contribution will be not only instrumental (doing chores) but also emotional (uplifting the family mood). They will help create family morale, identity, and unity.

Discipline

The Bible uses words such as *love* and *honor* to describe the ideal parent/child relationship. Various Old and New Testament passages also discuss the importance of guidance and correction and promise that good training will pay off because children will not depart from it. They learn from sound discipline and eventually become self-disciplined, responsible adults.

One helpful method of discipline is the concept of natural and logical consequences espoused by Rudolf Dreikurs (1991) and discussed in chapter 6. This method is familiar to us because God dealt with the children of Israel in a similar way. God's people had to face the consequences of their choices and behaviors. There are consequences to be reckoned with when we disobey. The blessing of the covenant was conditional in that they reaped what they sowed (although God's gift of love and grace was unconditional). God has laid down laws such as the Ten Commandments to guide us in rightful living, which will bring meaning to our lives. God has our best interests in mind and knows what will bring fullness and peace and purpose.

In the same way, children learn best through the consequences of their behavior, especially if they realize that the rules are a product of their parents' love and concern for them. This is in contrast to training children primarily by punishing their negative behavior, an approach that puts all the responsibility on the parents—they alone make the decision to wield punitive power when they are displeased. It is more helpful for children to come to understand that their misbehavior has specific consequences and that the ultimate responsibility rests with them.

Take the example of five-year-old June in a rocking chair. Rocking back and forth brings pleasure and joy, but if she rocks too hard or becomes too rambunctious, the chair falls over and she suffers the consequences of her action. This experience helps her monitor herself the next time she rocks in the chair. Children find their own limits through these consequences. As they self-correct and set appropriate boundaries for themselves, they are taking responsibility for their actions.

How should parents go about the business of setting up fair and reasonable rules (with logical consequences) to help their children learn limits and eventually become responsible for their own behavior? Basically, children should be given a reasonable limit and told that a specific consequence will be applied if they go beyond that limit. For example, to prevent Bobby from running into the street, his parents might tell him not to go beyond an imaginary line in the yard; if he does so, he will have to come into the house for a certain amount of time. At first one of the parents must stay close by. As soon as Bobby tests the limits of the rule (puts his foot over the line), the parent must firmly let Bobby know that he has overstepped the limit and therefore the consequence applies (he must come into the house).

Notice how the consequence is logically related to the misbehavior and carried out in a clear and pleasant manner. There is no need for a verbal reprimand, which might well lead parent and child into a useless power struggle and would also sidetrack attention from the child's responsibility for the consequence. The main point is that the parent does not need to scold or punish but must see to it that the child becomes fully aware of the consequences of the behavior. This allows the child to accept limits and eventually to achieve self-discipline.

Obviously, a crucial point is how the consequences are set up and carried out. The consequences should, of course, be appropriate to the child's age and maturity. Also parents should not be unduly restrictive and punitive by making rules and regulations that seem unfair or unreasonable to the children.

Here the idea of the family council comes into play. When children are old enough, they should be included in setting up the rules and the consequences of failing to keep them. The family decides together what are reasonable rules and expectations for everyone. It must be an equitable arrangement. For example, if the family rule is "no dishes are to

ALBERT AND I JUST LOVE TO TEACH THE CHILDREN BY MEANS OF NATURAL CONSEQUENCES.

be left in the sink after supper," then every family member must submit to the consequence. Therefore, if the father forgets, he, like any other family member, must wash the dishes the next morning.

When assigning chores, wise parents are flexible and listen to every family member. Perhaps someone is too fussy about how the beds are made, and another too careless in mowing the lawn. These matters need to be discussed together openly in the family council. This is the time and place to set up assignments that are age appropriate and fair. The family council provides an opportunity for children to learn the democratic principles of equality, freedom of speech, and fairness. All members should have input as to whether the emotional needs of the family are being met. Even the youngest child can point out that the family is not spending enough time together having fun and give suggestions for remedying the problem. Or the teenagers may need to point out that since they are older and can handle more independence, it is time to make some changes in policies.

The mode of discipline we have suggested entails personal empowering. The ultimate goal is mutual empowering among all family members. Of course, the onus of responsibility will initially be on the parents. They will need to take time with the family, listen to each member, and consider the uniqueness of each child. The parents must be willing to forgive and be forgiven, set an example by submitting to the same requirements asked of the others, and model love and caring behavior, fairness, and consistency. Wise parents allow a child the right to choose a behavior in spite of the consequence to be faced. They know when to step back and allow the consequence to do the correcting, as well as when to intervene to prevent a destructive consequence from exacting its toll.

These principles of the empowering process involve serving and being served. They are built on a foundation of unconditional loving and commitment, operate most successfully in an atmosphere of acceptance and forgiving grace, and result in intimacy through deep knowledge of and communication with one another. People who have been empowered have a competence and self-esteem they can share both in the family and with their community, society, and the world at large.

Once again God's covenant serves as an analogy. Unconditional faithfulness and love form the foundation. Even though we deserve the consequence of our failure and sin, God offers grace and forgiveness when we fail to meet expectations. Moreover, God provides the Holy Spirit to encourage, empower, and enable us to live according to the law so that the blessing may be ours. Finally, we are renewed and revitalized by the hope of intimacy and relationship with the Almighty One. As we grow in this circle of covenant, grace, empowering, and intimacy, we experience a deeper and more intense level of God's love and of our love for one another. And so too does the love within a family deepen as its members implement the empowering process.

8

FAMILY SPIRITUALITY

Nurturing Christian Beliefs, Morals, and Values

I N TRADITIONAL FAMILY systems, grandparents played a central role in the spiritual development of the young. The decline of an extended (three-generation) family system changed that, leaving the isolated nuclear family solely responsible for spiritual formation. For the most part, busy modern families have relinquished the responsibility of teaching moral beliefs and values to their children to other institutions (church and school). Without question, social institutions play a vital role in inculcating values, yet parents are the ones who are directed to "train children in the right way" (Prov. 22:6). We believe spiritual formation begins in the home through everyday interaction practices and patterns of modeling that occur in day-to-day living. Marjorie Thompson (1996, 21) asserts that "families intentionally communicate the values and vision of faith in two basic ways . . . through the *natural opportunities* of life together—occasions that simply characterize the relational fabric of family life . . . [and] through *intentional practices*—simple but specific structures and patterns that support the spiritual potential within families of faith."

The family is indispensable when it comes to building character in family members. How parents live out their faith in the context of the family relationship has an enormous impact.

In this chapter we use the term *family spirituality* as an umbrella concept to refer to all the ways family members cultivate an understanding of biblical truth, moral beliefs, and values in children. Moral values are based on underlying beliefs concerning *right* and *wrong*. Ideally the internal formation of becoming Christlike is manifested in attitudes and behavior that are truly transformative. Although the word *faith* can refer to one's religion, we use it to refer to a personal relationship to God the Father, the Son, and the Holy Spirit. We begin this chapter with a discussion of moral and faith development, using trinitarian concepts as a model for family interaction, and conclude with an examination of family spirituality as an essential aspect of faith communities.

Moral Development

Building on Piaget's assumption that children reason differently at different stages of development (see chapter 7), Lawrence Kohlberg (1963) suggests that moral development is best understood in an analogous way. During early childhood, moral decisions are made in terms of *obedience and punishment*. The child obeys rules because to disobey results in punishment. The second stage of moral decision making—*individualism and exchange*—is slightly refined as the child becomes aware of his or her own individual needs as well as the self-interests of every other family member. This realization is accompanied by a sense of fairness, and the child is motivated to make moral decisions that show impartiality to each person involved. The capacity to think more abstractly in early adolescence moves one toward the *interpersonal relationships* stage. During this third stage, personal intentions and character traits are taken into consideration in terms of how they affect the relationship when one makes decisions. The fourth stage of moral development involves *maintaining social order*. Now a person comprehends the more complex way moral judgments maintain social order through laws and societal responsibility. This more abstract understanding values the fact that laws exist to serve a greater social order.

However, in the next stage—*social contract and individual rights*—the person recognizes that social order does not always equal societal goodness. Therefore, one searches for a criterion higher than the existing social order when making moral decisions. At this point, a person moves on to the highest level of moral reasoning—the *universal principles* stage. Here all people are valued equally, and therefore one bases moral judgment on the principle of justice for all.

It is clear that Kohlberg's major focus is the *form* of a person's moral reasoning, not the content. His model is epigenetic in that the sequence of moral development moves forward through these stages, never skipping a stage or reverting to an earlier stage. Although stages of moral development might approximate chronological age, Kohlberg acknowledges that it is possible to "get stuck" in a specific stage of moral development and never move forward. Therefore, he reasons, only a small minority reaches the more advanced stages of moral reasoning.

Carol Gilligan (1982), a former student of Kohlberg, challenges his model and accuses it of being male oriented. She argues that women typically view moral decision making in the context of personal relationships rather than that of rights and justice issues. Currently some social scientists are interested in getting beyond a cognitive approach by looking at the importance of *moral identity*—one's self-identity as a morally responsible person.

The Handbook of Spiritual Development in Childhood and Adolescence (Roehilkepartain et al. 2005) proposes that moral identity is formed by social influence and most importantly through relationships with others. The authors insist that moral development is not merely a reflection of cognitive ability but primarily the result of a *personal relationship*. Anne Colby and William Damon (1995) point to *moral exemplars*—people, who by their action, devote their lives to the good of others—as major contributors to moral identity. Moral exemplars can be famous people such as Mother Teresa or Martin Luther King Jr., or simply people who have forsaken personal ambitions to devote their lives to the good of others. Their inspirational stories tell of life-changing experiences, such as serving the poor, that have transformed them (Reimer 2003). While cognitive development is certainly an important dimension of moral decision making, the role of moral identity has a profound personal impact on a person. Having a relationship with a person of strong moral character is a transformative experience in and of itself.

Therefore, we conclude that a holistic understanding of moral development includes content, cognitive reasoning, and relationships with moral exemplars. What is important for family spirituality is that values, norms, and rules be based on biblical truths and lived out in family relationships.

Faith Development

James Fowler (1981) brings cognitive development theory to his "faith process" model. He argues that faith is always relational. There is always someone to trust in or be loyal to. It is important for family spirituality to note that Fowler squarely relates the capacity to have faith to the bonding process between parent and child:

In the interaction of parent and child not only does a bond of mutual trust and loyalty begin to develop, but already the child, albeit on a very basic level, senses the strange new environment as one that is either dependable and provident, or arbitrary and neglectful. Long before the child can sort out clearly the values and beliefs of the parents, he or she senses a structure of meaning and begins to form nascent images . . . of the centers of value and power that animate the parents' faith. As love, attachment, and dependence bind the new one into the family, he or she begins to form a disposition of shared trust and loyalty to (or through) the family's faith ethos. (1981, 16–17)

As parents model covenant love to their children, they expose them to a way of seeing and being in the world. Their provision of a safe, trustworthy environment allows the child to experience loyal and faithful connection, which opens up a meaningful structure for the child. Fowler understands faith as developing through six sequential stages. Infancy begins with *primal faith*, which is derived from the infant's initial experience of being sufficiently cared for by parents. The formation of secure or insecure attachments establishes the foundation on which faith is built. The first stage, *intuitive-projective faith*, emerges during early childhood as language acquisition and emotional development allow a child to imagine through stories. Since imagination is not controlled by logical thinking, reality and fantasy are undistinguishable during this stage. Children begin to form a conscious image of God. The *mythical-literal faith* stage emerges during middle and late childhood. As children begin to reason in a more logical and concrete manner, they can distinguish between fantasy and reality. Children's understanding of God is largely a projection from human characteristics they find present in "godly" characters in stories. Adolescence is characterized by a *synthetic-conventional faith* that allows children to integrate their abstract religious ideas and concepts into a coherent belief system. Developing a personal identity spurs teenagers to incorporate God into that identity, while an increasing capacity for intimacy in personal relationships leads to a desire for a personal relationship with God. Stage 4, *individuative-reflexive faith*, emerges as adolescents transition into young adulthood. The process of anchoring faith within the self is often accompanied by examining and questioning the unexamined conventional, community-referenced faith of the previous stage. Individuative-reflexive faith tends to be both consciously chosen and intellectually based.

Advanced chronological age is no guarantee that one has automatically moved to a new stage of faith. In fact, a majority of young adults do not advance to the *conjunctive faith* stage. During this fifth stage, the need for a rational, intellectually consistent faith is replaced by the acceptance of a faith that includes paradox, ambiguity, and mystery.

The black-and-white certainty of the previous stage is replaced by the reality of gray areas.

At this time, one moves toward a deepening of one's relationship with God through spiritual disciplines and practices. It is a time when young people take up a clear devotion to God as their own personal quest rather than riding on their parents' coattails.

The highest developmental stage is *universalizing faith*, reached by few and then rarely before middle to late adulthood. Universalizing faith is characterized by a commitment to overcome division, violence, and oppression, and an ability to transcend specific belief systems. Fowler suggests that a quest for universal justice that moves beyond self-interest can be observed in the lives of people such as Mother Teresa, Martin Luther King Jr., and Mahatma Gandhi.

Although these specific stages of faith development are helpful markers, Fowler maintains that children enter into the faithing process through the relationship with their parents and primary caregivers, which is so persuasive. Children who are deprived of trusting and caring relationships are therefore hindered in the development of a mature and trusting relationship with God. The ability to experience God as a loving and trustworthy Father is related to personal experiences of loving and trusting in and through family relationships. The Christian family plays a crucial role in the development of faith.

A Trinitarian Model of Family Spirituality

The more recent emphasis on the relational nature of moral and faith development brings the understanding of spirituality to a richer level. Drawing on the insights of James Loder (1998) and a trinitarian theological perspective, Balswick, King, and Reimer (2005) present a view of moral and faith development that is more relational, less linear, and less cognitively dependent than the models of either Kohlberg or Fowler. An advantage of the trinitarian relational model is that it allows us to move beyond the individual to the interactional level of conceptualizing morality and faith.

Utilizing a trinitarian focus on relationality, we suggest that the core aspect of family spirituality centers on each family member achieving a *differentiated faith*. Differentiated faith in the context of family life is multilayered: first, each family member is differentiated (identity) in Christ; second, each member establishes spiritual differentiation in the context of the family; and third, a differentiated family spirituality develops, which serves as a unifying and transforming process in the life of each family member.

Differentiation in Christ

Differentiated in Christ refers to the New Testament emphasis on each believer finding his or her identity and reference in relationship with Christ rather than with other human beings. Trusting in Christ's death on the cross for salvation and looking to the Holy Spirit for indwelling and transformation starts the process. Surrendering one's will to the will of God places Christ at the center of each family member's identity. As the Spirit enters, this individual family member takes on a Christ-centered focus. The apostle John expresses it this way: "He must increase, but I must decrease" (John 3:30). Each family member's personal relationship to Christ and growth in the Spirit enhances family spirituality. Mutual commitment to spiritual transformation keeps family members consciously aware of how God is working in and through each of them and how it affects the family as a whole.

Spiritual Differentiation in the Family

Miroslav Volf (1998) utilizes trinitarian theology to develop a model of the church as a Christian community. We draw on Volf's insights in developing a relational model of family spirituality. Volf explains the New Testament concept of *perichoresis* as the reciprocal *interiority* of the divine persons mutually indwelling and permeating one another. He writes that "internal abiding and interpenetration of the Trinitarian persons . . . determines the character both of the divine persons and of their unity" (p. 208). In a similar way, we suggest, a family's spiritual character is defined and developed through the internal interdependence and mutual indwelling (interpenetration) of the spiritual lives of its members. Just as the members of the Godhead do not cease to be distinct persons in their unity, neither do family members cease to be distinct spiritual persons in the family. As Volf further explains, "The distinctions between them are precisely the presupposition of that interiority, since persons who have dissolved into one another cannot exist in one another" (p. 209). In other words, differentiation makes interiority and interdependency possible.

If family members absorb into one another spiritually, they cease to be a distinct spiritual presence to one another. We call this *spiritual enmeshment*. When members dissolve into one another, they cannot offer a unique spiritual perspective. At the other extreme, when the spirituality of family members has little or no mutual impact, spiritual interiority and interdependence are nonexistent. We might call this *spiritual disengagement*. When family members distance or disengage from one another spiritually, they cannot draw on the spiritual resources that could enrich their spiritual lives as a family.

Family members being responsible to one another while not being responsible for one another's spiritually—an important distinction—characterizes healthy family spirituality. Spiritual differentiation means that each member is ultimately formed through a personal relationship to Christ and God's Spirit.

In spiritual enmeshment, the spiritual trials or doubts experienced by one member precipitates a crisis that threatens the faith of the whole family. Honest differences are hard to tolerate because members are overly invested in being of one mind on spiritual matters. Any expressed difference sends members into a reactive panic mode, and honest doubt and questions are interpreted as a personal affront to the family faith. Such a state of spiritual fusion puts all family members under duress, leading to shaming and judgmental tactics to bring the straying member back into the fold. It might be helpful to make a distinction between spiritual *overdependence* and spiritual *interdependence* among family members.

The opposite end of spiritual fusion is spiritual disconnection and indifference. In this case, a low level of spiritual differentiation leaves family members cut off from one another's spiritual lives. In spiritually disengaged families, individual spiritual lives are kept private. Spiritual joys and struggles are not shared, resulting in disconnection. The family misses out on the spiritual meaning that emerges when members openly express their beliefs and spiritual vision. What is needed is neither spiritual *independence* nor spiritual *dependence* but rather spiritual *interdependence*.

The spiritually differentiated family, in contrast to the spiritually fused or disengaged family, allows members to share their spiritual lives in a way that *expands* and *connects*. Family *relationships* themselves become the means for growth because spiritual differences become a catalyst for spiritual differentiation. In a spiritually differentiated family, the personal faith of each family member can remain firm regardless of what is happening in the life of another member. At the same time, the doubts, struggles, and questioning experienced by one family member can serve as a catalyst for dialogue and personal self-examination before God for the others. Interest, concern, and support are given for the others' spiritual lives. Bringing resources to bear creates a beneficial balanced perspective.

The family with adolescent children is at a stage when family spirituality will most likely be tested. Patrick Leman (2005) found that an authoritative (as opposed to an authoritarian) parenting style (see chapter 6) resulted in children who were more likely to think that adults justify moral rules in terms of equality in social relations, while a permissive parenting style resulted in children who feel adults legitimize their decisions. When parents are secure in their own personal faith, the result is a healthy family spirituality that allows for parental support and guidance when children struggle in their personal faith.

Family Spirituality and Sanctification

We believe that healthy spiritual differentiation within the family and between members offers the greatest potential for a transforming experience. Because of the sheer magnitude of shared life experiences, no other human arena is as potentially powerful to form the inner spiritual life. In a parallel sense, there is no other human arena in which living a Christlike life is more difficult. In the family we are more exposed than anywhere else, and it is nearly impossible to wear a mask in front of other family members or to fake a spiritual life. Individual spiritual growth is an ongoing and sometimes painful journey that takes place in the demands of actually living together as family. The family can became a resilient vessel in which a spiritual metamorphosis occurs. Family relationships can become the catalyst for members to grow and to change in response to one another.

It should be noted that family tensions and conflicts can also be the catalysts for healthier forms of spiritual differentiation. Although not pleasant, family tensions and trials allow one to understand oneself more clearly and take responsibility for one's own growth. The family is a safe place where we can encounter others honestly and deal openly with spiritual differences and disappointments. When the family is an unsafe arena, spiritual stagnation results.

Family members become acutely aware of their human frailties in the context of relating to one another. However, living out the biblical components of *unconditional love*, *gracing*, *empowerment*, and *intimacy* offers the deepest possibility of being transformed into the image of Christ.

Dealing with Differences in Faith

In this section, we address the issue of diversity of faith commitments within a family. Although one should not assume that the lack of a common faith automatically negates the possibility of family spirituality, it certainly makes it more challenging. Differences in faith commitments can seriously limit family spirituality or place a family at a distinct disadvantage in this area. Under the conditions of diverse faith commitments, spiritual differentiation within a family becomes even more important. Since the adolescent is typically at a development stage in which she or he is trying to develop a personal faith, we use the family with an adolescent child to illustrate this point.

In a spiritually enmeshed family, the teenage child must either conform to the family ideal or risk the dire consequence of fracturing the family's spiritual unity. Spiritually enmeshed families have a low threshold for allowing members to think differently about issues of faith and spirituality. The unfortunate cost for such "spiritual unity" is that the adolescent does not form a personal faith and may be especially vulnerable when he or she leaves home.

We remember when our fourteen-year-old daughter, Jacque, announced at the dinner table that she no longer believed in God. We gulped, tried to remain calm, and listened with interest to what she was saying. We asked questions to help her sort out her ideas. Instead of giving pat answers, we responded to her questions by sharing our beliefs. A few weeks later from our living room, we overheard a conversation Jacque was having with two of her high school–age friends on the front-porch swing. To our amazement, Jacque was reiterating some of our beliefs as well as expressing more clearly her own belief in God. We realized others were challenging her faith, and she was searching for answers. Much of her questioning about religion during her teenage years was an attempt to make personal a faith she had learned from her parents and church. We were not always cool parents when our teens expressed doubts. It is difficult for parents to tolerate their own anxiety and keep from bombarding them with the right theology. However, we learned to trust in God to be at work in them and through others as well. We will always be thankful to Charlie, the youth pastor, and Thomps, a sixty-year-old mentor, who allowed our son, Joel, to grapple with faith and ask honest questions without fear. This is how he finally came to a personal faith in Christ.

Spiritual insecurity is likely to be at the heart of family spiritual enmeshment. Insecurity about spiritual differences tends to set up defiant and hostile attitudes toward other family members. Parents may be tempted to ridicule or put down their child's tender beliefs in their attempts to cajole or coerce their child to believe a certain way. Parents may even have a need to punish their wayward child for not conforming to what *they* need him or her to believe. Having a child who holds to a religious belief different from their own may cause them to feel defeated as Christian parents or to be apprehensive about their status in the church community when their children are not following the faith. These self-focused concerns diminish a genuine concern about their child's spiritual well-being.

At the opposite extreme, spiritually disengaged families take a "hands-off" approach in the name of respecting faith differences. Although such evasive tactics succeed in eliminating religious conflict (each family member is allowed to go his or her own independent way), it does little to enhance family spirituality. Consciously ignoring the spiritual differences, doubts, questioning, and struggles of other family members renders them "ships passing in the night." Compartmentalizing spiritual dimensions may prevent spiritual conflicts, but it also stifles sharing spiritual joy and meaning as a family unit.

When there is a high level of family spiritual differentiation, children can share their spiritual and faith questions with their parents, free of the fear of being rejected. Of course, it is always disheartening when your child seems to be rejecting God. Yet knowing your children can honestly come to you with doubts and questions means they are secure in your love. This gives you the best of all possibilities to be with them in their journey of faith.

Family Spirituality Embedded in Supportive Community

Although a family may be able to survive on its own spiritually, we believe it will never thrive without a supportive community. Stanley Hauerwas (1981, 283) describes the church as the *first family* of every Christian by pointing out that we learn "fidelity and love in a community that is sustained by a faithful God." When the family stands alone, it is difficult for it to withstand the onslaught of spiritual distortions from a secular society.

As we noted in chapter 1, the relationality exemplified in the Holy Trinity is a model for congregational life as well as the family. Miroslav Volf (1998, 16) declares that if the church is truly a reflection of the divine Trinity, relationships will be *reciprocal* and *symmetrical*, with all members expressing their gifts for the good of all the others. Secure identity in Christ at the congregational level means there is a healthy degree of *connectedness* as well as a healthy degree of *separation*. Permeable boundaries show respect for individual, couple, and family needs as they participate in the life of the church. This is a community where themes of reconciliation, transformation, restoration, and spreading peace and justice are lived out.

Church members reflect the trinitarian model by maintaining a differentiated identity in Jesus Christ. Being differentiated in Christ means we are therefore ultimately empowered by and accountable to God Almighty. Yet as members of the body of Christ, we live by the faith of the risen Lord and are therefore accountable to love, forgive, and empower one another in all our relationships.

A faith community must be invested in the spiritual maturity of all believers (1 Cor. 12:7–12). Baptized by one Spirit into one body, members acknowledge their interdependency and mutual submissiveness (Eph. 5:21). When one stumbles, everyone is affected, just as the healing of one brings blessing to the entire congregation. Members are called to accountability for destructive patterns of relating and empowered through care and challenge. The church is a place where a family's differentiated faith is nourished and preserved. It supports the making and keeping of the family members' covenant commitments to one another. Through its multiple resources, the church supports the family's growth through instruction and enrichment opportunities. Colossians 3:12–15 provides a model for the church: "As God's chosen ones, holy and beloved, clothe yourselves with compassion, kindness, humility, meekness, and patience. Bear with one another and, if anyone has a complaint against another, forgive each other; just as the Lord has forgiven you, so you also must forgive. Above all, clothe yourselves with love, which binds everything together in perfect harmony. And let the peace of Christ rule in your hearts, to which indeed you were called in the one body. And be thankful."

The deep undertone of hyperindividualism in modern society is an enormous barrier to faith. It is nearly impossible to hold on to community values in a society that promotes the "I" and the "me" over the "we" and the "us." In fact, community words such as *co-humanity*, *reciprocity*, *interdependence*, and *mutuality* are undervalued and rarely used. This self-focused mentality goes against the Christian ideal of forsaking self for the sake of other. This in itself is a compelling reason for families to join a community of faith that upholds biblical principles. We need all the help we can get to be God centered and relationship centered. Being part of a Christian community of care is not just a wise thing to do; it is a necessary spiritual discipline.

Family Spirituality as a Process

The foundational element of family spirituality is covenantal love, in which shortcomings are responded to with grace, and personal gifts and strengths are used to mutually empower, resulting in an intimate relationship. Family spirituality is not a static state to be achieved but a relational process to be lived out.

In introducing the model of family relationality, we stressed that such a form should be found not only inwardly but also outwardly. As family members are called to love unconditionally, forgive, and empower one another in moving toward greater intimacy, so they are called to do the same to those outside the family. Thompson (1996, 119) warns that "there is a strong tendency in our churches and in society at large to view interior spiritual disciplines as somehow antithetical to active service." The greatest evidence of strong family spirituality can be seen in the way families reach out to minister to the needs of others.

Family spirituality is an evolving process that corresponds to the major developmental issues of living together as a family. The early stages of marriage establish the foundational spiritual practices; with the arrival of children, family life is recentered around and immersed in teaching and modeling faith; when children become teenagers, parents and children negotiate the meaning of an independent faith; after grown children leave home, both those children and the parents redefine what it means to relate as adult to adult and honor one another's spiritual beliefs. Later in life, a couple's faith extends to grandparenting and elder-care roles, while in the last stage of family life, the finality of death is faced in light of one's faith. At each stage of family life, the potential for individual spiritual growth or stagnation is a reflection of the health of family spirituality and the nature of its corresponding relationality.

The relationship between Jesus and his Father serves as a model. Jesus proclaims in John 17:22–23, "The glory that you have given me I have given them, so that they may be one, as we are one, I in them and you in me, that they may become completely one, so that the world may know that you have sent me and have loved them even as you have loved me." God's desire for family life is for Christ to indwell each family member so that his or her unique spiritual gifts mutually serve and empower the other members. Christ, the cornerstone of faith, is the grounding force that permeates family relationships and the life of the family with a sacred meaning.

In anticipation of his death on the cross, Jesus offers us a glimpse of the spiritual differentiation between the Father and the Son. In his time of greatest spiritual anguish, Jesus tells his disciples, "I am deeply grieved, even to death; remain here, and stay awake with me" (Matt. 26:38). He reprimands them for falling asleep rather than joining him in prayer. In his humanity, Jesus seeks comfort and support from his disciples. After they fail him, Jesus prays, "My Father, if it is possible, let this cup pass from me" (v. 39). Then Jesus faces the anguish of being torn to the breaking point. He desperately wants to be relieved of the upcoming suffering but also agonizes about being separated from his Father in death. But in the intimate connection of prayer and assurance of his Father's love, he willingly submits: "Yet not what I want but what you want" (v. 39). The text reveals that the Son and the Father have wills. Yet the Son's desire is that his will be one with the Father's will. Does the Father feel the anguish and the "sorrow unto death" of the Son? We have no doubt that he does. In a fatherly sense, he certainly dies with Jesus in and is very present through his love. However, it is the Son, not the Father, who physically dies on the cross. In a spiritual sense the Father is there for the Son, without depriving the Son of his spiritual purpose. And in the end, after the resurrection, Christ is fully transformed as he becomes one with God. Here we have a glimpse of the differentiated spiritual unity between God the Father and God the Son that can be a model for spiritual differentiation in human family relationships.

9

ADOLESCENCE AND MIDLIFE

Challenging Changes

THE GREATEST CONFLICTS within the family are likely to occur when children are in their adolescence. One reason is that at the very time children are in the difficult period of adolescence, their parents are likely to be reaching midlife. Recent research on adult development has shown that reaching midlife is often a crisis for adults. Thus the conflict that frequently occurs during the strain of adolescence must be viewed in light of the parental strain as well. Both teenage children and their parents are likely to be undergoing challenging changes simultaneously.

A systemic approach helps us understand the interactive effect; adolescent stress does not merely add to parental midlife stress but multiplies it, just as midlife challenges affect and are constantly being affected by adolescent changes. Whenever two or more family members are going through a period of personal crisis at the same time, the potential for conflict increases exponentially.

This chapter presents the stressful challenges of adolescence and midlife separately and then considers the special problems that arise when they happen concurrently. We begin with an examination of the factors contributing to the rise of adolescent and midlife strain in our society. "What's the big deal?" the reader may be asking. "People pass through adolescence and midlife in every society. Why make such an issue about them?" But this is not, in fact, the case. True, people in every society pass through the chronological ages corresponding to adolescence and midlife, but these are not distinct stages of life in most societies. We will attempt to explain why our society seems to produce more adolescent and midlife strain than most others.

Adolescence

The Origin of the Adolescent Stage

Prior to the Industrial Revolution, youth were viewed as young adults. To recognize this, one need only recall how children appear in medieval paintings. They are commonly depicted as miniature adults, with adultlike arms, legs, and general physical features. We also know that the Puritans treated their children like adults—they were expected to sit still for long hours at church and then to exhibit the same disciplined behavior at dinner.

Only within the last three hundred years has childhood come to be recognized as a distinct stage of development. Children are now viewed as being qualitatively and not just quantitatively different from adults. They don't think like adults, they don't have a mature conscience, they don't view reality in the same way, and they don't have a well-developed emotional system.

Western societies initially had the cultural equivalent of puberty rites. Prior to the Industrial Revolution, youth learned to farm or acquired a trade by developing skills through the apprenticeship system. As they both lived with and worked under the watchful eye of the master craftsman, apprentices occupied clear-cut positions. Once the skills were mastered, one was ready for adulthood and marriage. Mastering the skills of one's future trade was the rite of passage into adulthood.

Urbanization and industrialization brought about a slower and more ambiguous passage into adulthood. With the development of factories, the apprenticeship system declined. Factory work did not require a high degree of skill, so youth could begin working independently at an early age. Children began to leave their homes to work in urban factories. Because of the extremely low pay, most of them lived in slum apartments. As a result of being alienated from the rest of society, they increasingly became a problem to society. Because these adolescents were disenfranchised from adult life, an adolescent culture emerged.

What in the beginning included just a few urban youth for a brief period of their lives has grown to include virtually all young people in our society. The period of time involved—the gap between childhood and adulthood, which we call adolescence—has also expanded. There are several reasons for this phenomenon. First, as our society has become increasingly technologically oriented, more jobs have been created at the highly skilled level and fewer at the lower level. Thus young people must continue their education and delay their entrance into the full-time workforce, which would normally award them adult status.

Second, most work is now done outside the home (the exception being farm families). Thus parents are unable to provide a visible work model for their children, which further alienates children from the everyday functioning of society. This isolation is aggravated by the high degree of mobility. The average American moves so often that the family structure lacks community control and support.

Third, the extended family has been replaced by the nuclear family because of this high mobility. The nuclear family is a small, fragile unit isolated from relatives who could give young people a sense of stability and belonging. In many families divorce, separation, or the need for parents to work long hours in the marketplace further complicate the situation.

A fourth factor contributing to the expansion of adolescence is the affluence of youth in Western societies today. Either because they earn their own money or because their parents give them money, many young people possess a degree of independence not experienced by any previous generation. The greater independence of youth today goes hand in hand with a loss of parental and societal control. Although these factors did not produce adolescence, they have been instrumental in furthering it.

Adolescence came about because social structures developed that retard the movement of youth toward adult status. Concomitant with this arrested development is a lack of meaning in the lives of young people today. Locked out of adulthood, they find their lives void of the meaning that is a part of adult roles. It is from this vantage that the creation of adolescent subcultures can best be understood.

But what about other societies? "Why adolescence?" is the precise question that anthropologist Margaret Mead tried to answer when she reported on her years of research among peoples of the South Sea Islands. In *Coming of Age in Samoa* (1928) and *Growing Up in New Guinea* (1935), she states that these societies were free from the adolescent stress and strain of Western cultures. There was, in fact, no adolescence. Rather, there were only two categories of people—children and adults.

In the cultures Mead studied, children were treated like children, free from adult responsibilities and excluded from making adult decisions. Adults were treated like adults, having both rights and responsibilities that were not a part of childhood. There was no question as to who were children and who were adults, for when the children in New Guinea or Samoa reached puberty, between the ages of eleven and thirteen, they were put through a series of puberty rites. For our purposes, the exact details of these puberty rites are unimportant, since they varied from society to society. What is important is that successful passage through these rites was an infallible indication that one was no longer a child but an adult. They can be thought of as the initiation into adulthood. Youngsters left the village as children and returned as adults. To have completed puberty rites was tantamount to wearing a sign that read "Adult."

What is absent from these and most other non-Western societies is the ambiguity associated with being a teenager in the United States. Being a teenager in our society is like being Alice in Wonderland—not knowing what the rules and expectations are. If asked whether a teenager is a child or an adult, most people will say, "Both," or "Neither." The underlying element here is that the beginning of adulthood has not been clearly defined.

There is evidence that, because of a combination of biological and social factors, adolescence is beginning earlier and lasting longer, resulting in the identification of an emerging adulthood stage between adolescence and young adulthood (Arnett 2000). Formal attempts to define the beginning of adulthood in contemporary society do very little to dispel this confusion. For example, the legal age at which one may marry varies from state to state. In terms of voting privileges and military service, an eighteen-year-old is judged to be an adult. In most states, a sixteen-year-old is permitted to drive. It is enlightening to note the age at which a person is regarded an adult when financial profit is involved. Movie theaters, airlines, and most public establishments that require an admission fee consider a twelve-year-old to be an adult. Teenagers are asked to pay adult prices, but when it comes to seeking adult privileges, they are told to wait until they grow up.

To grow up in the United States can be a free-form experience. It can be compared to a jam session in which jazz musicians play without a score. They simply improvise as they go along. With no clear cultural norms, adolescents similarly improvise new ways of behavior. This explains the rapid change in adolescent fashion and style, whether it be clothes, hairdos, or language.

Adolescence as an Identity Crisis

Although adolescence can be explained as resulting from the social conditions of Western cultures, its effect is most profound at the individual level, where it is often experienced as an identity crisis. In societies in which young people are given meaningful, clearly defined roles, such as those cultures described by Mead, youth have a clear sense of who they are. Similarly, some youth in our society never experience the stress and strain of adolescence because they have a clear sense of identity early on. This is most likely to be the case with young people who have a consuming passion, such as dedication to being an outstanding athlete, musician, or scholar. Others do not experience an identity crisis because they are given adult status at a very young age; farm youths, for example, begin to take on adult responsibilities in their teens. Our discussion of adolescent stress needs to be tempered by the fact that the media are quick to report on all that is wrong with adolescents but rarely give positive examples illustrating the good things adolescents do (Damon 2004).

The creation of an adolescent subculture is an attempt to establish identity. One learns from peer groups what to wear, what music to listen to, what movies to see, what language is in, and so on. The greater the adolescent's insecurity, the greater the slavish obedience to doing all the right things sanctioned by the peer group.

During the process of differentiation and identity formation, the adolescent is often caught between the family and the peer group. We might think of the family and the peer group as being alternative gravitational forces around which teenagers are orbiting satellites. Young children orbit quite closely around their family, but the orbit becomes wider and wider as the children grow older. As they approach their teenage years, they are increasingly drawn by the alternative gravitational pull of their peer group. As the pull from the peer group intensifies, they sometimes retreat from the family and reorient themselves around the peer group. Parents know quite well when this has happened, because their young adult children usually give more weight to the opinions of their peers than to those of their parents.

The generation gap of which we often speak can be understood as the result of the identity crisis faced by most adolescents. The task of establishing one's identity in today's society might be compared to driving a car. Many teenagers are restless because their parents are still in the driver's seat, running their children's lives. These parents fear that their children's restlessness and rebellion against established norms are signs of rejecting them and their values. In most instances, however, the young person wants nothing more than to get behind the wheel—to gain more control over his or her life and to share in determining where it is going. Parents hesitate to yield control to their teenage children for fear they will make bad decisions, while the teens wonder how they are supposed to learn to make decisions if they are not given the chance. The solution to this dilemma is to be found in relationship empowerment of teenage children, an issue we address at the close of this chapter.

Midlife

Adults continue to pass through individual stages of development throughout their lifetime. One of the most widely recognized stages is the onset of midlife, which is experienced by many as more a crisis than a transition. The rapidity of social and technological change shocks us, and we wonder how we can keep up with the vast changes of our post-modern world. Personal crises develop because we are not prepared for the enormous change we experience as we look to the future.

Adults in the labor force are especially vulnerable when they realize that the job they are trained to do, and have been doing for most of their adult life, is becoming obsolete. Automobile workers quite understandably experience a crisis when they realize that robots can do much of their work. A similar anxiety plagues management and other people in the business world. They fear being overtaken by younger, better-trained college graduates, especially in the computer age.

Midlife transition may also be a crisis for people who begin to realize that they will not reach the lofty goals they set years before, goals that represent self-esteem. Others may feel that they did their best work at an earlier age and that life is now less challenging or even boring. The term *career burnout* refers to such situations. Other people compare the progress of their careers with the progress of others of a similar age and become discouraged because they have not accomplished as much. Such people experience a crisis because they feel that they are not on schedule. Women who enter careers after their childbearing years often feel there is no way to make up for lost time. Some adults go through the agonizing experience of losing their jobs because of a variety of circumstances and fear no one will hire a person of their age.

Still others who have worked long, hard hours at their jobs reach midlife only to realize that they have spent little time with their children, who are now nearly grown, and have had little actual influence over them. Some of these hardworking people find that when they do want to relax with their families, they are unable to do so. The crisis in this case is that one has become a slave to work and career.

In his study of career-oriented men, Daniel Levinson (1978, 209–44) has identified four polarities of midlife transition:

1. Youth/Age. Many men in midlife occupy a marginal status: they feel past their youth but not ready to join the rocking-chair set. They attempt to appear young by the way they dress or to improve their physique by running or lifting weights.
2. Destruction/Creation. Having experienced conflict on the job and being battle scarred and hurt by others, men in midlife may resort

to the same tactics. They are aware of the death of friends their age, but at the same time they have a strong desire to be creative as they enter what often proves to be the most productive years of life.

3. Masculinity/Femininity. Concern over a physically sagging body is coupled with a desire to become more nurturing.
4. Attachment/Separateness. A continued need for bonding with others is balanced by a need to prove that one can get by alone.

Levinson believes that although these polarities exist throughout the entire life cycle, they are accentuated during transition periods. Men who have dealt with these polarities throughout their lives, having met minor crises on a regular basis, do not experience the midlife transition as a crisis period. By contrast, men who have not dealt with them are candidates for a major midlife crisis.

Although much of this is also true of women, Levinson (1996) suggests an important gender difference. For women, midlife transition is less pronounced than for men. This is especially true for women not employed outside the home. Women employed outside the home engage in *gender splitting*, simultaneously holding dichotomous identities. Four common types of gender splitting are *domestic/public*, *homemaker/provider*, *women's work/men's work*, and *femininity/masculinity in individual psyche*. Most of these splits in identity involve women wanting to uphold a traditional view of marriage while also holding an antitraditional view that allows for more independence and equality with men when participating in the public world.

For the woman whose only role has been mother and wife, midlife may be traumatic for other reasons. She may feel her role is being phased out—her maturing children have less need of her, and her husband may no longer appreciate what she is doing in the home. For the woman whose whole identity and self-esteem are based on being a supermother and a superwife, this can be a devastating blow.

Parent/Adolescent Relationships

Having considered the stressful aspects of adolescence and midlife, we are now in a position to consider the interaction between them. To begin with, it should be noted that a family with adolescents is likely to have a double inferiority complex. Both the teens and the parents feel insecure about who they are. This will have an enormous impact on the parent/adolescent relationship.

It helps when parents have compassion for their adolescent children, who are in the process of resolving a multitude of changes during this

DAD, IF YOU'D JUST HIT THE BALL A LITTLE DEEPER,
I'D HAVE A HARDER TIME CHARGING THE NET.

stage of development. While the major task concerns identity formation, Jacquelynne Eccles and Jennifer Gootman (2002) identify the following four additional tasks: working out a mature relationship with parents in assuming greater responsibility in the community; developing a solid gender and sexual identity; cultivating friendship, tolerance, and intimate relationships with peers; and developing greater economic self-sufficiency and life purpose. Parents who are confident in themselves are a source of stability by accepting these struggles as a natural part of their adolescent developing a mature self. Parents in the midst of their own identity crisis, however, may not be as understanding or psychologically prepared for the changes. They may personalize the problems and feel angry, rejected, and/or overwhelmed. In reaction, they may place unnecessary restrictions on their teenagers and dampen their ability to find their own way. It only complicates matters when personal needs in both cases put inordinate strain on the relationship.

One of the factors in parent/adolescent conflicts may be that the parent in midlife and the adolescent are experiencing contrasting physical changes. At a time when the adolescent is developing the physical characteristics of adulthood, the parents are beginning to lose theirs. While the adolescent boy finds his muscles growing and his physical strength increasing, the father finds his muscles shrinking and his strength declining. While the adolescent girl begins to develop a nice figure, her mother is fighting hard to keep her figure intact. The adolescent is developing greater physical beauty and capabilities; the parent is losing them. That fact strikes home when the daughter tells her mother to hold her stomach in, and the mother replies disgruntledly, "It is in!"

There are a variety of other reasons for parent/adolescent conflict. David Demo (1991) cites low degrees of cohesiveness in the family and inadequate self-concept in the adolescent. The disagreement peaks in mid-adolescence, then becomes less intense when realignment occurs in the relationship. Interestingly, parents tend to view the relationship as more positive and the conflicts as less severe than do the adolescents. The relationship parents maintain with their teens have important consequences for their future relationship. A recent study found that "fathers who rate their work lives as more successful than their sons' have elevated self-esteem only when they also report being very close with the children" (Carr 2005, 240).

Parental Stimuli of Adolescent Rebellion

Adolescent strain and rebellion is often escalated by sociocultural factors. But while these factors help explain the emergence of adolescence as a general phenomenon in societies around the world, they do not entirely explain why some adolescents go through a period of rebellion and others do not. Evidence suggests that parenting style and structural components within the family contribute to adolescent rebellion (Balswick and Macrides 1975; Steinberg, Blatt-Eisengard, and Cauffman 2006).

Unwise child-rearing practices. In chapter 6 we compared the effect of four socioemotional parenting styles. A study in Scotland sheds some light on how these alternative parenting styles affect adolescents in their schooling and psychological well-being (Shucksmith, Hendry, and Glendinning 1995). Consistent with what might be expected, the authoritative style was associated with success in school and mental well-being. Adolescents who received little support and control from their parents showed the most dissatisfaction with school and were the least fit psychologically. A study of 1,355 fourteen- to eighteen-year-old serious juvenile offenders likewise confirmed the superiority of the authoritative parenting style (Steinberg, Blatt-Eisengard, and Cauffman 2006). Youth reared in authoritative homes were found to be "more psychosocially mature, more academically competent, less prone to internalized distress and less prone to externalizing problems"; youth reared in neglectful homes were "less mature, less competent, and more troubled," while "juvenile offenders who characterize their parents as either authoritarian or indulgent typically score somewhere between the two extremes" (p. 47).

The relationship between parental restrictiveness and adolescent rebellion is far from simple. Adolescent rebellion is highest in very permissive and very restrictive homes, and lowest in homes with a balanced approach to discipline. This may be related to the important task of differentiation. Adolescents are challenged to develop a self in relation, that is, establishing a separate self (attitudes, beliefs, and values) while remaining connected with their family. Finding and asserting a clearly defined self is critically important because it is the only way one learns to establish a genuine relationship with parents and others. When an adolescent feels confident as a separate self, he or she has a new capacity to interact in meaningful ways with others.

Ideally, the child moves from complete dependence on the parents to semidependence to relative independence from them. The change from dependence to independence tends to proceed smoothly if the parents are moderate in their disciplinary practices. Although younger children seem to thrive on structure, when they become teenagers, they need far more breathing space. If parents continue to be very restrictive, adolescents are likely to rebel out of frustration. Overly restrictive parents hold the reins too tightly and do not allow for a gradual development of self. This creates a situation where independence can be achieved only by a drastic break from the parents. Restrictive parenting fails to provide enough structure/support in the child's process of developing a self. Children in such families may become frustrated or aggressive toward their parents and society in general, acting out in rebellious behavior.

In another scenario, teens from overly restrictive homes may choose to break away through subtle forms of rebellion such as eating disorders, depression, isolation, or creating a fantasy world. In effect the child is saying, "I'm in control, and you can't do anything about my behavior!" This is a drastic form of rebellion (acting in), since it can lead to bodily and psychological harm. Parents feel totally helpless to deal with such symptoms; however, the behavior may actually indicate an effort by teens to establish a different relationship with the parents.

Extremely permissive parents fail to set appropriate limits and guidelines that help the child develop a social self. Teenagers in chaotic homes with unlimited permission are frustrated because they have no idea what their parents expect from them. They struggle to find some sort of structure so they don't waffle throughout life. When parents fail to provide clear guidelines and set limits, the child's only option is to test the limits by behaving in increasingly extreme ways to discover precisely what the rules are. In a permissive home, there is a great deal of ambiguity about how the child is expected to behave. This ambiguity leads a teen to search for norms, which may take the form of rebellious behavior.

Teenagers have a great need to know what the rules are, even though they may not agree with those rules. They interpret permissiveness as lack of interest in them. Having reached such a conclusion, teenagers often rebel as a way of gaining attention from their parents. Thus the incidence of teenage rebellion is high in both restrictive *and* permissive homes.

Families with teenagers need the right amounts of cohesion and adaptability. As children advance through their teenage years, they move away from the family influence and closer to the norms of their peer group. When the family can tolerate an appropriate amount of separateness but also remain sufficiently connected, the teenager will be less prone to polarize family and peer group and will make a smooth transition. Teenagers in an enmeshed family either have trouble leaving home or end up making a rather dramatic break. Teenagers in a disengaged family may join a community in an effort to find a sense of belonging and camaraderie. This is a vulnerable and scary time for young people as they oscillate back and forth to discover the right balance between dependence, independence, and interdependence. Here family adaptability comes into play. When the family is flexible enough to tolerate these fluctuations, teenagers will eventually find a better balance for themselves.

Unsatisfactory division of parental authority. It is no secret that there is currently much controversy about the best authority pattern in the home. Studies show that the incidence of rebellion tends to be high in homes where either the father or the mother is dominant, moderate where the parents share equal authority, and low where one parent has slightly more authority. We believe that extreme inequality in parental authority results in a state of confusion for the teen. When authority is perceived as being primarily in the hands of one parent, the child may have problems interacting with both parents as authority figures. Excessive authority on the part of one parent is frustrating to the child and may result in aggressiveness. The teen has the distorted view that one parent is all good and the other all bad. This, in turn, sets up a conflict between the parents.

A different type of confusion may be experienced in the egalitarian home, where the child is not sure where the ultimate authority resides or tries to pit one parent against the other. This is why parents need to agree about discipline and stand together as a united front. Children need to be crystal clear about their parents being the coleaders in the home. The balance of parental power means that parents consult each other about final outcomes. Both parents discipline, guide, teach, nurture, and empower their children. The key is that parents work in tandem though they sometimes act separately in disciplining their children.

The strongest parental subsystem is one in which the mother and the father are both actively involved in the *coparenting* of children (Ehrensaft 1990; McHale, Khazan, and Erera 2002). The studies cited here found that coparented children, compared to those who had not been coparented, had a greater sense of trust; more successfully adapted to brief separations from the mother; had closer relationships to both mother and father; developed better social discrimination skills, such as discerning who can best meet their needs; displayed greater creativity and moral development; had less animosity toward the other gender; were better able to develop strong bonds with friends of both genders; and displayed fantasies of sustained connectedness. Also, in coparenting homes mothers are less likely to be enmeshed or overly involved with their children. The ideal pattern entails a moderate amount of cohesion. This enables teenagers to remain emotionally connected, even as they are differentiating from their family.

Empowering Adolescent Children

Although they may not realize it at the time, parents play an extremely important role in the lives of their teenagers. Pamela King and James Furrow (2004) found that young people having a strong sense of shared beliefs, values, and goals with their parents is related to their being altruistic and empathetic toward others. Youth are less apt to engage in delinquent behavior and achieve greater academic success when parents monitor their behavior. Positive effects were found for such parental monitoring as setting clear boundaries, establishing clear expectations, and being aware of when their teens left and returned home. Pamela King and Ross Mueller (2004) found that parents significantly influenced their teenager's religiosity.

When it comes to delegating responsibility, parents may feel nervous about letting go. To trust one's child to make the right choices and decisions and to act responsibly is perhaps one of the hardest things a parent is asked to do. Parents hesitate for two basic reasons: (1) the child's reaction to the delegation of responsibility is a true test of whether the child is mature; and (2) it is a true test of the parents' success in the empowering process. Let's not be afraid to let go but stand firmly with our teens as they reach their full adult status.

Children will, of course, make mistakes; this is part of the learning process. Because of the prevalence of parental determinism—the view that good parenting can ensure that children will turn out well—many parents feel unwarranted guilt when their children make mistakes. If parental love and discipline could ensure that children will turn out well, God would have nothing but perfect children.

The success of adolescent empowerment depends on both parents and children. Parents giving responsibility and adolescents acting responsibly mutually reinforce each other. The reverse is also true: adolescents acting irresponsibly and parents failing to give responsibility mutually reinforce each other. We should bear in mind that attitudes toward adolescents often act as self-fulfilling prophecies. The belief that teenagers are incapable of acting responsibly actually brings about irresponsible behavior; the belief that teenagers are capable and responsible is usually confirmed.

Our entire society needs to be reoriented so that young people can participate earlier and more meaningfully. This is no less necessary in the church than in any other social institution. The youth programs of many churches do a good job of entertaining the young people and keeping them busy but do little in the way of bringing them into responsible positions within the church community.

Adults are an often-overlooked source of empowerment for adolescents. In fact, there may be times of emotional turmoil in the parent/teen relationship when another adult can be more influential than the parents. King and Furrow (2004) found that both formal mentoring relationships and informal school, neighborhood, or church relationships are most effective when the relationship between adult and teen is positive and trustful, with open communication and a shared sense of value. Again, adults most positively influence teens when they provide a balance between accountability and guidance on the one hand, and encouragement and affirmation on the other. A study of adolescents with strong caring behavior by Colby and Damon (1995) found that they had benefited from adults who affirmed their gifts and encouraged their vision in serving others.

The empowering process will be most successful, we believe, in parent/child relationships based on covenant commitments. The true test of unconditional parental love occurs when the child reaches adolescence. Where unconditional love prevails, the family lives in an atmosphere of grace. Where there is grace, there is room for failure and the assurance that one will be forgiven and afforded the opportunity to try again. This deepens the intimacy between young people and their parents and makes mutual empowering possible.

10

THE JOYS AND CHALLENGES
OF FAMILY IN LATER LIFE

FAMILIES IN LATER life are those that have passed beyond the child-rearing years. The typical single parent or couple whose children are in their twenties or thirties can expect to live one-third of their lives in this particular family life stage. Because of the increase in life expectancy, this stage can last several decades. Many find this time of life an awesome, complex, and arduous journey, especially when there are four or even five generations of family members to deal with.

The "sandwich generation" describes those caught in the middle of several generations. Around the age of fifty, people who are at the peak of their earning capabilities may find it necessary to provide emotional and economic support to both young adult and elderly family members. The responsibility of caring for parents and/or adult children can come as quite a shock, especially after looking forward to a time of freedom to enjoy the fruit of one's active years of labor and raising children. Hoping for a breather after adult children have finally left home, fifty-year-olds may find it burdensome to meet the increasing needs of their adult children and elderly parents. On the positive side, although the phenomenon of living longer results in greater complexity in family relationships, it also opens up the possibility of increased cross-generational family interaction, support, and connection.

In this chapter we describe three separate stages of later life: launching, postlaunching, and retirement. We will clarify the unique aspects and typical dynamics of each of these stages.

The Launching Stage

The launching stage is the period when adult children leave home to establish an independent life outside the family. Tasks to be accomplished include (1) achieving autonomy in caring for oneself, managing finances, and being a responsible citizen; (2) developing meaningful relationships and support systems; and (3) finding a personal purpose and spiritual meaning in life. If all goes well, young adults prove able to manage their own lives effectively, think and act on their own behalf, take responsibility for their choices, and accept the consequences of their decisions. Another indicator of maturity is the establishment of relationships within and outside the family that lead to mutual interdependence and respect; we should also mention settling into a career and lifestyle that give personal meaning and satisfaction.

We noted in chapter 7 Erik Erikson's thesis that identity and intimacy are key developmental goals to be achieved by young adults on their way to maturity. Subsequent research has shown that while this sequence holds true for males, the reverse holds true for females. During adolescence males are more likely to be members of an identifiable peer group, while females are more likely to have made a few close friends. For males one's rank in the peer group helps to form personal identity, while for females the emotional bonding and communication between close friends develop intimacy. As a result of these differences during adolescence, the average male enters young adulthood with a firmer sense of identity, while the female has more fully developed intimacy skills. This difference explains why, among those who marry young, husbands struggle more with achieving intimacy and wives with identity. Working on those areas in which one is deficient is essential for young adults at the launching stage.

Adulthood is defined in most cultures as the time when people are held accountable for their behavior in society. It must be remembered that each culture, with its particular beliefs, traditions, and values, determines the pace of the launching period. We must not judge all families by the Western ideal but respect how each unique culture helps its young adults reach the point of accountability. Many circumstances influence the launching of each individual young adult, so we must pay attention to cultural diversity as well as individual differences and oscillations throughout the process from dependence to independence and eventually to mature interdependence.

In chapter 9 we identified some of the normal tensions that arise when parents are grappling with midlife issues just as their children enter adolescence. How well the launching goes is in large measure determined by how well parents and adolescents have addressed and resolved these tensions. We might speak of a smooth launch when the adult child who has left home orbits around the family at a safe distance; good connections are maintained, and there are mutually gratifying touchdowns. In a recalled launch, everyone seems prepared and ready for the big day, yet complex family circumstances prevent the adolescent from actually getting off the ground. More time is needed to make necessary repairs or to right wrongs before a successful launch can be accomplished. Sometimes there is clearly a blastoff, fueled by anger and dissension that propel the young adult to a distance beyond the gravitational pull of the family. In such cases, the premature cutoff leaves young adults floundering without support, and it is not surprising that they come crashing back, often having an impact on everyone in their path. Thus there are sad and incomplete leavings, just as there are happy and satisfying leavings. Perhaps one of the most reliable predictors of the chances for a successful launch is the level of differentiation a youth has achieved while in the home.

Differentiation is the process whereby an individual assumes his or her unique identity as separate from while remaining connected to the family. Those who approach the launching stage without a clear self-definition can be overly dependent or too cut off and disengaged from their parents. Without a solid, sufficient sense of self, they either pretend that they don't need anybody, or they lack the confidence that they can succeed on their own. In contrast, differentiated young adults can assume an interdependence in their relationships because they are both separate from yet stay meaningfully connected to their parents.

Transition Tasks

Paulina McCullough and Sandra Rutenberg (1989) have identified four tasks that, when accomplished, contribute to a successful transition through the launching stage. First, the parents who are married must refocus on their marriage relationship. When the marriage is doing well, an adult child's leaving home unites rather than divides the parents. However, if unresolved issues have caused ongoing tension and disagreements, the marriage may be on shaky ground. If the couple has focused solely on their parenting role, whether through trials or delights, the loss of that role puts them at jeopardy. They may need to face each other and their relationship in new ways. This can lead to growth and a stronger marriage if the couple is able to refocus on their partnership.

If not, there is little to keep the marriage vital, and it may disintegrate. Adult children feel the freedom to go forward with their own lives when they are assured their parents have a substantial marriage.

The second task is related to the first: parents and children need to learn to relate to each other as adults. Part of the letting go involves allowing the child to take on a new adult role. Respecting young adults and acknowledging their adult status can be a challenging task for parents. It is especially problematic when the parent/child relationship was based on authoritarian practices; affirmation of the child's adulthood is more difficult for controlling parents. Easing into an adult-to-adult relationship is more natural for those working from an empowering model, since there has been continual affirmation as the child developed toward maturity.

A third task for successful launching is for parents to develop good relationships with their adult child's mate. Often the daughter-in-law/mother-in-law relationship is the most conflicted. One reason may be that mothers tend to be more heavily involved in the lives of their married children. This may be exacerbated when the husband compares his wife to his mother on such matters as cooking, cleaning, and parenting. These comparisons put the daughter-in-law in a no-win situation since the husband defines "good" in terms of his family of origin. The new wife naturally operates according to her family's traditions and tastes.

Also prone to conflict is the relationship between the son-in-law and the mother-in-law. The popular stereotype of a mother-in-law interfering may serve as a self-fulfilling prophecy. The expectation that she will interfere serves to increase the son-in-law's reaction to her involvement with her daughter. The conflict in the son-in-law/father-in-law relationship seems to be centered in the father-in-law's view that the son-in-law is inadequate to provide for his daughter. Indeed, when the son-in-law is perceived by the father-in-law as a good provider, the chances are good that this will be a positive relationship. The least conflictive relationship seems to be between the daughter-in-law and the father-in-law. This relationship is often characterized by mutual acceptance and well-intended humor. Perhaps the relational skills of the daughter-in-law give her an ability to get along with her father-in-law.

The fourth task for successful launching is to resolve issues pertaining to the older generation. When parents have been consumed and drained by the emotional and economic needs of their adult children, the problems presented by their own aging parents may come as a disturbing reality. Having fewer resources to give may fuel resentment about the needs of aging parents. Taking time to anticipate and prepare for the needs of the elder generation can alleviate some of the frustration.

Contemporary Obstacles to Successful Launching

Clearly, the process of leaving home is not as easy as it once was. In a highly technological society, the majority of well-paying jobs demand a high degree of education, training, and skill. Even adequate entry-level jobs may require a college degree at a minimum. Given the high cost of education and training, the adult child today often needs additional economic help. The pattern of adult children leaving home only to return a few months or years later has given rise to the term *boomerang children*.

The cost of housing also makes it difficult for newly married couples to move into their own home. This means that adult children frequently ask for financial help from their parents even after they have established themselves in a career and a significant relationship. Given this trend of continued financial need on the part of children who have already been launched, the contemporary urban family may be returning to the more traditional extended-family structure.

The Postlaunching Stage

Whenever we visited Jack's parents, a predictable ritual would take place. Dad Balswick would gleefully announce, "I think it's time we washed your car!" Clean cars were a priority for Dad, and our car was sure to need a good washing after traveling three hundred miles. The car-washing ritual dated back to when Jack was a little boy. Dad would hold the hose and give the instructions as Jack did the grunt work of soaping down and scrubbing the car. Now, as an adult, Jack moved back into his little-boy position, while Dad assumed his "father knows best" position. Although this was an innocent ritual, one that Judy thoroughly enjoyed because her father-in-law winked at her as he bragged about how he got Jack to wash the car, it points to an area of struggle during the postlaunching phase. Old patterns of relating can sometimes be hard to take and even more difficult to break during family reunions, especially if the parents fail to relate to their children as adults to adults.

Leaving home is definitely a challenge for both parents and adult children. The fact that launching has taken place doesn't mean that all issues have been clearly worked out between family members. In fact, working out these family relationships is a lifelong process. Making adjustments is difficult, because the family is a network of patterns and roles so predictable that they seem to be cut from a pattern. And even greater adjustments are required when adult children bring their partners and children into the mix. Old routines will be tested, and new coalitions will bring a mosaic of different interactions and interconnections. Expectations and unspoken messages can leave the new spouse feeling excluded. If parents and their adult children are to have a successful relationship during the launching and postlaunching stages, new roles and patterns must be established. The family should endeavor to create new ways of relating that are also inviting to and include the new members.

An aspect of being differentiated is the ability of launched children to be objective about their family and resist the pull that hooks them into the old patterns. Instead of responding in predictable ways of the past, parents and adult children alike need to find appropriate new ways that work best in the current circumstances. A flexible environment allows changes that enhance all relationships so that there is a feeling of well-being and harmony among family members. Rodney Clapp (1993, 86) comments insightfully: "When family is not the whole world, parents can let children go and in turn find themselves reclaimed as parents. Truly letting a child go is hard, not only because of the pain of separation, but because a child fully released will reclaim and reshape the relationship in a way that may not be entirely to the parents' liking." This opportunity for change and growth can increase interconnectedness and renew the relationship.

Grandparenting

Grandparents have long been depicted as gray-haired, slightly frail, sitting in their rocking chairs, and passing out sugar cookies to their adoring grandchildren. Such stereotypes do not fit our modern picture of grandparents between the ages of fifty and sixty-five who dress in blue jeans and tennis shoes as they actively engage with their grandchildren. In view of the amount of financial and emotional support given by grandparents, it is now accurate to describe the North American family as a modified extended family.

Research has provided insights into the changing nature of how grandparents contribute to their grandchildren as they develop and mature from childhood to adulthood. Infants and toddlers benefit most from secure bonding with grandmothers who provide physical and emotional care. During the early school years, grandchildren value what grandparents do for and with them, such as showing love, giving presents, taking them places, and having fun together. In preadolescence grandchildren continue to value indulgent grandparents but focus on the feelings of connectedness and the family pride they derive from the relationship (Ponzetti and Folkrod 1989).

When the relations between parents and teenagers become strained, grandparents can be sensitive, nonjudgmental listeners to their grandchildren. It is especially important that grandparents of teenagers listen to the problems relating to self-esteem, affirm their grandchildren's strengths, and demonstrate their caring by attending special school events and other performance-oriented activities. An intimate, meaningful relationship between grandparents and teenage grandchildren can be mutually beneficial, contributing to both the grandparents' mental health and the grandchildren's efforts to resolve identity issues. Adult grandchildren and great-grandchildren can benefit from the emotional support given by grandparents and great-grandparents.

What goes around comes around, for those grandparents who actively bond with their grandchildren when they are young can expect their grandchildren to be emotionally supportive and concerned about them when they are old. Although granddaughters and grandsons bond equally well with their grandparents, there is a tendency for both to be closer to maternal than to paternal grandparents and to be closer to grandmothers than to grandfathers (Hodgson 1995). Since women traditionally take on the role of keeping up relationships with extended-family members and kin, this finding is not surprising.

In traditional nonindustrial societies, most grandparents were highly involved in the lives of their grandchildren. Since parents devoted much of their time to work, the care of children as well as the inculcation of morals, beliefs, and values were frequently the province of grandparents. Indeed, Scripture emphasizes the grandparents' spiritual role of passing on the faith: "I am reminded of your sincere faith, a faith that lived first in your grandmother Lois and your mother Eunice and now, I am sure, lives in you" (2 Tim. 1:5). But because of both the decline of the extended family and the high geographical mobility of industrial society, few grandparents have daily involvement with their grandchildren, let alone the opportunity to pass on their faith. Moreover, in our society not only the parents but also often the grandparents work outside the home.

The extent to which contemporary grandparents are involved in the lives of their grandchildren varies greatly. Differing circumstances create different styles of grandparenting that can include varying elements; grandparents can be fun seekers, parental surrogates, reservoirs of family wisdom, or even distant figures. Margaret Mueller, Brenda Wilhelm, and Glen Elder (2002) found that grandparents who were most influential and supportive were usually part of a highly cohesive family, had more education, fewer grandchildren, and lived closer to them. Grandparents with a more traditional view tend to be formal figures who take on the role of defining moral behaviors and rules. Grandparents who live a great distance from grandchildren pack a lot into brief visits once or twice a year. They are prone to engage in fun-seeking interaction during those visits but remain background figures for the rest of the year. Grandparents who live with or close by their grandchildren usually have frequent contact with them. It may be that they serve as surrogate parents for a variety of reasons. In this case, it goes without saying that they have a great impact on their grandchildren. Heartwarming stories are told by many adults who credit their grandparents with providing the love, prayer, values, faith, and beliefs that made all the difference in their lives. The sad news is that when grandparents are divorced, they, and particularly grandfathers, are less involved in the lives of their grandchildren (King 2003).

Most grandparents make quite an effort to connect with their grand-children, even if they are geographically distant. Interest, support, and concern can be communicated through phone calls, cards, e-mail, pack-ages, visits, summer trips, and vacations. Regardless of the grandpar-enting style, most grandparents can be counted on for support in one way or another. Most adult children turn to their parents for help dur-ing times of stress and crisis. Grandparents are called on to fill in the gaps and provide a significant amount of support to their children and grandchildren when divorce occurs. The role of grandparents in the lives of grandchildren can be especially meaningful at those transition points, such as leaving home, when the tensions between parents and child are at their highest. Think of the advantage for a child of any age who can draw on unconditional support and love from both maternal and paternal grandparents.

Multigenerational Households

Multigenerational households, consisting of three or more genera-tions living together, are most common during the postlaunching stage. In extended-family systems, such as those in Asian societies, the family by its very nature is multigenerational. In the nuclear-family system of Western societies, multigenerational households are of two types. First is the postlaunching multigenerational household of married children and their offspring who live with their parents or return home after they have been on their own for some time. A second type of multigenera-tional household forms during the retirement stage, when elderly parents move in with their married children. The dynamics of these two types of multigenerational households may be extremely rich and rewarding or extremely stressful and disruptive. In most cases there is a mixture of rewards and stress.

In general, families that have not coped well with major transitions in the past are likely to find that multigenerational living amplifies the strain. The stress will be less intense in those multigenerational families characterized by good health, emotional maturity, and self-differentiation. Other factors that can help alleviate stress include adequate material assets, financial security, a house of ample size, access to transportation, and availability of community resources. Among the more beneficial community resources are elder-care programs, day care centers for young children, and a network of extended family, friends, and church members who can step in to provide assistance when needed.

Establishing appropriate boundaries helps combat one of the most potentially troublesome areas within multigenerational households. The homeowners will quite naturally feel that it is their right to establish household rules and boundaries with their adult children, grandchildren, and elderly parents. These rules and boundaries are likely to concern questions of space, household responsibilities, child-rearing or elder-care practices, and time schedules. Although most of the space in the house may be understood as a common living area, it is wise to establish clear guidelines before living together. Taking time for mutual consideration of each individual's needs will help with the negotiation.

During our postlaunching period, our married daughter, son-in-law, and two young grandsons came to live with us for three years. Although we developed clear spatial boundaries from the start, we experienced some humorous moments. Much of the rather large house was open to everyone, but Curtis and Jacob had to be reminded that Grammie and Grampie's bedroom and upstairs living-room areas were private space that was off limits when the doors were closed. We soon learned that our grandsons lived by the letter of the law, so when the door was open just a crack, they would rush in with all the exuberance of young children. One morning, as our grandsons were trying out Judy's hairbrush, comb, perfume, and other items of interest while she was getting ready for work, it was necessary for her to explain that these things belonged to Grammie and were not to be "messed with." After listening to Judy expounding on the boundary rules, Curtis piped up with a serious expression on his face, "And Grammie, when you're in our room, you don't mess with any of our things either!" It was a lighthearted moment, but Judy was quick to reply, "Yes, Curtis, that is right! Grammie and Grampie will knock before we come into your room and ask if we can play with your things!" The boys had learned that boundary issues are a matter of mutual respect.

Other rules concern the responsibility for household tasks such as cleaning, yard work, and meal preparation. In the three years we lived as a three-generation household, our son-in-law took responsibility for house repairs, Jack did the yard work, our daughter cleaned the common living area, and Judy planned the meals, to which we all contributed by cooking and cleaning up. Similarly, when elderly family members move in, it is vital that they contribute to the household in any way they can. For some it may simply be doing a little dusting or clearing the table or gardening or making their bed; the very act of participating gives them meaning. Those unable to help physically can say a prayer or contribute through their presence at family gatherings. They should be affirmed for what they contribute to the family and be told how much they are appreciated.

An area of potential conflict and misunderstanding is caretaking. When it comes to discipline of children, for example, grandparents may tend to take charge. Having strong ideas about parenting since they have already been through the experience, they may find it tempting to criticize the parents' methods. The task facing grandparents is learning how to share knowledge without undermining or disrespecting the parents. Grandparents must also acknowledge that adult children have both the right and the responsibility to raise their children their own way. A sacred rule for us was to never interfere with our daughter and son-in-law as they were actively parenting but to share any concerns or suggestions with them in private. Of course, when they were not in the home, we clearly took the leadership role.

Different ideas about caring for elderly parents can also become a serious area of conflict between a married couple. Making good judgments about what is needed, without being over- or underprotective, is the key. When there are differences that can't be resolved, it is wise to protect the marriage by bringing in substitute caretakers who can ease the load.

When an elderly family member moves into the home, it is essential to discuss some important issues (Brubaker 1985). First, talk openly and honestly about feelings, expectations, strengths, and limitations as you anticipate caring for an aging parent. Get together with one or two close friends to talk through the hopes, fears, and doubts that having this particular parent in the home raises. Discuss the parent's physical and emotional needs and your ability to meet those needs. Consider the role that your sense of obligation plays in the decision to care for your parent and be willing to examine any resentment you may have. It is also vital to spend time reflecting on how the decision will affect your life and your significant relationships. Are there hidden expectations about the extent to which others (spouse, siblings) will be involved? What fears are there about becoming emotionally distant in your relationships as you focus on the needs of the elderly parent? Clearly voicing these concerns helps you be as realistic as possible about the decision. Periodic discussion about how things are going ensures that necessary and appropriate changes are made.

A second set of questions concerns the family as a whole. These questions center on the family's relationship with the aging parent and the impact of the decision on each member. Do they all get along with the elderly individual? Are there particular concerns with any family members that put them at special risk? How will they deal with illness? What feelings of intrusion or resentment are present? These and other questions should be processed in a family meeting. Letting family members voice their fears and concerns as well as their positive attitudes about the decision allows everyone a chance to make it a successful venture.

A third set of questions deals with the adequacy of living space, privacy, and financial resources. Finally, investigating the community resources that can contribute to the well-being of the elderly members of the household will benefit everyone. Such community resources might include transportation programs, senior-activity centers, home-delivered meals, housekeeping services, and home health care.

The Retirement Stage

Marital Satisfaction and Challenge

Most couples report retirement to be a satisfying phase of marriage. Those couples who are most satisfied have reserved time for themselves and engage in rewarding activities. They have fulfilling marriages and a sexual relationship that is founded on mutual expressions of affection, open communication, and ability to resolve conflicts. David Olson (1988) found good communication and compatibility in marriage to be most important in preventing stress during retirement. Highly satisfied couples are also fairly healthy, financially secure, and involved with church and friends. Couples in long-term marriages report more affection and intimacy and fewer marital problems, conflicts, and negativity than do couples who have been married fewer years (Cooney and Dunne 2004).

At a time when approximately one out of every three marriages ends in divorce, it is particularly important to discover reasons for long-term marital success. A study of couples who had been married from forty-five to sixty-four years (Lauer, Lauer, and Kerr 1995, 39) reports that essential to success in marriage is an intimate relationship with a mate whose company one thoroughly enjoys. Almost as important are commitment, humor, and the ability to agree on a wide variety of issues. In their review of literature on long-term marriages, T. Cooney and K. Dunne (2004, 138) report that "the same things that make a given couple happy or unhappy early in marriage tend to make them happy or unhappy later in marriage."

Of course, retirement brings with it some notable changes in the marital relationship. As the relationship becomes more equal in power, wives become more assertive, and husbands more concerned with interpersonal relationships (Long and Mancini 1990). Given the additional time that retired couples have to focus on each other and their relationship, it is not surprising that most of the research reports an increase in marital happiness after retirement.

But retirement also tends to highlight the negative qualities of a couple's marriage (Brubaker 1985, 33). Role loss is an inevitable challenge. A workaholic (whether in the home or outside it) who has defined self-worth purely in terms of work will find retirement a difficult time of life. Also, involvement in work may have kept spouses from developing a more satisfying marriage. With time on their hands, a retired couple must confront unresolved marital issues head-on. An annoying habit that was previously tolerated may become unbearable when one must deal with it on a constant basis. Another difficulty for some retired people is insufficient financial resources to maintain their accustomed lifestyle. The most challenging part of retirement involves health and aging bodies. Illness and physical and mental deterioration can sap vitality and much of the joy of living.

Minor tensions can arise because the retired husband spends so much time at home. One elderly woman compared her marriage to the Bobbsey twins: "He's always right there under my feet! I'm not used to it, and I don't know what to do with him being home all day long." His constant presence interfered with her freedom to socialize with female friends and to run the household on her own. A retired husband with few interests outside the home and few friends may find himself at a loss as to how to fill the day and become overly dependent on his wife in retirement.

Retired couples have two major crises to face: illness and death. The first crisis occurs when one of the spouses becomes seriously ill, making it necessary for the other spouse to become the caregiver. Since husbands are usually older than their wives and women have a longer life expectancy, the wife is more likely to find herself in the caregiver role. Even minor illness can provoke tension when one spouse assumes the burden of caring for the other. The healthy spouse also lives with the fear that the other will get worse and die.

Both physical and emotional illness can greatly affect the quality of a marriage relationship. The increase in life expectancy means that a larger number of people will suffer a debilitating condition such as Alzheimer's or Parkinson's disease. It is estimated that 50 percent of all marriages will reach a point where one of the spouses develops some form of dementia.

As a couple's time and energy focus more on a debilitating illness, their involvement with other couples and friends decreases. At this time, they need assistance from adult relatives. Without help from other family members, the caregiving spouse can become overburdened and stressed beyond the ability to cope. Needless to say, when both spouses are too ill to care for themselves, the extended family must enter the picture to arrange for care.

The death of a spouse is the final phase. Although death can be a relief in the case of a severe illness, it usually comes as a numbing shock to the surviving partner and other family members. Free from the responsibilities of children and work, the lives of elderly partners usually revolve around each other, resulting in mutual emotional and physical dependency. Thus the death of a beloved partner often leaves the surviving spouse seriously depressed. Frequent crying, withdrawal, loss of appetite, sleep disturbances, fatigue, declining health, and lack of interest in life are common symptoms. It is not unusual for a surviving spouse whose health is also failing to give up on life and die shortly after the death of the partner.

Although we might expect that people who are most dependent on their spouses will be more devastated by their death, this is not necessarily the case. A recent study found that "women who were most emotionally dependent on their spouses had the poorest self-esteem while still married, yet evidenced highest levels of self-esteem following the loss. Men who were most dependent on their wives for home maintenance and financial management tasks experienced the greatest personal growth following loss" (Carr 2004, 220). From this we conclude that highly dependent spouses during marriage have the capacity to gain self-confidence when they are forced to manage on their own.

Caring for Aging Family Members

When chronic illness or death strikes, adult children are called on to care for their dependent elderly members. In extended-family systems, the care of elderly parents by adult children is taken for granted. In nuclear-family systems, care for elderly parents may be more problematic. After their children leave home, parents pride themselves on their desire and ability to live their remaining years by themselves. Single adult children and those in dual-career families are not able to stay home to care for elderly parents. Some are also caring for boomerang adult children, a situation that leaves little time and energy to take in elderly parents. Health and financial problems may also deter adult children from caring for their elderly parents.

A new perspective on adult children caring for aging family members has been described as *intergenerational ambivalence* (Willson, Kim, and Elder 2003; Pillemer and Luscher 2004). Intergenerational ambivalence is a theory in family gerontology that addresses positive *and* negative features of intergenerational relationships. Ingrid Connidis and Julie Ann McMullin (2002, 565) define ambivalence as "socially structured contradictions made manifest in interaction." Family members with fewer options are more likely to resolve ambivalence through acceptance rather than confrontation. Family members exercise agency as they negotiate relationships within the constraints of social structure.

By comparing and contrasting alternative models of intergenerational family relationships, Vern Bengtson and his colleagues (2002) identify the likely path to intergenerational ambivalence. They conclude that intergenerational relations begin with *solidarity*, the bonds of cohesion that hold a family together, followed by *conflict*, as the ideal relationship evolves into reality, with the intersection of solidarity and conflict resulting in *intergenerational ambivalence* (p. 575).

Modern industrial societies seem to consist largely of modified extended families in contrast to truly nuclear families. Even though parents may live apart from their adult children and grandchildren, they are interdependent and receive emotional, social, and economic support. Thus the care of aging parents is more a question of how it is to be done than whether it is to be done. The children will inevitably be involved in one way or another.

Although the inclusion of dependent elderly parents can greatly enrich family life, it can also be a psychological, social, and/or financial burden. As more people live longer, an increasingly larger percentage of health-care costs comes in the last years of life. The statistics are staggering. According to the 1990 census, 13 million Americans were age seventy-five or older. It is estimated that by the year 2040, one in every five Americans will be sixty-five or older (Hargrave and Hanna 1997, 42). There is concern whether Social Security will have sufficient funds to take care of the needs of the elderly in the future.

The cost of placing an elderly person in a convalescent home averages between $30,000 and $50,000 a year. A couple who have worked and saved money over a lifetime may see their nest egg vanish in a matter of years. The inability of such couples and their families to meet the costs is merely the tip of the economic iceberg and a serious concern for our nation.

It is worth noting that there is a gender gap when it comes to taking care of elderly parents. Studies consistently show that adult daughters spend more time giving assistance to their elderly parents than do sons (Sarkisian and Gerstel 2004). Using a social exchange perspective, Michael Raschick and Berit Ingersoll-Dayton (2004) found that women must bear more caregiving costs than men, and adult children of the elderly receive more rewards than their spouses in the caregiving process. Although some of the gender difference involves employment obligations, we believe sons as well as daughters should share the responsibility so that women are not overly burdened in the caregiving process.

In chapter 1 we discussed the ideal of a mature bilateral commitment in which the unconditional love shown by parents to their children is reciprocated when the parents age and become socially, emotionally, and physically dependent on their adult children. When this happens, family life has truly come full circle. The Bible speaks of the family's responsibility to care for its most needy members. That this includes elderly parents is made clear in 1 Timothy 5:4: "If a widow has children or grandchildren, they should first learn their religious duty to their own family and make some repayment to their parents; for this is pleasing in God's sight." Lest the reader fail to get Paul's message, he continues with this warning in verse 8, "And whoever does not provide for relatives, and especially for family members, has denied the faith and is worse than an unbeliever."

In the social economy of the early church, it was primarily the responsibility of the family rather than of the church to care for the elderly. First Timothy 5:16 reads: "If any believing woman has relatives who are really widows, let her assist them; let the church not be burdened, so that it can assist those who are real widows." The reason given is that the church will then be better able to care for the dependent elderly who do not have family. The clear social ethics found in Scripture is that we are to care for our own family members as well as for those in need through the community of faith.

Within reason, the elderly person should have a say in the matter and their preferences should be taken into account. The elderly parent must be treated with dignity at all times.

Caring for elderly parents is both a privilege and a priority for Christian families and the church community. Granted, making decisions about how to best care for elderly parents is a complex process, and we must do so with respect, honor, and integrity.

Regardless of the social structural arrangements utilized to care for the elderly, efforts to foster independent living is an important goal. In addressing theological issues in caring for the elderly, Balswick, King, and Reimer (2005, 233–36) suggest that the family create *zones of proximal capabilities*. In chapter 7, we referred to Vygotsky's *zone of proximal development* concept to describe the range of skills to be accomplished in assisting children. In a similar way, a zone of proximal capability helps establish the range of skills an elderly person can accomplish on his or her own or with the help and support of others. As a mirror image of empowerment, family members will increase the scaffolds or helping structures as needed to allow the elderly to continue to be as independent as possible. Sometimes outside caregivers can empower and model patience because family members have a hard time seeing a loved one struggle in an attempt to be independent.

Given the biblical emphasis on community, one can argue that the entire community, rather than merely a few family members, is responsible for the elderly. Some religious groups and denominations are well known for establishing excellent retirement communities to provide for the aging. The overarching biblical principle here is that family members care for their own. How this is done, within the household or within an elder-care community, depends on social, psychological, physiological, and economic circumstances. God can honor a number of alternative social arrangements. Both approaches—household and community care—have their unique strengths and limitations. The important thing is that the dependent elderly be nurtured and loved unconditionally as family, regardless of who is providing the day-to-day care.

PART 4

GENDER AND SEXUALITY

Identity in Family Life

T HIS SECTION FOCUSES on two major sources of personal identity: one's gender and one's sexuality. In chapter 11 we discuss the impact of changing gender roles on the family in our society. We examine current explanations of gender differences and then offer a Christian viewpoint. We also offer practical ideas on how Christian families and the church can provide leadership in this area.

In chapter 12 we expound on the fact that God created us as sexual beings and pronounced this very good. God intended that we be authentic and whole in our sexual relationships. After noting sociocultural influences on the development of our sexuality, we present a theological understanding. Finally, focusing on four important aspects of sexual expression—sex and singlehood, masturbation, sexual preference, and marital sexuality—we offer some practical guidelines for achieving wholeness in a broken world.

11

CHANGING GENDER ROLES

The Impact on Family Life

IN MOST SOCIETIES throughout history, being a man or a woman was taken for granted. Males and females developed into their respective roles quite naturally. This is certainly not the case today! Our society is embroiled in debates over what constitutes masculinity and femininity and what the appropriate roles are for each gender. This redefinition of gender roles has caused disruption in the family. The marital dyad, where husbands and wives are struggling with conflicting definitions of marital roles, has suffered the most. Redefining gender roles also extends to parent/child relationships as parents come to grips with how to raise their sons to be men and their daughters to be women in an age when traditional definitions of manhood and womanhood are being challenged.

The fact that more than half of all married women work outside the home today raises a concern over the adequacy of parenting. This is a crucial concern since the family is the arena in which a child's personal character and gender identity are formed. A little boy learns how to be a man by observing not only the behavior of his father and older brother(s) but also what is expected of him by his mother and sisters. Likewise, a little girl learns how to be a woman by viewing the behavior and expectations of family members of both sexes. For this reason, we have chosen the family as the context for our discussion of changing sex roles.

We note the reasons gender roles are changing today and then consider some of the explanations for gender differences. Finally, we explore the effect that redefinition of gender roles has on the family. In the process, we reflect on these changes in light of our hermeneutical understanding of the relevant scriptural texts.

Why Gender Roles Are Changing

There are several reasons why traditional definitions of sexual roles are currently being called into question. The social sciences have demonstrated that many of the traditional characteristics of masculinity and femininity, formerly assumed to be the result of natural development, are in reality a result of cultural conditioning. Increased observation and dialogue with people from various parts of the world have also informed us that most differences between masculinity and femininity are culture bound.

The explosion of technological culture is another reason gender roles are changing. Before the machine age, the physiological differences between the sexes determined one's work role. Being larger and stronger than women, men were expected to do most of the heavy work. Since

I CAN OPEN MY OWN DOOR, MACHO MAN!

women give birth to babies and nurse them during infancy, they were more involved with child care. With the emergence of electronics and computers, however, the most valued work is no longer manual labor but work that demands the development of the mind. That men and women are equally qualified in this realm has opened the job market for women. The development of contraceptives has also freed women from giving birth to large numbers of children.

Explanations of Gender Differences

For years there has been an argument as to whether gender differences are due to environment or heredity. This controversy began with the emergence of modern science. With the development of the biological sciences, it was discovered that genetics plays a key role in determining the nature of both plants and animals. Furthermore, not only physical features but also traits of temperament were traced to the genetic packages that children inherit from their parents. Although each individual genetic package was understood to be unique, males and females were thought to possess decidedly distinctive genetic packages.

Behavioral scientists challenged this notion, explaining that gender differences are acquired after birth as a result of cultural conditioning. Both sides of the debate initially assumed an either/or approach, arguing that gender differences are either a result of hereditary factors or a result of environmental factors. As the dividing lines between scientific disciplines have broken down, explanations for gender differences have become less an all-or-nothing proposition. Contemporary explanations of gender differences are much more complex, and both theoretical sides point to the interactive effect between heredity and environment. Let us look at some of these explanations and then at some of the theories propounded by the women's movement in the late twentieth century.

Evolutionary Psychology

Evolutionary psychology, sometimes referred to as sociobiology, explains the differences between the sexes in terms of the gene pools that have developed through a natural-selection process over thousands of years. As stated in the introduction of *The Handbook of Evolutionary Psychology* (Buss 2005, 5), "The long term scientific goal . . . is the mapping of our human universal nature." Since reconstructing a narrative explaining the emergent differences between the sexes remains speculative, there are different versions. One version that is especially relevant in explaining male/female involvement in the family proposes that men bonded together because of the need to hunt wild animals. In the process, they also developed a sense of adventurousness and protectiveness toward their family. Women developed nurturing abilities through the bearing and rearing of children.

One may ask, what prevented women from going with the men on the hunt? Some women did in fact hunt with the men, but because of the dangers involved those who did so were more prone to lose their offspring. Also, women who spent their time at home giving birth and caring for children were more desirable as marriage partners. Consequently, these were the women whose genes were passed on to future generations. The men who were desired as marriage partners did not stay around the compound to care for children; rather, they were successful on the hunt. Thus, it was not the men with nurturing tendencies who contributed to the gene pool, but those who acted on their hunting instinct.

Evolutionary psychology also has an explanation for why men are more sexually promiscuous than women. Sexual motives and actions are understood as attempts to maximize the possibility of passing on one's genes. Since men have an unlimited number of sperm, it is in their self-interests to "diversify" by having sex with as many women as possible. Women, however, have a limited number of eggs and when pregnant must carry the child for nine months before birth. Thus a woman has nothing to gain by being promiscuous but becomes a "careful shopper," having sex only with a male who shows promise of supporting her and her offspring. This tendency for men and women to come together to assure the survival of a common offspring is known in evolutionary psychology as *pair bonding*. Men bond with women because they realize this is the most effective way of assuring that their offspring will survive. Herein is the evolutionary explanation for the emergence of *monogamy* as the most common form of marriage around the world.

The result after thousands of years of natural selection is that men and women have different genetic packages that influence temperament. Women are more nurturant and capable of emotional bonding with small children. Men are more adventurous, strong, and protective. While evolutional psychologists admit that we no longer live in a society dependent on hunting dangerous animals, and the differences between the sexes are no longer a matter of our prime function in life, they believe these genetically produced differences are real and cannot be dismissed.

Christians differ in their assessment of evolutionary psychology as an explanation of the temperament differences between the sexes. Some are rather favorably disposed, while others categorically reject any evolutionary explanation of these differences. Ironically some Christians and evolutionary psychologists agree regarding existing temperamental differences between the sexes but differ in their explanation, viewing it, respectively, as an act of God's creation or as a natural-selection process. The question still remains regarding the *desirability* of differences between females and males. Thus, Mary Van Leeuwen (2002, 146) notes that "in contrast to a biblical world view and the theologies that have been built on it, evolutionary psychology has no basis for sorting out what is created from what is fallen in human behavior."

Socialization Theory

Socialization theory holds that from the time children are born, they are taught both explicitly and implicitly how to be a man or how to be a woman. In learning to be a man, boys in American society come to value masculinity as expressed through physical courage, toughness, competitiveness, strength, control, dominance, and aggressiveness. In learning to be a woman, girls are taught to value gentleness, expressiveness, responsiveness, sensitivity, and compliance. When parents rigidly enforce these values, male children fear being caught doing anything traditionally defined as feminine. Girls avoid appearing too aggressive, boisterous, or tomboyish, for fear of being labeled unladylike.

Peer groups continue to perpetuate the gender stereotypes as well. According to studies of male subcultures such as school groups or street-corner gangs, if a boy is affectionate, gentle, or compassionate toward others, he is not invited to be one of the group. Girls are ostracized in a similar manner for being too tomboyish or assertive. The mass media also reinforce the traditional stereotypes in subtle yet powerful ways.

The message of how to be female or male is deeply imprinted in the cultural patterns of every society. The family, peer groups, and the media converge to persuade young people to take on stereotypical behaviors. By the time they reach adulthood, they have been socialized into clearly defined sexual roles.

Neopsychoanalytic Theory

Nancy Chodorow (1999) presents an explanation of gender differences consistent with both Freudian theory and feminist thinking. She believes that women rather than men do most of the parenting as a result of social structures rather than as an unmediated result of physiology.

Chodorow contends that while the mothering process enhances a girl's nurturing capacity, it inhibits a boy's. Both boys and girls begin their lives with an emotional attachment to their mother, but boys must learn to identify with their father by denying this special attachment to their mother. Girls, however, can continue to identify with and attach to their mother in a natural way.

A girl's relationship to her mother and a boy's relationship to his father are significantly different. The girl is likely to be continually involved with her mother in the home. That the father is probably absent from the home for most of the day means that the boy must derive notions about masculinity from his mother and the culture at large, rather than from a close relationship with his father. One might say that girls get an inside look at what their role in the family will eventually be; boys, on the contrary, must learn their role from external models. As a result, females take an active part in family life; males see themselves as outsiders.

The close ties developed with their mothers means that girls will most likely desire to be nurturers. Boys who are not closely tied to their fathers must deny the attachment to their mother for the sake of defining their own masculinity. Consequently, when they become fathers, they are likely to be emotionally distant from their children.

In summary, neopsychoanalytic theory, which is a specialized type of socialization theory, explains that gender differences are a result of girls' experiencing a warm, close relationship with their mother and boys' experiencing a cool, distant relationship with their father. A helpful assumption is that male and female temperaments can actually be changed through the parenting relationship.

Feminist Theories

The women's movement has generated several feminist theories, each of which attempts to explain the conscious as well as unconscious dominance of males over females. Although each accepts the goal of ending sexism by empowering women, there is much disagreement about how to accomplish this (Lindsey 2005). The majority wing of the movement consists of liberal feminists who generally explain gender differences in terms of the socialization theory.

Liberal Feminism

Liberal feminists emphasize that inequality of opportunity has been perpetuated by a social structure in which men are the dominant class and women are the underclass. Although liberal feminists do not deny some innate dissimilarities between the sexes, they believe that most of the difference is socially determined. They believe that every individual has unique skills and abilities that have nothing to do with gender.

On the basis of assumed equal potential, liberal feminists believe that gender should not be a factor in determining involvement in any familial or societal task. All individuals should be allowed to pursue their own goals, irrespective of gender, and to participate in any task or activity they choose. Liberal feminists argue that a variety of family forms is a constructive and healthy consequence of modernity. It is desirable for a society to honor different family arrangements in which individuals of both sexes have a free choice in their wage-earning and housekeeping roles. For example, a couple may decide on any one of three options: male wage-earner/female housekeeper; female wage-earner/male housekeeper; or dual wage-earners/dual housekeepers. Every couple should be allowed and encouraged to develop the type of living arrangement that is best for them. Liberal feminists abhor the bondage and constriction of family life dictated by rigid definitions of female and male roles.

In the area of sexuality, the active male/passive female dichotomy is viewed as culturally determined. Liberal feminists would elevate the role of both females and males, believing that both genders are responsible for their own sexuality and sexual fulfillment.

Marxist Feminism

Advocates of Marxist feminism believe that gender equality is possible only in a classless society. In their view, class differences and the concomitants of those differences, such as private property, perpetuate the oppression of women. Within capitalism, upper-class women are reduced to useless, perfunctory roles. They are viewed only as beautiful objects to be adorned with fine clothing and costly jewelry, thereby remaining helplessly dependent on the men who provide for them. At the same time, lower-class women are overworked, exploited, and made to bear the worst of the burden. Marxist feminists believe that if capitalism were defeated, women would gain equal jobs. To accomplish this, women must join men in the labor force in the struggle to overthrow capitalism. At the same time, housework needs to be valued and esteemed as the economically productive activity it is.

Although Marxist feminists accept the sexual and emotional aspects of monogamy, they would eliminate its economic aspects. As an instrument for channeling wealth and power from one generation to the next, monogamy helps perpetuate upper-class dominance. This means of keeping women economically oppressed must, they claim, be put to an end.

Radical Feminism

Radical feminists argue that the oppression of women is inherent in the nature of male/female relationships and predates the emergence of private property. Contrary to Marxist feminists, radical feminists do not believe that the abolition of class-based societies will end the oppression of women. Rather, sexism is understood to be rooted in the very fabric of all societies; consequently, it will not diminish apart from radical structural change.

Radical feminists seek change in at least three areas: (1) Presently held in economic bondage to men in a society geared to reward the male rather than the female, women must form their own economic associations and businesses. Women's progress to date is seen as mere tokenism—only a few women have been given premier positions in the business structure. Capitalist organizations controlled by men reinforce the economic subordination of women. (2) Women must be allowed to be sexually free and to establish spontaneous relationships with those they choose. This means putting an end to the hypocritical double standard that gives much more sexual freedom to men. (3) Women need to be freed from the burden of rearing and caring for children. This task should be shared by society as a whole.

Socialist Feminism

Accepting the major arguments of both Marxist and radical feminism but rejecting the exclusivity of each, socialist feminists argue that both economic oppression and the fundamental structure of male/female relationships are primary causes of sexism. Like Marxists, socialist feminists reject the dichotomy between homemaking and work. They believe that domestic work must be considered real work, that is, it must be considered productive work. The lower-class wife, in releasing her husband from housework, is contributing to what Marxists call surplus value. Accordingly, housewives should be paid a wage by the state.

The family in its present form must be eliminated, because it represents the private sphere and functions to aid capitalism and perpetuate sexism. Only by eliminating the existing familial and societal structures can the dual evils of economic and sexual oppression be eradicated.

Socialist feminists see an additional dimension in the problem of sexism. They argue that although all women are oppressed, they are oppressed in different ways. Working-class and third-world women are more oppressed than upper-class women. The most oppressed are lower-class women living in the poor societies of the world, for they must bear both international economic exploitation and sexism.

Critical Feminism

Critical feminism grew out of critical theory, a sociological analysis of power in relationships. According to critical theory, power is based on having the resources to dominate and control and is thus always being negotiated and reconstructed to keep the dominant group (race, gender) in charge. Thus critical feminism is the analysis of how men use institutional and informal power to dominate and control women. As a sociological theory, critical feminism focuses on the relationships between men and women more than on particular male and female characteristics.

Central to critical feminism is the idea of hegemony, the process whereby men keep power by ensuring that everyone sees the world from their point of view. While men are the dominant group, and women are the subordinate group, neither of these categories is homogeneous. Only certain men have what the masculine or patriarchal ideology defines as the most desired characteristics: financial independence, physical strength, good looks, toughness, and social status. These men possess hegemonic masculinity. Men who lack these particular masculine characteristics are considered to be of lower status and may be labeled wimps or nerds.

Although all women are a part of the subordinate group, they too differ greatly in relative status. Women who possess the characteristics defined as desirable by the patriarchal ideology (i.e., a pretty face, a shapely body, emotional warmth, submissiveness) experience privilege because they approach ideal femininity. But regardless of how closely a woman approximates ideal femininity, she can never obtain hegemony, for she is not male. Theological, political, and philosophical ideologies combine to justify barring women from powerful positions. For instance, certain religious ideologies maintain that only men can occupy ecclesiastical positions that carry the greatest power.

A unique aspect of critical feminism is that it offers hope for change. Regardless of their circumstances, women and men can think critically and act together as agents of change to transform the oppressive system. Critical feminists also believe that the dominant group will be tenacious in its efforts to retain power by suppressing such change. When pressured, a patriarchal structure will make token concessions in an attempt to appease female discontent, but access to the resources on which male power is based will be carefully guarded. Therefore, it will take relentless work to change the patriarchal system. But when men and women work in tandem toward this end, there is great potential for change.

Biblical Feminism

Based on a biblical understanding of gender, biblical feminists are women and men who advocate legal and social changes that would establish the political, economic, and social equality of the sexes. They are committed to empowering women to identify, develop, and use their gifts for the advancement of God's reign on earth. This is to be done responsibly and without regard to sexual stereotypes.

Judith Plaskow (1980) broadens the definition of sin and argues that women's sin has been self-denigration and lack of self-affirmation, which has led to excessive dependency and powerlessness. Sin manifests itself in the social and political systems of patriarchy, keeping women dependent on men. Sexism, like racism, is embedded in a sinful social system that perpetuates practices that discriminate against women and keep them subordinate. Sexism is sinful and needs to be eradicated through changes not only in individual attitudes and behaviors but also in the social and institutional systems themselves.

Another useful analysis is *After Eden* (Van Leeuwen et al. 1993), authored by a five-member study group sponsored by the Calvin Center for Christian Scholarship. Wedding the ideas of critical feminism to biblical feminism, the book provides an insightful understanding of the structural barriers hindering gender equality. It also presents a biblically informed basis for gender equality as a matter of fundamental Christian justice.

Biblical feminists are committed to raising the consciousness of people within the Christian tradition. They challenge the inequality of hierarchical structures by promoting the ordination of women and inclusive language, by attending to the special needs of the disadvantaged poor, and by fighting against the physical and sexual abuse of women and children.

Christian feminists seek reform in and through the church. They urge Christian communities to acknowledge the human suffering of women and to find solutions. They demand that the church encourage all people, regardless of gender, to recognize and affirm that they are endowed by God with gifts and responsibilities to strive for love and justice through service to one another in all realms of life and in all parts of the world.

Organizations such as Christians for Biblical Equality (CBE) have provided a strong voice for evangelicals who advocate equality for all human beings. Their methods include issuing challenges, setting up remedial processes, and promoting reconciliation and change. The central difference between evangelical feminism and other types of feminism is that its authority is biblical revelation. As men and women reconciled in Christ work together for worthy goals, they will transform the kingdom of God on earth. Biblical feminists are concerned with establishing justice through living one's faith. The essential message of CBE is stated in the introduction to its sponsored book *Discovering Biblical Equality: Complementarity without Hierarchy*: "Gender, in and of itself, neither privileges nor curtails one's ability to be used to advance the kingdom or to glorify God in any dimension of ministry, mission, society or family" (Pierce, Groothuis, and Fee 2005, 13).

A Radical Proposal for Reconciliation

All feminist theories have in common (1) the fervent goal of eliminating sexism and (2) the view that gender differences are the product of the fabric of society and culture. Patriarchy has been an obstacle throughout history, blocking the affirmation of women as persons. Frustrated by this obstacle, feminists see the necessity of altering the social and institutional structures that perpetuate the subordinate status of women. Liberation for both women and men from their respective restrictive roles as oppressed and oppressor is the corrective needed to overturn the damage done by patriarchal structures.

Theologian Miroslav Volf (1996) has issued a challenging proposal about what it will take to reconcile two groups that have had such a long history of hostility. He advocates both personal and spiritual reconciliation.

Volf's compassionate but tough model of reconciliation offers a powerful ideal for gender reconciliation. The theological starting point is found in the "offense of the cross." It seems outrageous to us that Christ would make himself totally vulnerable on the cross to create a space in himself for those who were his enemies. Yet he opened his arms and invited the offenders in (Volf 1996, 126–29). Applying Christ's model to the relations between men and women, Volf believes that a "reconciliation with the other will succeed only if the self, guided by the narrative of the Triune God, is ready to receive the other's alterity" (p. 110). Until each gender makes a space for the other, true reconciliation between them will not be possible. The seriousness of the offense must be acknowledged and never minimized. The wrongs must be named, for repentance is required. Each gender has offended the other in different ways: men must repent of their sins as oppressors, while women "need to repent for what was done to their souls as a result of the disempowerment" (p. 117).

In this radical approach to reconciliation between men and women, Volf is careful to clarify that forgiveness is not a substitute for justice. In fact, asking for forgiveness draws attention to the offense, wrongs that justice alone can never satisfy. The offense cannot be rectified, for once done, it cannot be undone. What makes confession and repentance so powerful in this situation is the very idea that injustices are being dealt with in the presence of God. His invitation to women and men to let go of the rage and its destructive consequences that eat away at their very souls is crucial, because only God can truly forgive. Of course, the choice to no longer see the other as the enemy puts one in a vulnerable position.

However, it also means that one is no longer defined by the offender, and that one has a new ability to remember rightly. When women and men get beyond excluding each other and reach the point of embrace, there is great hope for the future.

At the heart of the cross was Christ's decision to heal brokenness by no longer keeping offenders as enemies. Volf offers this as a model for groups who define themselves as enemies. For just as God makes room for us, there is hope that when "guided by the indestructible love which makes space in the self for others in their alterity, which invites the others who have transgressed to return, which creates hospitable conditions for their confession, and rejoices over their presence, [women and men will with God's help keep] re-configuring the order without destroying it so as to maintain it as an order of embrace rather than exclusion" (Volf 1996, 165).

Toward an Integrated View of Gender Differences

On the basis of both physiological and social-science research, we can concluded that both *nature* and *nurture* are important contributors to the formation of femininity and masculinity. We must challenge both evolutionary psychologists and social scientists when they too vigorously argue for a single-factor *deterministic* explanation of gender differences.

A biblical perspective on being human assumes human agency. Human beings are active agents, not passive objects influenced by internal genetic forces or acted upon by the external environment. Further complexity is added by evidence that physiological and sociocultural factors have an *interactive* effect on gender formation. For instance, higher levels of testosterone have been correlated with more aggressive behavior. Although this is true among both males and females, males on average have significantly higher levels (10:1 ratio) of testosterone. Research shows a higher rise in testosterone level among men who were spectators at a sporting event in which their team won when compared with men whose team lost (Bernhardt et al. 1998). Here we have an example of an interactive effect between physiological and sociocultural factors.

Another example of the interaction between nature and nurture is found in the capacity for nurturing behavior. Research reveals that even during infancy girls have a higher degree of sensitivity to touch, sound, and odor; are more drawn to human faces; and exhibit greater responsiveness to the nuances of facial expression. Girls also develop more quickly than boys in the areas of language, verbal fluency, memory, sensitivity to context, and picking up and processing peripheral information. This evidence leads Alice Rossi (1984) to conclude that females have a head start in developing the capacity to care for children. Although women enjoy a genetic advantage in the caretaking of infants, their physical ability to nurse children is also an advantage. The time spent in infant care further develops caretaking abilities. Although fathers have a physiological disadvantage in caretaking, fathers who do engage in the care of their children develop greater nurturing qualities. In other words, the act of engaging in caretaking changes one's capacity and ability to nurture.

The most compelling evidence that biological factors account for some gender differences can be found in correlations between the social behavior and the physiological attributes of each sex; gender differences in infants and young children prior to socialization; the emergence of gender differences with the onset of puberty, when physiology and hormonal secretion change rapidly; stability of gender differences across cultures; and similar gender differences among the higher primates (Rossi 1984, 4). Whereas these findings may seem to reinforce traditional gender stereotypes, they do not deny that these tendencies are accentuated through the socialization process.

The evidence suggests that males and females are born with general dispositions but not directional predispositions. These genetic tendencies are then exaggerated by patterns of socialization to fit with the prevailing definition of masculinity and femininity. (See figure 13, where the distance between the horizontal lines represents the difference between male and female behavior.) We suggest that culture, not biology, molds

FIGURE 13 **Differences between Male and Female Behavior**

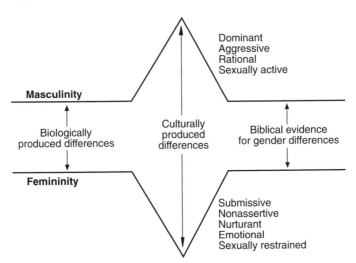

males to exhibit primarily dominant and rational characteristics and shapes females to appear submissive and emotional. It is essential for Christians to keep this in mind when they ask the fundamental question, "What is God's intention for the development of full manhood and womanhood in modern society?"

As Christians we must be careful not to defend cultural images of gender differences. This is precisely what happens when we argue for the preservation of traditional gender roles. It is also important to guard against a wholehearted embracing of the modern androgynous ideal. What we must do is accept the evidence of biology and social science and then interpret those data in light of the biblical pronouncements.

Genesis 1:27 records the creation of Adam and Eve: "So God created humankind in his image; in the image of God he created them; male and female he created them." One important implication of this verse is that God created male and female as distinct human beings. We are left to determine exactly what that means and how such differences are to be expressed in male/female relationships. We must turn to the Scriptures for further elaboration on this distinctiveness and then interpret what we find there in light of social-science findings on gender differences.

When we examine the Bible, we see little evidence that God desires sharp normative differences in temperament and behavior between males and females. Christians who argue for rigidly separate roles for men and women can do so only by misconstruing the overall message of Scripture. Some use a proof-texting method that ignores the context of the verses cited. Another faulty use of Scripture is to view historical descriptions of gender roles as if they were normative.

The Bible has more to say about Christian temperament in general than it does about distinctions between female and male temperament. Paul writes in Galatians 5:22–23: "The fruit of the Spirit is love, joy, peace, patience, kindness, goodness, faithfulness, gentleness, and self-control." It is noteworthy that our culture considers these attributes to be feminine. On the basis of these verses, we would argue not only that males and females should be more alike but also that males need to develop the qualities that have traditionally been defined as feminine.

Still another means of viewing gender roles from a Christian perspective is to examine the person of Jesus during his earthly ministry. That is to say, what was Jesus really like as a human? To begin with, we read about a person who experienced a wide range of emotions, but compassion and love were pervasive. Jesus's compassion is seen in his relationships with the blind man, the lepers, the bereaved widow, the woman at the well, and the children. Consider also his actions toward people in need—feeding the hungry, healing the sick, and reaching out to the lost as to sheep without a shepherd.

The compassion of Jesus was also expressed in his sorrowful emotions during experiences of despair and loss. Jesus wept over Jerusalem because of the unbelief of its people. When he saw Mary and Martha grieving over the death of Lazarus, he openly cried and expressed his own sadness. At other times, Jesus was elated and expressed great joy. When the seventy he had sent out to witness returned, Jesus "rejoiced in the Holy Spirit" (Luke 10:21). He also told his disciples that if they would abide in his love, his joy would be in them (John 15:10–11).

In addition to meekness, Jesus openly expressed anger and indignation. In a world under the curse of sin, he responded appropriately with anger. When he witnessed unbelief, hypocrisy, and acts of inhumanity, he took action. Jesus openly expressed his emotions, whether it was to nurture the little children or to overturn the tables in the temple. The picture that emerges is that Jesus was not traditionally masculine or feminine by current cultural standards but, rather, distinctively human. He incorporated the characteristics of both masculinity and femininity and presented to the world a model of an integrated and whole person.

Changing Gender Roles and Family Life

As we mentioned earlier, the current redefinition of gender roles is causing confusion and disruption in family life. In response, some Christians have retreated out of fear to a traditional patriarchal form of family life in which gender roles are sharply separated. While it may be tempting to return to a time that appears to have been less disruptive, this course of action offers a false sense of comfort, for women had a very difficult life in the past. Christians need to see the present disruption as an opportunity to put in place a more biblically based form of family life. In doing so, we must avoid both excessive individualism, which can culminate in a cult of self-fulfillment, and an overemphasis on the group, which can lead to worshiping the family.

Women in Family Life

Women have traditionally acquired status in our society through being wives and mothers. However, this situation is rapidly changing as women assume extrafamilial responsibilities, particularly in the workforce. Many women experience contradictory expectations when they begin to pursue professional careers or work full time outside the home. Magazines, films, and television add to the confusion by encouraging romance, marriage, and childbearing and at the same time glorifying the independent, career-oriented woman.

The message given to women is that they must have it all. In an effort to do it all, they become superwomen who suffer stress and frustration, especially if they attempt to balance a career and motherhood. This might best be illustrated by the recent titles of popular books written to women—*The Wall between Women: The Conflict between Stay-at-Home and Employed Mothers*; *The Working Gal's Guide to Babyville: Your Must-Have Manual for Life with Baby*; *Mommy Wars: Stay-at-Home and Career Moms Face Off on Their Choices, Their Lives, Their Families*; *Every Mother Is a Daughter: The Never-ending Quest for Success, Inner Peace, and a Really Clean Kitchen (Recipes and Knitting Patterns Included)*; *Childlessness, Ambivalence, and How They Made the Biggest Decision of Their Lives*; and *Perfect Madness: Motherhood in the Age of Anxiety*.

Other books critique the "momism" expressed in these books. In *The Mommy Myth: The Idealization of Motherhood and How It Has Undermined All Women* (2004), Susan Douglas and Meredith Michaels suggest that there is a "new momism" consisting of a set of standards of success that any mother will find impossible to meet—devoting herself 24/7 to her children with a professionalism that includes the skills of a therapist, a pediatrician, a consumer products safety inspector, and a teacher. In *The Myth of the Perfect Mother* (2004), Carla Barnhill urges mothers to parent without fear or guilt by reclaiming their personhood in Christ. This means viewing motherhood as a spiritual practice and not as a calling. A mother should be judged less on how her children turn out than on how her spiritual practice of mothering is exemplified by the virtues of love, mercy, humility, peace, justice, and compassion. Rethinking the spirituality of mothering goes a long way in combating the cult of the perfect mother.

Whereas husbands may encourage wives to do it all, they often do not pick up the slack, so the woman is left with a double-duty workload—a second work shift. The result has been confusion and disruption for wives, husbands, and their families. We believe that Christians should pursue a path of dual leadership and coparenting. Husbands and wives should be on the cutting edge in working for the liberation of both women and men from oppressive norms.

Men in Family Life

The traditional definition of the male role encourages toughness, inexpressiveness, and competitiveness. Accumulated evidence demonstrates that this traditional definition of manhood is very costly for women, children, and men themselves. In the 1980s, several books were written by women describing the dilemma facing women who have emotionally invested themselves in a relationship with a man only to find that his masculine restrictiveness does not allow him to love fully in return. Books such as *Women Who Love Too Much* (Norwood 1985) and *Men Who Hate Women and the Women Who Love Them* (Forward and Torres 1986) tell of women caught up in relationships with men who cause them tremendous pain. Men are described as either intimidating through verbal outbursts or withdrawn into angry silence; switching from charm to anger without warning; belittling a woman's opinions, feelings, and accomplishments; and even humiliating her in front of others and withholding sex, love, money, or approval as a form of punishment or control.

The traditional male has also been hammered by emerging research on men. Men are described as so emotionally restricted that they are often strangers to their wives; fathers are so emotionally absent that they are often more a "phantom man" than a "family man"; boys grow into manhood with a "wounded father" within resulting from an emotionally distant father they never knew; and what men learn about power, achievement, competition, and emotional inexpressiveness results in their entering relationships with other men with great caution and distrust.

David Blankenhorn (1995) documents the negative effect of distant and nonresidential fathering on children, especially sons. Approximately 40 percent of American children go to sleep at night in fatherless homes. He argues that the decline of the father's role as caregiver, moral educator, head of the family, and breadwinner has been enormous. Although we are cautious about offering a single explanation, Blankenhorn gives a wealth of research evidence suggesting that the diminished presence of the father is responsible for increases in a variety of social ills: juvenile delinquency, youth violence, domestic violence against women, child sexual abuse, children living in poverty and economic insecurity, adolescent childbearing, and unwed pregnancy (pp. 25–28). This bleak report on fathering should be tempered by other evidence that many fathers, especially younger ones, have begun to invest more of themselves in relating to their children. In his review of research on fathering, Scott Coltrane (2004, 238) explains this contradiction by suggesting that "two ideal types—of involved and marginalized fathers—are likely to continue to coexist in the popular cultural and in actual practice."

It is significant that a major challenge to the traditional masculine role comes not only from the secular feminist and men's movement but also from a number of parachurch organizations. Among the earliest to show concern was James Dobson's Focus on the Family, which emphasized the need for strong Christian fathering in the home. The Christian men's movement Promise Keepers has also strongly emphasized emotionally involved fathering as a major plank in its construction of Christian manhood. Promise Keepers burst on the popular scene in the early 1990s, led by the successful college football coach Bill McCartney, with the message that above all Christian men need to be keepers of promises. Men need to be *committed*—especially in their relationships—to Christ, family, and the church. The extraordinary emphasis Promise Keepers placed on being a servant husband to one's wife and a dedicated father to one's children surprised even the most hardened critics of gender roles in conservative families. A number of Christian organizations continue to work to strengthen the father in the home.

Evidence suggests that this emphasis on strong fathering within the evangelical community may be having a positive effect. Bradford Wilcox (2004) notes that when compared with fathers who do not attend church and fathers from mainline churches, fathers in evangelical churches are warmer, more tender, and more expressive in their fathering. This contradicts some feminist literature that suggests that conservative Christian churches encourage thinking that can lead to physical and emotional abuse. Based on their review of the literature, Dollahite, Marks, and Goodman (2004) report that the higher a father's religiosity, the more positive a child's outcome.

A major part of the "culture wars" debate centers on the issue of family values. Evangelicals have come to focus on the family as *the* ideological ground on which to distinguish themselves from the culture at large. Family values have become the key markers of evangelical identity (Gallagher 2003). A legitimate question to ask is to what degree do evangelical family values and ideology correspond with how men *behave* in family life. Melinda Denton (2004, 1151) notes that "while conservative Protestants espouse a traditional gender-role ideology, their marital decision-making practices are not significantly different from those of other religious groups. . . . Theologically liberal Protestants have more egalitarian ideology while reporting decision-making practices that are not significantly more egalitarian than those of conservative Protestants." In other words, evangelical husbands may be more equalitarian in behavior than the stated ideology would lead one to believe. However, it should also be noted that Wilcox (2004) found that married fathers who express the most traditional gender-role beliefs, and whose wives also work outside the home, spend about three hours *less* on household labor each week than do the equalitarian fathers.

Distinguishing between *soft patriarchy*, which holds that husbands should lead as suffering servants, and *hard patriarchy*, which maintains that they should be in charge, may be helpful in interpreting these findings. Wilcox (2004) uses the term *soft patriarchy* to describe the "softening effect" on men who are regular attendees of conservative churches, shown by greater emotional engagement with wives and children.

Christians in the early church were known for their love of one another. The same should be said of Christian men today; they should be known by their love. This is especially crucial because of the male propensity to dominate and lord it over others. Authentic Christian manhood is found, on the contrary, in behaviors that "seek to support rather than dominate women, empower rather than control younger men, and mentor and complement rather than compete with other men" (J. O. Balswick 1992). A study by Valerie King (2003) found that religious fathers are more involved with their children and have a higher-quality relationship with them. In these homes, a higher degree of marital satisfaction was reported and the fathers espoused more traditional values.

Coparenting: The Need for Mothering and Fathering

At present most parenting is, in reality, mothering. Fathers need to be jointly involved in child-rearing efforts for the benefit of both sons and daughters. The contribution made by the father must be significant enough to establish deep emotional bonding with his children. Research has shown that the more exclusively a boy is parented by his mother, the greater his need to be superior to women and eliminate any behavior that appears to be feminine (Chodorow 1999).

Children who live in coparented families have the best of all worlds since they have the presence and involvement of two parents in their lives. Couples who share parenting and household roles experience a high degree of marital happiness, whereas couples who both work but do not share roles at home experience distress. The commitment coparents make to work through various issues about gender-specific parenting and household roles teaches their children about mutual respect, gender equality, and cooperation. Coparenting not only enhances the marital bond but also sends a clear message to children that the parental bond cannot easily be disrupted. Thus children sense a security that stabilizes the family relationship (Ehrensaft 1990; McHale et al. 2002).

In a study of parenting during infancy, it was found that fathers displayed more supportive coparenting, while mothers displayed more intrusive behavior (Lindsey, Calder, and Colwell 2005). Randi Cowdery and Carmen Knudson-Martin (2005) found that parents construct alternative models of parenting. In the traditional model, parents believe that mothers have the greater *natural connection* with a child, resulting in the father stepping back and allowing the mother to organize their time around the child as she assumes continual responsibility for the child. In fact, one study found that a key barrier to greater involvement of fathers with children was the mothers' "gatekeeping" stance, based on their belief that fathers should be less involved than mothers (McBride et al. 2005).

A coparenting model begins with the assumption that parenting responsibility should be shared. While recognizing that the mother may have an initial advantage in emotional connectedness through birthing and nursing, fathers can compensate by making special efforts to bond with children. Mothers need to encourage this and resist the temptation to intervene. Cowdery and Knudson-Martin (2005) believe that coparenting will happen only if parents intentionally move toward collaborative parenting, in which fathers are open to learning tasks traditionally reserved for mothers and mothers allow fathers to learn "on the job."

Fathers who become involved in the parenting process find that their socioemotional and relational sides develop. This has a positive effect on the sons as well, for when fathers set an example of expressing their feelings, their sons also become more expressive (J. O. Balswick 1988, 101–19). In contrast to the world of work outside the home, where decisions are expected to be based on the rational rather than the emotional, taking care of children inclines men to consider personal and emotional issues, which will affect their work roles as well.

If we take seriously the evidence suggesting that modern society has become increasingly cold, heartless, and impersonal, then the need for the family to be an intimate, nurturing, and caring environment becomes even more obvious. Fathers do daily battle in this impersonal and heartless society, and they often return battered and bruised to the confines of their self-contained, emotionally isolated nuclear family. At the same time, the social supports for family members—extended families, neighborhood networks, community embeddedness—have been largely eroded by the cultural move toward modernity. The result is that the nuclear family is often the sole source for meeting its members' emotional needs. Because of all these social and cultural changes, men need and are emotionally needed by their families more than ever before.

Family roles cannot be altered without altering work roles. Therefore, the second type of needed structural change involves the demands that the workplace makes on men. In working full time outside the home, most fathers have little opportunity to establish deep bonds with their children, even if they so desire. Fathers must usually crowd any attempts at establishing intimacy with their children into a few hours at the end of the workday (when their emotional resources for doing so are probably lowest) or into increasingly busy weekends. Their efforts are typically limited to excursions for milkshakes after dinner, quick-ending games, jokes, and bedtime stories.

By playing down the father-child relationship, the legal system sets up further barriers to the development of deep, meaningful bonding between a father and his children. Divorce courts usually give the mother custody of the children and relegate the father to the position of periodic visitor.

Fathers can be brought into court for failing to support their children financially, but little is done about the absence of emotional support from fathers. It will take a prodigious effort to overcome these various obstacles to effective fathering.

In their landmark book, *The Case for Marriage*, Linda Waite and Maggie Gallagher (2000) document that when men marry, they fare better in almost every respect—physical health, mental health, earnings, life expectancy, and so on. After examining the literature on men in family life, Van Leeuwen (2002, 208) surmises that "children of both sexes need to grow up with stable, nurturant adult role models of both sexes to better develop a secure gender identity that then—paradoxically—allows them to relate to each other primarily as human beings, rather than as gender-role caricatures."

A Concluding Comment

The traditional pattern of segregated gender roles—women in the home and men in the workplace—serves to keep males and females overly dependent on and distant from each other. While women are kept economically dependent on men, men are emotionally dependent on women. Christians need to encourage men to devote more time to tasks that require emotional input. If men committed only half as much time to relating to their children as their wives do, their relational ability and sensitivity would be greatly enhanced, not to mention the positive effect on their children. Some of the needed structural changes have already been initiated by women redefining their roles in society. Now is the time for men to commit greater amounts of their energy to activities that will produce deeper emotional bonding.

The Christian community is currently far from united in its evaluation of the change in gender roles; some Christians say that women should return to their rightful place in the home, while others argue for increased participation by women in all occupations, including the ordained ministry. It is important for us to grasp the intentions God had in mind in creating humanity as distinctly male and female (Genesis 1–2). The fact is Christians can hold to a high view of biblical authority and yet differ on the role of women and men in the family, the church, and society. In her essay "Toward Reconciliation: Healing the Schism," Alice Mathews (2005) credits David Scholer with noting that the biblical text one chooses for one's starting point in the study of a doctrine or issue in Scripture becomes the lens through which one looks at all other texts. The difference between the two positions reflects a difference in hermeneutics—to gain, through careful exegesis, the original intent of

Scripture and to apply it to contemporary life. Both positions recognize that culture can bend or alter gender distinctions in ways that were not intended by the Creator.

In his recent book John Stackhouse (2005) attempts to reconcile these two evangelical positions by suggesting that both sides are wrong—and right! First, egalitarians need to concede that in some of his writing "Paul is maintaining a patriarchal line" (p. 68). Stackhouse goes on to remind his "complementarian friends that the task is to make sense of *all* that Paul says, including the apparently equalitarian verses, some of which appear *in the same passage*" (p. 68). He suggests that, for a reason similar to why Paul did not directly write against the practice of slavery (see Philemon), he at times did not directly write against the patriarchal structure of New Testament times. Stackhouse presents two principles in his paradigm: *first*, "men and women are equal in every way" (p. 35), and *second*, "some things matter more than others" (p. 38). This leads him to a *holy pragmatism*: in the unfolding of history, some things are to be sacrificed (that men and women are equal in every way) in the interest of the greater good (the furtherance of the gospel message).

Stackhouse's paradigm provides a new way to read and understand such double-pattern passages as 1 Corinthians 11, Ephesians 5, and 1 Timothy 2. Those supporting gender hierarchy may object that Stackhouse is suggesting total gender equality for North American society. In response Stackhouse points to the irony of "Christians lagging behind society and still requiring a submissive role for women, a posture that now is a mirror image of the scandal that egalitarianism would have caused in the patriarchal first century" (p. 72). Those supporting an equalitarian position may object that his paradigm tolerates the oppression of women and thus tolerates sin. To this he replies, *"If this paradigm is to be believed, then the church should not only tolerate but also comply with patriarchy today in the many parts of the world that still practice it—and that seems repugnant"* (p. 92).

The current clash between traditional and modern definitions of gender roles confuses women and men alike. Many Christians are tempted to react defensively against the current redefinition. But the present situation should be viewed as an opportunity for both women and men to become more fully developed human beings as God intended. For this to happen, women and men need to talk to one another about the changes in gender roles.

We believe that Christians should be actively working to liberate men from traditional definitions of masculinity that have hindered them from developing healthy male/female, male/male, and father/child relationships. For there to be a true liberation of women, there must also be a men's liberation. When men are secure in their masculinity, they can support increased freedom for women. Secure Christian manhood means that a man is mature enough that he doesn't need to confirm his masculinity at a woman's expense. Such a man works with women as equals as well as under their supervision. Within the family, he is willing to be equally involved in household chores and child care. Secure Christian womanhood means that a woman is mature enough to establish her own identity, priorities, and personal values in the workplace and at home.

True Christian womanhood and manhood are not mere reflections of traditional definitions of femininity and masculinity. To help achieve the ideal of true manhood and womanhood, cultures can continue to recognize the distinctions between men and women and at the same time encourage individuals to meet their potentials and goals in life through equal opportunities and responsibilities. The Scripture proclaims, "There is no longer Jew or Greek, there is no longer slave or free, there is no longer male and female; for all of you are one in Christ Jesus" (Gal. 3:28). The essential question that we should be asking is at what point our cultural norms prevent both men and women from becoming the fully human persons God intended them to be (Fee 2005).

Once again our theology of relationships is pertinent. Men and women must be willing to interact with one another in a cycle of covenant, grace, empowering, and intimacy. There must be a joint commitment to one another in a covenant of love working toward the goal of equality. This entails a willingness to forgive and be forgiven of the oppression and antagonism that have existed between the sexes. It takes grace to acknowledge and accept differences of opinion in this area. Another element is a mutual serving and empowering of one another. Women and men are both in need of liberation from the gender stereotypes that have hindered growth in personhood. Finally, men and women will achieve intimacy in same-sex and opposite-sex relationships as they become free to know and be known to one another. This requires communication and a desire to understand the other so that we may cherish and value who we are as brothers and sisters in Christ. As we become fully developed men and women, others will know from our love for one another that we are Christians.

12

BECOMING AN AUTHENTIC SEXUAL SELF

T HE SEARCH FOR authentic sexuality often starts with an attempt to understand how we are to behave as sexual persons. Achieving authentic sexuality, however, depends more on understanding who God created us to be as sexual persons. How we behave sexually certainly influences how we define ourselves as sexual beings and vice versa. However, an understanding of what it means to be created as sexual persons in God's image involves much more than a simple assent to or an ability to live according to specified behavioral standards.

Sexuality includes such factors as biology, gender, emotions, thoughts, behaviors, attitudes, and values. Authentic human sexuality is not something that just develops naturally. The word *authentic* is defined as "real, genuine, believable, and trustworthy." We use the term to indicate that sexuality is meant to be a congruent and integral part of a person's total being. Our sexuality must be a real, genuine, believable, and trustworthy part of ourselves, so that we can embrace what God has created and declared to be "very good."

Our sexuality is a product of God's design, but it bears the taint of our fallen nature. In a multitude of ways, this good gift of sex has become perverted and warped in our world. The inauthentic sexuality inherent in our fallen human condition is shaped by an interplay of societal attitudes and beliefs, cultural structures, and biological factors. In this chapter, we examine some societal and cultural influences on the development of our sexuality. We also present some ideas on how Christians can become more authentic in their sexual personhood and expression.

Societal Attitudes toward Sexuality

Human sexuality is profoundly affected by prevailing societal attitudes. The predominant attitude in the United States has changed throughout history. Our past is often regarded as a time when sexuality was repressed; our modern society, by contrast, attempts to throw off all sexual inhibitions.

The Puritans have traditionally been blamed for some of the uptightness of past generations. By the standards of seventeenth-century European culture, however, the Puritans had a quite healthy view of sexuality. They did, of course, hold to a standard of celibacy for the unmarried and monogamy for married people, but they advocated a wholesome sexual expression in the marriage relationship. An example comes from the Groton church in 1675. When a husband announced that he would abstain from having sexual relations with his wife for a year as personal penance for disobeying God, the church leaders pronounced that he had no right to deny his wife her rights to sexual fulfillment. Sexual expression between spouses was regarded as good, natural, and desirable and therefore not to be withheld. This is in accord with 1 Corinthians 7:1–5 (Doriani 1996).

The Victorians, on the contrary, held many sexual taboos, so it may be more valid to blame some negative attitudes toward sex on them. The Victorian philosophy was to repress anything that appeared to be sexual. For example, not only were people required to cover their arms and legs in public, but even the legs of the living-room sofa and chairs were covered with little skirts. Bare legs on furniture were considered a symbol of sexual immodesty.

The Victorians also drew a sharp line between sexual desire and love. A virtuous man was encouraged to wed a woman for whom he had pure thoughts, which meant no sexual desire. Husbands were told that if they really loved their wives, they would refrain from having sex with them too often, for even in marriage sexual relationships were considered degrading to women.

The expert medical opinion of the day asserted that any sexual desire in a young woman was pathological. In 1867 the surgeon general of the United States proclaimed that nine-tenths of the time decent women do not feel the slightest pleasure in sexual intercourse. The advice columnists of the day indicated that the more a woman yielded to the animal passion of her husband, the more he would lose respect for her. It is not coincidental that one of the most popular songs at the turn to the twentieth century began, "I want a girl just like the girl that married dear old Dad."

The dichotomy between sexual desire and love led to a dual arrangement: a man had his sexual needs met by a bad woman but would marry only a good woman. During the first half of the twentieth century, especially during the 1920s, shifting attitudes ushered in an era of permissiveness with affection. Now it was perfectly acceptable to engage in sex, provided both people felt affection for each other.

For a period of time following World War II, Americans had what can only be described as a preoccupation with sex. This began with the publication of the Kinsey reports: *Sexual Behavior in the Human Male* (1948) and *Sexual Behavior in the Human Female* (1952). Later Hugh Hefner left his job as a copy editor at *Fortune* magazine and started *Playboy*. *Playboy* found an eager audience of young adult males who were ready to jump on the sexual-freedom bandwagon. By denying the multiple facets of womanhood, they proceeded to reduce women to a single dimension, the sex object. *Playboy* had great appeal for insecure men who were terrified at the thought of relating to a multidimensional woman. They were told how to dress, what music to put on, how to mix a drink, and when to turn the lights down. In short, the message was how to get the woman into bed and emerge free of any emotional attachments.

C. S. Lewis (1960b, 75) has compared a society obsessed with sex to a hypothetical society in which people pay good money to view a covered platter sitting on a table. At an assigned time and to the beat of drums, the cover is very slowly lifted, and the object underneath is exposed for all to see. To everyone's great delight, a pork chop is revealed. Lewis makes the conclusion that something is obviously wrong with a society so obsessed with food. The point is well taken. Something is radically wrong with a society so obsessed with sex.

In the 1980s, a slight backlash resulted from sexual overexposure, and a trend toward a new virginity emerged. Christian young people made a pledge of celibacy before their parents and God with a "promise ring" representing their determination to maintain their chastity until their wedding night. Women began to question what they had bought into with their newfound sexual freedom; many felt their deeper desire for emotional intimacy had been completely sabotaged. College students wore large red buttons declaring "NO" to casual sex. Cable television experienced a sharp drop in the audience for X-rated movies. Raw, explicit sex had lost its appeal as a shock and stimulus, and people began rebelling against the use of sex for entertainment purposes and recreation. Many took a second look at how sexual freedom undermines relationships. The fear of AIDS reinforced this trend to stop promiscuous sex and begin safe practices.

The backlash in the 1980s proved to be short lived. If we were to use C. S. Lewis's analogy, we might say in regard to sex in the twenty-first century, the platter is no longer covered. Explicit sex is depicted in most forms of popular culture, movies, television, popular music, and so on. The Internet allows people to privately consume eroticism and pornography. In this electronic computer age, children as well as adults are inundated by a culture saturated with sex. As harmful as exposure to nudity and sexual innuendoes may be, an even greater harm may come from dishonest messages that depict sexual promiscuity and nonrelational sex as having few or no negative consequences.

The Origin of Sexuality

Not unlike the human personality, human sexuality does not emerge in full bloom in a person. One becomes a sexual being through a multidimensional developmental process. It is evident from social-science research that human sexuality is partly a reflection of the culture within which a person is socialized. We are taught to respond sexually to certain objects and symbols in our environment, and this influences how we define ourselves sexually. Our sexuality is also a product of biological, psychological, and experiential factors. We must resist the temptation to give a simplistic explanation of sexuality, one that relies only on either sociocultural or biological explanations.

Human sexuality emerges as part of an interactive development process between biological and sociocultural factors. Presented in figure 14 is an *interactive developmental theory* of human sexuality; biological factors are represented on the left side and sociocultural factors on the right, with the arrows between the two sides indicating directions of influence and interactions between them (Balswick and Balswick 1999).

If figure 14 appears to be complex, it is because human sexual development is a complex process. As part of the maturation process, both biological and sociocultural factors contribute to sexual development. Not only do biological and socioemotional-cultural factors individually influence sexual development, but they also have an *interactive* effect on sexual development. By an interactive effect, we mean that the two factors *join together* in sexual development. In figure 14, the one-way influences are represented by one-way (➞) arrows, the interactive influences by two-way (➞ ➞) arrows. We will build on figure 14 by giving a few examples of how sociocultural and biological factors have an interactive effect on sexual development.

FIGURE 14 **An Interactive Developmental Model of Sexual Development**

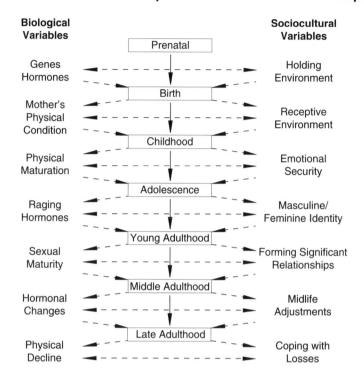

As a first example, we focus on the prenatal stage, when a crack baby is born to a drug-addicted mother. That baby is born physiologically addicted to the drug through the biological system of the mother. While crack babies are physiologically normal in genetic and chromosomal makeup, the sociocultural factors (poverty, abuse, depression, etc.) of the mother abusing drugs results in a chemical dependency in the newborn infant that affects his or her future. Without intervention, this will undoubtedly lead to physical, emotional, and cognitive problems in the development of the child.

A second example involves the development of sexual desire. In response to erotic stimulation (sociocultural), the brain (biological) organizes the behavior that will lead the body to sexual involvement. Incoming sensual stimuli are encoded in the cortex of the brain. The hypothalamus then determines if the stimuli are painful or pleasurable. This determined, the message is sent to the pituitary gland, which controls the adrenal glands and the female and male gonads. If the incoming sexual stimuli are pleasurable, the pituitary gland will command the gonads to produce the necessary hormones to begin sexual arousal. However, if the stimuli are painful, the pituitary gland will close the system down. Thus the brain, which is a bio-logical organ, is greatly influenced and affected by the social environment. It is also true, however, that hormonal levels can greatly alter the power of external sexual stimuli to bring about erotic arousal within the sexual system. Needless to say, social and biological factors interact with each other in ways that make it difficult to assess the effect of each separately.

A third example is taken from the prepubescent stage, when a variety of changes begin to shape boys' and girls' bodies in different ways, not only between genders but within gender. During this age period, boys learn a *boy code* that teaches them to be strong, competitive, and sexu-ally aggressive, while girls learn a *girl code* that teaches them to be nice, cooperative, and sexually modest. There will be differences among boys and among girls, however, to the extent to which these sex-typing codes are learned. Some parents make sharp distinctions between boy behavior and girl behavior, while others encourage their child to value and emulate both male and female characteristics. At the same time, however, there are significant differences in hormonal levels among boys and girls. High testosterone levels among some boys and high estrogen levels among some girls set the stage for early development of secondary sexual char-acteristics (pubic hair, breast and hip development, etc.). The range of gender-typical and atypical behavior during prepubescence can best be understood in terms of both biological and sociocultural influences and the interaction between both. The fact that some boys prefer male-typical rough-and-tumble competitive play and others prefer more female-typical relational or nurturing play is most likely the result of both biological *and* sociocultural influences and the interactive effect between them.

The previous example comes during adolescence, when the hormones begin to rage. For some youth, it begins as more a trickle than a rage. In regard to socioemotional factors, most boys find their masculine identity in male-typical behavior and girls in female-typical behavior. Some boys, however, would rather play a violin than football, and some girls would rather play soccer than prepare a dinner. This is to say, there is a wide range of gender-typical and atypical behavior among teenagers. Examples of interactive effects are many at this stage of sexual development. One study of male adolescents found a positive correlation between testoster-one level and sexual promiscuity (Udry 1988). While this finding should in no way justify sexual promiscuity, it does illustrate the relationship between biological and sociocultural factors.

Sociocultural factors are responsible for many, but not all, of the differences between male and female sexuality. By the time males and females reach adulthood, males are observed to be more sexual than fe-males, to be stimulated more by sight, and to think about sex more often. Sociocultural explanations can be given for these differences because in nearly all societies culture places more restraints on females than on males. Parents take a more protective stance toward their daughters. Girls are warned to show modesty in their apparel; they are instructed to keep their dresses down, their breasts covered, and to guard themselves against sexual advances by boys.

Our final example of the interactive effect between biological and sociocultural factors is taken from late adulthood, when the range of sexual interest and involvement varies greatly. Research has found an interactive effect between hormonal level and sexual interest and involvement. Increases in hormonal level can elevate sexual interest and involvement, but engaging in sexual activity can also increase hormonal level. Researchers refer to this as the "use it or lose it" phenomenon.

Although the interaction of the biological and sociocultural contributors to human sexuality is complicated, we offer the following generalizations (Balswick and Balswick 1999). First, the evidence is insufficient to make causal statements in explaining the development of human sexuality. Rather than writing about causation, it is more accurate to cite the factors that *contribute* to the development of human sexuality. Second, biological factors serve as necessary but not solely sufficient contributors to the formation of human sexuality. An intact biological package prepares one to develop authentic male or female sexuality. However, this biological given is not enough to secure authentic sexual development. Third, sociocultural factors serve as sufficient, but not necessary, contributors to the formation of human sexuality. The person who has an intact biological package, sufficient sociocultural factors, and an effective value system will have the greatest potential to develop a healthy sexual self. Fourth, human sexuality emerges as part of a developmental process. Physiological, psychological, social, and cultural factors all make their separate, unique contribution at crucial points to guide the developmental process.

The Meaning of Sexuality

Explanations of sexuality are important but nevertheless incomplete. Moving directly from biological and sociocultural information to value judgments about sexuality is a premature leap. It is one thing to examine sexual behaviors and norms and quite another to make decisions and judgments about moral issues. To this point, we can identify the major factors contributing to "normal" sexual development, but to speak of "authentic" human sexual development, it is necessary to understand the meaning of sexuality. These last three generalizations focus on the meaning of sexuality.

The fifth generalization is that, while biological factors are most crucial in establishing sexuality early in life, sociocultural factors become increasingly significant as the child matures. As children develop the capacity to use language, they correspondingly learn the meaning of sexual attitudes and behavior. An understanding of God's design for human sexuality becomes increasingly important if the individual is to construct a truly meaningful world. Because the meaning of sexuality is learned within a social context, it is imperative that the family and community powerfully live out and communicate God's design for human sexuality.

Sixth, families, churches, communities, and societies vary in the degree to which they reflect God's design and meaning for human sexuality. Since every individual belongs to a variety of groups, many of which offer competing perspectives on human sexuality, internalization of contradictory views is likely. The more the various groups to which the individual belongs consistently reflect God's ideal for sexuality, the more internally consistent will be his or her development of authentic sexuality. Where contradictions exist, our nature as choice-making creatures with emotive, volitional, and moral qualities can help us achieve authentic sexuality.

Seventh, authentic sexuality and inauthentic sexuality are dichotomous only in a moral sense and thus should never be used as descriptions of given individuals. Authentic sexuality is not totally represented in any one person. Being part of a fallen creation, each human is sexually broken and lacks perfect wholeness in various ways.

It is enlightening to note the relationship between one's theological position and the relative credence given to sociocultural and biological explanations of human sexuality. In general, people with a conservative Christian theology tend to emphasize biological factors when explaining male/female differences; they believe that God uses biology to imprint different sexual codes in females and males. But these same people tend to emphasize environmental factors and discount any genetic explanations when they make value judgments about homosexual behavior. In contrast, people with liberal theologies tend to do the reverse. They de-emphasize genetic explanations for male/female differences, but embrace genetic explanations when addressing homosexual orientation and behavior. It is important to be consistent in the credence one grants to social and biological explanations of sexuality.

A Biblical Perspective on Human Sexuality

With this understanding of the development of sexuality, we are now in a place to expand on the biblical meaning of human sexuality. Theologically, human sexuality can be understood as a reflection of God's design for creation. Genesis 1:27–28 declares: "So God created humankind in his image; in the image of God he created them; male and female he created them. God blessed them, and God said to them, 'Be fruitful and multiply, and fill the earth and subdue it; and have dominion over the fish of the sea and over the birds of the air and over every living thing that moves upon the earth.'" This passage shows that males and females are distinct in God's design, yet in God's sight they are also equal and united as sexual beings. Both men and women are commanded to be fruitful, to subdue the earth, and to rule over the rest of God's creation. The beginning point includes an acceptance of one's unique sexuality, with the ability to acknowledge and be thankful that it is part of God's creation, design, and intention. Our sexuality is good in God's sight.

The biblical account, however, does not end with the *creation* story; it is followed by the *fall*, and then *redemption* and *restoration*. The following six principles provide a summary as follows: First, human sexuality is established in the differentiation of male and female and the unity between them. The first chapter of Genesis informs us that there are two ways to reflect the image of God—as a male and as a female. Male and female were created by God as separate persons who form a differentiated unity. Human sexuality is complete in the unity between a man and a woman. Second, sexuality is a good gift meant to draw us to deeper levels of knowing (ourselves, others, and God) and being known. Our bodies are equipped with a nervous system, hormones, physical sensations, and an emotional capacity to help us find connection with others. God has created us for community. Third, humans are born with an innate capacity for sexual pleasure; this capacity can best develop within an emotionally caring, trustworthy family environment. Fourth, sexuality and spirituality are intricately connected. They cannot be separated, and this is why deep religious meaning brings the two together in a profound way. Fifth, after the fall, sexuality was distorted and in need of redemption. And sixth, Christ offers restoration and renews our potential for authentic sexuality.

In the beginning, Adam and Eve were perfect sexual beings just as God created them to be, yet they fell from that perfect state. All human beings inherit this fallen nature, which includes inauthentic sexuality. It is clear from the Genesis account that the fall has affected both sociocultural and biological life. Forever after, humans must face physical death and various mental and physical consequences of the fall, such as pain in childbirth and physical exertion in work as predicted in Genesis 3:17–19: "Cursed is the ground because of you; in toil you shall eat of it all the days of your life; thorns and thistles it shall bring forth for you; and you shall eat the plants of the field. By the sweat of your face you shall eat bread until you return to the ground, for out of it you were taken; you are dust, and to dust you shall return."

Sociocultural factors were also drastically affected by the fall, and as a result, human relationships are broken. Brokenness is evidenced in the home, the place where sexual attitudes are established. Family structures, along with other social and community structures, all play their part in contributing to the distortion of a person's sexuality. It becomes difficult to achieve an authentic sexuality in the midst of these distorting influences. The comprehensiveness of the fall means that achieving an authentic sexuality involves conflict and struggle for everyone.

We have seen that God allows human sexuality to develop through sociocultural and biological factors, yet because these systems are imperfect, we are also imperfect in our sexuality. Some people suffer from deficiencies in the genetic package they have inherited; some lack a sexual wholeness because of inadequate socialization in the home and community; some are victims of societal ills such as sexual abuse and pornography. Everyone at some level must deal with the sexual distortions of the fallen world.

Despite all the obstacles, the sexual authenticity God intended for us is a goal worth striving for. Authentic sexuality is most attainable for those who are born with a normal genetic and physiological makeup, who are socialized in a home where parents display healthy attitudes regarding sexuality, and who live in a community where societal values are consistent with biblical teaching.

Inauthentic sexuality can take a variety of forms as a result of differing combinations of sociocultural, biological, and spiritual factors. Some people have the disadvantage of living through circumstances that result in a devastating sexual brokenness. This is especially true when sexual encounters have been deeply harmful, creating scars that make healing a long-term process. The good news of the gospel is that we can find hope and wholeness in Jesus Christ, who, having once been wounded for us, shows compassion for and heals our wounds.

Sexual Wholeness in a Broken World

The preceding analysis points to the development of sexuality as a complex process of multidimensional factors. Achieving sexual authenticity in a broken world is equally complex. We all have wounds that need to be healed as we struggle to authentically express our sexuality in relationship. In the remainder of this chapter, we will address four aspects of sexual expression that are important concerns to the Christian community: sex and singleness, masturbation, sexual preference, and marital sexuality.

Sex and Singleness

Not wanting to wrestle with the difficult question of sex and singleness, churches sometimes seek an easy out by declaring that single people should deny their sexuality or by completely ignoring the question. Christian singles are often left with insufficient guidance as to how they are to live as sexual persons in a singles' subculture that endorses standards in direct contradiction to biblical values.

As a starting point, we present the three principles of sexuality introduced by Lewis B. Smedes (1994, 29):

1. The sexuality of every person is meant to be woven into the whole character of that person and integrated into his (her) quest for human values.
2. The sexuality of every person is meant to be an urge toward and a means of expressing a deep personal relationship with another person.
3. The sexuality of every person is meant to move him (her) toward a heterosexual union of committed love.

Living out these principles keeps sexuality and personhood connected at every level. It also calls to mind our theology of relationships. Sexuality is to be exercised within a context of covenant, an unconditional commitment to a personal relationship. We are challenged to work toward deepening this personal relationship by establishing an atmosphere of grace (acceptance and forgiveness), empowering one another, and increasing the level of intimacy. As Smedes suggests, "Sexual fulfillment is achieved when a personal relationship underpins the genital experience, supports it, and sustains a human sexual relationship after it" (1994, 25–26). This will be our basic premise in discussing premarital sexual relationships.

In the United States today, there are four major standards of premarital sex: (1) sexual abstinence, (2) the double standard, (3) permissiveness with affection, and (4) permissiveness without affection. Although sexual abstinence is the traditional Christian value (and one of the two most strongly held beliefs in the general population), when it comes to behavior, a majority in today's society do not adhere to it. The double standard, which allows premarital intercourse for males but not for females, has declined during the last hundred years. Permissiveness with affection is the viewpoint with the greatest number of proponents in Western societies today. Permissiveness without affection, which allows casual and recreational sex between two consenting adults, had been growing as a standard in the past few decades. However, the AIDS epidemic has reduced the number of single people willing to live by this philosophy. The risks involved have led formerly promiscuous people to declare, "I like sex, but I'm not willing to die for it."

We believe that Christians should celebrate their freedom in Christ and be bound by no rules other than those given in Scripture. Starting with the Ten Commandments, it is clear that the Bible holds adultery to be contrary to God's will. While the term *adultery* is usually defined as sexual intercourse between a married person and a person other than the lawful husband or wife, some theologians argue that the term is broader in intent, referring to any intercourse between two people who are not married to each other.

The New Testament word *porneia*, which is translated "fornication" or "immorality," has traditionally been interpreted as sex outside marriage. Those holding to the position of situational ethics (the guiding principle of which is to maximize love) argue that "fornication" refers to a depersonalized, body-centered sex. Such a definition promotes freedom to engage in sex as long as it is not depersonalized (love with affection). Although the word may have this meaning in some passages, *porneia* almost always refers to sexual intercourse outside the marriage union.

We interpret the Bible as restricting sexual intercourse to the marital relationship. Depending on how engagement and betrothal are defined, specific application of this principle may vary from one society to the next. Historically, girls were often very young at the time of engagement. In contemporary society, however, the trend is to marry at a later age, making it more difficult for single people to meet the biblical standard.

Another contrast with the past is that societal structures used to help young people meet the standards, but in modern society people of all ages are bombarded with explicit sexual stimuli. The mass media sanction sexual expression before marriage, creating an unrealistic situation. At the very height of their sexual urges, people who have committed themselves to abstinence before marriage are besieged by such messages.

To add to the confusion, singles must grapple with the gray areas of determining the amount of physical and sexual involvement they will engage in during dating and courtship. This can mean anything from merely holding hands to genital contact just short of sexual intercourse. While the Bible advocates physical affection between Christians in the form of greeting one another with a holy kiss, it does not tell us what makes a kiss holy or how to express affection in a relationship that goes beyond friendship. It is indeed difficult to set up hard-and-fast rules regarding premarital sexual involvement since many factors enter into the situation, such as the couple's age and maturity, the level of their commitment, the length of the engagement, and the closeness to the marriage ceremony.

It is natural and good for a single person to physically express affection for the one he or she loves. Touching is a means of communicating acceptance, love, and care. We learn this from children, who are free to express themselves through touch and open themselves up for expressions of affection. Single adults more often withhold expressions of affection, an important means of affirmation, out of fear of being misunderstood. Unfortunately, this leaves many singles longing for intimate relationships with others that are free of such sexual connotations. Singleness presents a wonderful opportunity for both men and women to develop deep friendships. Reaching an appropriate level of vulnerability in emotional and spiritual and physical relationships with others brings richness to one's life.

Of course, when there is a sexual element to relationships, this must be negotiated by the couple. It is essential at this point for both individuals to determine to what degree they will be involved, what is appropri-

BUT, CAROLYN, PAUL WROTE IN SECOND CORINTHIANS THAT WE SHOULD GREET ONE ANOTHER WITH A HOLY KISS.

ate at this point in their relationship, and how to proceed in mutually agreed-upon goals. To assist in making these decisions, we present the following guidelines:

1. The degree of sexual intimacy should correspond to the degree of love and commitment present in the relationship. Where there is no commitment, a high degree of sexual intimacy is inappropriate. Physical intimacy is meant to enhance the expression of love and commitment. When the personhood of the other is the primary focus, the sexual expression is merely a by-product, as C. S. Lewis observes (1960a, 132–38). Where there is commitment, being with the person is more important than the pleasure derived from the physical intimacy. In covenant love, commitment to the person and the relationship takes precedence over sexual expression.

2. The law of diminishing returns is as applicable in sexuality as in physics. This law states that to achieve an effect a second time, a stronger force must be applied. Think of the effect of one's very first kiss. It is an exhilarating experience. However, as time passes and one becomes used to kissing, the effect diminishes. We tend to desire increased intensity in physical lovemaking and progress to more intimate expressions to be stimulated. The ultimate sexual expression is orgasm. The closer a couple gets to that point, the harder it is to retreat to a previous level. The couple needs to be aware of this fact so that they can determine appropriate limits for their physical involvement. These limits should reflect their level of commitment and the stage of the relationship (as our first principle stated).

3. Both partners must test their personal motives for the physical involvement and activity. Is the motive for physical involvement to express affection or to sexually excite one's partner and oneself? It does something for the ego of both men and women to know that they can sexually excite another person. Most people feel a sense of power and control when they get another person to the point where they cannot be resisted. As the motive behind physical involvement, such ego gratification has a way of separating sex from personhood, since the goal is not a deeper personal connection but satisfaction of one's personal needs.

4. The two people involved must continually communicate about all areas of the relationship. A couple should tread cautiously when the physical dimension develops out of proportion to the social, emotional, psychological, and spiritual dimensions. When the sexual aspect dominates, the other important dimensions are undernourished, and the relationship becomes lopsided, vulnerable, and weak. A full relationship requires a communication process in which both partners share and get to know all aspects of each other's lives. Getting to know another person intimately requires that one listen and come to appreciate all dimensions

of the beloved. The relationship itself is strengthened through intimate sharing. This includes enjoying each other's company through fun and play, laughter and activities; sharing about hurts, disappointments, joys, and successes in the past and the present; planning and dreaming about a future together; praying and developing a spiritual life; and working toward mutual goals. Spiritual oneness will come as the couple seeks God's presence and blessing in their current togetherness and future union.

5. Both partners should take responsibility for establishing guidelines and setting physical limits. Christian males must reject the societal norm that males should go as far as they can sexually, since it is up to the female to set the limits. Both partners are responsible for their sexual involvement. This needs to be discussed early on when the couple is able to rationally set up clear guidelines. There must be a mutual keeping of the boundaries. When one partner wavers, the other can call for accountability to the agreed-upon limits. There will be no need to argue about the standard, since the commitment was made at a prior time. This eliminates the possibility that in the heat of passion one partner will give in to the other—an action both partners will later regret.

There may be times when a couple will want to rethink an established boundary or to set a more stringent limit. They will need to find a place and time to look honestly at the pros and cons of the proposed change in standards. In this way, there will be mutual agreement and commitment through a clear decision-making process in which both views are respected and taken into consideration. Once again the relationship will have priority.

6. The two people involved must agree to abide by the limits proposed by the partner with the more stringent standards. Such an attitude of respect and caring places the person above the desire for sexual activity. In an authentic relationship, there is a willingness to honestly express one's own ideas about standards and to learn what a particular limit means to one's partner. Neither person tries to dominate by judging the other's standards as prudish. In the end, honoring the limitation shows that the partner is valued and cherished, and a deepening of emotional intimacy will result. It is also important that the partner with less rigorous standards not be judged. The essential thing is that each partner be willing to listen to and try to understand the other. Recognizing and accepting differences in each other helps the couple to make whatever adjustments may be necessary for the relationship to succeed.

To sum up our guidelines: the sexual dimension must be put in proper perspective. In 1 Corinthians 6:12–13, Paul says: "'All things are lawful for me,' but not all things are beneficial. 'All things are lawful for me,' but I will not be dominated by anything. 'Food is meant for the stomach and the stomach for food.' . . . The body is meant not for fornication but for the Lord, and the Lord for the body." There are, then, no hard-and-fast laws to govern premarital sexual expression; rather, there is a freedom in Christ to make responsible decisions that are in accordance with God's word. We must bear in mind that not everything is good or beneficial for us; this is especially true of behavior that comes to have a grip on us. Once again, if sexual involvement becomes the overriding concern, it can lead to the demise of a relationship.

In thinking about premarital sexual involvement, a due amount of attention should be given to the matter of sexual lust and sin. That is to say, we must neither ignore the subject nor overly concentrate on it. When Paul speaks out against fornication and immorality, he does so in a list of sins that includes greed and overeating. Some people make the mistake of magnifying sexual sin out of proportion. To them it is the great unpardonable sin, but this is not the biblical view. Others yield to the ethics of secular society and minimize sexual sin. It is not easy being single in a sexually oriented society that promotes norms beyond biblical teaching. Single people need to be enfolded into family and community life in ways that accept them as sexual persons with needs for love and intimacy. In turn, they have much to contribute to the community, as they struggle along with everyone else to realize the full potential of their humanity, which includes their God-given nature (see Hsu 1997).

In a mature relationship there is a mutual responsibility for sexual behavior. This mutuality helps each partner set limits on sexual expression. Leaving the matter up to chance is irresponsible.

Although chronological age does not guarantee maturity, it is a general indicator of one's development and differentiation. The younger the person, the more underdeveloped his or her sexuality, and the more confusing sexual involvement can be. Few teenagers are mature enough to sustain a relationship as demanding as marriage. In fact, statistics show a high percentage of teenage marriages in the United States end in divorce. We have found that while many Christian young people have deeply ingrained beliefs about the value of abstinence, their behavior doesn't coincide with those beliefs (Balswick and Balswick 1994). Many who engage in premarital sex do so for the wrong reasons, such as using sex as a substitute for emotional intimacy, to keep a relationship going, or to satisfy a partner. Although sex may offer physical pleasure, fixation on the external act does not satisfy the deepest internal cravings for an intimacy based on covenant love.

However, mutual commitment allows single adults to respond to each other with maturity and respect. A mature sexual relationship incorporates the elements of covenant, grace, empowering, and intimacy in an ever-deepening cycle that continues throughout life. People who achieve authentic sexuality do not separate sex and personhood but understand that their sexuality is an integral part of who they are. Lauren Winner (2005) argues for the importance of premarital sexual chastity by stressing that sex is communal rather than private—"doing sex in a way that befits the Body of Christ, and that keeps you grounded, and bounded, in the community" (p. 123).

Masturbation

In the most extensive study of human sexual behavior ever conducted, Alfred Kinsey found that prior to marriage 92–96 percent of males and 60 percent of females have masturbated to orgasm (Kinsey 1948, 499; 1952, 141–42). This study was conducted in a relatively inhibited period. Recent studies have revealed even higher percentages. Masturbation seems to be a nearly universal practice for both males and females.

In the past, various attempts were made to discourage people from masturbating. Folk wisdom claimed that masturbation had unpleasant consequences: hair loss, warts, pimples, even blindness or impotence. Many young people lived not only with the fear of these physical consequences but also with intense guilt.

How are Christians to view masturbation? What should parents teach their children about it? Obviously, parents should alleviate the fears and guilt that the myths of the past may have perpetuated. It is very natural for children to explore their physical bodies and come to have an awareness of their anatomy. They need to feel positive about their bodies and the sensations they experience when they touch themselves. Healthy attitudes about sexuality begin in the home. Children who get a good start there will grow up with an appreciation of God's gift of sexuality.

It is important to recognize that the Bible is completely silent on the topic of masturbation, and that any case a person builds either for or against it is based on inference. There are three major opinions about the place of masturbation in a Christian's life. The restrictive position is that masturbation under any circumstance is sinful. The permissive position holds that masturbation under any circumstance is healthy and morally permissible, harmful to no one, and a good way to be aware of ourselves as sexual beings. The moderate view holds that masturbation can be both healthy and morally appropriate but also has the potential to be unhealthy and morally inappropriate as well.

We hold this moderate position as most reasonable. Masturbation can be a healthy way for a person without a marital partner to experience sexual gratification or release. God has created humans as sexual beings, so masturbation is one means for them to be in touch with their sexuality. Accordingly, many Christians need to be released from the guilty feelings they have about masturbation. Studies have shown that the incidence of masturbation greatly increases among college students just before final exams as a common way to relieve tension.

But masturbation is not always psychologically and morally healthy. Compulsive masturbation can lead to addictive, self-defeating patterns. Within marriage, masturbation can be a negative factor if it deprives one's spouse of sexual fulfillment or is used as a way of evading relationship problems. When married partners have different desires regarding the frequency of intercourse, however, masturbation may be a healthy outlet and a loving solution. The relationship must always take priority, however, and the couple needs to face sexual problems rather than try to escape them.

Another issue to contemplate is the connection between masturbation, fantasizing, and lust. Jesus teaches about this in Matthew 5:27–28: "You have heard that it was said, 'You shall not commit adultery.' But I say to you that everyone who looks at a woman with lust has already committed adultery with her in his heart." Lusting after a particular person may lead to acting out one's desire. This is adultery, and adultery is sin. Lusting should not necessarily be equated with fantasizing, however. Most people fantasize about future possibilities, and masturbation with one's spouse or future spouse in mind can be a helpful way to remain celibate and faithful. Lusting has more to do with inordinate, inappropriate desire and finding ways to fulfill it. In fantasy, by contrast, one's wish is more general, and there is usually no specific attempt to achieve it. The one who is doing the lusting or fantasizing is usually aware of the difference. If an inappropriate fantasy turns into lusting, there is real trouble. The person, for example, who masturbates while fantasizing about having sex with a neighbor's wife turns the lust into action when he makes an advance to her the next day. In this case, fantasy is a precursor to a sinful act. It behooves us to pay attention to our fantasies, so that we can keep them within God's intended purpose.

It may be that a person who craves power fantasizes about sexual conquest. Bringing such a fantasy to awareness makes it possible to consider whether this is God's intended purpose. This particular fantasy disregards God's commandment to love others and not do them harm. In the same way, people who masturbate while viewing erotic pictures ought to consider the moral question of sexual exploitation and judge whether the dehumanizing aspect of the erotic material is in keeping with God's intention for humanity. The rising concern about pornography involves these issues, since the distorted attitudes about women and sex in our culture may lead to an increase in rape and other violent crimes. Again, the Bible admonishes us to cherish and value one another rather than to degrade others.

These are the kinds of issues that Christians must consider when trying to decide what one is free to do and what is good to do. Each one of us must determine the appropriateness of our fantasies and the effect they have on our whole life. It is possible to monitor our thoughts in the area of sexuality, just as it is possible to make choices about other things we allow to affect us. A person who reads a novel or sees a movie and experiences a romantic fantasy needs to consider if it takes away from the spouse and the marital relationship or increases responsiveness to the spouse in a positive way. The single person needs to decide whether a particular fantasy enhances the hope for a future relationship with a partner whom God has intended or overidealizes a phantom person that no ordinary person can fulfill. The important thing is that we are able to admit when our fantasies are not in keeping with God's intention and to change them to conform with God's plan for us.

In the past, the Christian community has magnified the sins of the flesh out of proportion to other wrongs and given the erroneous impression that sexual sins are far worse than any other sins. It is important to remember that we have been created in the image of God, and we are the children of God who have been made righteous through the blood of Christ. All our sins are forgivable. Regardless of what our past sexual life has been, we can come before God, ask forgiveness, and claim sexual purity in Christ. At the same time, we are responsible for our behavior and must earnestly seek God's help to become whole persons in every aspect of our lives, including sexuality.

Sexual Preference

Although most people have a preference for the opposite sex, an estimated 1 to 2 percent of the population in the United States has an erotic preference for the same sex. On the basis of biblical texts such as Leviticus 20:13, Romans 1:26–27, and 1 Corinthians 6:9–11, the Christian community has traditionally condemned homosexuality as sin. Today, however, most Christians believe that homosexual orientation is not to be condemned, although homosexual behavior is condemned. Some Christians are tolerant of monogamous homosexual expressions between consenting adults but contend that this is not what God initially intended. A few even place homosexual expression on a par with heterosexual expression and advocate a marriage arrangement for homosexual couples. They believe that sexual orientation is determined quite early in life and is beyond a person's choice. Therefore, it is "natural" for homosexuals to express themselves sexually to a member of the same sex. The scriptural passages that condemn "unnatural" affections do not, it is alleged, apply in such cases. Whatever one's position, most Christians uphold a standard of committed monogamy for both heterosexual and homosexual couples, as opposed to casual sex or a promiscuous lifestyle. The AIDS epidemic has reinforced the monogamous lifestyle. Both homosexuals and heterosexuals are choosing between celibacy and commitment to one person.

A simple definition of homosexuality is a sexual attraction and orientation toward members of the same sex. At a young age, homosexuals come to feel that they are different from their peers, and many do not conform to traditional gender roles (Ben 1996). This can be a very painful time, for such children have a great fear of being different and are often cruelly labeled "queer" by their peers. Identification as gay or lesbian occurs over considerable time.

There may be a period when homosexuals hide their orientation and have great fear of being discovered. This is an understandable fear, because our society exhibits considerable contempt for homosexual men and women. Homophobia is an excessive or compulsive hatred or fear of homosexuals. Homophobic reactions often stem from insecurity about one's own sexuality or from ignorance about homosexuality and homosexuals. It is important for Christians to understand the great pain many homosexuals have experienced and to have compassion for them.

Researchers report that although no firm evidence has established the origin of homosexuality, biological factors probably act in concert with cultural factors. A literature review on explanations of sexual identity yields contradictory conclusions (Omoto and Kurtzman 2005; Friedman and Downey 2002). As our model presented earlier in this chapter illustrates, sexual development is a complex process. This is not less true in understanding sexual identity issues. Thus we believe it would be premature to state with certainty the cause of homosexuality.

Some attempts to explain homosexuality concentrate on psychodynamic factors such as a cold, distant relationship with one's parent of the same sex or having a domineering parent of the opposite sex. Most Christian ministries hold out hope that one's sexual orientation can change (see Comiskey 2003; Nicolosi 1997; Payne 1996). The beginning point with such redemptive ministries is that a person must want to change and believe that he or she can. Cognitive-behavioral change strategies are usually combined with an emphasis on group support and accountability, prayer and inner healing. Many testify that change in sexual orientation is a process of recognizing the false premise of attempts to fill childhood deficits through sexual encounters. Some who go through these ministries choose celibacy, while others marry.

Christians need to acknowledge the lack of clear evidence explaining how homosexual orientation develops and to develop an approach to homosexuality based on a theological and biblical perspective. We began this book with our theology of relationships, which is built on the premise that the original intention of God's creation was heterosexuality. In the Genesis account, the ideal is a complementarity of the male and female: we become one flesh for the purpose of intimacy and procreation. However, since the whole human race is fallen, none of us achieves sexual wholeness in accordance with God's high ideal. Everyone falls short. Homosexuals and heterosexuals alike must strive to find a wholeness in their lives in a less than ideal world. All struggle in their own ways for sexual authenticity. In their struggle, some gay Christians believe that God's best for them is to commit themselves to a lifelong, monogamous homosexual union. While our compassion supports all people as they move in the direction of God's ideal for their lives, we hold to the model of a heterosexual, lifelong, monogamous union.

We believe that God can lead each one of us closer to sexual wholeness. This will, of course, be a more painful and difficult process for some than for others. It is a tragedy when people who struggle with sexual identity find more love in the homosexual subculture than in the Christian community. By balancing *truth* and *grace*, the Christian community is called to be a place where the world knows we are Christians by our love. Christ is willing to grant to everyone the privilege of walking through that process of finding sexual wholeness with him.

Marital Sexuality

Sexuality is only one aspect of the marriage relationship. It is authentic and healthy when it is well integrated into a comprehensive pattern of intimacy between the partners. Several principles will prove helpful for couples who want to achieve authentic sexuality in their marriage.

First, the foundation for authentic sexuality in marriage is mutuality. This idea is presented in 1 Corinthians 7:4–5: "For the wife does not have authority over her own body, but the husband does; likewise the husband does not have authority over his own body, but the wife does. Do not deprive one another except perhaps by agreement for a set time, to devote yourselves to prayer, and then come together again, so that Satan may not tempt you because of your lack of self-control."

Here we see that the Bible urges full mutuality. "By agreement" is a translation of the Greek phrase *ek symphomnou*, which literally means "with one voice" (cf. the English word *symphony*). The mutuality mentioned in verse 5 is consonant with Ephesians 5:21, where husbands and wives are told to "be subject to one another out of reverence for Christ."

Authentic marital sexuality can be achieved only if husband and wife are in agreement about their sexual interaction. There is no room for the misguided view that the husband initiates and dominates while the wife submits in obedience. Rather, 1 Corinthians 7:4–5 and Ephesians 5:21 assume mutual desire for and interest in sexual expression. This requires sensitive communication between the couple about their sexual desires. Just as an orchestra plays "with one voice" when each instrument contributes its own unique part and the music is brought together in harmony, so a married couple reaches sexual harmony through communication and sensitive understanding of each other's needs.

Second, husband and wife need to verbally communicate their sexual feelings and desires. Each spouse needs to know what the other desires sexually; this is not the time for guessing games. Although sexual desire can be communicated nonverbally, the communication needs to be verbal as well. It is important for couples to communicate about how they can best fulfill each other's sexual needs and desires. Guiding each other through touch and brief words of encouragement during the sexual encounter can be helpful. However, it is also essential that the couple take time to talk about their sexual relationship, so they can evaluate how each is feeling and what may need changing. This is difficult for most couples to do, but if it is not done, dissatisfactions are never addressed and may take on more disruptive forms. Open discussion about sexual matters contributes to sexual enjoyment. Obviously, the couple will need to invest time and effort in working together on matters that will enhance the sexual relationship.

Third, there must be no game playing in the sexual encounter. Total openness is essential. There must be no hiding of one's true sexual feelings and desires for the sake of personal advantage. Much of the game playing plaguing relationships is motivated by an inadequate sense of self-esteem. Thus, an individual who does not feel attractive may continually bait the partner into affirming him or her in this area. Another kind of game playing is alternately showing signs of sexual interest and of disinterest in one's partner. This behavior is often motivated by the need to be pursued or the desire to be in control of the relationship. Yet another form of game playing is sexual teasing. One partner teases about desiring sex and then resists or is very passive when the other responds with sexual advances. These games end up having a negative impact on the relationship.

Fourth, marital sexuality should include an element of playfulness. Although game playing is destructive, a sexual relationship benefits from a sense of uninhibited engagement and non-self-conscious interaction. A healthy view of oneself and one's body and feelings of comfort with one's partner are vital ingredients of freedom in a sexual encounter. Accordingly, the level of fun in a relationship is often a good measure of the degree of intimacy.

One of the benefits of playfulness is that it prevents couples from making a production out of sex. Controlling the sexual encounter in such a way that it becomes contrived and serious makes it impossible to respond to each other freely. A spirit of fun, however, keeps the sexual encounter spontaneous and relaxed.

Fifth, it is essential not to become spectators in the sexual encounter. When partners assume a spectator role during coitus, they tend to lose sight of each other. This is a particular problem in a technologically oriented society that emphasizes the importance of using the right methods. This attitude reduces sex to little more than an exercise in techniques. When this happens, sex is similar to the once-popular paint-by-the-number kits. The detailed instructions of a sex manual virtually dictate a couple's lovemaking. Just picture a scene in which the wife turns to her husband during lovemaking and says, "Turn back a page, Henry! We must have missed a step because I'm not feeling anything." The whole experience is inauthentic because there is no creative and spontaneous interaction between the spouses. In a very real sense, the personhood of each spouse is lost in the effort to make love by the book. Naturalness between lovers has been replaced by an effort to be technically correct.

When partners take on a spectator role, they separate themselves from their sexuality. They are so overly conscious of their performance that they fail to be involved in the lovemaking experience. This removal of self from the sexual event defeats the whole purpose.

In authentic sexuality, by contrast, the spouses allow natural feelings, inclinations, and actions to occur without a conscious evaluation of the performance. Both husband and wife are spontaneously engaged in the sexual encounter. Both partners are giving and receiving as they encounter each other in the moment.

Sixth, the greater the sensory pleasure in a relationship exclusive of coitus, the greater the sexual adequacy. This principle refers to the pleasure derived from foreplay, which involves the stimulation of erogenous zones prior to coitus. The lyrics of the popular song *Slow Hand*, by the Pointer Sisters, expresses this principle: "I want a man with a slow hand; I want a lover with an easy touch." Touch communicates tenderness, affection, desire, warmth, comfort, and excitement. When a couple takes time to touch in ways that invite and increase responsiveness, they find more mutual satisfaction.

Seventh, the more secure the partners feel in their commitment to each other, the more complete their sexual response. Research shows that women and men are most able to invest themselves sexually when they feel secure about the relationship. Inversely, when trust is in question, spouses are less able to make an adequate sexual response. Men as well as women desire a sexual involvement that makes them feel warm and secure. Here again we see that trust helps bring about sexual responsiveness and authenticity.

Our discussion of marital sexuality calls to mind our theology of relationships and the four related principles (Balswick and Balswick 1999).

1. A sexual relationship is meant to be based on an unconditional covenant commitment. A commitment of this nature gives a couple the security to be open and responsive to each other sexually. Such trust is a necessary foundation for healthy marital sexuality.

2. A spirit of grace rather than blame or shame leads to healing and renewal in covenant relationships. To accept each other's unique sexual needs and desires and to work through different sexual preferences takes an attitude of grace. The dimension of forgiveness is also crucial. Disruptions in the sexual relationship that cause disappointment or anger require a forgiving attitude.

3. A sexual union is meant to be part of a relationship in which spouses use their personal resources and gifts to affirm rather than control the other. Spouses ought not make unreasonable demands on each other sexually but rather mutually empower each other.

4. A sexual union is meant to be part of a relationship in which one makes oneself known more deeply. Understanding, valuing, and cherishing each other will lead to this deeper intimacy. This includes acceptance of each other's views and limitations, a desire to know and be known by each other, and the willingness to be vulnerable.

All these aspects of sexual intimacy come through covenant commitment, which leads to emotional closeness and oneness. Sexual satisfaction is a wonderful by-product of a total relationship. As a marriage grows in commitment, grace, service, and intimacy, the couple will move ever closer to God's ideal of authentic sexuality.

PART 5

COMMUNICATION

The Heart of Family Life

THIS SECTION DEALS with the important dimension of communication. Communication is the heart of family life in that family members interact through verbal and nonverbal exchanges to express their thoughts, wishes, and core emotions. Through their honest expressions of thoughts and emotions (love and anger), family members come to know one another in very personal ways. When family members communicate and express themselves in their own unique ways, family relationships grow and deepen.

Without the ability to communicate effectively, the family unit quickly becomes a mere collection of individuals whose thoughts, feelings, and desires are nobody's but their own. With an increased ability to communicate, however, the family can become a vibrant system whose members learn to engage in meaningful interaction. In this sense, communication is truly the heart of family life, a place where members have both the freedom and the skills to deepen their relationship.

Chapter 13 begins with a discussion of why the expression of love is so important to family intimacy. We indicate the fears family members have about communicating love and the obstacles that interfere with becoming emotionally connected. We follow with a section on why expressing love between family members is essential in deepening levels of knowing and being known. We then conclude with a poignant example of an expression of love between Jesus and Peter.

Chapter 14 deals with the important topic of conflict in family life. Conflict is indeed a normal part of family life, yet there are destructive and constructive ways to work through problems. We present some "fair fighting" rules to guide family members in their inevitable skirmishes. There are five major styles people tend to use when they engage in conflict; we describe these styles to help family members recognize the pros and cons of their unique styles. Effective families learn to respect one another's styles but at the same time adjust their ways of dealing with conflict for the good of the relationship. This creative effort is the difference between a satisfactory resolution that connects family members and an unsatisfactory one that distances them.

13

Expressing Love—Achieving Intimacy

Intimacy, described by Abraham Greeff and Hildegarde Malherbe (2001, 248) as "behavioral interdependency, fulfillment of needs and emotional attachment," sets the stage for this chapter. Being able to share thoughts and feelings with other members is crucial to effective family living. By expressing emotions and sharing needs, family members develop an emotional attachment and create opportunities for mutuality and interdependence. The expression of emotions, whether it be anger, hurt, love, joy, sadness, or affection, is essentially how family members become more intimately acquainted with one another.

Building intimacy in family relationships is one of the most important yet one of the most difficult tasks to do well. Sharing honestly about what is going on internally places one in a vulnerable position. Therefore, the family must be a safe place for members to share themselves. If it is unsafe, members will feel personally threatened and guard others from knowing their true feelings or expressing their real needs. When the fear of being ridiculed or rejected is more than members can risk, they will undoubtedly protect themselves by keeping their feelings and thoughts to themselves. This creates a distrustful atmosphere in which no one knows what the others are thinking and feeling. Many misunderstandings result from this state of affairs, and family members are stymied in their interactions. As members keep their distance and remain self-contained, the capacity for significant bonding becomes increasingly remote.

Achieving intimacy is more complex in marriage and family life today than it was in the past. A number of characteristics of modern society have increased the sense of alienation and loneliness. The prevalence of anonymity and impersonalization in our society leads to superficial relating. Thousands of people live together on the same city block, but most of them know very little about their neighbors, let alone establish any semblance of relationship with them.

Mass society in a computer-driven world is characterized by special-ization of tasks coordinated by social structures. Bureaucracies place people into neat, categorical relationships, and the individual's rights and responsibilities are defined in terms of one's position in the organizational chain of command. As a result, we begin to treat one another as objects occupying a position rather than as human personalities. We become part of a faceless crowd, recognized and treated as mere numbers.

As far back as 1950, David Riesman aptly titled his book *The Lonely Crowd*, indicating a deep desire for intimacy in people because so much of life is impersonal in the external world. In the face of this heartless world, the family becomes a refuge where we hope to find comfort, care, and intimacy. The increased expectation of meeting emotional needs in modern/postmodern marriage and family relationships makes the expres-sion of love an essential ingredient today (Flora and Segrin 2003).

We believe that intimacy is desirable in marriage and family relation-ships not only as a refuge from the impersonality of society but as a reflection of the biblical ideal. Genesis 2 describes a pre-fall condition in which intimacy, knowing and being known, brings a deep sense of relationship joy and mutuality. The trinitarian concepts of relationship unity and particularity provide a model for family members to make room in their hearts and lives for each unique family member and their emotions, needs, desires, and thoughts. Dialogue, mutual regard, inter-est, and engagement among members leads to increased understanding and interdependent unity.

Expressing Feelings of Love

It is ironic that the three little words "I love you," which ought to be the most effortless and pleasurable phrase for us to say to those we love, are actually very difficult for most people to utter. Everyone surely knows that nothing would make another person happier than to hear such an expression, yet family members may be reluctant or feel strangely un-comfortable when speaking of their love for one another.

The extent of emotional discomfort is evident in the following illustra-tion. One afternoon the movie *Romeo and Juliet* was shown to a crowded auditorium of high school students. The roles of Romeo and Juliet were played by sixteen-year-olds, and many of the students could identify with the tragedy of young love impeded by family relationships. However, during the death scene, it was surprising to hear laughter among the males, intermingled with the tears of most of the females. Obviously, the young males had sidetracked the emotional impact to cover up what they had been conditioned not to express.

The Effects of Expressing Love

You may ask why it is so important to express the affection you feel to one another in the family. Most importantly, it assures them that they are loveable and encourages relationship bonding. Human beings need to hear and to receive overt expressions of love from the time they are born until the day they die.

Studies of infant deprivation suggest that babies who do not receive expressions of love will be unable to receive or express love during their entire lifetime. Many children who are not given sufficient affection, even though they may receive adequate physical care, suffer from marasmus, a disease in which the body simply wastes away. Marasmus is prevalent among war victims and orphans. A child with marasmus fails to develop socially, psychologically, and physically; death is frequently the outcome. What is most important for our purposes is the cause of marasmus: a deprivation of love. This fact makes it clear that children need to be held, cuddled, caressed, kissed, and hugged.

It is well established that children develop their self-image on the basis of their perceptions of how others view them. Children are able to love themselves if their parents have expressed love to them both verbally and physically. No one ever outgrows the need for affection and love. As we mature from infancy to adulthood, we have an increased need for verbal affirmation and physical expressions of love.

It is emotionally rewarding for all people to engage with others at a personal and emotional level. Doing so indicates the desire for interaction and interdependency. Psychologically speaking, keeping emotions to yourself actually puts you at risk of losing touch with yourself and others, inhibiting the potential for developing a close, emotional connection with those you love.

Articulating our feelings helps us acknowledge and accept our emotions. When they are not articulated, we remain removed, uncertain, and unclear about what we feel. Just as talking over a problem with someone is a way to better understand that problem, articulating emotions helps us to conceptualize what we are feeling.

Expressing love is important for all relationships. Just as mutual commitment (covenant) is the basis of secure bonding, communication is the basis for intimacy. Communication is a two-way street. Some family members make valiant efforts to engage, but they find themselves in a dead end if the other member is unwilling to respond or reciprocate. Some people explain away the problem with dismissive statements such as, "He is just like that" or "She is shy" or "It's in the genes, so I can't expect much." While personality and even shy genes may be part of inexpressiveness, the fact remains that lack of emotional sharing develops into patterns of stifled communication. The possibility of intimacy is crushed, and the relationship stagnates emotionally.

Unfortunately, when one gets very little response, it is natural to stop making attempts at connecting. Without engagement or feedback, a person is on a one-way street. Intimacy requires reciprocity. For instance, when a father never expresses love for his son, the son soon wonders where he stands with his father. In frustration, the son tries any means (even misbehavior) to get his father's attention. He may use manipulative means to evoke some kind of response from his unengaged father. That behavior may elicit a negative reaction (anger), but even that is better than nothing at all.

Nonverbal Expressions of Love

The expression of love can be communicated nonverbally as well as verbally (Turner and West 2002). Individuals who have difficulty expressing feelings verbally may ask, "Can't body language, physical actions, or symbolic gestures be used to show love?" It is assuring to know that there are alternative means of expressing love. Family members can express feelings for one another in a number of ways. A person can show affection through a hug, a pat on the back, a wink, or some other symbolic gesture. The fact is we do communicate through our facial expressions, posture, and general body movements. Researchers note that people indicate open- or closed-mindedness through body language. A person who assumes an open and relaxed body posture is likely to be open-minded about the ideas being discussed by the family. A family member who sits stiffly upright, tense, with legs crossed and arms folded, is likely to be closed-minded and defensive.

It is certainly possible to express affection in many ways, but we must also ask the question, "How far can nonverbal types of communication carry a love relationship?" The answer to this question is complex. If one family member is communicating only by nonverbal means, the others must be able to read the hidden meaning in the nonverbal messages. When a conscious effort is made, they may be quite successful in interpreting the real meaning in a grunt, a sigh, a cough, or a glance. It takes a lot of work for the skilled interpreter to accurately decipher the wishes and feelings of a nonengaged family member. The obvious problem with nonverbal expressions of love is that ambiguous messages often result in guessing games and misunderstandings. More importantly, people who fail to express themselves verbally are deprived of the deepest levels of intimacy that can be attained only through mutuality and reciprocity.

Gestures of love such as giving a dozen roses, sending a love note in a suitcase, surprising a spouse with two tickets to a play, or taking the family to a ball game are ways of reaching out. They represent the thoughtfulness and affection of the giver. Such gestures are received with great delight and enthusiasm. Love can also be expressed in written form: a letter, a poem, or a song. One need not be a fine poet for family members to cherish a poem written especially for them. The main thing to remember is that family relationships are enhanced through a variety of expressions of love.

People who find the verbal communication of feelings difficult may be tempted to argue that nonverbal forms of communication are sufficient. It should be noted, however, that verbal communication has two distinct advantages: preciseness and personalness.

Body language, for example, can be misread. The receiver of the message may wonder, "What does that gleam in her eye really mean?" Physical expressions can be misinterpreted as well. A parent may question, "Is my son hugging me so tightly because he loves me or because he wants me to delay his bedtime hour?" Symbolic expressions may conjure up suspicion: "Why did he send me these flowers today? Did he just have his secretary order them, or has he really gone out of his way to pick them out?" or "I wonder what's behind all this special attention I'm getting from her tonight." The point here is to take the crucial next step of clarifying the intended meaning so the nonverbal message is crystal clear.

Although a high degree of precision can be obtained, a genuinely personal element is hard to achieve in written communication. E-mails may be exact and to the point, but they are usually read when the writer is not present. Feelings of love and affection are communicated more completely, personally, and precisely by direct speech. The personal vulnerability that goes along with face-to-face contact allows for an immediate response and exchange between two people. This is a more vulnerable engagement with more potential for person-to-person intimacy.

Love has been compared to a finely cut diamond that can be appreciated in its entirety only if it is seen from many angles. Each angle gives a different view and shows a different facet of the unique beauty of the diamond, and yet the diamond is only one piece. The same may be said about love. The depth and dimensions of love are communicated by body language, physical actions, symbolic gestures, and written *and* oral communication. Although all expressions of love are wonderful, the whole package develops the deepest capacity for knowing and being known.

Obstacles to Expressing Love

Family members have difficulty expressing feelings of love for several reasons. After considering some of the general reasons for inexpressiveness, we consider why males, in particular, are less likely than females to show their vulnerable sides.

Fear is perhaps the number-one reason family members fail to express their love to one another. When we express ourselves freely, we open ourselves up to be vulnerable to the response of the other. It is not just our feelings that we reveal, but our feelings for the other person. When we communicate love, we place ourselves in an exposed position. It is as if we were emotionally naked, having stripped off our protective armor as we bare our feelings of love for that person. When we let another person know of our love, we may fear he or she won't accept it or reciprocate it.

This can be a source of dread if we fear we will be ignored, discounted, or, worst of all, rejected. Experiences of being rejected in the past make it difficult to freely expose ourselves in the present.

The fear of expressing love is partly a symptom of low self-esteem. When family members believe they have little to offer, they feel their expressions of love have no worth. When self-esteem is extremely low, there may be an inability to love oneself. And when self-love is absent, loving someone else becomes a needy love. So even if love is felt, people with low self-esteem may have difficulty expressing that love.

Another obstacle to the expression of love is embarrassment. When certain patterns have been established, introducing new ways of communicating can be awkward. Parents who have verbally communicated love from the day their children were born generally have no trouble communicating love when the children are grown. Parents who have not established such a pattern feel embarrassed about verbally expressing their love when their children are grown. Although grown children may want to tell aging parents of their love, it is most difficult to break through the barrier. However, sometimes as people age, they become more free to express their love for family members. Perhaps they have a desire to make their love known before they die.

Family members use uncanny ways to get around intimacy. Talking about trivia is an example. Continual chatter is a defense mechanism that serves to keep a person from communicating on a deep emotional level. Another defense is the practice of intellectualizing feelings. Some people become very skilled at analyzing or critiquing to avoid expressing their innermost emotions.

Another barrier to family intimacy is the lack of time spent together. Acts of love are usually expressed naturally when people spend quality time together. Cultivating intimacy within which love can be expressed comfortably takes much time and intentional effort. Expressions of love will be inadequate and seem forced when family members have not invested themselves in the relationship. If the relationship is superficial, the expression of love is insincere.

Some family members never express themselves vulnerably simply because they are not in touch with their feelings. Although they may actually feel something, they have such a weak understanding of the feeling that they cannot identify, acknowledge, or express it. When they do attempt to express feelings, they do so indirectly. An inexpressive husband who loves his wife but has trouble identifying the feeling as love may say something like, "I guess I knew what I was doing when I picked you." This is an indirect way of saying how much he loves his wife. Sadly, lack of awareness keeps people removed from others, making it almost impossible to develop intimate relationships.

Finally, traditional cultural expectations inhibit people from expressing emotions. In fact, this may be the most significant factor. Cultural norms about appropriate expression of feelings is part of the socialization process. Inborn tendencies, for example, shyness, are reinforced by cultural and gender norms. These expectations become part of the child's self-image and a self-fulfilling prophecy.

Boys in many societies come to value so-called expressions of masculinity and to eschew expressions of femininity. They are taught that love, tenderness, and gentleness are feminine. When a young boy expresses his emotions through crying, his parents are quick to assert, "You're a big boy, and big boys don't cry!" or "Don't be such a sissy; be a man!" In various ways, they indicate to their son that a real man does not show tender emotions. Other expressions of masculinity that reinforce these messages are statements like, "He's all boy," when referring to aggressive or mischievous behavior.

As the boy moves out from the family and into the sphere of male peer groups, the taboo against displaying any of the feelings characteristic of girls is reinforced. To be affectionate, gentle, and expressive toward others is to forfeit becoming "one of the boys." The mass media convey a similar message. In movies, music, television, and advertising, the male image does not accentuate affectionate, softhearted behavior.

Although females also grow up in environments that inhibit their expression of love, the male receives messages that tie his inexpressiveness to his male identity. These messages need to be combated in family and society if change is to be accomplished.

The Expression of Love in Parent/Child Relationships

The emotional bond between child and parent is the most important factor in the development of a child. Children who are denied a strong emotional bond with their mother and father must go through life compensating for this lack. In reality, the most extensive problem for both boys and girls is the lack of a strong emotional bonding with their father.

In keeping with their distinct societal roles, mothers and fathers differ in relating to their children (Maccoby 1999). Evidence suggests that these differences begin very early and increase through the child-rearing period. Studies show, for example, that mothers tend to engage their babies directly, to stimulate responses, and to display affection, while fathers tend to read to or watch television with their children. Mothers are also more likely than fathers to hold, smile at, and speak to their infant.

Parents, especially fathers, have been found to treat their sons and daughters differently. Fathers set narrower boundaries of sex-appropriate play for twelve-month-old boys than for girls. It has also been found that the disparity in the father's treatment of sons and daughters is greater when the mother is present.

The pattern that seems to emerge from the research on parenting is that mothers are more evenhanded in the affection they show daughters and sons, while fathers treat sons and daughters according to sexual stereotypes. Further, while the disparity in the father's approach toward sons and daughters begins when the children are infants, it increases as they grow older. By the time children reach their teenage years, fathers view a daughter as someone to be treated in a gentle manner, held, hugged, and affirmed, while a son is treated in a standoffish way. It is not surprising that more daughters than sons rate their fathers high in nurturing and giving affection. Fathers seem to be preoccupied with the masculine development of their sons, while they encourage femininity in their daughters.

Men struggle with intimacy because they have not experienced warm relationships with their fathers. The process of individuation is particularly difficult for boys because they must first psychologically separate from their mother and then identify and bond with their father, who in all too many cases is rejecting, incompetent, or absent. Discouraged from going to the mother for help and turned aside by a cool and distant father, many boys are forced to deal with their confused feelings and problems by themselves. It comes as no surprise, then, that when these boys grow to manhood, they find it difficult to share their feelings with others (Maccoby 1999).

All these findings suggest that boys and girls come to have different capacities for expressiveness because of their parents' role modeling and expectations. Research consistently shows that adolescent and adult females are more expressive of their feelings of love than are males. However, there are exceptions, and when fathers are very expressive, so are their sons. With the leadership of both parents modeling expressiveness, family members can learn to express their feelings.

The Expression of Love in Marriage

When it comes to expressing love in a marital relationship, men face a dilemma. On the one hand, society teaches that to be masculine is to be inexpressive; on the other hand, marriage requires a sharing of affection and companionship, and the ability to communicate and to express feelings.

James Cordova, Christina Gee, and Lisa Warren's (2005) research demonstrates that a couple's ability to identify and communicate emotions is related to marital adjustment. A number of studies also indicate that husbands tend to be less expressive than their wives. When a couple expresses feelings about equally, the marriage tends to be well adjusted (J. O. Balswick 1988, 151–71). Regardless of the total amount, similar levels of self-disclosure point to a healthy marriage. Great dissatisfaction and problems are likely to emerge when there is an imbalance in the amount of self-disclosure.

Although the husband is typically less expressive than his wife, some factors work against a wife's being open and sharing. First, over a period of time the wife's verbal expression of love will diminish. Many a wife begins marriage with expansive declarations of love for her husband, but without reciprocal expression, she will express her feelings less frequently.

A second factor is unequal levels of vulnerability, resulting in less self-disclosure. In their research, John Gottman and Joan DeClaire (2001) find that one spouse will offer a statement to the other as a *bid* for greater intimacy, for instance, "I feel like I don't know you." When one spouse reveals himself or herself in such a way and the other stands aloof, refusing to up the *bid* toward greater vulnerability, the spouse offering the bid will cease taking steps toward greater intimacy. Without unilateral *bids* toward mutual sharing, the hope for real intimacy diminishes between a couple.

Another possible factor is the birth of a child. Carrying this additional emotional burden, the wife may express herself less to her husband. As time passes, the child may be able to fill some of the emotional needs of the mother. It is natural for a mother to express herself to a child who returns love in contrast to a husband who rarely returns affection.

Wives may also become less expressive of their tender feelings in a bid for marital power. Although commitment is the ideal basis for marriage, in actuality marriage is often more an ongoing struggle for control. Male inexpressiveness can be a form of *sexual politics* in which the husband deliberately hides feelings as a way to have more power in the marital relationship. If a wife perceives that her husband's inexpressiveness is a conscious effort to control her, she may withhold her expression of affection as well. Withholding affection becomes a power play in which both spouses lose.

Another scenario can occur in which the husband is relatively uninterested in the marriage and the wife overly dependent on it. The wife dares not make too many demands for fear that her husband will terminate the relationship. He can have his way by being demanding and by threatening to leave unless she yields. In a relationship of this type, her expressions of love amount to a loss of power. Saying "I love you" is interpreted as a sign of dependence. When an uninterested husband can take his wife's love for granted, she is powerless. The wife who finds herself in such a situation learns to feign a lack of interest in an attempt to gain some power. Unfortunately, these power games ultimately lead to distance and dissatisfaction in marriage.

A Biblical Model of Expressiveness

In our first chapter we noted that the last recorded exchange between Jesus and Peter (John 21) is a perfect picture of the intimacy desirable in family relationships. It is also a model of expressiveness and the communication of love. Peter and some of the other disciples have been fishing during the night on the Sea of Galilee. They come to shore just as day is breaking and find Jesus with a charcoal fire ready. He invites them to join him for breakfast. Jesus then begins a curious quizzing of Peter about his love. Three times Jesus asks Peter, "Do you love me?" After each query, Peter replies, "Yes, you know that I love you." We are told that Peter was grieved after Jesus asked him this question the third time.

Jesus had a definite reason for posing the question three times: Peter had earlier denied Jesus three times; Jesus is now giving Peter the opportunity to assert what he had previously denied and to reaffirm his love three times. We have no way of knowing whether Peter had asked forgiveness for his denial, but Jesus does offer Peter at this time both forgiveness and an opportunity to express his feelings of love. Peter certainly has a need to express these feelings and to reaffirm his love, for he will soon be one of a small group left on earth to carry on the work that Christ had started. Jesus cares for Peter; and because he does, he draws Peter out to the point where he is able to share his feelings of love toward Jesus.

With this experience Peter changed from an intimidated coward during Christ's crucifixion to becoming a fearless witness after Jesus's ascension. People struggling today to find intimacy in an impersonal society need to realize that they too can change by expressing love. For as the Word of God teaches, "There is no fear in love, but perfect love casts out fear; for fear has to do with punishment, and whoever fears has not reached perfection in love. We love because he first loved us" (1 John 4:18–19).

14

Expressing Anger—Negotiating the Inevitable Conflicts

Strong families are not those that never experience conflict but those that successfully manage conflict when it does arise. When we meet a couple who tell us that they never have any conflicts, we assume one of several possibilities: they have not been married very long, they don't know each other very well, they don't talk to each other very much, or they are lying. Although conflict is a normal part of intimate relationships, exposure to frequent and intense parental conflict can "result in greater emotional distress, psychopathology, and health problems in children" (Clingempeel and Brand-Clingempeel 2004, 245).

Simply put, a conflict is a difference in opinion. Family conflict can be individual (i.e., between two family members) or collective (i.e., between two sets of family members). Individual conflict can arise within a family subsystem (e.g., between a husband and a wife) or between subsystems (e.g., a father in conflict with a son). Collective conflicts can occur between family subsystems (parents against children) or irrespective of subsystems (e.g., mother and daughter in conflict with father and son). Extended-family conflict involves conflict between parents-in-law and their children and children's spouses or children. Thus multilevels may need to be addressed.

Although family conflict stems from differences between people, it is usually related to the ways in which individuals are part or parts of larger family systems or subsystems. That is to say, most family conflict is systemic in nature, centering around changes within and between family systems (Sillars, Canary, and Tafoya 2004). Marital conflict, for example, is most likely to occur during the initial years when the spousal system is being formed or during transitional periods involving family restructuring or re-forming (Rogge and Bradbury 2002). As would be expected, parental conflict has the most negative effect on children when it is focused on parental differences in child rearing (Clingempeel and Brand-Clingempeel 2004, 245).

Regardless of the marital stage, conflict is greatest when spouses are under stress (Noller and Feeney 2002). Parent/child conflict is less likely when the parental and sibling subsystems are on solid footing, and more likely when these two subsystems are in flux, such as when children reach their teenage years, when stepfamilies are formed, and so on.

It should also be noted that conflict between subsystems can cause secondary conflict between individuals in the subsystems. For example, parent/teenager conflict can intensify conflict between the husband and the wife around issues of discipline. In stepfamilies, conflicts between child and stepparent bring added tension into the spousal subsystem. Externally, an ex-spouse's dealings with children can cause havoc in the remarriage. However, conflict between subsystems can unify a subsystem, such as when conflict with parents leads children into coalition or when the remarried couple joins forces to present a united front when dealing with their children or ex-spouses.

A conflict between two family members frequently entangles others (triangling). Strong emotional ties and investment in the outcome make it difficult for the others to stay out of the skirmish. A triangle is formed when noninvolved family members are brought into a conflict to help one member gain power. This side-taking complicates the situation, since the matter of the third party's loyalty now intensifies the relationship dispute.

Before proceeding to the next section, we note recent research that indicates physiological differences in how men and women handle conflict. Gottman (1994) reports that men were more likely to be negatively affected physiologically by highly emotional conflicts. A man's greater increase in heart rate and rush of adrenaline lead researchers to conclude that men need a twenty-minute cooling down period before they can adequately deal with conflict. Another study (Loving et al. 2004) investigated the impact of marital power on endocrine responses to marital conflict. The researchers discovered that less powerful spouses displayed elevated hormone responses in a conflict discussion. They also found that shared power has a beneficial effect on the wives' hormone response level but doesn't seem to affect the husbands'. From these studies we recognize that men and women are affected physiologically and must take the needed steps to resolve conflicts between them.

Levels of Conflict and Offense

In a helpful essay on forgiveness and family life, Anne Borrowdale (1996) distinguishes four levels of conflict or offense that damage family relationships. The particular level of offense is directly related to the possibility of forgiveness. The least serious level consists of everyday failures in relationships, such as being late for dinner, not picking up dirty clothes, or eating the last cookie in the cookie jar. At this level, family members need to decide which offenses truly matter and which ones can be ignored. When small offenses are regularly repeated, however, the accumulative irritation must be addressed. A generosity of spirit, forgiving, and refusing to hold grudges over minor offenses can quickly move the family on to more important matters (p. 206).

The second level of offense involves negligence or deliberate acts that disrupt family relationships. These more serious offenses must be acknowledged as wrongs committed against family members, even when they are done in ignorance. They need to be put right through forgiveness as well as some form of restitution or punishment. By working through the problems, family members can achieve healing.

Third-level offenses involve physical, sexual, or emotional abuse that results in extreme personal and relational harm, putting the very fabric of the family in danger. Borrowdale is convinced that many families do not understand what is required to address problems at this level. If the offender is insufficiently aware of the depth of the personal damage done and does not repent, forgiveness will be superficial and nothing but a sham. Making these relationships right is not merely a matter of the offender admitting regret; it is a matter of dealing directly with the offending behavior, the one who was offended, and the entire family system for not preventing the offense from occurring (Borrowdale 1996, 213).

Fourth-level offenses involve, not particular acts, but societal tolerance of gross neglect or abusive treatment. When children's basic needs are unacknowledged, overridden, or disregarded, we must question societal attitudes and customs that allow for such offenses. A different sort of forgiveness is required here. As a start, the victims must be allowed to rage at such injustices and seek justice from parents, systems, and society at large. Forgiveness is difficult in these cases and may never be possible for some. Healing, however, can come through the power of faith, which gives victims an extraordinary ability to forgive the wrongs committed against them.

A Destructive Approach to Conflict: Denial

While conflict in itself is neither good nor bad, the way in which it is handled can be destructive or constructive. Denying or failing to deal with conflict is invariably destructive to family relationships. Denial of conflict is like sweeping dirt under a rug. It only appears to eliminate the problem; it does nothing about the behavior that brought about the conflict in the first place. The problem, like the addictive use of drugs, intensifies because the conflict-producing behavior never changes. Denial is destructive not only on the relational level but also on the personal level, since those who deny the conflict are also forced to deny their feelings of hurt, disappointment, and anger.

There are several ways in which family members can deny conflict. One common method is displacement: a family member angered or disturbed by another conveniently vents frustrations on a third member. The comic strip "Family Circus" once depicted an excellent example of displacement: the boss lashes out at the husband, the husband comes home and shouts at his wife, the wife scolds the oldest child, who crabs at his younger sister, who bawls out the dog. The string of displaced conflict ends with the dog chasing the cat, and the cat catching and eating a mouse. In the end, a victim suffered the final blow.

Powerful family members use displacement to take out their frustrations on the less powerful. The younger members on the receiving end often come to the mistaken belief that they are bad and deserve punishment.

Another common form of denial in the family is disengagement. In this case, family members avoid conflict by sidestepping sensitive and controversial issues. Disengagement might be initiated by a burst of anger followed by withdrawal, such as when a husband gets mad at his wife, storms out of the house and drives away in the car, and then returns two hours later as if nothing had happened. The husband and the wife never talk about what caused the blowup and collude in the cover-up. Disengagement serves as a barrier to growth in the relationship, and the unresolved conflict may well lead to a severe crisis later on.

A more subtle form of denial is disqualification, a quick discounting of one's angry reaction. A mother may get mad at her children only to disqualify the legitimacy of her angry feelings by reasoning that she would not have gotten mad if she had slept better the night before. Disqualifiers tend to cover up angry emotions rather than admit them. Like the other forms of denial, disqualification is a barrier to growth and is destructive to family relationships.

Constructive Approaches

The first step in dealing constructively with conflict is to admit that the conflict exists. The second step is to decide how the conflict is to be handled. While there is little disagreement regarding the need to recognize and admit angry feelings, opinions differ as to how to go about resolving the anger. There are three basic constructive approaches: fair fighting, conflict resolution, and conflict management.

As early as 1968, George Bach and Peter Wyden suggested that conflict be handled in a fair fight. Perhaps because of the seeming contradiction in terms such as *constructive conflict* and *fair fighting*, many people have vehemently reacted to this proposal; they believe that fighting is always destructive. Others have found the analogy of a fair fight helpful.

The second constructive approach is conflict resolution. Its advocates wholeheartedly accept many of the rules of fair fighting but reject the concept itself because of the negative connotation of words such as *fighting*. It can be dangerous to endorse such terms in a society such as ours where there is so much physical abuse in families.

The third constructive approach is conflict management. It emerged in reaction to conflict resolution, which suggests that there is an end to conflict. Its proponents argue that a more realistic model views conflict in human relationships as an unending process involving constant change. There is a sense in which conflict is never completely resolved but needs continuous management.

Fair Fighting

Before the concept of fair fighting was introduced, the tendency was to view all conflict as destructive and undesirable. Fair fighting developed as a reaction to the opposite extremes of denial and avoidance, on the one hand, and confrontation and attack, on the other hand. We believe there is wisdom in reviewing the rules of fair fighting (see table 6). We have made no attempt to identify the source of each rule; some appear in Bach and Wyden's original work, some have been formulated by a number of other writers, and some are our own reformulations.

1. *Identify the issue.* The first rule in fair fighting is to identify the real issue in a conflict. This can be a very difficult task, because most family conflicts involve more than a single issue. There is also the likelihood that family members will differ as to what the central issue really is.

Table 6

Rules for a Fair Fight

1. Identify the issue.
2. Choose the right time.
3. Choose the right place.
4. Begin with a positive stroke.
5. Stick to the issue.
6. Do not bring up the past.
7. Do not hit below the belt.
8. Take the other seriously.
9. Express anger nonabusively.
10. Do not play games.
11. Do not be passively aggressive.
12. Avoid asking for explanations of behavior.
13. Avoid labeling and name calling.
14. Avoid triangles.

Little progress can be made until each person involved knows how the others define the conflict. When there are multiple issues, the first task is to agree on which one to tackle first and to try to understand how they are all interrelated.

2. *Choose the right time.* If time is available and if emotional intensity does not preclude a reasonable argument, some conflicts can be constructively resolved when they arise. In most cases, however, family members need a period for cooling off and must schedule the main event for a time that is mutually convenient for everyone involved. If a sixteen-year-old son arrives home at midnight, one hour past his deadline, the parents would be well advised to wait to deal with the issue, for they will be tired and angry. Perhaps a brief explanation from the son together with an expression of concern by the parents and a promise to discuss the issue the next day is the best plan of action.

In our own marriage, we have learned never to schedule a fight for the early morning as Judy is barely functioning then. Likewise, to schedule a fight late at night is to risk Jack's noninvolvement. Through our many years of marriage, we have learned to schedule our conflict discussions for early evenings.

3. *Choose the right place.* Fair fighting needs to take place on neutral territory. The father's workshop is an inappropriate place, as is the wife's study or the child's room. Seek out a neutral area where all parties involved are on equal footing and where the family can be free of interruptions.

4. *Begin with a positive stroke.* The discussion will proceed much more smoothly if one begins by giving a positive stroke. For example, suppose that Sally has been remiss lately about hanging up towels and picking up her clothes when she uses the family bathroom. Her parents might

confront her by saying, "Sally, we're tired of your throwing towels and dirty clothes all over the bathroom floor; so shape up!" Or they could begin with a positive stroke: "Sally, you are generally very good at following the family rules, but you seem to have forgotten the agreement regarding bathroom tidiness. We would really appreciate it if you would pick up your clothes and hang up the towels after you bathe." This is a clear indication of discontent as well as an honest request, but the positive stroke gives Sally the benefit of the doubt and does not label her actions as intentional or antagonistic. There is no need to berate her for the infraction of the rule, and the positive stroke may well elicit a positive feeling and response.

5. *Stick to the issue.* Once conversation has begun, it is essential to stick to the issue. This may be hard to do, especially when someone brings up a related point. If that point is truly pertinent to the issue at hand, the discussion may need to be widened. However, no one should be allowed to diffuse or sidetrack the major issue. Left-field issues, since they only muddy the water and forestall resolution of the problem, should immediately be declared off-limits.

When the family gathers to work out a conflict, it is important that everyone participate. The group has come together to listen to each member and to try to understand one another's involvement in the conflict. Each person needs to ask how he or she is contributing to the problem and what can be done individually and collectively to solve it.

6. *Do not bring up the past.* In the heat of an argument, it is tempting to dredge up past hurts and complaints. Some people have a habit of storing all their anger and frustrations rather than dealing with them directly. This is sometimes called gunnysacking. These individuals will unload their past anger and disappointment on others during a fight. The experience of being dumped on is devastating and will, in fact, negate any progress toward conflict resolution.

7. *Do not hit below the belt.* In a fair fight, verbal attacks on areas of personal sensitivity are prohibited. Each of us has emotionally vulnerable areas where even a mild punch would be a shattering blow. Family members generally know each other's sensitive areas. For example, a reference to weight may be a hit below the belt. So too a reference to stinginess. However, some family members are so overly touchy that important issues cannot be addressed without their calling foul. These people wear their belt around their neck!

8. *Take the other seriously.* Ridiculing or laughing at another family member during a fight is inappropriate. Such behavior does not take the other person seriously and sends the message that the other's opinion is worthless, stupid, and not worth considering. This obviously precludes any problem solving.

ARE YOU SURE "DO NOT LET THE SUN GO
DOWN ON YOUR ANGER" IS TO BE TAKEN
LITERALLY?

9. *Express anger nonabusively.* It is important to be reminded that the Bible does not say that anger is a sin. Ephesians 4:26 reads, "Be angry but do not sin; do not let the sun go down on your anger." There are two ways, however, in which our anger can become sin. First, if we deny our anger or hold it in, never expressing it to the one with whom we are angry, it will smolder and build within us. This is allowing the anger to become sin. Unexpressed anger can lead to resentment, hate, and revenge. Second, anger becomes sin when it is expressed in abusive ways, either verbally or physically. Physical abuse is, without doubt, sinful behavior. But it is also true that verbal abuse is psychologically damaging and sinful. The familiar saying, "Sticks and stones may break my bones, but words will never hurt me," is clearly not true, for abusive words certainly do hurt.

A healthy expression of anger includes a clear statement of just how one is feeling. It is important to use the first person. Thus one would say, "*I* am angry because of such and such," rather than, "*You* make me feel so angry!" When we can admit our anger, we take personal responsibility for our feelings rather than blame them on others. The party being addressed is not made to feel defensive or wounded by a personal accusation. Clear first-person statements make it possible for the individuals involved to work together on the behaviors or situations that are contributing to the anger.

10. *Do not play games.* Game playing is a barrier to fair fighting. One of the most common games is to play the martyr. In response to criticism, a person may cry, "I just can't do anything right," or "I guess it's all my fault." Another common game is to feign weakness, inability, or neediness and thus trick others into doing favors. Some family members like to play the "poor me" game or "kick me" game to get sympathy or assistance.

11. *Do not be passively aggressive.* Passive aggressiveness, which aims at getting back at another person in indirect, devious ways, is one of the more effective methods of sabotaging fair fighting. Picture a Sunday morning when Mom and Dad are trying to hurry everyone so the family will not be late for church. Dad has managed to herd everyone to the car except Greg, who happens to be mad at his parents. In response to Dad's call, "Hurry up or you will make all of us late!" Greg very slowly walks to the car, placing one foot in front of the other as if they were made of lead. This is an example of passive aggressiveness—denying one's anger while acting it out in an indirect manner. Since others cannot deal with the anger openly, no resolution is possible, and the anger continues to be acted out in passive ways. The person who behaves in this manner wields a great deal of control in the family.

12. *Avoid asking for explanations of behavior.* Asking others to vindicate themselves is counterproductive in fair fighting. More often than not, such questions are construed as attempts to place blame. It is frequently the case that the person being quizzed cannot give a satisfactory explanation. In this situation it is better to back off from the question and try instead to work on solutions.

13. *Avoid labeling and name calling.* A sure way to antagonize another person and destroy any chance of reasonable discussion is to engage in labeling or name calling. Examples include calling another person stupid, ignorant, silly, dumb, square, childish, spoiled, compulsive, conceited, or some other derogatory adjective. Using such labels traps people in a box or category from which they cannot escape. It is disrespectful and prohibits any serious efforts to deal with the conflict.

14. *Avoid triangles.* Suppose thirteen-year-old Kathy and fifteen-year-old Chad are arguing at the supper table. Kathy turns to her mother for support: "Isn't that so, Mom?" She has just attempted to entangle her mother in the argument she is having with her brother. If the mother is wise, she will not allow herself to be drawn into the argument. It is a common practice for two people who are fighting to attempt to bring in a third party to gain an advantage in the argument. In some homes, this has developed into a fine art that thoroughly disrupts the family.

Now that we have reviewed the basic rules of fair fighting, the question arises: Should parents fight in front of their children? Raise this question with a group of parents, and a variety of answers will be forthcoming. Some parents carefully monitor their disagreements so that their children do not hear the slightest word of conflict between them. Others openly argue with each other even if children who may be emotionally stressed by the conflict are present.

We believe that children should be exposed to fair fighting by their parents. Children learn to accept conflict as a natural part of relationships when they observe their parents in the process of working out their differences. Obviously, it is best when children learn effective ways of resolving conflict. Unfortunately, parents often model ineffective or destructive ways of dealing with conflict. It can be very frightening and unsettling for children to watch their father refuse to talk and angrily walk out of the house in a huff every time he has a disagreement with their mother. Worse still, those children are likely to imitate that behavior in their own disagreements. Keeping all arguments behind closed doors can be equally frightening and disruptive, because children have an uncanny sense of what is happening when in their presence parents give each other the silent treatment. Such behavior can have destructive effects.

We offer two qualifications to our general position that it is healthy for parents to fight in front of their children. (1) The parents must engage in constructive dialogue rather than destructive bickering. (2) Certain matters are strictly personal and should not be shared with the children. Especially when children are very young, it is best not to burden them with financial worries as they may easily misunderstand the nature of the problem. Conflicts concerning sexual matters and other highly personal concerns should, as a rule, be private. However, some of these adult matters may be discussed with the family after the parents have dealt with them satisfactorily. For example, financial difficulties can be openly explained in a way that removes the mystery surrounding problems that children tend to sense and worry about on their own level. Bringing the children in on the problems at an appropriate time allows them to participate and contribute to the problem-solving process.

Conflict Resolution

Conflict resolution is in many ways a systemization of fair fighting under another name. Research on conflict resolution suggests that it is a process that moves through several stages. In applying this research to the family, Kathleen Galvin, Carma Bylund, and Bernard Brommel (2003) identify six stages:

1. *Prior-conditions stage*: the problem arises
2. *Frustration-awareness stage*: a family member comes to realize that satisfaction of some need or concern is being blocked by another family member
3. *Conflict stage*: a series of verbal and nonverbal messages is exchanged
4. *Solution (or nonsolution) stage*: the problem is resolved (or an impasse is agreed on)
5. *Follow-up stage*: the conflict reerupts, or hurt feelings and grudges develop
6. *Resolve stage*: the conflict no longer affects the family system

Although conflict resolution is a worthy goal, it is part of a difficult process. John Oetzel and Stella Ting-Toomey emphasize "constructive conflict management from a communication perspective" (2006, xi) as the key element in conflict resolution.

Conflict Management

While some conflict can be resolved, there are perpetual issues in marriage and family that are never really resolved. In fact, Gottman (1999) found that most marital conflicts are never completely resolved but need to be managed. Therefore, *conflict management* is one of the most realistic approaches to handling conflict (Oetzel and Ting-Toomey 2006). Family life is too complex to be understood in neat cause-and-effect terms. And conflict is so much a part of this system that it cannot be viewed simply as something that arises within and is then purged from the family. Rather, conflict continually feeds back into the system as a whole. It is, therefore, more realistic to think of conflict as a process to be managed rather than a situation to be resolved.

As can be seen in figure 15, there are five major styles of conflict management: (1) Avoidance, which involves a low degree of both cooperation and assertiveness, is characteristic of individuals we might describe as withdrawers. (2) Accommodation, which involves a high degree of cooperation and a low degree of assertiveness, is characteristic of yielders. (3) Competition, which involves a low degree of cooperation and a high degree of assertiveness, is characteristic of winners. (4) Collaboration, which involves a high degree of cooperation and assertiveness, is characteristic of resolvers. (5) Compromise, which involves negotiation, cooperation, and assertiveness, is characteristic of compromisers. It should be noted that these five styles of conflict management are basic theoretical types. In the real world, styles of conflict management can fall at any point in the figure.

FIGURE 15 **Styles of Conflict Management**

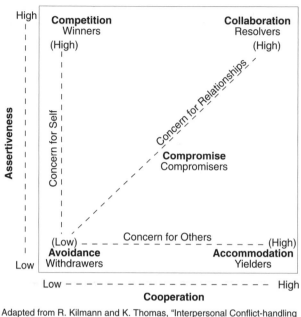

Adapted from R. Kilmann and K. Thomas, "Interpersonal Conflict-handling Behavior as Reflections of Jungian Personality Dimensions," *Psychological Reports* 37 (1975): 971–80; and Joyce Hocker and William Wilmot, *Interpersonal Conflict* (Dubuque, IA: William C. Brown, 1985), 40, 52.

Each style of conflict management entails specific levels of concern for oneself, for other family members, and for family relationships. The style of conflict management that evidences little cooperation and little assertiveness (avoidance) shows little concern for self, others, and relationships. The style with a high degree of cooperation and a low degree of assertiveness (accommodation) shows high concern for others, less concern for relationships, and little concern for self. The competitive approach shows high concern for self, less concern for relationships, and little concern for others. Compromise and collaboration show high concern for relationships and, accordingly, a balanced concern for self and others.

Much research has accumulated in support of the ideas depicted in figure 15. Unfortunately, most of the research has been based on bureaucratic organizations that are larger and far less personal than a family. Two questions need to be asked at this point: (1) Are the data consistent with the biblical view of how to handle conflict? and (2) Are they applicable to family conflict?

In answer to the first question, we believe the data on conflict management to be consistent with what the Bible says about how Christians are to handle conflict. The Bible most directly addresses this issue in Ephesians 4:25–29:

> So then, putting away falsehood, let all of us speak the truth to our neighbors, for we are members of one another. Be angry but do not sin; do not let the sun go down on your anger, and do not make room for the devil. . . . Let no evil talk come out of your mouths, but only what is useful for building up, as there is need, so that your words may give grace to those who hear.

Contained in these verses is support for being assertive. We are told that when there is conflict, we should speak truthfully about it. The implication is not to withdraw ("Do not let the sun go down on your anger") or become aggressive ("Be angry but do not sin. . . . Let no evil talk come out of your mouths"). The text lends support to a direct confrontational style that shows concern for self, the other, and the relationship.

The verses also point toward cooperation as the ideal for Christians—we should speak the truth because "we are members of one another." If there is anything that should be characteristic of the body of Christ, it is a spirit of cooperation and collaboration. First Corinthians 12:12 reiterates this idea, "For just as the body is one and has many members, and all the members of the body, though many, are one body, so it is with Christ." We believe that the Bible stresses both assertiveness and cooperation. The best way to deal with conflict is a collaborative style with equal concern for self, the other, and the relationship.

How well do the data on conflict management fit the family? One way of answering this question is to examine how closely they fit with our theological model of family relationships. This model began with an emphasis on a two-way covenant commitment. The data on conflict management similarly stress the need to be concerned with both self and others. Second, just as an atmosphere of grace is essential to our theological model, reciprocal forgiving is an essential part of fruitful conflict management. Third, collaboration can be viewed as a type of mutual empowering, as two people work together toward common goals. The fourth phase in our model is intimacy, which entails compassionate caring for one another. In conflict management, likewise, there is an emphasis on concern for the self, the other, and the relationship.

While we have argued that the social-science evidence on styles of conflict management is consistent with the biblical view, we also believe that different situations call for different styles. It is unhelpful to suggest that one style is inherently superior to another. We believe there are times when it is appropriate to take the part of a withdrawer; at other times it is appropriate to be a winner, a yielder, or a compromiser. When one style is the dominant or the only way an individual can react in conflictive situations, it inhibits creative responses. Thus, the husband who always withdraws or the wife who always yields in a marital conflict makes it very difficult to deal with the conflict openly and adequately. They each need to adjust their styles so they can resolve the matter.

Each style of handling conflict has both advantages and disadvantages and, depending on the situation, may be more or less appropriate. As we discuss each style, we will give an example from the life of Jesus to show that he used that style. He was, variously, a withdrawer, a winner, a compromiser, a yielder, and a resolver.

Withdrawers. Although avoidance was not Jesus's usual style, at times he did withdraw. When he healed the man with the shriveled hand on the Sabbath, he greatly angered the Pharisees, who "conspired against him, how to destroy him" (Matt. 12:14). Jesus surely could have confronted the Pharisees, as he had on other occasions. But instead, when he became aware of the Pharisees' plotting, he departed (v. 15). There was a similar reaction during the final hours before his arrest, when Jesus anticipated the upcoming conflict. As he and his disciples went to the Mount of Olives, he said to them, "'Pray that you may not come into the time of trial.' Then he withdrew from them about a stone's throw, knelt down, and prayed" (Luke 22:39–41). We are also told in Luke 5:15–16 that when crowds of people pressed on him with their needs for healing, Jesus would withdraw to deserted places to pray.

There will be times when family members need to withdraw from a conflict to think more clearly about the issue. Sometimes emotions of anger run so high that conflict resolution is impossible. There are other times when trivial conflicts need to be set aside for the sake of more pressing family matters. Avoidance can be destructive, however, so the person who withdraws for a time needs to be accountable by promising to come back to deal with the conflict after taking the needed break. In the absence of such a promise, withdrawing sends a signal that the individual does not care enough to work out conflicts.

Winners. At times Jesus adopted the approach of a winner. This can most clearly be seen in Matthew 21:12–13: "Then Jesus entered the temple area and drove out all who were selling and buying in the temple, and he overturned the tables of the money changers and the seats of those who sold doves. He said to them, 'It is written, "My house shall be called a house of prayer"; but you are making it a den of robbers.'" In this situation there was no yielding, withdrawing, or compromising. Rather, Jesus acted authoritatively and decisively. The reason for this action, as Matthew makes clear, was that the law of the Lord was being violated.

There will be times when family members disagree on the basis of their principles and assume that the family is strong enough to survive the competition. The danger here is that the real issue may get lost in the battle over principles, and the conflict may degenerate to a personal level at which each party feels the need to win the point to save face. Such competition between family members escalates rather than decreases conflict. It takes a strong family system to survive. Winners often win the battle (the point) but lose the war (the relationship) in the process.

Compromisers. We tend not to see Jesus as a compromiser. Yet when the Pharisees sought to trap him by asking if it was right to pay taxes to Caesar, Jesus replied, "Give therefore to the emperor the things that are the emperor's, and to God the things that are God's" (Matt. 22:21).

Compromise can be the best way to handle conflict when there is inadequate time to work out a collaborative effort. When used too often, however, compromise is too easy an out, leaving all family members less than satisfied. Some family conflicts can be handled best by compromise, such as disagreements about when to serve the evening meal, where to go on vacation, and what television programs to watch. On other issues, compromise is not the best solution. For example, the Kakimotos are planning to move to a different region of the country. Annette wants to live in the heart of the city, where they both will work, while Duane wants to find a twenty-acre plot of land in a rural area some distance from the city. To compromise by living in the suburbs would leave both spouses unhappy. They will need to work together toward a resolution that will afford both of them the essential advantages they are seeking. It will take some creative thought to find such a solution.

Yielders. In the greatest conflict Jesus had to experience in his life on earth, he yielded himself to be arrested, falsely convicted, and finally crucified. His yielding is evident in the account of his arrest in Matthew 26:50–53. After Jesus had been arrested, one of his companions struck the servant of the high priest and cut off his ear. At that point Jesus stepped forward saying: "Put your sword back into its place; for all who take the sword will perish by the sword. Do you think that I cannot appeal to my Father, and he will at once send me more than twelve legions of angels?" (vv. 52–53).

Yielding may be appropriate when an issue is far more important to one family member than to the others or when it threatens a relationship. Yielding can also be a self-giving act of putting another person's wishes ahead of one's own. However, when yielding is motivated by a desire to show others how self-sacrificing one is, it can be a form of manipulation. Similarly, yielding out of a fear of rejection or a need to be liked can be detrimental. Yielding to another may also not be in the best interest of that person. The parent who gives in to a child's demands for more candy or wish to stay up late may be doing the child a disservice.

Resolvers. During his earthly ministry, Jesus elicited strong reactions. Toward those who reacted against him, such as the scribes, priests, and Pharisees, Jesus assumed a confrontive style. Toward those who reacted positively, he assumed a collaborative style, which can best be seen in his long-term commitment to his disciples.

Since family relationships are long-term commitments, most family conflicts can best be dealt with through collaboration. The advantage of this style is that it offers maximum satisfaction to everyone. The disadvantage is that collaboration takes a lot of time, effort, and emotional energy. It also affords a family member who is verbally skilled the advantage. In conflicts between siblings, the elder may be able to manipulate the younger one into the worse end of a deal. Five-year-old Carol may be able to resolve a conflict by offering three-year-old Eddie five big nickels for his four small dimes.

In general, family systems benefit from having at least one resolver around who will see to it that conflicts are not swept under the rug. The resolver is often very intense in working through conflicts and will be frustrated when others do not cooperate or have the same amount of determination to settle things. There may be family disruption if the resolver is unable to rest until there is closure on an issue. When the resolver pursues the issue too intently, the others will distance themselves and intimacy will be impaired.

Each one of the five styles of handling conflict will prove, at one time or another, to be the most appropriate. It is imperative, then, that family members not get locked into any one particular style and thus lose their flexibility and capacity for finding creative solutions.

At the systemic level each particular combination of different types of styles produces its own chemistry and problems. Picture, for instance, a marriage between Barb, a resolver, and Mike, a withdrawer. This type of marital system, in which one partner pursues and the other withdraws, can turn into a cat-and-mouse game. Each partner's style may also be reinforcing the style of the other and thus perpetuating the imbalance in the relationship. The more she pursues, the more he withdraws, and vice versa. It is inevitable, of course, that every individual will tend to use the style learned in his or her family of origin. The challenge is to expand one's horizon and to consider the possibility of using other styles, giving up the tendency to always select the style that comes naturally. To return to our example: Barb may get further if she stops pursuing and persuading. If she is able to relax and let go of some of her intensity, Mike may well take more initiative and work with her toward conflict resolution.

One can only imagine the dynamics when a yielder is married to a winner, a winner to a winner, a compromiser to a yielder, and so on. Add to this the various styles of all the individual members of the family, and there is an even greater challenge. The more complicated the situation, the greater the need to be flexible and responsive to different ways of dealing with conflict.

To this point we have considered individual styles of conflict management. This has been necessary because individual family members differ in the ways they handle conflict. Family conflict must be understood, however, as involving not only the individual members but also the entire family system. Consider, for example, how conflict management in a disengaged family might be different from conflict management in an enmeshed family. Or consider the difference between rigid and chaotic families.

In disengaged families the bonding between members may be so weak that there is little direct confrontation when conflict arises. Conflict is most likely dealt with by ignoring it and hoping it will go away. In the highly enmeshed family it is impossible for conflict to involve just two family members. The whole family is so intertwined that every member is quickly drawn into the conflict. By contrast, a healthy approach to conflict is most likely found in families that are moderately cohesive, possessing a balance of separateness and connectedness.

In rigid families, patterns of behavior and communication are fixed, meaning that there is little room for negotiation or a search for creative solutions when conflict arises. Conflict is likely to be handled through the existing power structure, with those who have the greatest power either dictating to or manipulating the others.

In chaotic families, the system is so unstructured that family life is an endless series of shifting negotiations and rearrangements. Given the lack of structure and basic ground rules, there is little possibility that conflict will be handled well. Living in a chaotic family is like playing in a baseball game in which each team has its own set of rules. One team considers three strikes an out, and the other two. For one team a fly ball caught in foul territory is an out; for the other it is merely a strike. One team permits the runner to lead off base before the pitch; the other team does not. The problem in chaotic families is not that communication is cut off but that there is little possibility of finding a solution since there are so many different ways of playing the game.

By contrast, family systems that are moderately adaptable are best able to handle conflict. They have both the needed structure and the flexibility to successfully negotiate disputes.

Family systems, as well as individual family members, develop styles for dealing with conflict. Families that are inclined to avoidance rarely deal with their conflicts. Families with a competitive style may be a little better off, because they at least talk about their conflicts. While families with an accommodating style may appear to be healthy, there may also be many unexpressed personal wishes, opinions, and needs that go unfulfilled.

At times the needs of the family will be met at the expense of the needs of individual family members; at other times the needs of the individuals will be met at the expense of the needs of the family. Families characterized by compromise and collaboration are the most successful in balancing the needs of individual family members with the needs of the family as a whole. Healthy families also have the combined strengths of flexibility and structure, separateness and connectedness, as well as open and clear channels of communication that permit them to alter their approach to fit the situation.

PART 6

THE SOCIAL DYNAMICS OF FAMILY LIFE

IN THIS SECTION we turn our attention to the social dynamics of family life. Power within the family, stress, and divorce will be the major topics of concern.

Working out the issue of power in family relationships is a difficult process. In chapter 15 we will examine different types of power as well as where power should reside and how it should be exercised in family life. We argue that empowerment, that is, the use of power to enable all family members to realize their potential, is the biblical prescription.

Family stress is the topic addressed in chapter 16. Every family encounters stress in one form or another. We present a model for understanding stress and demonstrate how family members can work together to solve problems and cope with catastrophes. Christian beliefs and values are crucial resources in times of family stress, providing hope in the midst of despair.

Divorce is a stressful time for families. The high divorce rate in America means that millions will experience the pain and loss that divorce entails. Some of the factors that contribute to this breakdown in family life are discussed in chapter 17. We address the effects of divorce on both the couple and the children, concluding this chapter with a discussion of the single-parent family. Chapter 18 is devoted to complex families in contemporary society that are a result of remarriage and the blending of families into reconstituted families. We conclude with a plea for compassion for those family members who attempt to rebuild their lives, noting that Christianity offers the survivors of divorce the hope of restoration and renewal.

269

15

BECOMING POWERFUL
THROUGH EMPOWERMENT

ONE OF THE strongest human tendencies is the will to dominate, to
be in control not only of oneself but also of others. Consequently,
power is a dimension found in all human relationships. Our desire for
power undoubtedly stems from the basic self-centeredness that is a part
of our human creatureliness. In formal organizations such as businesses,
schools, and government agencies, power is clearly charted in elaborate
hierarchies. In informal and impersonal relationships, such as interaction with a sales clerk, power is more ambiguous and perhaps less important. In intimate relationships between family members, however, a
power system is present and operative even if it has not been formally
established or is not officially recognized by the family. The concept of
power is important to an understanding of family relationships.

Although many dimensions of the use of power within the family
have been researched (Allen et al. 2001; Hsiung and Bagozzi 2003), the
concept of empowerment, which we introduced in chapter 1, seems
to have been neglected. One notable exception is an article directed
to marital therapists on how to help a couple construct a narrative of
shared relational and position power (Blanton 2001). The purpose of
this chapter is to explore the distribution of power within the family and
the effects of empowerment.

Power is the ability of one person to influence or to have an effect on another person's behavior. Rightly understood, power is actually the capacity to influence and not the exercising of that capacity (Levine and Boster 2001). A person may have a very powerful influence, for example, but choose not to exercise it directly. In fact, such an individual often does not need to act in order to be influential, for others have come to trust that he or she has their best interests at heart. The result is responsiveness, a willingness to be influenced and empowered.

We will see that power is a dynamic process operating in both marriage and parent/child relationships. Power in the marriage relationship is an especially timely topic because of the shift in marital authority. Our society has been moving from a patriarchal system, in which the man is head, to an egalitarian system, in which husband and wife exercise power as partners.

Power in the parent/child relationship is also an important issue. The tensions between parenting responsibilities and the child's differentiation process occurs throughout the stages of growth. Battles often erupt over when parents should relinquish power as their children become empowered to make their own decisions.

Since the dawn of history, there have been power struggles between family members. The first was the rebellion of Adam and Eve against God. And in the first recorded act of aggression, Cain killed his brother Abel out of jealousy. These power struggles remind us of the distortion that occurs in all relationships as a result of the fall. Genesis speaks of the husband dominating his wife and an enmity between them resulting from sin. What God had ordained and created to be perfect became broken and distorted. However, the message of restoration and renewal is seen throughout the Old and New Testaments. Through the power of the resurrection and the empowering of the Holy Spirit, God has provided a way for us to lead lives of mutual empowerment and service. We are called to the building up of others; this is the task and privilege of the empowering process.

Types of Power

Authority and Dominance

One reason there is so much confusion surrounding the issue of power in the family is that power can be conceptualized in several ways. One of the most important ways to categorize it is on the basis of its legitimacy. Simply put, legitimate power is authority, and illegitimate power is dominance. The person whose power is sanctioned by society possesses authority. For example, most societies grant parents authority over their children until the children reach the age of majority. Although the age of majority differs from culture to culture and even from state to state, parental power is regarded as legitimate by most societies.

Dominance, however, is power that has not been sanctioned by society but, instead, is taken without consensus. It is, therefore, illegitimate power. For example, some parents and some spouses go beyond the boundaries of legitimate power given them by society. Society then makes a second judgment, and people who are guilty of child neglect or spouse abuse are (at least in an ideal situation) denied further exercise of the legitimate power originally granted to them.

In addition to societal sanction, authority is based on valued resources. In the absence of power, a person may resort to intimidation or brute force in an attempt to influence. The power-through-intimidation approach advocates that an individual without skills and resources can gain power by intimidating others. Clever tricks are suggested: dressing in a certain manner to enhance one's image, controlling the situation by meeting people on one's own turf (i.e., in one's own office), purposely making others wait a few minutes for an appointment, or prearranging with a secretary to interrupt the meeting so that the guest sees how important and powerful one is. These manipulations are designed to give one the upper hand.

The empowering model we have in mind is the direct opposite. By building others up and valuing who they are and what they contribute to the situation and relationship, family members achieve mutual respect. Parents who have the respect of their children have legitimate power (authority) and influence. Parents who do not have the respect of their children often resort to force and coercion (dominance).

In some societies, legitimate parental power is acquired merely by becoming parents. Such power is ascribed on the basis of one's position. It is not earned but is merely possessed because one has a given status in society.

Other societies hold a democratic view of parent/child relationships. Here the mere fact of being a parent does not automatically guarantee legitimate parental power. The possession of resources is an important condition of parental power. Such resources as wisdom; love; nurturing skills; and the ability to provide food, clothing, and shelter, when recognized and valued by children, are the basis of parental power. Such power is achieved rather than ascribed. Power is not an automatic given with parenthood; parents must prove worthy through their faithful behaviors and loving actions toward their children.

Traditionally, in rural societies power is ascribed; in modern urban societies it is much more likely to be achieved. Accordingly, most of the power exercised today has been earned. It is the reward for behaving in ways that are respected and trusted by others. Obviously, there are positions of power in any society that are assigned on the basis of status, but people in these positions must prove their worth if they are to keep their power.

Orchestrative Power and Implemental Power

Another way of categorizing power is to distinguish between orchestrative power and implemental power. Orchestrative power involves making decisions and delegating responsibilities to others. Implemental power involves carrying out those decisions made and responsibilities delegated by the one who has orchestrative power.

In some families headed by the husband, it may seem that the wife actually wields most of the power and makes the more important decisions. However, she may simply have implemental power that was delegated to her by her husband, who has orchestrated her role and duties. In reality, he is still the seat of power.

There appears to be an inverse relationship between how powerful one is and how active one must be in order to be influential. A really powerful person can be influential without trying to be, while a less powerful person has to work very hard to be influential. For instance, some parents need speak a request only once and their children obey, whereas others must raise their voices and bark out a series of threats to bring about compliance.

Power must be understood from a systemic perspective. The individual who appears to make the important decisions is not necessarily the most powerful person in the family. There may be a hidden power in the system or a silent delegation of power. Laura Flurry and Alvin Burns (2005) utilized *social power* theory to understand how children both actively and passively influence family decision making. The smallest child can use disruptive behavior to influence the whole family system. For example, a well-timed temper tantrum can be a powerful distractor, making the family ineffectual.

It is important that parents be clearly in charge and responsible for the family. When they are not, chaos abounds. In effective family systems, the parents are united and take on the executive function. Single parents need to take on this role as well.

Parental authority does not mean that the children should not be involved in problem solving and decision making. Empowering parents listen to, understand, and value the points of view of each family member. They then incorporate these views so that the family works together for a satisfactory solution or decision.

Table 7

Models of Family Power

	Basic Assumption
Traditional Patriarchal	God has determined that ultimate power resides in the role of the husband.
Democratic Exchange	Power does not reside in any one individual, but rather in the family as a whole operating as a democracy.
Hedonistic Self-Interest	Each family member watches out for self.
Empowerment	Family members use their gifts and resources for one another.

Basic Models of Family Power

There are four basic models of family power (see table 7). The patriarchal model has been dominant in the past. However, changing social conditions, such as women working outside the home combined with the spread of individualistic and democratic ideals, have led to the emergence of the democratic-exchange model. The power in most American families today probably reflects a combination of the traditional patriarchal and the democratic-exchange model. The hedonistic self-interest model is an unfortunate result of hyperindividualistic emphasis, which characterizes contemporary societies. The empowering model embodies biblical principles.

The Patriarchal Model

The patriarchal model operates in many societies today. John Zipp, Ariane Prohaska, and Michelle Bemiller (2004) found that even wives who earned more money than their husbands were more likely than husbands to agree with their spouse's decisions, a phenomenon these researchers call "the invisible power of men" (p. 933). Ideological justifications that attempt to go beyond mere cultural tradition usually defend the patriarchal model as being God's intent. The man has been placed in the position of headship for the sake of resolving disagreements in the family.

In some extreme cultural versions of the traditional patriarchal family, the husband has dictatorial rule, ordering his wife and children around as he sees fit. In versions that have been tempered with Christianity, his rule is usually more of a benevolent dictatorship. In the most authoritarian of Christian versions, the father is placed just below God in a chain of command extending downward to the mother and then the child. The father is in a position of absolute power over his wife and children. Children are to submit to both father and mother, the wife is to submit to her husband, and the husband is to submit to God. Noticeably absent are the concepts of mutual submission and the suffering-servant role modeled by Christ (Phil. 2:5–8). In less authoritarian Christian versions of the patriarchal model, the husband is seen as head of his wife as Christ is head of the church; in this case, the husband is to emulate Christ's role as the Suffering Servant. The husband remains head in that he is expected to make decisions and assign responsibilities.

The Democratic-Exchange Model

The democratic-exchange model, which has emerged in recent years, is based less on the notion of ascribed power than on the assumption that power resides in the family unit as a whole. The notion that power resides in one individual on the basis of his position is rejected. Family policy is determined by negotiation and bargaining. The exercise of power is understood as a balance between the democratic ideal of each family member having an equal voice and the reality that parents have more resources with which to bargain and negotiate for power. Therefore, parents have the final say in the decision-making process.

The issue of family power is much more complex in the democratic-exchange model than in the traditional patriarchal model, where power is ascribed. Achievement rather than ascription determines who has power. Power in the democratic-exchange model can best be analyzed in terms of its bases, processes, and outcomes (see figure 16). Analysis of the bases of power is most relevant to our purposes.

In the democratic-exchange model, every family member gets a hearing and is very much a part of the decision-making process. Power is still determined, however, by the distribution of resources within the family. The types of resources that can be converted into power are many and varied, differing according to the specific needs of family members. The most obvi-

FIGURE 16 **An Analysis of Family Power**

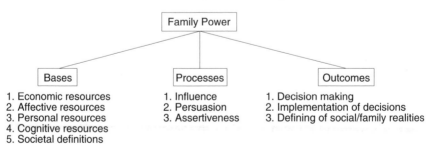

Adapted from Gerald McDonald, "Family Power: The Assessment of a Decade of Theory and Research, 1970–1979," *Journal of Marriage and the Family* 42 (1980): 844.

ous type of resource that can be converted into power is economic. Being without their own economic resources, children are dependent on their parents and are thus less powerful in deciding matters involving money. When children are employed outside the home, they experience a new independence and become more powerful as a result. Likewise, a wife who does not earn money outside the home has less power than her husband, who is the sole financial contributor to the family. Research demonstrates, on the contrary, that wives who work outside the home experience an increase in power and input into decision making (Yount 2005).

But family members have needs that go far beyond the economic. Therefore, resources can come in the form of emotional nurturing, support, protection, and the like. Some couples are fairly equal in power not because both make equal economic contributions to the marriage but because one has the ability to provide the affection and nurturing that the other needs.

If the family values certain natural endowments, such as physical appearance, musical ability, athletic prowess, intelligence, or manual skills, those children who possess or develop these gifts (resources) will become powerful. In some cases, power may be diverted to a child who is sick or acting out as a way to focus attention away from other family problems. For example, if the marriage relationship is disrupted, the children have an uncanny way of diverting attention from the marital problem to themselves. Everyone feels more secure when distracted from the possibility of divorce, which threatens the entire family system.

The Self-Interest Model

The individualistic and materialistic values of modern society have led to self-interested hedonism. In family life, as in mass society, everyone watches out for number one. Personal interests and needs come before any collective interests or needs of the larger system. This philosophy is not characteristic of cultures that highly value the extended family.

In families that adopt the self-interest model, everyone vies for a place of authority. Cooperation is incidental; family members work together only as a way of getting personal needs met. These homes are often chaotic because individualistic thinking separates members rather than bringing them together for the good of the whole. This tends to disengage members, since there is little mutual support among them.

Empowerment

Our last model of family power is empowerment. It assumes that the task of the more powerful family members is to enable the less powerful family members. Even though empowerment is rarely recognized in the sociological literature, we believe it is exemplified in Christian family life at its best.

The Basic Nature of Empowerment

The concept of empowering involves the use of power. Most research on the use of power has focused on attempts to influence or control the behavior of others. The underlying assumption has been that people who use power are not seeking to increase the power of the person(s) whom they are trying to influence. Rather, they use power to ensure the maintenance of their own more powerful position. Although we do not deny that many uses of power are motivated by this selfish inclination, we also believe that power is best defined as building up others.

Empowering may be described as an attempt to develop power in another person. As we have already noted in chapter 1, empowering does not necessarily involve yielding to the wishes of another person or giving up one's own power to someone else. Rather, empowering is the active and intentional process of helping another person become powerful. The person who is empowered has gained power because of the encouragement of the other. There is an interactive process between the two.

One of secular literature's rare recognitions of empowering can be found in Rollo May's classic book *Love and Will* (1969). He identifies five types of power: (1) exploitative—influence by brute force; (2) manipulative—influence by devious sociopsychological means; (3) competitive—influence based on the possession and use of personal resources; (4) nutritive—influence such as that of a parent on a child (this power eventually outlives its usefulness); and (5) integrative—the use of personal power for another's sake. What May calls integrative power is clearly what we refer to as empowering. May points to Jesus and Gandhi as examples of people who used integrative power. In stating his central message, Jesus said, "I came that they might have life, and have it abundantly" (John 10:10). Gandhi maintained that the goal of his nonviolent resistance was to empower not only the oppressed but also the oppressor.

Another recognition of empowering is found in Maximiliane Szinovacz's (1987) brief discussion of family power and the construction of family members' self-images. Building on previous descriptions of power as the potential for shaping another person's identity and self-concept (McLain and Weigert 1979), Szinovacz interprets this shaping of another's self-image as an attempt to impose one's own values. One way to develop another's self-concept is to tell that individual not what to be but who and what he or she is. Szinovacz concludes: "It would seem essential that family power researchers pay more attention to such control situ-

I SOMETIMES THINK THIS EMPOWERING THING
GETS TO BE A LITTLE ONE-SIDED AT TIMES.

ations. If A is able to shape and modify O's identity and self-concept, his/her control is likely to extend to a broad range of behaviors, to be long-lasting, and to involve relatively few costs since O is made to believe that [A] acts in [O's] own interests" (p. 683).

The socialization of children has been described as the process of getting them to want to do what they have to do. From this perspective, empowering can be understood as the process whereby external control (the wishes of the more powerful, e.g., the parent) is transferred into internal control (the child actually wants to do what the parent desires). One is left with the impression that empowering is selfishly motivated. At best it is a type of paternalistic pronouncement: "You may think you know what is best for you, but I really know what is best, and I'll see to it that you come to feel that way also." This is an inadequate view of empowering.

Another inadequate view is the perception that power is in limited supply. Most analyses of the use of power are based on such an assumption. Social-exchange theory, for instance, is based on the belief that there is a set number of power units available in any relationship. Thus power in marriage may be represented as 100 units to be divided between the husband and the wife. Now the husband may have all the power (100 units) and the wife none (0 units), or the wife may have slightly more power (60 units) than the husband (40 units), or (in the egalitarian marriage) 50 units may be allocated to each spouse. In this scenario one spouse must command at least 51 power units to be in a position of control.

In promoting the ideal of empowerment, the Bible disproves the view that power is in limited supply. The message of the Bible is that the power of God is available to all human beings in unlimited amounts. Thus the family member who empowers benefits another and at the same time will be benefited in the very act of empowering. Empowered family members mutually build up one another. Therefore, increasing another person's power does not decrease one's own but, instead, multiplies one's potential for further empowering.

Empowerment as a Component of Utopian Societies

A virtually unanimous finding of sociological studies is that humans use power as a means to suppress and control others. The most effective instruments of suppression and control are social structures, leading to the suggestion that much of human history can best be understood as a record of domination built on classism, racism, and sexism.

As a dominant group begins to use power, reification takes place; the rule of the powerful comes to be regarded as justifiable and is incorporated into ideology. The subordinate group is no longer considered oppressed but is seen as rightfully subject to the rule of the powerful because of inequality in abilities. Any attempt at building a utopian society must deal with the problem of inequality. It is noteworthy that two originators of utopian ideologies, Jesus Christ and Karl Marx, incorporated the practice of empowering into their image of an ideal society.

What Jesus taught about power was so central to his mission that it serves as an ideal for all human relationships. To the request of James and John that they be permitted to sit on his right and left hand in glory, Jesus replied, "But whoever wishes to become great among you must be your servant, and whoever wishes to be first among you must be slave of all. For the Son of Man came not to be served but to serve, and to give his life a ransom for many" (Mark 10:43–45). By his teachings and life, Jesus redefined power. He rejected the use of power to control others and instead affirmed the use of power to serve others, to lift up the fallen, to forgive, to encourage responsibility and maturity, and to enable the unable.

The relationship of Jesus to his disciples is a perfect example of empowering, which extended even beyond his ascension. When preparing his disciples for his leaving, Jesus encouraged them by promising that the Holy Spirit would come to comfort and help them accomplish their ministry (John 16). Later he assured them, "But you will receive power when the Holy Spirit has come upon you" (Acts 1:8).

It is worth noting the type of community the disciples developed after Jesus's departure. Acts 2:44–45 states: "All who believed were together and had all things in common; they would sell their possessions and goods and distribute the proceeds to all, as any had need." They took seriously Jesus's message of servanthood and mutually gave up the very resources on which conventional power is based, for Jesus had modeled a power that served rather than controlled others.

Although an avowed enemy of religion, Marx, like Jesus, found it necessary to radically alter the conventional definition of power. Marx believed that the traditional use of power is, in fact, exploitation and results in an abuse, namely, private ownership of property. Marx's solution was amazingly similar to that of the early Christians: own all things in common and give to each according to his or her needs.

Marx held that in a property-based society, people inevitably seek to use power to control, but in his utopian society they would use power to build up one another. The Marxist slogan of "power to the people," rightly understood, involves empowering. In Marx's view, this empowering must begin among the underclass (proletariat) in the form of consciousness raising and will end only when all members of society are part of a classless whole.

Given the competitive economic system of our society, it is not surprising that power within the family is usually exercised as a self-centered social exchange. But the time has come to realize that such perception of how power is to be used is debilitating. As Szinovacz (1987, 682) suggests, "To avoid interpretations that 'eternalize' present societal constraints, we may further profit from in-depth analyses of couples or families who have themselves, at least to some extent, transcended these constrictions."

Empowerment in the Family

We believe there is something fundamentally wrong with the way in which power is typically used in the contemporary family. The social-exchange theory was originally proposed because it seemed to explain the way in which family members utilize power—the aim is to maximize personal rewards and minimize personal costs. However, the social-exchange theory has become reified and has come to represent what is considered the ideal way for families to operate. This is unfortunate because a view emphasizing that power is to be used to control ultimately prevents family members from reaching their full potential. We propose empowering as the model for the use of power in family life. Empowering transcends the oppressive effects of racism, classism, and sexism.

As a model for marriage, the concept of empowering transcends the regressive approach inherent in a system of social exchange. Every couple begins marriage with similar and dissimilar (complementary) resources and skills. In a hedonistic, self-oriented relationship, each partner jealously guards personal resources, attempts to accumulate more power, and in the process keeps the other person dependent. In an empowering relationship, each partner's primary concern is how best to build up and encourage the other to reach his or her potential.

Under the traditional patriarchal system, servanthood was expected only from the wife; the husband assumed the position of master. In an effort to do away with this type of oppression, our society has too often opted for self-centered marriages in which both partners seek to be master and want to be served by the other. An even more radical change is needed: both spouses must devote themselves to empowering and serving each other.

Marital empowering can be direct, such as when spouses share a skill, expertise, information, or abilities with each other. One partner teaches the other how to cook, how to read a map, how to interact socially, how to balance a checkbook, or how to share feelings openly. The aim is to help each other overcome personal deficiencies that may be keeping the other person dependent. It may be that personal resources are gained through education or specialized training. Whatever the means, family members are encouraged to be all they can be.

The goal of empowering within marriage could conceivably be construed as bringing two people with different skills and abilities to the point where they are mirror images of each other. This would be a mistake since God gives different gifts to different people. Moreover, part of the complementary quality of the marital relationship is the ability to appreciate and enhance each other's gifts. Empowering means not that each partner's strength must be duplicated in the other but that there is a willingness to build up the other and a commitment not to control or keep the other dependent.

With regard to empowering, cross-cultural research indicates that women are more likely than men to use their resources for the good of the family as a whole. While men spend a large share of their earnings on themselves, women spend more of their earnings for the welfare of their children than for personal pleasure (Blumberg 1991). This is yet another indication that male power is used to dominate women in marriage. We suggest that society adopt two changes that would promote marital empowerment between men and women. First is the adoption of an ideological structure that would allow men and women equal access to the valued resources of power. While most models have concentrated on resources within the family, we believe it is equally important for men and women to have equal access to resources in the wider community. When men are affirmed and awarded power for their nurturing ability, and women are affirmed and awarded power for their intellectual ability, there is potential for radical change.

Second, the social conditions that predispose people to seek to control rather than to empower must be challenged. In societies in which women are kept in a subordinate position, boys and girls grow up considering it normative for men to control and women to be controlled. To break this pattern, children need to see models in which mutual empowerment is the norm (Balswick and Balswick 1994).

Since chapter 6 offers an in-depth discussion of parental empowering of children, we will make only a few additional comments here. Trust is a key component of the empowering process. Parents who do not trust their children seek to maintain control over them. The trust that parents place in their children encourages the children to be trustworthy; in time they also learn to trust themselves and others. A child who does not experience trust will most likely develop a negative self-image—"I am a person who can't be trusted." Of course, circumstances may work out the other way: children may abuse the trust. When this happens, parents need to be mindful of the faithfulness of God. Despite the repeated failings of the children of Israel, God remained faithful, longing for them to come back of their own accord and grasp what it means to be empowered through a relationship with their creator God. The heavenly Father refused to be a controlling parent; desiring his children to grow to spiritual maturity, God demonstrated persistent and persuasive actions of love. The hope was that one day the children would understand that the Ten Commandments were meant to empower them to live life in rightful relationship.

16

THROUGH THE STRESS AND STRAIN
OF FAMILY LIFE

A NY GROUP WHOSE members have a strong attachment to one another, interact on a regular basis, and go through various changes
together can expect to experience stress. The family is such a group.
Family stress can be defined simply as an upset in the regular routine
of the family and can vary from a minor irritation over someone's being
late for dinner to a major crisis, such as the death of a family member.
Moreover, similar events can trigger completely different reactions in
different families and their members. What may seem a minor irritation
in one family can be major in another. It's also the case that families
handle stressful situations differently.

When not dealt with effectively, family strain can have an accumulative destructive impact. For instance, it has been found that many
parents who abuse their children were themselves the victims of abuse
when they were growing up. Although this finding does not excuse the
abusive behavior, it drives home the point that unresolved feelings of
powerlessness in parents can take a secondary toll on their children
(Holden and Banez 1996).

A Model for Understanding Family Stress

Attempts to study family stress can be traced back to the Depression
of the 1930s and World War II, when millions of fathers were separated

from their families. Reuben Hill (1949) proposes that family stress can best be analyzed by considering the interaction of three factors: (1) the stressful event itself; (2) the resources or strengths that a family possesses at the time the event occurs; and (3) the family's perception of the event. In a sense, the event itself (the war) is the necessary cause but is not sufficient in and of itself to cause family stress. For example, if the alcoholic father is a source of tension in the home, his separation from the family may be perceived as a relief. This is especially true if the mother has sufficient resources to carry out the functions usually performed by the father.

Most models of family stress elaborate Hill's seminal work about how these three factors interact. A good overview of these models can be found in chapters 9 and 10 of *Family Communication* (Segrin and Flora 2005). The major refinement in these models has been an endeavor to understand the coping abilities of the family when it is confronted by a stressful event. This has placed the focus on the family's recoverability instead of its troubles and on the family's resources instead of the crisis itself. A model of family stress that focuses more on the effects of serious individual trauma on the family, such as death, murder, or terrorism, can be found in two books by Don Catherall: *Handbook of Stress, Trauma, and the Family* (2004) and *Family Stress: Interventions for Stress and Trauma* (2005).

Stressful Events

Before we consider how families cope, it is important to gain an understanding of the various types of stressful events that affect most families. A major distinction can be made between predictable events (usually transitions to new stages in family life) and unpredictable events (unexpected and unplanned events). Happy and anticipated events can also be stressful (weddings, births, adoptions, forming new families, leaving home, etc.) because they usher in emotional and physical changes that must be dealt with. Although it is true that the predictability of an event does not eliminate stress, families can make the needed effort to prepare for changes. Transitions in family life not only change each member, but the family itself also changes with the entrance and exit of members. The family, a system of maturing and changing individuals, is challenged by these events. The stress generated by the family system causes stress to individuals, and likewise the strains on individuals introduce tension into the family system.

Among the unexpected events that have such a devastating impact on families are environmental disasters such as floods, hurricanes, fires, famines, and earthquakes, as well as societal afflictions such as war, ter-

Table 8

Stressful Events

	Level of Stress
1. Death of a spouse	100
2. Divorce	73
3. Marital separation	65
4. Detention in jail or other institution	63
5. Death of a close family member	63
6. Major personal injury or illness	53
7. Marriage	50
8. Being fired	47
9. Marital reconciliation	45
10. Retirement	45
11. Major change in the health or behavior of a family member	44
12. Pregnancy	40

rorism, and economic depression. Individual families have little control over such adversities. These unexpected disasters take a great toll because families and communities are powerless against them. Help is needed from outside sources on a national and international level.

There are various ways to classify stressful events: maturational/situational, usual/unusual, developmental/environmental, or volitional/nonvolitional. We ask questions such as: Do they originate inside or outside the family? Are they chronic or acute? Mild or severe? Isolated or cumulative? (Boss 1987, 699). These categories help to clarify the situation, but we need a better understanding of family dynamics in coping with stress.

In a study of experiences that disrupt life (Holmes and Rahe 1967), forty-three stress-producing events were ranked on a scale from 0 to 100, with a score of 100 representing the greatest amount of stress. It is noteworthy that of the twelve most stressful events, eight directly involve family life (see table 8). Obviously, the major source of personal stress for most people is the family.

A series of stressful events can have a cumulative effect on the family system, especially if the family is unable or unwilling to deal with each event as it occurs. Stress can build up, and eventually a relatively minor incident can burst the floodgates. For example, a teenager who has been irresponsible at home, on detention for skipping school, may easily meet his parents fury when he comes home drunk. A family under financial strain may react out of all proportion to their teen's minor accident because it puts undue stress on the budget.

Resources

A family's ability to cope with stress is directly related to the resources it possesses. Some of these resources are personal in that they reside in the individual family members themselves. An obvious example is the ability to earn an income. Education is a resource that contributes to one's earning power, enhances prestige, and instills self-confidence. Personal maturity coupled with a good education can provide helpful skills in such areas as problem solving, goal setting, and strategic planning. Physical and mental health are also valuable in times of stress; they provide the needed strength to handle the stressful situation. Characteristics such as self-esteem, a positive disposition, and clearheadedness are resources that can make a difference in a crisis.

The most important resources in coping with family stress, however, are those that reside in the family system itself. The ability of a family to handle stress is closely related to its degree of adaptability and cohesion. Effective family systems are structured yet flexible. Families that are chaotic or rigid are ill prepared to handle stressful events. A degree of separateness is needed for family members to perceive the stressful event objectively, while cohesion allows the family to provide the needed

HI, I'M DOING A STUDY ON FACTORS WHICH
CAUSE FAMILY STRESS.

emotional support. The balanced family can operate as a sound functioning unit under stress.

Clear and open communication is a strength families draw on during times of crisis. The family that can honestly express ideas and feelings openly can work together to make the needed adjustments.

Some families possess many resources, but the shock of the crisis leaves them stifled and ineffective. They need time and often hope offered by others so they can marshal their resources to move forward. The external networks the family has established are the support systems—friends, neighbors, coworkers, church and community groups—they can draw on in time of special need. The necessity of cultivating such outside resources is one reason geographical stability is so important to the family system. A family without such resources is highly vulnerable.

Family Responses to Stress

Families respond to stress in two general ways: coping and problem solving. Although the literature on coping is more directly related to the issue of family stress, we believe that the literature on problem solving is invaluable because it conceptualizes the family's response to stress as taking place in stages.

Coping

Coping refers to what the family and its individual members do with their resources in the face of stress. Pauline Boss (1987, 695) agrees with Hill (1949) that stress is the result of the interaction between the event, the family's resources, and their perception of the event. Since the degree of success in coping with stress varies significantly from family to family, she proposes the following strategy.

The first step is to marshal all available resources. Coping strategies may consist of direct action aimed at changing the stressful conditions, a rethinking of the whole situation (including how the stress might be turned into a benefit), or a combination of both of these processes. Take the case of an elderly grandmother who is no longer able to live independently. First, the family considers all the family and community resources available to help with this crisis, for instance, retirement homes, eldercare facilities, and health programs. One of her children and his family may decide to have her move in with them. While they must consider the initial stress and the adjustment to be made by everyone involved, they also take into account the family strengths and the resources that family members have to offer. It can be a wonderful opportunity for members to extend themselves in new ways. They also see Grandmother as a resource for the family and recognize all the ways each member will benefit from her presence.

If family members are depleted because of other mitigating circumstances, they are not in a position to be a resource in this crisis. For instance, if the husband is frustrated in his job, the teenage daughter is acting out, and the family dynamics are disruptive, they are in no position to take on the grandmother. This would be a poor environment for the grandmother and most likely the demise of the family system.

Functional coping involves successful management of stressful events by both the family system and each individual in the family (Boss 1987, 701–8). Coping patterns may vary by culture or ethnicity and be passed down from family to family through the generations.

Problem Solving

Much research has been done in the area of problem solving within families. Irving Tallman and Louis Gray (1987) have suggested that five stages are involved:

1. The family becomes aware of and defines a situation as a problem. The greater the threat to the family's welfare, the more the situation will be perceived as a problem. "The most salient problems for the family as a unit will be either external threats to its ability to care for and protect its members or internal threats to its viability and functioning" (Tallman and Gray 1987, 13). It is also true that the more immediate a situation, the more likely it is to be perceived as a problem. Thus a serious threat to the family's survival, such as spousal abuse, may temporarily have lower priority when the family must deal with a more immediate problem, for instance, a burst pipe in the bathroom. Tallman and Gray summarize these two points: "Some degree of threat is necessary at least to the extent that the actor is uncomfortable with the existing state of affairs; and the situation must be sufficiently immediate to make the action implicit and problem awareness meaningful" (p. 16). It seems that families that consider themselves effective problem solvers are quick to perceive threatening situations as problems. Families that lack confidence in their ability to deal with problems are more likely to deny the seriousness of the situation.

2. The family decides to try to solve the problem. This decision is more likely if the family members believe they can really do something about the situation. The greater the family's confidence that they can solve the problem, the greater their motivation to act.

Although stress is often a motivating factor in a family's decision to solve a problem, families are less likely to recognize and act on problems when stress is very low or very high. Studies have found that under very high stress, families engage in defensive avoidance instead of constructive problem solving. Examples of defensive avoidance include selective inattention, forgetfulness, distortion of the meaning of warning messages, and wishful rationalizations that minimize the severity of the problem. During a time of severe crisis, a family may panic and require assistance from external resources such as a family therapist, service agencies, or their community of faith.

Families are more likely to engage in problem solving if the aim is to correct a negative situation rather than to improve their status. Parents, for example, will be motivated to attend a seminar on parent/child communication if they think it will reduce the stress in that relationship, but not if the goal is simply to enhance the relationship. This may explain the reluctance of couples to engage in premarital counseling. Most couples seek counseling only after marital difficulties arise. It is ironic but true that families are more motivated to act if the matter is framed in negative rather than positive terms. By implication, then, ministry to families is more effective if it promises to help them cope with an existing problem rather than avoid a potential one.

3. The family searches for and processes information relevant to effectively solving the problem. On the basis of the information gathered, the family decides which among the many options is the most effective way to resolve the problem. In general, they will select the solution that entails the least inconvenience, that is, the least time, money, energy, and resources. Thus, the family will search not necessarily for the best possible solution but rather for a satisfactory one. Once they have found a satisfactory solution, they will give up their search. For example, once the parents of a rebellious teenager believe that the solution to the problem is to spend more time with their child, they will stop considering other solutions that may be more directly related to the problem behavior, such as adjusting the restrictions on the teenager or changing their parenting style.

4. When the selected solution has been tried, the family evaluates its effectiveness. They may decide that the chosen strategy should be continued, revised, or discarded in favor of an alternative strategy. Many families, unfortunately, lack the patience to wait for a solution to work. It is helpful to remember that stress is usually heightened, rather than reduced, during the problem-solving process. However, making needed adjustments to ensure a good solution is also a wise strategy.

5. At this point the family either knows that the problem has been solved, or that it needs to go back to the drawing board and try another solution. Flexibility ensures that families make needed adjustments or

discard what isn't working and try something new. They stay with it until a satisfactory solution is working.

Coping with Catastrophes and Ambiguous Loss

A catastrophe is a stressful event that is sudden, unexpected, and life threatening. The circumstances are beyond the family's control and leave them in an extreme state of helplessness. Because catastrophes occur infrequently, most families are not prepared to cope with them. Wars, terrorist attacks, hurricanes, tsunamis, earthquakes, or epidemics can wipe out whole segments of a populated area without warning. Survivors are devastated by the losses.

Catastrophes differ from other stressful events in a number of ways (Figley and McCubbin 1983, 14–18): (1) a family has little or no time to prepare for a catastrophe; (2) the family has no previous experience to help it deal with the situation; (3) there are few resources to draw on to help manage the resulting stress; (4) few other families have experienced a similar disaster so that they could provide suitable support; (5) the family is likely to spend a long time in a state of crisis; (6) the family experiences a loss of control and posttraumatic stress syndrome resulting from a heightened sense of danger, helplessness, disruption, destruction, and loss; and (7) a number of medical problems (physical and emotional) are likely to occur.

Ambiguous loss is a concept coined by Pauline Boss (2000) to refer to unresolved grief that lingers in a family because there is no closure. Examples of ambiguous loss include a parent with Alzheimer's, an alcoholic spouse, a long-lost child, or a family member missing in action or a prisoner of war. There are two type of ambiguous loss: one involves a family member who is missing, but there is no proof of death or even knowledge of where the person may be if still alive; the other involves a person who is present in body but whose mind is not, such as the case with severe dementia, depression, mental illness, or addiction. Boss describes ambiguous loss as *frozen sadness*, what a family feels when it cannot really know what it has lost.

Substantial research has examined the various emotional stages that a family in crisis goes through. Best known is Elisabeth Kübler-Ross's (1970) five-stage process an individual or a family typically goes through when confronted with a loss through death (see figure 17). First is the denial stage, which is usually characterized as a state of shock. Family members may appear calm and collected, exhibiting emotions that are fairly inappropriate given the severity of what has happened.

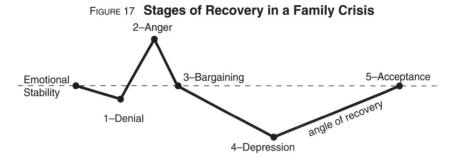

FIGURE 17 **Stages of Recovery in a Family Crisis**

There are acute underlying feelings of loneliness, guilt, conflict, and meaninglessness.

As family members get in touch with their feelings about what has happened, they enter the anger stage. To the outside observer, the increased emotional intensity characterizing this stage may appear to be regressive. In truth, it is a necessary and healthy step along the road to emotional healing. The anger is an honest reaction to the reality of the loss.

After the emotional expression during the second stage, the family often enters into a bargaining stage. Still unable to accept the magnitude of the loss, they may try to minimize it through bargaining processes (e.g., a family that has suffered financial bankruptcy may promise to give more to the church if only God will restore a portion of what has been lost). When the family members come to realize the full extent of the catastrophe, they tend to feel the loss and become depressed. At this stage, the family reaches its lowest emotional point. Depression is actually an expression of deep sadness and grief about what was lost. The passage from depression to acceptance, the final stage, is known as the angle of recovery. It can be depicted as a very steep incline, pointing to a speedy emotional upturn, or as a gradual slope, representing a long, drawn-out recovery period. The angle of recovery depends on the resources the family has at its disposal.

On reaching the acceptance stage, the family may be quite different than it was before the catastrophe occurred. Reaching the acceptance stage does not mean that family members no longer feel any of the emotions of the other stages (denial, anger, sadness), but they are no longer immobilized by them. Having been empowered, they can experience increased self-reliance as they make the needed adjustments and plan for the future. Needless to say, in the case of ambiguous loss, the possibility of a family moving toward recovery can be severally hampered.

A crisis can happen to an individual in the family or to the whole family. What is most important is for help to be given in a way that empowers rather than keeps others dependent. One must treat the person/family with deepest respect rather than taking over under the assumption that the victim is totally incapable and helpless.

When an entire family suffers a crisis, its members are often drawn closer together by the common experience. In such a situation, each member mutually gives and receives support. The isolated nuclear family is especially vulnerable during such times, and the Christian community can be invaluable. Jesus radically redefined the concept of family when he said, "Here are my mother and my brothers! Whoever does the will of God is my brother and sister and mother" (Mark 3:34–35). The challenge is for us to be family to one another, so that we can offer Christ's love and support in emotional and physical ways during times of crisis.

Families in Pain

Sometimes the disruptive effect of an event is felt so deeply by the family that the term *stress* is an inadequate description. When family members have been hurt to the core of their being, they are in *pain*. Such pain has a far-reaching impact on the life of the family and if not addressed may continue from one generation to the next in even greater tragic scenarios.

Like the disciples who asked why the man whom Jesus was about to heal had been born blind, families today often ask similar agonizing questions about their pain. Jesus firmly answered that the man's blindness was not a consequence of anyone's sin. Jesus then took action by responding to the needs of the man in pain (John 9). Like the blind man, we need the one who has the power to heal our deepest hurts. We need his strength to offset our vulnerability. We need a belief in God that gives meaning and a perspective to help us survive and eventually get beyond the pain. We need to feel God's compassionate presence suffering with us and lighting the way through our darkest hours.

By banding together, families can constructively work through the deep hurts of life (Balswick and Balswick 1997). In 1 Corinthians 12:26–27, Paul says that all believers are part of the body of Christ; thus "if one member suffers, all suffer together with it." It works this way in the human family too. When one person suffers, the entire family suffers. Our son, Joel, has a chronic liver disease; every time he is hospitalized, each one of us who love him is affected in an intense way. The responses of all the family members and the interactions between them during a family crisis need to be acknowledged and reckoned with. A family must not only look for their collective strengths in time of trouble but also deal with those weaknesses that prevent them from helping the one who is hurting.

Working together and placing Christ at the center, family members can begin a process that will help them regain wholeness:

1. Each family member should gather the courage for a self-examination of his or her feelings, thoughts, and behavior under the trying circumstances.
2. The family should ask honest questions about how each member is doing, how each one is affecting the others, and how the family is coping as a whole.
3. Every family member must be allowed to feel the painful experience; the emotions of anger, sadness, and fear about what has happened must be acknowledged rather than denied.
4. Grieving over the losses that have occurred, the family must find the strength to relinquish the concerns they cannot control and to let go of past injuries in order to focus more fully on the present.

Families will be empowered to take responsibility for their behavior once they understand clearly how past events and injuries have contributed to the present pain. Oftentimes, family members will see how their behavior is telling a story of unmet needs, of fears, and of resentments they're trying desperately to resolve. When appropriate, forgiveness will complete the healing and lead to substantial restoration of relationships. Although forgiveness can take many forms and serve different purposes, it should never be superficial or offered lightly. As part of the healing process, forgiveness helps us release the bitterness, anger, and hurt that stifle healing. In some instances, forgiveness of self is the hardest part. Although forgiveness may seem quite an outrageous idea from the human point of view, with God's strength and mercy it is not only possible, but it will also prove to be exactly what is needed to bring transforming power to anguished lives.

Christian Belief and Response to Stress and Pain

Our perception of stressful events and our ability to cope with them are strongly influenced by our belief system (Boss 1987, 715–18). The particular influence that Christianity has had in this regard varies over a broad continuum from passive resignation to self-reliant attempts to achieve mastery over catastrophe. At one extreme is a fatalistic view that abuses Paul's teaching that Christians should be content in whatever state they find themselves (Phil. 4:11). Most Western versions of Christianity, in contrast, are very action oriented, emphasizing the responsibility and capability of the believer to take whatever action is needed to alleviate the threatening situation. These two conflicting extremes reflect the current narcissistic thinking of our society and deny the legitimacy of stress and pain within the Christian life.

A current example of the fatalistic view is the theology of positive thinking. It comports well with the societal emphasis on each individual's ability to mentally create his or her own perfect world. Positive thinking comes close to promising a life without any difficulties, but this is incompatible with the reality of a world tainted by sin. To live in a fallen world is to experience stress and pain. In our humanness, we are capable of causing all sorts of burdensome situations for ourselves and for others.

Clichés that admonish us to "turn every stumbling stone into a stepping stone" and to "turn scars into stars" must not be used to deny the very real disruptions families face. Rightly taken, however, positive thinking can help reduce stress and keep problems in perspective. To view scars as stars, that is, to change one's perception of a painful event, is healthy when combined with both an awareness of the potential damage the crisis can inflict and a realistic assessment of how the family can manage with the resources available. Such an approach enables the family to take action rather than deny or be paralyzed by disaster.

No less narcissistic than positive thinking is the opposite extreme—the view that stress or pain is the direct result of a specific sin and is therefore capable of being overcome instantaneously through an act of divine healing. In reality, most of the events and conditions that distress families, including alcoholism, eating disorders, job loss, parent/child conflicts, and illness, are caused by complex physical, social, and psychological factors. In a general sense, of course, all these stressful conditions stem from our living in a fallen world tainted by sin. But to insist that the cure lies simply in taking action against the sin in individual lives is to fail to comprehend the pervasiveness of evil and the role that social structures play in producing stress and pain in the world.

True, to deal with stress and pain, we must take action against the sin in our lives, but we must not ignore other realities such as dysfunction within families, unjust economic systems, the oppressiveness of poverty, and so on. We must adopt a multifaceted approach that recognizes the complexity of the anxieties and pressures of life in the modern world. Awareness of this complexity will make us extremely cautious about claims of instant healing for the deeply painful experiences in life.

In our pill-oriented society, we want instant relief and cure from all that ails us. One aspirin advertisement promises relief "when you don't have time for the pain." Our society promotes the quick fix over the long, hard work required to overcome most of the stress in today's world. To become whole, a healing process must take place in the believer. This healing process, which includes growth in faith and in our relationship to God and others, usually works at a gradual pace.

To think that Christians are immune to stress and pain is not only an unrealistic view but also bad theology. Scripture includes numerous examples of disaster falling on the just and the unjust alike. We need look only at the life of Job to know that evil circumstances come to the righteous and that instant cure is not the norm. What is guaranteed is the compassion of God in every circumstance. God will be present with us through the body of Christ and in the power of the Holy Spirit.

The two extreme responses to stress that we have examined lead, respectively, to a theology of escapism, in which the Christian tends to withdraw in the face of crisis, and to a theology of activism, in which the Christian tends to be self-reliant to the point of rendering God a mere bystander in the process. What is the biblical response? Scripture suggests that when confronted by a crisis, Christians should not fatalistically resign themselves. For example, when Paul was arrested, he did not meekly succumb. Instead, he asserted his status as a Roman citizen in order to deliver himself. Examples from the life of David point to a balance between passivity and activism in the midst of stress. At times David fell on his knees before the Lord, acknowledging that his situation was hopeless without divine intervention. At other times, David took forthright action in the face of extreme difficulties. The balance between passivity and activism can be seen in the story of David and Goliath. Fully aware that without God's help he had no chance against the Philistine, David equipped himself with his sling and five smooth stones.

The same combination of passive reliance and active assertiveness can be seen in the life of Jesus. Faced with imminent arrest, trial, and crucifixion, Jesus retreated to the Garden of Gethsemane. Distressed and agitated, he told his disciples that his soul was "deeply grieved, even to death" (Mark 14:34). In his despair Jesus prayed to his Father, "Remove this cup from me; yet, not what I want, but what you want" (v. 36).

It is important to recall that this very same Jesus had previously gone into the temple and assertively driven out the money changers. Enraged at the hypocrisy of the Pharisees, he called them whitewashed tombs, snakes, and a brood of vipers. His language was equally severe when he called Herod a fox, unreceptive audiences swine, and false prophets savage wolves. Nor did he restrain himself from taking direct action against the social evils of his day.

Christians need an able response to crisis. An unavoidable part of living in a fallen world, stress should be approached as a time to draw especially near to God and others for support. Although God has not promised an escape from stressful situations, he has promised to be our "refuge in the time of trouble" (Ps. 37:39).

It is often the case that stressful events shake up the family system in a way that disrupts the stagnant comfort of routine life. This can be an occasion for growth as Christians. It can also be a time of increased intimacy among family members and with the body of Christ as a whole. When people are vulnerable, they are often more receptive to the support and love of others. It is essential, then, in periods of adversity to choose a direction that, with God's help, will lead to deeper levels of intimacy, commitment, forgiveness, and empowering. To help achieve and maintain a balanced perspective, we might also keep in our hearts the simple yet profound prayer of Reinhold Niebuhr (1987):

> O God, give us serenity to accept what cannot be changed,
>   courage to change what should be changed,
>   and wisdom to distinguish the one from the other. (p. 251)

17

DIVORCE AND SINGLE-PARENT FAMILIES

F AMILIES ARE AMAZINGLY resilient. Even in the face of challenging external pressures and intense internal conflicts, they are often able to adapt through a built-in survival mechanism. From an outsider's point of view, a given family may face insurmountable challenges, and yet to the members within, it is their only source of identity and security. Waite and Gallagher (2000) conclude, "There is substantial evidence that, on the average, being in a satisfying marriage enhances the physical, psychological, social and economic well-being of adults, and that divorcing may involve considerable risk" (p. 323).

There is a concerted effort today to emphasize the benefits of marriage even when trouble exists between spouses. In a study released in 2002, Waite and five colleagues analyzed data from the University of Wisconsin's National Survey of Family and Households. They discovered that adults who said they were unhappily married in the late 1980s and got divorced were on average still unhappy or even less happy when interviewed five years later as compared to those who stayed in their marriages. Most of those who stayed in their marriages had on average moved past the bad times and reached a happier stage. After controlling for race, age, gender, and income, the researchers found that divorce usually did not reduce symptoms of depression, raise self-esteem, or increase a sense of mastery over one's life. The general conclusion is that divorce does not make unhappy married people any happier. Therefore, people who stay in an unhappy marriage are at least as well off as those who divorce.

One could argue, then, that there is no benefit to leaving a marriage if you're unhappy because these marriages may be happy at a later stage (Nock 1998).

A point does come, however, when spouses divorce because life together is no longer a viable option for them. This often occurs after a fairly long period of disillusionment or denial when spouses have ignored their problems. Eugene O'Neill's play *Long Day's Journey into Night* provides a good look at a family engaged in collective denial. They keep talking about each other in totally unrealistic terms. Such defense mechanisms deflect debilitating conflict for the time being, but ultimately they keep the family from instituting needed change. When built-up anger and bitterness disrupt into violent abusive interactions, marriage is no longer a safe haven. Without help, the spouses will likely divorce.

In this chapter we investigate the statistics and complex causes of divorce. Because of the large number of divorces in contemporary society, we give special attention to single-parent families and the impact divorce has on children. We conclude this chapter with a Christian mandate asking faith communities to do what they can to promote strong marriage and family life, as well as provide a place of compassion and support during divorce recovery. Given the fact that most people who divorce eventually remarry, the next chapter is devoted to the reconstituted family.

Divorce

Demographics

Among developed countries, only Russia has a higher divorce rate than the United States. As shown in figure 18, the annual divorce rate steadily rose from a low of 1 divorce for every 1,000 married couples in 1860, to a high of 22.5 in 1979. Immediately following World War I, the divorce rate rose noticeably; similarly, following World War II there was a dramatic rise in the divorce rate. These increases reflect both the stress placed on marriages by forced separation and the large number of unstable marriages contracted during the wars. The drop in the rate during the Depression years reflects the costliness of legal divorce. The most dramatic rise in the divorce rate occurred between 1965 and 1979. It was especially pronounced among people under age forty-five.

Since 1980, there have been approximately 1.2 million divorces each year, slightly less than half the number of marriages. Since that time the rate of divorce has been moderately declining to a rate of 17.7 divorces for every 1,000 married couples in 2005. The best estimate is that approximately four out of every ten current marriages will end in divorce,

Figure 18 **Annual Divorce Rate**

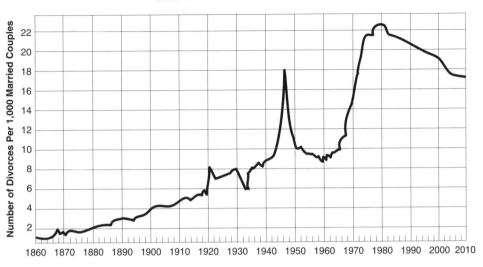

From H. Raschke, "Divorce," in *Handbook of Marriage and the Family*, ed. Marvin B. Sussman and Suzanne K. Steinmetz (New York: Plenum, 1987), 844; and U.S. Bureau of the Census, Current Population Reports, Series P-25, Population Estimates and Projections, nos. 311, 519, 917, and 1000. D. Popenoe and B. Whitehead, *The State of Our Unions: The Social Health of Marriage in America, 2005.* www.marriage.rutgers.edu/Publications/SOOUT/TEXTSOOU2005.htm.

with the likelihood of divorce being lowest among those who have been married the longest. The average length of marriages that end in divorce is seven years; the rate of divorce is highest for marriages of two to three years' duration.

Although the decline in the divorce rate since 1980 is encouraging, it should also be noted that in part this trend can be explained by the number of people choosing to cohabit rather than marry. Although a high percentage of cohabiting couples separate, such breakups do not affect the divorce rate. The later age at first marriage (twenty-five for women, twenty-six for men) also contributes to the declining divorce rate. Those who marry in their midtwenties tend to have the most stable marriages. Although it is hard to document, we believe that the positive marriage movement emphasizing the importance of premarital counseling and marital enrichment also accounts for the declining rate of divorce.

Although there is no sure way of predicting whether a marriage will succeed, research has found correlations with a number of demographic factors, such as age, ethnicity, income, occupation, social class, and level of education, that may have a bearing. A 2001 Centers for Disease Control and Prevention report shows that 20 percent of first-marriage divorces now occur within five years. Those who marry young, especially in their teens, are much more likely to divorce than those who marry in their twenties. A number of interrelated factors may also be at work here. Couples who marry young are typically from a lower socioeconomic class (which increases the probability of financial difficulties); they marry after a very short engagement and perhaps because of a pregnancy. Given their stage of individual development, most teenagers are socially and psychologically unprepared for a relationship as demanding as marriage. Inadequacies in role performance, unfaithfulness, disagreement, lack of understanding, and low companionship satisfaction have been found to contribute to divorce among those who married while very young.

Next to teenage marriages, the most unstable marriages are those of people who marry after age thirty. Among these divorces, the most common complaints are a lack of agreement and the tendency of the spouse to be domineering and critical. The underlying dynamic here is perhaps that those who marry late in life have become so set in their ways, they have a hard time adjusting to the expectations of a spouse.

The divorce rate is low among men with little education, increases among those who have had some high school training, and declines among men who have a college degree. In terms of ethnic differences, the divorce rate is highest among blacks, moderate among whites, and lowest among other ethnic groups, particularly those of Far Eastern origin. In terms of religion, divorce rates are lowest among Jews, moderate among Catholics, and highest among Protestants. Finally, heterogeneous marriages are more likely to end in divorce than are homogeneous marriages. Thus divorce is more likely when there is a sizable age gap or differences in religion, social class, or ethnic origin.

Causes

There is no single cause of divorce. The reasons are multiple, complex, and interrelated. Some are related to the idiosyncrasies of the individuals; others involve social and cultural factors such as the demographics we have just examined. Other things being equal, the lower the quality of the marriage, the greater the likelihood of divorce. Therefore, absence of any of the requisites for a strong marriage (e.g., commitment, family support, differentiation, adaptability) discussed in prior chapters could contribute to marital failure. Gottman (1994) claims to be able to predict divorce simply by observing how couples deal with marital conflict. Couples who learn conflict management skills are more likely to work out their differences and stay married.

The most frequent motives given for divorce center on relational issues, behavior problems, and problems about work and the division of labor in the home. It seems "we are moving into an era in which the 'normalization of fragility' will become central to people's intimate relationships" (Hughes 2005, 69).

A number of factors at the sociocultural level may contribute to a *culture of divorce* and a divorce-prone society. Based on their research on divorce in the Netherlands, deGraff and Kalmijn (2006) observe three important trends in modern societies: the normalization of divorce, the psychologization of relationships, and the emancipation of women. Other factors contributing to a culture of divorce include a decline in viewing marriage as an unconditional commitment, a decline in the social stigma of divorce, the liberalization of divorce laws, increased opportunity for males and females who work together to become romantically involved, and changing gender roles that make wives less dependent economically on their husbands (Hughes 2005; Yodanis 2005).

David Popenoe and Barbara Dafoe Whitehead (2003, 2004, 2005), of the Institute for American Values, believe that the cumulative effect of divorce has eroded the foundation of American society. They believe the impact of the no-fault divorce policy has made it far too easy to divorce and contributes to a culture that is comfortable with divorce. The modern/postmodern preoccupation with individualism and self-fulfillment versus covenant commitment and personal sacrifice place inevitable tension on marriage today. Also unrealistic expectations, lack of egalitarian practices, loss of a community base to support family life, and the emergence of materialism as a dominant value take a toll on marriages. Clearly, there are a multitude of reasons, some direct and some indirect, some conscious and some unconscious, some personal and some societal, why people divorce.

The Process

The divorce process can be a highly conflictive time. Any antagonistic or abusive pathology that has previously existed is likely to escalate during and immediately after divorce proceedings, increasing the threat of harm to the children. Ava Seigler (2005, 61) found that divorce and custody proceedings are often accompanied by "a destructive spectrum of adversarial, antagonistic, and abusive behavior between cohabiting adults."

From a legal standpoint, divorce is enacted on a specific date; however, the ending of a marriage typically stretches over several years. As both a public and a private process, divorce is most often a crisis-producing event. It involves the death of a relationship, and as with most deaths, pain and crisis are common by-products. Although both suffer immensely, the man is generally affected most negatively in the sociopsychological sphere and the woman in the economic.

The divorce process typically follows a four-stage sequence. The first stage is the period before separation, sometimes referred to as the emotional divorce or the erosion of love, which conjures up feelings of anger, disillusionment, and detachment. The second stage is the point of actual separation, which often is accompanied by bargaining tactics, sadness, regret, and depression. The third stage, the period between the separation and the legal divorce, involves legal issues, economic readjustments, continued mourning, coparenting arrangements, reorientation of lifestyle, and a focus on one's own identity and emotional functioning. The fourth and final stage of personal recovery includes a restructuring and restabilizing of lives, opening oneself up to new possibilities and goals. This time may include a "second-adolescence" phase of being single and being involved in the dating scene again.

The emotions people experience in the four stages of a divorce are like the emotions experienced during the stages of coming to grips with the death and dying of a spouse. However, although the marriage has come to an end, the two individuals are still alive, and their relationship with their children has not ended, keeping them involved with each other after the divorce.

The Effect on Children

Once spouses have children, the divorce outlook becomes a more serious concern. All things being equal, we believe children need and deserve to grow up in a family with two parents who love them and who love each other. The covenant commitment extends to our children. Since divorce hurts the relationship between parents and kids, it will always be a drastic last resort. We also acknowledge that when there is a high level of violence in the home, divorce sometimes saves lives and the sanity of children.

The crucial question is, "What is in the best interest of children?" The long-term impact of divorce on children has been debated for the past forty years. Some researchers are more optimistic than others about the adaptability and resilience of children, while others point to the negative effect divorce has on them. Up until the late 1970s, there was some attempt to downplay the negative effects of divorce on children. This attitude was based on research suggesting that children may be better off in a happy one-parent home than in an unhappy two-parent home. The home supposedly became a more stable, less disruptive environment once the neglectful or abusive father or mother was removed.

At this time, research indicates that children from divorced homes fare worse than children from intact homes. However, the reason for this can be debated. One view is that the real harm to children comes from a conflicted marriage, in which children have experienced trauma created by the psychopathology of their parents. In support of this view are Robert Gordon's (2005) findings that the direct negative effect of divorce is more short term, with children of divorce appearing less harmed after long-term adjustment. Gordon believes that the impact of divorce on children is fleeting and that the long-lasting psychological problems displayed by children of divorce in adolescence and adulthood reflect more the preexisting marriage and the continued conflict between ex-spouses. Lisa Strohschein (2005, 1286) reports that even before the divorce, children whose parents later divorce exhibit higher levels of anxiety/depression and antisocial behavior than children whose parents remain married. She did note, however, that there were "divorce specific" increases in anxiety and depression. Another study (VanderValk et al. 2005, 533) reports "a further increase in child anxiety and depression but not antisocial behavior associated with the event of parental divorce itself."

One of the more complete pictures of how divorce affects children is a report on a randomly selected sample of fifteen hundred young adults from divorced and intact homes, reported by Elizabeth Marquardt (2005). She found that the children of divorce were four times more likely than those from intact families to agree with the statement, "My father has done things I find hard to forgive." Although the difference was less dramatic, children of divorced parents were also more likely than those from intact homes to agree that their mother had done things they found hard to forgive.

Most researchers agree that the trauma created by the divorce itself and the resulting anxiety and uncertainty is harmful to children. A well-documented longitudinal study by leading divorce researchers Mavis Hetherington and John Kelly (2002) found that the changes in everyday life following divorce do have an initial negative impact on the children. The greatly altered behavior of their parents during and soon after divorce (dating phase) is a particularly difficult time. It takes most parents two or more years to recuperate from divorce, and during this time of adjustment both parents struggle with personal self-esteem needs. Some spouses were prone to sexual acting-out, vengeful deeds against the former spouse, emotional outbursts or periods of depression, and fearful concerns about their future and their finances. This period of transition takes a toll on the children because parents are often not available to help them make emotional adjustments.

Children also have adjustment problems in the first year after divorce, and they may exhibit acting-out or acting-in behaviors. Girls frequently recover in the second year, while boys may continue to have adjustment problems through adolescence, especially if they live with their mother in a single-parent home. Though dependent on her, boys go through coercive cycles and tend to be more aggressive and noncompliant. Single-parent mothers and daughters tend to become very close emotionally until the onset of adolescence, which brings conflict over sexual behavior and individuation (Hetherington and Kelly 2002).

Rather than continuing the argument, we believe the body of divorce research supports both views, namely, children are harmed by what transpires in unhappy and conflictive marriages, but they also suffer because of the divorce itself. The term *double-exposure effect* refers to how the *divorce event* and *parental distress* contribute *independently* to child and adolescent distress (Storkson et al. 2006). Regardless of the source of the harm, the evidence indicates that children of divorced homes are burdened more than children of intact homes.

Long- and Short-Term Divorce Adjustment

Hetherington and Kelly's longitudinal project spanning three decades led them to conclude that divorce should not be viewed as a momentary event but rather "as a lifelong process that has a continuing influence throughout the stages of divorce, single parenthood, remarriage, and stepfamily life" (2002, cover). They admit that going through a divorce takes a toll on all family members because of the many changes, challenges, and losses they experience during that time. The years immediately before and after the divorce especially carry high risks in terms of emotional, personal, and health issues. Among Hetherington and Kelly's most important findings on divorce are that the father's absence is more disruptive to boys than to girls, persistent symptoms among children may be linked to postdivorce conflict between parents, and the father's withdrawal from child rearing may damage the child's recovery.

Hetherington and Kelly report that by six years after divorce, over half of the women and 70 percent of the men had remarried, with over three-quarters of them believing the divorce had been the right thing to do. They contend that the vast majority of children of divorce (75–80 percent) are resilient and doing well. They criticize studies that take averages—for example, "20–25% of kids of divorced families have behavior problems compared to 10% of non-divorced"—because these studies capitalize on the "twice as many" but fail to point out that 75–80 percent are not having problems and therefore the vast majority are doing well (Hetherington and Kelly 2002).

Judith Wallerstein's (2005) groundbreaking longitudinal research dating back to 1997 indicates that the tumult of parental breakup continued throughout adolescence and even into adulthood. In summarizing these findings, Wallerstein concluded that "stressful parent-child relationships in the post-divorce family together with the enduring effects of the troubled marriage and breakup lead to the acute anxieties about life and commitment that many children of divorce bring to relationships in their adult years" (p. 401). Later in life, children of divorced parents seem to be at greater risk for divorce (Segrin, Taylor, and Altman 2005, 361). Another study reports that mothers raised in divorced homes had lower income levels and lower levels of education compared with their counterparts from intact families (Nair and Murray 2005, 245). The same study found that these mothers were more likely to use authoritative parenting styles compared with mothers raised in intact families, a factor related to attachment insecurity.

A study in the Netherlands found a negative association between divorce and social integration (Lucas 2005, 455). It revealed that divorced people report lower levels of life satisfaction than do married people, suggesting that this is both a result of preexisting differences and lasting changes following the divorce. These studies note the accumulation of evidence that suggests divorce has a lasting effect throughout both the individual and the family life cycle. Paul Amato and Jacob Cheadle (2005, 191) found that "divorce in the first generation was associated with lower education, more marital discord, weaker ties with mothers, and weaker ties with fathers in the third generation."

In light of the long-term effects of divorce, we would do well to heed Connie Ahrons's (2004) suggestion that "good divorces" allow adults and children to continue to live relatively harmoniously as a family. She notes that divorce reorganizes a family but does not destroy it. In fact, many children of divorce believe that their parents' decision to divorce was the right one, and most do not wish their parents had remained married.

Judith Wallerstein and Sandra Blakeslee (2003) encourage parents to observe how their children are doing and seek professional help when they see them struggle with education, emotions, or behavior. Because of multiple changes in roles that occur after divorce, parents, grandparents, and children benefit from regular and intentional communication in family meetings or family therapy.

When conflict between parents continues after the divorce, children are often caught in the middle. Paul Amato and Tamara Afifi (2006, 222) conclude that "research on divorce has found that adolescents' feelings of being caught between parents are linked to internalizing problems and weaken parent-child relationships." These children also had a lower sense of overall well-being. These researchers speculate that since being caught in the middle likely fades with time, in the long run these children may be better off than children of parents who continue to live together in a highly conflictive relationship.

After reviewing research on divorce, Jan Pryor and Bryan Rodgers (2001) conclude that divorce has a negative impact on both children and parents—especially during the years right after the divorce. In his review of divorce research, Paul Amato concludes that "research in the 1990s consistently demonstrated that children do best when they grow up with two happily *and* continuously married parents" (2004, 276). However, some marriages not only lack happiness but also rip apart the fabric of family life through conflict, strife, and abuse. While remaining pro-marriage, some would argue that divorce can unfortunately be the best of two bad alternatives.

Amato contrasts two major perspectives on divorce. The *family deficit perspective* assumes that "any departure from the nuclear family is deviant and therefore deleterious to children's well-being" (2004, 272). In contrast, the *family pluralism perspective* assumes that "family structure has few intrinsic consequences (negative or positive) for children's well-being and that children can develop successfully in a variety of family forms" (p. 272). Finding a middle ground between these two perspectives, Amato suggests a *contingency perspective*, which views divorce as a "stressor and a risk factor for subsequent academic, behavioral, emotional, and social problems" (p. 276). In this perspective the effect of divorce is "dependent on family circumstances before and after divorce, and depending on the presence of a variety of protective factors in children's environment, divorce may be harmful or benign to children" (p. 276).

Best-Case Scenarios

From a Christian perspective, we must ask what the best-case scenario can be for spouses and children when divorce becomes a reality. Here we focus on conditions under which divorce is least troubling. It has been established that children adjust better when parents discuss the possibility of divorce beforehand and continue to discuss the situation after the divorce occurs. Obviously, the less hostility between the parents during divorce, the better the child's adjustment. Divorced parents who maintain an affable relationship with each other and show continuous love and support of their children lessen the disruptive effects of their divorce. The quality of the parents' postdivorce communication is essential to good adjustment in children (Lamb 1997).

Another key indicator of how well a child will adjust to divorce is the custodial parent's effectiveness in the role of single parent. When custodial fathers expect obedience and good behavior and operate with mutual respect and affection, children do better. Giving in to children and trying to make up for the pain of the divorce leaves them less secure than when the father takes a clear leadership role. It is vital that the parent who has not been awarded custody spend quality time with the children.

Joint custody and split custody are two creative attempts to promote continued involvement by both divorced parents in the lives of their children. The results have been mixed, but for the most part when both parents take cooperative and mutual responsibility, the children fare better. This arrangement can work well when a couple maintains a good relationship, but it does not fare well when parents continually fight and have disputes over the children and custody arrangements. Although children in joint custody tend to exhibit greater self-esteem than do those in sole custody, primary custody by the parent of the same sex in most cases seems to be a more beneficial arrangement for the child.

In split custody, each parent assumes the care of one child (or more). It is sometimes reasoned that girls need to be with their moms and boys with their dads. However, sibling separation and the formation of parent-child coalitions may in the long run hurt rather than help the adjustment process.

A Christian Approach to Divorce

Divorce, while not condoned in Scripture, has become common in today's world. For this reason, we want to offer a Christian response. Throughout this book, we emphasize that marriage and family relationships should be based on a mutual covenant. When two people marry, God intends for the relationship to be a two-way, unconditional commitment. God desires that covenant commitment lead to a relationship in which grace abounds. This means that both spouses will undoubtedly fail each other, and forgiveness is an ongoing aspect of marriage. Within this atmosphere of grace, spouses are challenged to strive for reciprocal engagement and empowerment through their interdependence. Bringing their unique talents and gifts to the union, they use their resources to build up their union. And out of this empowerment, spouses are compelled to know and be known in deeper ways that secure intimate bonding. God desires permanence in marriage, and married Christians must do all that they can to uphold their marriage. This ideal for Christian marriage is an honorable aspiration that can be achieved by God's grace and through the power of the Holy Spirit.

However, we would be remiss if we didn't acknowledge that there are no perfect people who completely live up to this ideal. All marriages are composed of two imperfect people who fail each other to one degree or another. All couples struggle with their relationship. While many learn to deal successfully with marital conflict and find the healing needed through therapy and community support, others are unable to overcome the obstacles of violence, disrespect, abuse, bitterness, addictions, cold detachment, and neglect. Brokenness is heaped on brokenness and anger; hurt and bitterness begin to take on a life of their own. These marriages tend to spin in reverse—from conditionality to emotional distance to possessive power to an atmosphere of law—and eventually the marriage is severed.

Although marital dissolution is surely a spiritual problem, we must resist the temptation to spiritualize in a simplistic way. Human beings are complex creatures, and there is a web of complicated social, psychological, and spiritual factors in the dissolution of any marriage. The marital struggle begins to eat away at the person as well as destroy the relationship. Sad to say, divorce is the radical choice. In their own eyes—and in the eyes of the Christian community—spouses confess they have failed. The question now becomes how we as a family of faith apply our theology of relationships to those who walk through that valley of the death of a marriage.

To begin with, we acknowledge that we live in a broken world in which we all fail in many aspects of our lives. Dwight Small (1977, 8) has noted, "We give people the right to fail in business, in school, in careers, but not always in marriage. We reserve a particular stigma for that. The redemptive side of failure is not applied as readily as it ought to be."

Jesus is the model for our response to failed marriage. Jesus did not condemn the woman at the well for her unsuccessful marriages but offered redemption and a new beginning (John 4). To be legalistic rather than offer forgiveness, love, and compassion is unacceptable. Ray Anderson and Dennis Guernsey (1985, 101) note that Jesus presented the basis of marriage from the perspective of the command of God: "Therefore what God has joined together, let no one separate" (Matthew 19:6). They conclude:

> In saying this, Jesus removed both marriage and divorce from the status of being under a law, and reminded his listeners that humans are accountable to God in thought, word, and deed, not least of all in the "one flesh" relation of marriage. Viewed from this perspective, it is clear that there can be no "rules" by which marriage can be dissolved, any more than there are marriages which can be sanctified before God by observing certain legalities.

Wherever Jesus talks about divorce (Matt. 5:31–32; 19:3–9; Mark 10:2–12; Luke 16:18), the clear thrust is that marriage is of the Lord and is not to be broken. Christ calls couples to fidelity in marriage as a lifelong commitment; he does not have in view, however, a marriage of legalism that entails only commitment to the institution and not to the relationship. Marriage is merely a human structure, and we must never focus more on preserving a structure than on caring about the individual spouses themselves. The Christian message of forgiveness and restoration must be generously offered to divorced people and their children. These members of our church body need us more than ever during this painful experience. We must be accepting and lovingly welcome them into our midst as God's family. We must never deny them hope for wholeness and restoration. As Garland, Richmond, and Garland (1986, 171) state:

> If it is the case that marriage was made for the blessing of humankind, and not humankind for marriage, it would seem that one who has failed in marriage might have another opportunity to remarry. Any moral superiority that the nondivorced person might feel toward the divorced who remarry is undermined by Jesus' claim that everyone who lusts after another is guilty of adultery (Matthew 5:28). Every spouse has broken commitments to the partner, and every relationship experiences alienation from unresolved differences.

Single-Parent Families

Single-parent households can be defined as either mother or father living alone with their children, bringing children into a cohabiting situation, or sharing living arrangements with others (extended family or other single or married people). The parent who lives in the same household with his or her dependent children is referred to as the custodial parent, while the noncustodial parent is the one who does not live with the children.

As trends of divorce have increased, so have single-parent homes. Every year approximately 1 million children become part of a single-parent home. The percentage of children under age eighteen living with a single parent has risen from 9 percent in 1960 to 28 percent in 2004. The changing proportion went from 22 percent in 1960 to 56 percent in 2004 among blacks and from 7 percent to 22 percent among whites (Popenoe and Whitehead 2005). Although the number of single-father homes has increased slightly, of the nearly 20 million children under eighteen living in a single-parent family in 2002, 83 percent lived with their mothers and 17 percent with their fathers (Popenoe and Whitehead 2003). In terms of the overall picture of children's living arrangements, approximately 68 percent live with both parents, 22 percent with mother and no father, 5 percent with father and no mother, and 4 percent with neither of their parents in the household (U.S. Census Bureau 2002). Divorced men are more likely to remarry and to remarry sooner than divorced women, although the majority of divorced women also remarry. Thus it should be noted that due to remarriage, many children in single-parent homes eventually become part of reconstituted families, a phenomenon we deal with in the next chapter.

The first two years following a divorce can be an especially fragile period in the single-parent home, as both the custodial parent and the noncustodial parent adjust to new roles. The degree of harmony or conflict between the parents is the major factor in how stressful this period will be. The hurt, anger, sadness, and depression that occur with a divorce affect the single parent at an emotional level especially in the first few years, making it more difficult for divorced parents to attend to the needs of their children. With their security undermined, they can feel unsure of themselves in many areas. The adjustment to being a divorced person with children is accompanied by two major stressors: *not enough time* and *not enough money*.

Not Enough Time

The common complaint of not enough time only intensifies when the solo parent is called on for double duty. At the practical level, this means something has to give. Single parents lack the time needed to juggle work, parenting, household tasks, and a personal life. Being deprived of a mate to share the parenting responsibilities, the single parent often feels both lonely and overwhelmed. Some single mothers give more to their children and take less care of themselves, which explains the common complaint among single mothers that they have little left over for themselves.

As hard as single parents try, their children are often shortchanged. The term *latchkey children* describes youngsters who are on their own and lack adult supervision for a large portion of time even when living with the custodial parent. Because of the difficult circumstances of single parenthood, living in a single-parent home can be a lonely existence for children and place inordinate responsibility on them. Given less attention and guidance than they require, such children are disadvantaged when it comes to educational, occupational, and economical provisions.

Noncustodial Parents

Potentially, but rarely in reality, the noncustodial parent equally shares parenting responsibilities with the custodial parent. Those parents who truly put the good of their children first find a way to overcome differences with the ex-spouse and remain involved, caring, and supportive parents. Sadly, face-to-face involvement by noncustodial parents in the lives of their children consistently decreases with time. A major cause of the declining involvement is often the development of a new relationship for the father.

Since children ordinarily do not live with their father after divorce, his absence can be detrimental to both sons and daughters (Carlson 2006). Seth Schwartz and Gordon Finley (2005, 207) found that, compared with children "from intact families, those from divorced families indicated lower levels of nurturant fathering and reported family involvement." The difference was especially pronounced for children from African American, Caribbean Islander, and foreign-born Cuban families and lowest for those from non-Hispanic white and Asian families.

Economic and emotional abandonment of children by their fathers may cause many of divorce's most damaging effects. Mothers rarely abandon their children when they abandon marriage, but fathers often move away and/or fail to pay child support. Popenoe and Whitehead (2003) report that only one in six children on the average saw their father as often as once a week in the first year after divorce. Ten years after the break up, more than two-thirds of the children report not having seen their father for a year. Income for mothers and children declines about 30 percent in contrast to fathers, who gain 10–15 percent in personal income.

In seeking to understand the impact of nonresident fathers on their children, Juliana Sobolewski and Valarie King (2005) report that fathers who are engaged in cooperative coparenting after divorce have more contact with their children, and in turn are more responsive fathers, with a reported higher-quality relationship with their children.

Boys who have little contact with their fathers may see an adult role modeled only by their mother and thus have some difficulty forming their masculine identity.

Not Enough Money: The Link between Single Parenthood and Poverty

The greatest difficulty experienced by single parents is a lack of economic resources. Divorce is one path to single motherhood, unwed pregnancy the other. Both paths unfortunately have a statistically high probability of leading to poverty. It is estimated that approximately two-thirds of single-parent mothers live below the poverty level. Evidence suggests that new laws, such as no-fault divorce, have had disastrous results. A study of the effects of no-fault divorce in California concludes that in ten years divorced women and their children suffered a 73 percent drop in their standard of living. Ex-husbands were actually better off; their standard of living increased 42 percent in the first year after divorce (Weitzman 1986, 338).

It is sobering that the majority of those who divorce live below the poverty level. Lack of sufficient education or skill often means that the single parent's employment demands physical and emotional energy with little left over for the care of the children. As a way to alleviate economic stress, some single mothers remarry prematurely, only to face a second divorce. Finding employment, especially when one is not educated or trained, is an enormous burden. On top of this, the single mother must deal with the logistics of making ends meet, perhaps face the need to relocate, and take care of the emotional and physical needs of the children, which means she has little time to maintain a social life.

The discouraging evidence is that falling into single-parent family status often begins a downward spiral to deep poverty that persists from one generation to the next (Blalock, Tiller, and Monroe 2004). Such single-parent families are caught in a *culture of poverty*, a concept denoting a way of life that ensues when people are forced to adapt to poverty. Characteristics of the culture of poverty can be seen at four levels.

At the widest level there is a disengagement from and nonintegration of the poor into the major institutions of the larger society. The poor feel disempowered when they are not part of the political, religious, or economic process and feel alienated from society at large. The second level of a culture of poverty is reflected in the lack of sociocultural organization in the slum or ghetto settlement. The community of residence is almost not a community in any integrative sense. Robin Jarrett and Stephanie Jefferson reveal a glimpse of this in their article, "Women's Danger Management Strategies in an Inner-City Housing Project" (2004). This article details the multiple types of violence and predatory activity constantly confronting single mothers and their children, not only from within the community but also from the outside. Although the women's nonconfrontational and family-focus responses to violence were effective in keeping themselves and their children safe, the lack of community organization meant that the prevalence of violence was not reduced.

The third level where a culture of poverty can be seen is in the *disintegration in family life* itself. Although children and childhood are strong American values, the family of poverty affords scant room for a protected childhood. Statistical data affirm that children in poverty are the most likely victims of physical and sexual abuse. The family life cycle among the poor is compressed or speeded up. Poor families lack the time and the means to provide children with the luxury of living a carefree childhood, as children are quickly thrust into the role of caring for their younger siblings or of fending for themselves. Children who grow up in poverty and in low-income families are often deprived of a normal childhood. In their summary of many qualitative studies, Lisa Dodson and Jillian Dickert (2004) conclude that when a single mother's income is low, children—most often girls—are called on to do many of the household chores. They surmise that "when earnings are low and social support limited, girls emerge as a prime substitute for parents . . . a survival strategy" that effectively robs girls of their childhood (p. 328).

In the case of unwed mothers, who themselves are often children of a single-parent family, single motherhood often begins with an early initiation into sex, pregnancy at an early age, childbearing out of wedlock, or marriage at a young age, all of which help to perpetuate poverty and an unstable family environment.

Finally, the culture of poverty can be seen within the personality of individuals. A culture of poverty leads to a sense of fatalism, helplessness, and dependence, as well as a feeling of inferiority and lack of motivation and achievement. These personal struggles are exacerbated by few social, emotional, and material resources and little family solidarity, recreating a fertile environment for the persistence of the culture of poverty.

Poverty has a most detrimental effect on children. This begins with the difficulties experienced by parents. Deborah Ghate and Neal Hazel (2002) report that parenting in poor environments is particularly difficult because of substantially worse physical and emotional health. In the case of solo parenting, statistical analysis demonstrates that poverty rather than marital status is the more significant factor elevating parenting difficulties. Compared to two-parent biological families, all nonbiological-parent family types (single-parent, stepparent, foster-parent, and kinship care) were found to be clearly disadvantaged in terms of resources. For instance, the annual household income in nonbiological-parent households was lower by about $16,800, and parents' educational attainment and occupational prestige were lower by two levels on a scale of attainment (Youngmin 2003).

David Armor (2003) found that in nearly all studies that correctly measured families' socioeconomic status, children from families with lower socioeconomic status had lower academic achievement, even from the earliest years of school. One study found that married mothers had more education, were older, showed better psychological adjustment, were more financially secure, and had more social support than cohabiting or single mothers (Aronson 2004).

This bleak account of single-parent families should be balanced by the fact that, in spite of the extreme difficulty resulting from the lack of economic resources and time, some single-parent families function quite effectively. This is especially true when the noncustodial parent contributes financially and takes an active role in the lives of the children.

Is Workfare the Answer?

In the 1980s a fear arose that the government welfare system was actually responsible for perpetuating helplessness and dependency among the poor. One of the most articulate and influential advocates of this position was Charles Murray, whose book *Losing Ground: American Social Policy, 1950–1980* (1995), blamed welfare programs for removing incentives to work, rewarding nonwork, and creating dependency. In responding to this allegation, William O'Hare (1996) provided data indicating that only 59 percent of the poor received any kind of welfare at all in 1985, thus concluding that welfare is neither a necessary nor sufficient condition of poverty. Nevertheless, a welfare reform movement ensued, culminating in the Personal Responsibility and Work Opportunity Reconciliation Act of 1996. This act imposed time limits on the receipt of federal cash assistance for poverty-level families with dependent children. Although there is evidence that this program had some positive effects on two-parent poverty-level families, the effect on single-parent families is another story. In effect, the new law placed the value of employment for single mothers above the care of their children.

Another study on the effects of workfare indicates both benefits and costs to single mothers and their children (London et al. 2004). The benefits included increased income, increased self-esteem and feelings of independence, social integration, and the ability to model work and self-sufficiency values for children. The costs included working without increased income, overload, exhaustion, stress, and less time and energy to be with, supervise, and support children. Overall, the women in this sample expressed considerable optimism about moving from welfare to work, yet they were compromising time spent with their children to receive only modest increases in total household income.

The central issue behind the welfare to workfare program lies in assessing the effect it is having on children. Sharon Hays (2003) points out the paradox in a "family values" position that encourages mothers to stay at home to care for their children but at the same time argues that workfare rather than welfare should be offered to single mothers. She challenges the idea that children should experience the benefit of an at home mother only when they are fortunate enough to have a father who supports their mother.

Sandra Danziger, Elizabeth Ananat, and Kimberly Browning (2004) report on the importance of child care for the single mother's successful transition from welfare to work. They conclude that increased use of subsidies by eligible families and greater funding for high-quality child care would help meet the demand for this important support for working-poor families.

Family Values and Valuing Families: A Christian Response

Applying family values to the single-parent home must begin with accepting, valuing, and supporting each family member. As evident in the research, children and single parents suffer most in an isolated family system. A biblical ethic of family must include the mandate that each member in society is to be cared for—that truly none must be left behind. Jesus's radical redefinition of family (see chapter 18) leaves no room for an ethic that allows Christians to draw the line at caring only for their own families. In a household of faith, we gladly reach out and freely give our resources. We recall again Jesus's response to his disciples when they let him know his mother and brothers were outside. Jesus replied, "'Who are my mother and my brothers.' And looking at those who sat around him, he said, 'Here are my mother and my brothers! Whoever does the will of God is my brother and sister and mother'" (Mark 3:33–35). The admonition for the church as the body of Christ is to be family to those who are in need.

A disturbing finding by Marquardt (2005) is that children found the church to be less than helpful in the divorce process. For those children attending church at the time their parents divorced, two-thirds said that no one, neither clergy nor congregational members, reached out to help. Some of the children from divorced homes in her study responded to the parable of the prodigal son by identifying their parents as the prodigal one who left them. These children had a difficult time imagining themselves with open arms, welcoming parents back after they left. In the words of one young woman, "I thought it was a nice ideal if it would ever really work to actually believe that you could just leave and the fact that love would always be constant. For me, it was like, if they love me, then why do they live so far away? Or why are they always going out with boyfriends? . . . I figured if I left and went away, when I came back my house would be gone" (p. 162).

Kristen Harknett (2006, 171) has identified private safety nets—"the potential to draw upon family and friends for material or emotional support if needed"—as a major advantage that some single mothers have over others. She found that single mothers who do not have such safety nets are more prone to depression and lack of self-esteem and self-confidence. The Christian community can serve as a safety net for single-parent homes and make a significant difference to these families.

Many families are doing well, even after the disruption that occurs as a result of divorce, death, or abandonment. When both custodial and noncustodial parents take their covenant to their children seriously, there will be great reward for all concerned. Extended-family members and church community members can take the role of mentor and empower children from single-parent families. Other resources in the larger community can bring needed support, such as Big Brother/Big Sister programs, after-school activities (sports, music, art), church youth groups, and tutoring services. Welfare agencies at the local, state, and federal level can also offer substantial help that can make a difference in the lives of those family members.

18

COMPLEX FAMILIES
IN CONTEMPORARY SOCIETY

W E CAN NO longer assume that a family consists of two parents and their children. Family types now include single parents with their children full or part time; stepfamilies with his, hers, and their children full or part time; foster families; cohabiting couples with children; couples without children; households of singles and married people with or without children; and multigenerational family structures. Holding a narrow definition of family undermines the importance of these families. In this chapter, we examine the complex dynamics that occur in newly formed families and note the important qualities that keep them resilient. Diverse conditions (individual differences, quality of relationships among members, family environments, unique stressors, cultural and religious beliefs) affect the success or the failure of these families to thrive.

In our postmodern era, newly formed families face unique challenges. Adopting creative living arrangements to meet the unique needs of each family and its members can be either the making or the breaking point. David Elkind (1994, 57) describes the postmodern home as resembling "a railway station, with parents and children pulling in and out as they go about their busy lives."

Embracing differences, irregularity, and diversity necessitates permeable boundaries. Making room for each family member and his or her significant relationships (coming in and going out) challenges the structure of these families. Adapting to the changing needs of the members is quite a balancing act. Establishing family togetherness in the midst of making space for noncustodial parents and extended-family members and friends is not an easy task. Increased options introduce increased stress among family members.

Our rapidly changing technological society impresses on us the need to be proactive in keeping all families functioning at an effective level. When the multifaceted interests, abilities, gifts, and talents represented by each member become resources for the good of the whole, the family has achieved a greater goal.

A View from Trinitarian Theology

The changing nature of newly formed family structures does not change the interaction principles introduced in our trinitarian theology. The reciprocal relationships may be not only more complex, but just as or even more essential. Foundational to all interactions, regardless of the family structure, are the biblical relationship principles of covenant (establishing trust, belonging, and security); grace (living in a constant state of acceptance and forgiveness); empowerment (building one another up to reach God-given potential); mutual interdependence (differentiated unity); and intimacy (communicating in ways that establish deep connections and intimate sharing among members).

Trinitarian concepts of diversity and particularity lead us to embrace the irregularities of newly formed families. Mutuality and equality are the centering qualities governing roles and responsibilities. Both fathers and mothers remain faithful in their covenant commitment to their children even when the spousal covenant has been broken. Every family member puts the best interest of other members as a priority. The interdependence of working together for the good of the whole strengthens newly formed families.

Interdependence means that these new family members must learn to depend on one another and work together. They will receive the benefits and blessings when they feel part of and responsible for working toward a well-functioning family. Indeed, grace (acceptance and forgiveness) must abound during the process of coming together and then living together. Mutual empowerment will become a primary focus as family members show respect for differentiation as well as engage in cooperative efforts for the good of the whole family. When each member makes a contribution rather than focuses on individual rights, interdependence will be achieved. Because all members have an important place and purpose in the family, each one reaps the benefits of intimate connection.

Newly Formed Couple

An estimated 80 percent of people who divorce eventually remarry. Although these marriages have a slightly greater risk of dissolution than do first marriages (Bramlett and Mosher 2001), being remarried seems to bring restoration and renewal to most. Linda Waite's research (2002) indicates that those who divorce or are widowed regain many of marriage's benefits when they remarry. Although parental remarriage can be difficult and even catastrophic for some children, most divorced men and women hope to be in a committed relationship with a spouse who loves, values, and supports their children.

Second-marriage transition is a unique challenge for newly married spouses, and many are ill prepared to meet it. The fundamental truth is that the newly formed marriage is the most fragile relationship yet the most important link in forming the new family. The newly married couple may feel shaky in light of several external factors that have an immediate impact on them. Yet being prepared for the reality of joining their two families means they must honestly anticipate the common challenges and stand solidly together as they enter this new phase of life.

Janet, a widowed woman of three years, began dating a widower of two years who fell head over heals in love with her. Their first marriages were strong, and each felt the profound loss of a beloved partner. They each had children who would be part of the remarried family. As they began to anticipate a future together, Janet noted that Terence had not fully grieved the loss of his wife. "I can live with her memory but I cannot live in her shadow," she told her counselor. A new marriage was not possible until the loss was fully grieved. She knew that living with an idealized ghost is a no-win situation. Janet was astutely aware she could never live up to an image nor could she or would she want to replace the deceased spouse. Her own differentiated sense of self gave her a solid place to stand on her beliefs. She challenged Terence that he and his children had not sufficiently grieved their loss and until they did they could never make room for her. She knew it was a setup for immediate failure. Also Janet's younger son, Curt, had formed a special relationship with his mother since his older siblings were in college. After his father's death, he had played an important role in his mother's life and was not ready to relinquish it at this point. Clearly, he was not ready for a relationship with a stepfather. Working these issues out in therapy gave this couple the best chances of all to take their time until there was a clear readiness for these two families to come together. Timing is everything.

In a divorce situation, a major chapter has ended, and each family must make numerous changes to separate from an old life and establish a new one. Similar to the grieving process accompanying death, there is also a grieving process of letting go of the past before one is able to embrace the future. After divorce, spouses are acutely aware of the pain of a broken covenant and the unfinished emotional business accompanying that relationship. The high divorce rates for second marriages are enough to keep people from entering a new covenant before they are ready. If the pain and grieving is denied or dismissed in the throes of a new romance, however, people may plunge into a new relationship before they are emotionally ready. This is a disastrous step because without insight and changed behavior, problems will only repeat themselves.

Fortunately, many enter a second marriage after personal examination and understanding about the past relationship that ended in divorce. They have developed a differentiated self and can thus choose more carefully the second time around. Instead of repeating patterns, they have done the emotional work required to enter the new marriage with valued assets. In cases of both divorce and death, the following reminders are helpful for family members to keep in mind as they grieve their losses.

Dealing with Loss and Grief

- Fear is often a by-product of loss.
- Anger is often a by-product of fear.
- Take time to talk about the losses.
- Take time to grieve the losses.
- Don't shortchange the process—take all the time needed.

Second-Marriage Dynamics

Modern cultural ideology and norms about stepfamilies can have a negative impact on relationships. The first five years of forming the new family are the most troublesome, and during this time the couple is at greatest risk for divorce. Therefore, it is important that the couple enter marriage with optimistic strength to face head-on the realities of forming a new family. Alert to second-marriage dynamics, they can avoid making common mistakes.

Knowing the value of and being skilled in communication and conflict resolution will put the couple on the right path of interpersonal relating. What both spouses have learned in the former relationship will pay off in second-marriage dividends. Such spouses are not foolhardy, approaching the marriage with blinders on, but are realistic and have their eyes wide open, aware of what it takes to make marriage work. Prior planning regarding living arrangements (his, hers, or a new home), financial provisions, dealing with ex-spouse(s), and extended-family visiting rights will help smooth a sometimes rugged path.

The marriage is the most fragile unit of the newly formed family and therefore must be protected through a covenant commitment that builds relationship security. In their study of fifty couples in long-term marriages (nine to fourteen years together, with two or more children), Wallerstein and Blakeslee (2003) asked the question, "What do you define as happy in marriage?" They found that the answers were straightforward and could be summarized as follows: "For everyone, happiness in marriage meant feeling respected and cherished. Without exception, these couples mentioned the importance of liking and respecting each other and the pleasure and comfort they took in each other's company . . . all felt they were central to their partner's world and believed that creating the marriage and the family was the major commitment of their adult life" (p. 329).

In this study, respect was based on moral qualities such as honesty, compassion, generosity of spirit, decency, loyalty to family, and fairness. Admiration involved being a sensitive, conscientious parent. They shared the view that the partner was special and the marriage enhanced each of them as individuals. Togetherness expanded their sense of self along with the ability to include the other while carving out an area of autonomy for themselves (i.e., differentiation as defined in earlier chapters).

Building a marriage grounded in sound biblical principles also renews enthusiasm. The couple is well beyond the romanticizing of younger days and brings both wisdom and knowledge to the family dynamic. Although living alone may have led to independent living, their desire and choice is to bring togetherness and separateness into a balanced interdependency.

Remarriage can be an incredible source of healing. Being accepted, cherished, and nurtured by one's new spouse enhances connection and is reassuring. A renewed sexual relationship, shared activities, and a meaningful life are a great contrast to the lonely days. Discovering a new couple identity and protecting it with all one's might is well worth the effort. David Knox and Marty Zusman (2001) found that lack of social and extended-family support was related to lower marital happiness, especially for second wives in stepfamilies. Thus reaching out for support from family and friends helps safeguard the sacredness of the new commitment.

Newly Formed Family

The terms *blended*, *binuclear*, and *stepfamilies* are used in the literature to refer to homes in which children from a previous marriage reside. Although we often refer to newly formed families as a way to acknowledge a variety of families (foster, cohabiting, etc.), we use *reconstituted* and *stepfamilies* interchangeably as terms that have developed over the years. Constance Ahrons (Ahrons and Rodgers 1987) coined the term *binuclear* to give a positive view of being part of a reconstituted family. Such a family has two nuclei, both of which are essential to the progress of the family as a whole and the well-being of the children.

Regardless of the terms we use, a major challenge facing newly formed families concerns *ambiguity of status*. A history of shared experiences that maintained the first families is missing. The boundaries of reconstituted families must be more permeable to include everyone invested

I UNDERSTAND THAT BOTH SUE AND GARY BROUGHT THEIR CHILDREN WITH THEM WHEN THEY REMARRIED, BUT WHY IS IT CALLED A BLENDED FAMILY?

and involved in the lives of family members. Adding to the complexity of ambiguity of status is the fact that parental authority and economic responsibilities shared by two households open up emotional battles of divided loyalties and affection. Thus even though family members yearn for less ambiguity, it is a condition that needs to be accepted and lived with.

The lack of clearly defined norms regarding newly acquired relationships can be daunting. Children can feel torn when living with a stepmother or a stepfather while their biological mother or father lives elsewhere. Moreover, ambiguity is also an issue for the former wife and her current husband (or a former husband and his current wife), children's grandparents, and family friends with which close ties have been established.

The task is to build a newly formed family with a distinct history that includes fresh traditions, rituals, and experiences that become unique to them. In the process of living together, the family creates an identity that becomes a shared blessing. Here are a few ways to begin forming a new family:

Tasks of Newly Formed Families

- Discover an identify of your own as a family.
- Create holidays and traditions unique to this family.
- Plan fun times/vacations/activities together.
- Experience faith practices and worship as a family event.

Unrealistic Expectations

Another source of difficulty in any newly formed family is *unrealistic expectations*. If romantic notions about families (e.g., based on *The Brady Bunch*) drive family members, each one will end up feeling like a failure, and the whole group will be disheartened before even getting started. Instead, talk together ahead of time about natural changes and struggles to keep members realistic but hopeful.

A natural source of difficulty is for stepchildren to be more tolerant of the mistakes of their natural parents than of the mistakes of the stepparents. Most likely their history with their biological parent gives them more familiarity and confidence in that relationship. Of course, the child may also have sustained serious damage by a biological parent, which keeps that child skeptical and distant. But, in general, society conditions children to trust their own parents, and therefore they will quite naturally be more suspicious, overcautious, and even resentful of the stepparent or foster parent.

Themes in children's literature put the wicked stepmother or stepfather in a bad light. Less often do we read stories or see films about the positive role a stepparent or a foster parent plays in the life of a child, so no matter how loving and caring, stepparents are often rebuffed. Knowing this will keep the stepparent/foster parent from trying too hard or pushing too soon for a relationship. Patience is the key. Resist the temptation to move quickly into a parental role and take time to be a friendly adult who cares about the children. A stepparent can never win if he or she tries to compete with an idealized parent who, in the eyes of the child, is perfect. Listed in the following box are some common unrealistic expectations that will add perspective. Most important is learning how to get along with stepchildren/foster children and taking time to develop a relationship with them.

Unrealistic Expectations about Stepfamilies/Foster Families

- Our stepfamily/foster family will function just like our first family.
- There will be instant love between all family members.
- Everything will quickly fall into place; adjustments will be easy.
- The children will be as happy about the remarriage/new family as we are.
- The stepchildren/foster children want a relationship and will be easy to get along with.

It can be immensely helpful for couples to anticipate the tough emotional and physical adjustments that are inevitable during the first few years. Rather than crumble under the illusion of unrealistic expectations, the couple establishes a united front to face the reality of the situation. Family cohesion is not the first goal for stepfamily success. The ability to stay flexible is the golden rule. This gives the family members the necessary time to gradually get used to one another so that they can define their roles and relationships accordingly. Family cohesion can be achieved only through the mutual respect and regard that occurs when the newly-formed family is living together. Bartolomeo Palisi and his colleagues (1991) found that the couple's being realistic as well as possessing negotiation skills that lead to united decisions regarding stepchildren are predictors of remarriage adjustment.

Parents Taking Leadership

How a family navigates structural change is influenced by cultural, socioeconomic, religious, and cross-generational values and attitudes. Regardless of these influences, family leaders must do whatever they can to protect and provide for the children. Inevitable environmental and relationship changes place the parenting roles in a continual state of flux. Maintaining sufficient structure and stability counterbalances the frequent moving between households. Although the leadership of the family lies with the biological parent(s) for the most part, stepparents and/or surrogate parents play an essential part in the leadership decisions.

Research indicates that it is extremely important for the biological mother and father as well as the stepparents to be involved in the lives of the children. Parenting values and practices are a key element to be negotiated in newly formed families. The literature shows that quality and quantity time spent with children has a positive effect on their overall health and resilience. Establishing a foundation of trust and a sense of belonging is crucial in the life of a child. Even after disruptions such as death or divorce, a secure attachment established early in life gives children the capacity to build on that initial bonding (Bell 1974; Bell and Ainsworth 1972).

Cooperation and collaboration place the emphasis on teamwork in reconstituted families. The leaders set the pace for harmonious interactions. Basic agreement requires constant communication, commitment, and mutual accountability. Learning to work through differences takes persistence and perseverance. Because children are often part of two family systems, they must learn to cooperate and fit in as contributing members in both homes. Teenagers may contribute by assuming a role in child care and younger children through performing household chores; the entire family may choose to prepare meals as a cooperative venture: everyone pitches in to clean up, and so on. Consulting with children and teens about family responsibilities and rewards brings them into the process as contributing members who also express their preferences and privileges. When family rules are determined in a democratic way, each member has input and takes responsibility in the cooperative venture. Schedules, lists, routines, and structure help organize the family, while adaptations are made in response to the needs of its unique members.

Communicating individual and family needs becomes the joint responsibility of every member and the family as a whole.

Guidelines for Leadership

- Be united in your leadership roles.
- Don't initiate major changes (rules and routines) too soon.
- Establish clearly defined rules in a timely manner.
- Be flexible and adaptable when possible.
- Use a weekly family council time to negotiate family goals.
- Stand together on goals and expectations decided in the family council.
- Create strategies for making decisions, negotiating solutions, and resolving problems.

Stepparents/Stepchildren

It will come as no surprise that the quality of the stepparent-stepchild relationship greatly affects the couple relationship. Age is a moderating factor in that the younger the children are during the remarriage, the greater the likelihood of success.

Children quite normally experience a strain between loyalty to their natural parents and to their stepparents. Stepparents who no longer live with the children from their first marriage may also struggle with loyalty issues. Perhaps moved by guilt to be better parents with the new family, they become more intense, which actually hinders establishing a relationship with their stepchildren.

Many studies indicate that children can and do form close emotional ties with stepparents. To be successful, stepparents must take sufficient time to form relationships with each child. This transition period provides the stabilization process in which stepfamily members experience and begin to think of themselves more as a family unit (Bray and Kelly 1998).

According to Hetherington and Kelly (2002), making a good transition into parenting involves the stepparents' ability to initially consider themselves as secondary parents. It is especially important for the stepparent to be a warm and supportive friend and refrain from taking on a strong disciplinary role in the beginning. The point is to let the biological parent continue in the disciplinary role and to simply back this role rather than be the one who determines it. The couple is the architect of the newly formed family, and when their spousal relationship is solid, their joint leadership sets the right tone for the rest of the family. Agreement between stepparents about the rules and roles are solid building blocks for discipline strategies and interaction with the children.

The positive stepparent-stepchild relationship keeps members connected and united rather than distant and fragmented. Establishing appropriate boundaries and working out a cooperative relationship with former spouses also goes a long way in keeping the marital dyad strong. In contrast, highly charged, conflicted, or negative relationships with former spouses negatively affect the new couples' relationship (Buunk and Matsaers 1999; Knox and Zusman 2001).

Stepfathers/Stepchildren

In most cases, it is the mother who brings children into the reconstituted family. Thus, the most problematic relationship is usually between the stepfather and the stepchildren. Stepfathers tend to be either very much involved with or disengaged from their stepchildren (Hetherington, Cox, and Cox 1982). One study found that children who live with stepfathers are as happy and successful as are children who live with their biological fathers (Bohannan and Yahraes 1979); another found children who live with stepfathers to be better off than fatherless children (Oshman and Manosevitz 1976).

Initially, both boys and girls tend to be somewhat resistant to a stepfather coming into the home. Over time he is likely to win them over, especially if he does not take a strict disciplinarian role but works hard to build a relationship with his stepchildren. Mavis Hetherington and her colleagues (1982) found that boys are generally more open to a stepfather, whereas girls tend to resist his intrusion into their special mother-daughter relationship. Teenage daughters of divorcées seem to have difficulty interacting in appropriate ways with stepfathers, even though they desire and seek male attention.

According to research, girls make a better adjustment after divorce if they are cared for by their mothers, and boys make a better adjustment if they are cared for by their fathers. It seems that girls in the custody of their fathers and boys in the custody of their mothers profit from remarriage. Their social development is enhanced with the arrival of stepparents (Santrock, Warshak, and Elliott 1982). Charles Hobart (1987, 274) found that, given the centrality of the mother in family life, the children of a husband's prior marriage receive less attention than do the children of a wife's prior marriage.

William Marsiglio (2004) did a conceptual analysis using in-depth interviews exploring stepfathers' experiences in claiming stepchildren as their own. Trying too quickly to construct an unrealistic "we-ness" or isolating oneself in the outsider position hinders the process. Because of the complexity of each situation, the stepfather needs to be wise in establishing a quality, stable connection with stepchildren. In this study, the majority of the men expressed a reasonably strong connection with their stepchildren and took responsibility in practical ways in the home regarding money, discipline, protection, guidance, child care, and affection. "It was shared daily contact and practical involvement in their stepchildren's lives that altered their views in almost imperceptible ways" (p. 37). A sense of "we-ness" was developed through joint activities in everyday situations. It seems stepfathers grew closer to their stepchildren as time went on and as they began to think of themselves in the fatherly role. Making an unconditional commitment to the stepchildren and gradually spending time with them helped the stepfathers see the stepchildren as their own.

The ten interrelated benchmarks that emerged in stepfathers claiming stepchildren as their own concerned timing, degree of deliberativeness, degree of identity conviction, paternal role range, solo-shared identity, mindfulness, propriety, work, naming, and seeking public recognition (Marsiglio 2004, 27). The biological mother's influence is also important to the stepfathers' success. When she encourages connection and expects him to take responsibility for her children, it opens an opportunity for him to develop feelings for them. In a real sense she is making it easy for the stepfather to have a relationship with her children when she asks him to pick up the kids after school, help with homework, and take part in the discipline.

Being a stepparent is an extremely demanding job. You must be relentless in your compassion for the children and refuse to view them as out to get you. Trying to create one big, happy family is an erroneous goal, so stepparents should live with the realistic goal to do everything possible to live in harmony in the newly formed family. The perseverance, courage, patience, and sacrifice usually offer great rewards.

Marital Tension over Stepchildren

The not-so-surprising news is that one falls in love with the person he or she marries but not necessarily with his or her children. Thus engaging each other's children may be the most difficult aspect of remarriage. Even when you know you have a lot to offer as a parent, your confidence is easily destroyed by the indifference or rejection of your spouse's children. Often the stepparent is seen as the unwanted intruder. Your attempts at nurture may be automatically spurned and even ridiculed by stepchildren. When children have been emotionally hurt and disillusioned with life, they hold on to unrealistic fantasies that parents will reunite and make everything better. They can be fiercely determined to defeat the stepparent. This is new territory for both parents and children. No one is ever prepared for such disruption, which has the power to devastate the new marriage.

Explosion over who has priority, the spouse or the children, creates startling tension between the remarried spouses. Similar marital struggles in a first marriage do not take on such emotional dimensions because the children are the couple's own. As good as the marriage may be, guilt, anger, and trouble over children can take a serious toll on any marital relationship.

In exploring the good parent/bad parent phenomenon in a stepfamily situation with adolescents, Susan Knower (2003) found that adolescent stepchildren polarized parents who were indulgent as compared to those who were disciplinarian into good and bad categories. Especially if the indulgent parent is the biological parent, the stepparent is put in the negative position of being the more demanding bad parent. Giving in to avoid stress leads to confusion about family rules and fails to establish maturity demands on the developing teen. The parental hierarchy becomes skewed quite easily because the biological parent naturally forms a close bond with his/her children. The stepparent is also seen as the enemy who is breaking the children's bond with their biological parent.

A further complication is that adolescents are entering the life stage when it is common to question, engage in conflict with parents, and challenge authority figures. Under these circumstances, adolescent stepchildren believe the new parent has no right to discipline them. Every attempt must be made to neutralize the dichotomous good parent/bad stepparent thinking so that stepparents can be effective in their leadership.

Lawrence Ganong and Marilyn Coleman (2004) found that stepfamilies are more complex than previously thought, and they can function successfully in different ways. However, when stepfamilies are able to construct an identity of their own and the members can establish relationships with one another, they are well on their way. The study shows that the nature and quality of the stepparent-stepchild relationship depend on several factors, such as the stepparent's investment in the relationship, the stepchild's willingness for the relationship, the relationship with the nonresidential parent, and time available (pp. 227–32).

Summary

Ronald Deal (2002, 70) uses the analogy of a crock pot to describe the stepfamily. He writes:

It takes time and low heat to make an effective combination of ingredients. When ingredients are thrown together in the same pot, each is left intact, giving affirmation to its unique origin and characteristics. Slowly and with much intentionality, the low-level heat brings the ingredients into contact with one another. As the juices begin to flow together, imperfections are purified, and the beneficial, desirable qualities of each ingredient are added to the taste. The result is a dish of delectable flavor made up of different ingredients that give of themselves to produce a wondrous creation.

Stepfamilies are a work in process! The concept of differentiation helps us put to rest the idea of a blended, bland family. Only when each member is able to contribute his or her distinctiveness will there be a rich flavor to taste. Relationships with stepchildren develop over time. They set a pace that cannot be hurried.

Take it one small step at a time. It takes time for each family member to adjust to new living conditions and new roles, rules, and responsibilities. It takes time to get to know one another, develop trust, and begin a shared history. It takes time to find a sense of belonging, interdependence, and identity as a newly formed family unit. Learning to trust the time factor gives spouses permission to relax, lower expectations, go with the flow, and enjoy the moments of progress. Be patient. Be ever ready to listen with compassion. Persevere, and remember to use humor, laughter, and play in developing relationships with stepchildren.

William Doherty (1997) reminds us of the difficulties all families experience in rearranging busy schedules to be together. It takes an even more intentional effort for stepfamilies to make these connections. It requires tremendous openness and flexibility to address the unique needs and desires of each member in the midst of establishing family routines and rituals that bond them together. A highly effective way to formulate a family identity is to create family traditions, rituals, and celebrations around significant holidays. When family members come together for such events, they each bring a unique presence. Be it a birthday celebration at a special restaurant, a church advent service, or an annual trip to the beach or the mountains, it brings history and harmony to the newly formed family.

Routines, Rituals, Traditions

- Invite the children to help create traditions and rituals.
- Welcome their ideas and follow their suggestions.
- Give adolescents leadership roles.
- Allow time for family ties to evolve.
- Make weekly, monthly, and yearly opportunities for connection.

Learning to apply the concepts and principles discussed throughout this book—empowerment, acceptance, grace, intimacy, and loyalty—will lead to stepfamily growth. Showing empathy and tolerance for one another, putting the best interest of others on a par with one's own, and giving of oneself out of care and concern for others develops not only character but also closeness.

The rewards are great when the members of the newly formed family can establish meaningful relationships and join in cooperative projects. Finding mutual meaning in spiritual life forges a bond that gives the family a significant purpose beyond itself. We suggest you refer to chapter 8, which discusses family spiritual life, for more ideas about this process.

PART 7

FAMILY LIFE
IN POSTMODERN SOCIETY

Any meaningful understanding of the family must integrate an analysis of the family at both the micro and the macro level. We have focused mainly on microfamily issues—looking inside the family for an understanding of its dynamics. We turn now to an analysis of macrofamily issues—looking outside the family to explore the relationship between the family and the wider social context. Through this exploration, we will see that many microfamily issues are, in reality, a reflection of macrofamily issues.

In chapter 1, we developed a theology of family relationships based on the biblical concept of covenant. Now we move beyond the family to examine the broader social context. The contemporary family lives in a world of urbanization, bureaucracy, and technology, developments that make covenant commitment increasingly difficult. Contemporary family life has been profoundly affected first by modernity and second by postmodernity. Rather than replacing modernity, postmodernity exists as a layer upon modernity, as both interact in their effect on the family. Chapter 19 introduces major aspects of modernization (an issue first addressed in the 1950s and 1960s) and their profound negative influence on contemporary family life. Not only has covenant commitment eroded within the family, but the very structures that were intended to support and maintain this ideal have collapsed. In chapter 20, we discuss postmodernity's effects on family life and present a biblical response to modernity and postmodern thought. We suggest ways in which covenant commitment can and must be incorporated into broad social structures. Only by recapturing the covenantal meaning of living in community, whether it is localized or universal, can the family be strong. We need a family-friendly society.

19

THE EROSION OF BIBLICAL TRUTH
IN A POSTMODERN WORLD

IT WAS THE best of times, it was the worst of times." Charles Dickens's description of revolutionary change in eighteenth-century France aptly characterizes the family in the United States and around the world today. It truly is the best of times and the worst of times. The contemporary family is an institution of contrasts and contradictions. Although the current divorce rate in modern nations is virtually as high as ever, more married couples than in the past report satisfaction in their relationship. At the very time that millions of children are living in broken families, there is also an unprecedented emphasis on love and intimacy in family relationships. And just as some are celebrating the freedom and openness brought about by new family forms, others are horrified at the decline of the family. Don Browning, M. Christian Green, and John Witte (2006) document how the major world religions are currently wrestling with questions of the purpose and meaning of marriage and family life in modern society. In focusing on the American family, Steven Tipton and John Witte (2005) suggest that the family is indeed in trouble and can be rescued only by reintegrating it into a just moral order of the larger community and society. They argue that beyond merely upholding traditional family values, we must come to terms with increasing family diversity.

The successive effects of modernity and postmodernity have also led to contradictions in the family. Our society has traditionally espoused a very optimistic view of the future, based largely on faith in progress. However, what was once heralded as the path to a utopian future is now being blamed for the decline of the family and the quality of life in our postmodern world.

Along with this lament for the family, we must also be cautious when valuing the family too highly at the expense of the "larger project." As Peter Selby (1996, 168) reminds us, we must be ever cognizant that God invites us "to become people who transcend our descent: we are to become children of God 'born not of blood or of the will of the flesh or of the will of a man, but of God' (John 1:13)."

Modernity Defined

A concept as inclusive and encompassing as modernity is difficult to define. One line of thought considers modernity to be closely tied to technological development. According to Marion Levy (1966, 190), "the greater the ratio of inanimate power sources and the greater the extent to which human efforts are multiplied by the use of tools, the more modernized is the society." Peter Berger likewise conceives of modernity as closely linked to technology. His view has been summarized by James Hunter (1983, 6): "Modernization is to be understood . . . as a process of institutional change proceeding from and related to a technologically engendered economic growth. . . . Modernity is the inevitable period in the history of a particular society that is characterized by the institutional and cultural concomitant of a technologically induced economic growth."

Other theorists understand modernization as social change in various spheres. Neil Smelser (1973, 748), for example, sees modernization as occurring

> (1) in the *political* sphere, as simple tribal or village authority systems give way to systems of suffrage, political parties, representation, and civil service bureaucracies; (2) in the *educational* sphere, as the society strives to reduce illiteracy, and increase economically productive skills; (3) in the *religious* sphere, as secularized belief systems begin to replace traditionalist religions; (4) in the *familial* sphere, as extended kinship units lose their pervasiveness; (5) in the *stratificational* sphere, as geographical and social mobility tends to loosen fixed, ascriptive hierarchical systems.

The sociological concept of modernization reflects both evolutionary theory and structural functionalism. Evolutionary theory assumes that a society advances from a simple to a complex state. This process is usually described as "development," with traditional agrarian communities with minimal technological innovation regarded as undeveloped. Modernization, then, is conceived as occurring in stages. We might imagine, for instance, a five-stage progression beginning with an *agrarian society*, *preconditioning for takeoff*, *takeoff*, *drive to maturity*, and finally *high mass consumption*.

Structural functionalism assumes that as economic development takes place, new social and cultural forms must emerge. It argues that new institutional forms are desirable and necessary in view of the changes in economic life. Some Christians, who see God-given ideals behind traditional social institutions, experience modernity as a threat. While the threat is real, modernity also affords the opportunity to examine existing social structures and re-create them in light of the biblical ideal.

The Crisis and Challenge of Modernity

A primary feature of modernity is the disintegration of traditional forms. Nathan Glazer has said that being modern involves "a sense of the breaking of the seamless mold in which *values*, *behavior*, and *expectations* were once cast into interlocking forms" (cited in Seeman 1957, 411). With this breakdown of traditional forms comes the responsibility to create new institutional structures. And with this opportunity come threats of social, moral, and intellectual chaos, making the creative task of reconstructing institutions overwhelming. We live in the tension created by the dual realities of choice and a series of modern deterministic factors that Jacques Ellul (1976, 27) characterizes as "a collection of mechanisms of indescribable complexity—technics, propaganda, state, administrative planning, ideology, urbanization, social technology." This tension leads us to see only the threats of modernization. Rather than facing up to modernity, as Peter Berger has advised, we too often retreat or try to avoid the issues.

Social scientists continue to debate the origins and moving forces of modernization. While some theorists believe that modernization is fueled primarily by economic and technological forces, others point out that ideological changes have made modernization possible. We believe that modernization unfolds in a dialectical manner, fed by both material and ideological aspects of life. No part of society and culture is autonomous; no social entity develops purely in terms of its own internal organization. This is true of every major structural unit of contemporary society—the church, the family, the economy, education, and politics.

Although there is interaction between all the major dimensions of life, the economic and technological are dominant in present-day Western society. The other dimensions of life have been cast into a responsive, rather than a leading, role. However, the various internal crises of modernization may lead to changes in the current balance of power. For example, the issue of moral legitimation in modern society may lead to a new role for religious and moral institutions. Many question whether a society built on moral pluralism and its attendant, moral uncertainty can maintain itself. As Berger (1983) has suggested, the crisis of secularization may lead to an awareness of the need for a new moral, if not religious, consensus in modern society.

In developing a framework to analyze the modern situation, we consider four dimensions of sociocultural life: consciousness, communication, community, and commodities (see figure 19, in which the solid arrows represent logical priority, and the broken arrows feedback between the various dimensions). Modernization is rooted largely in economic reality (commodities); changes at this level are reflected at the other levels of sociocultural life. Each level also sends feedback to the others. The dialectical model we are suggesting is similar to a general model of social structure in which each part is conceived as influencing and being influenced by every other part. We hasten to add that these dimensions should be considered as analytical constructs only. They should not be reified and considered separate components of reality.

In facing up to the challenge of being modern, we must address all areas of life. We have chosen these four dimensions because they are the settings in which major crises are occurring in our world today. We will first explore the general dilemma posed in each of these layers of sociocultural life and then turn our attention to the specific negative effects on the family.

Consciousness

Consciousness refers to the individual's subjective experiences, including thoughts, beliefs, images, and emotions. Crises in this area can occur both within and between individuals—both subjectively and intersubjectively.

Within the individual, consciousness is fragmented among different spheres of life. The individual must negotiate between the impersonal competition of the marketplace and the intimacy of friendship and family, between rationality in the school and faith in the pew, between the fast-paced solutions of multimedia and the routine open-endedness of daily life. Under such circumstances, even the best minds and the most

FIGURE 19 **The Four Dimensions of Sociocultural Life**

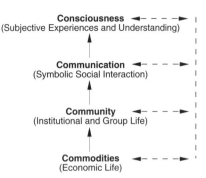

stable personalities can quickly lose a sense of centeredness, a clear grasp of meaning and reality.

This fragmentation of thought has resulted in a disjunction between faith and life. We ask the questions: How do our beliefs and values affect the structure of our lives? Do competing values and beliefs shape different areas of our lives? Do our commitments and beliefs as Christians distinguish us from other people?

Michael Billings (1982) suggests that people today live in a state of cognitive dissonance. We have adapted to apparently inconsistent beliefs and lack of congruency between values and behavior. For example, interpersonal commitments and intimacy are highly valued, but relationships are unstable. Many Christians speak about having compassion for the poor but avoid those in need. To paraphrase the apostle Paul, we are trapped in a sociological "body of death," doing not the good we want, but the evil we do not want—and we do not understand our actions (Rom. 7:15–25).

A diversity of worldviews is available to us. The more modern we become, the more we are aware of this diversity and the more relative our views appear. Berger (1983) refers to this as the pluralization of consciousness. For some, this opens the door for a challenging dialogue with others to help in the construction of one's personal value system. This can be an awesome and lonely task. Others try to mold a new consensus either by creating a new synthesis through dialogue or by cutting the dialogue short and imposing their own beliefs on the other participants. Another possible way of proceeding is subjectivization. As Hunter (1982, 40) puts it:

> When the institutional routines and ideologies are rendered implausible, modes of conduct and thought, *morality included*, are deliberated. If institutions no longer provide consistent and reliable answers to such ques-

tions as "What do I do with my life?" "How do I raise my children?" "Is it acceptable to live with a member of the opposite gender outside of marriage?" etc., the individual must necessarily *turn inward* to the subjective to reflect, ponder and probe for answers. The process of "turning inward" is the process of subjectivization.

As Hunter further suggests, the process of subjectivization is not negative—it is simply a structural feature of modern society. It can, however, foster "an incessant fixation upon the self . . . [an] abiding absorption with the 'complexities' of individuality" (p. 40).

Communication

Communication in modern society both shapes and reflects the fragmentation, pluralization, and subjectivization of modern consciousness. Significant symbols—terms that everyone understands in precisely the same way—are the basis of communication. But in modern society we cannot assume that everyone understands a term in precisely the same way. Even the words *family* and *church* have a variety of meanings that can arouse emotional debate. The denotative, or referential, meanings of words vary considerably; consider the multitude of meanings of the word *love*. The connotative, or associative, meanings are even more diverse. Lack of consensus on meanings creates a dilemma. On the one hand, our diverse backgrounds and uniqueness as individuals make communication more necessary than ever. On the other hand, our lack of significant symbols makes communication equally problematic.

A variety of questions arise in the context of our attempts to communicate: How can we communicate if we cannot assume that others will understand our words as we understand them? How is dialogue possible if there is no shared basis of interpreting language? Are our vocabularies authentic? How free are we to create new vocabularies and to give new meanings to words? What is the relationship between experience and language? Can we trust the very process of communication? Will language become, like advertising, one more technique to mystify and control others?

The difficulties of communicating are compounded today by the proliferation of technical and professional languages, which mystify the nonspecialist. We also see attempts to transcend the traditional means of symbolic communication through various forms of nonverbal communication. For the most part, everyday language and conversation are impoverished because of the difficulty of capturing complex and confusing realities in simple words.

Community

Phyllis Airhart and Margaret Bendroth (1996) conclude that although the ideal of community and family life might differ in the various faith traditions, modernity has fragmented the sense of community and family life. Many people have lamented the breakdown of homogeneous and geographically based communities as the major crisis of the modern era. Without such communities, we have no means of social control and are thus vulnerable to ourselves (to our own moral laxity) and to strangers around us. Peter Berger, Brigitte Berger, and Hansfried Kellner (1973) and others have spoken of the homeless mind: people are in search of a new home or community so that they can find meaning and purpose. What is often forgotten when we grieve the loss of traditional communities, however, is the provincialism and lack of autonomy that characterize them. Isolated villages and tribal groups are noted for their ethnocentrism.

Concurrent with the disintegration of community life is the centralization of economic and political functions in corporate and governmental bureaucracies. The picture that emerges is of the isolated individual and

IS THIS WHAT PAUL MEANT BY CHRISTIAN COMMUNITY, DAD?

the nuclear family confronted with the faceless image of mass society. The community that once mediated between the individual and larger institutions is no longer there. Judicial and political institutions are increasingly called on to settle family, church, and community disputes. Government encroachment into areas previously considered private or sacred has become a serious social question to which there are no apparent answers.

Some social scientists have suggested that networks are the modern substitute for traditional communities. Friends, coworkers, and social, educational, cultural, and religious groups—together these networks can satisfy all or almost all of the individual's needs. However, networks tend to be unstable and specialized and thus lack the virtues associated with community: unconditional commitment and a sense of belonging that encompasses the whole of a person's life.

There is a wide range of responses to the disintegration of traditional communities. At one extreme is the trend toward a self-contained individualism that denies dependence on others and makes no commitment to them. At the other extreme, we find people experimenting with various forms of communities focused around a common value such as economic sharing, family life, or religious devotion. In between these extremes are the many people searching for a sense of community in institutional contexts such as the church, where the community metaphor is familiar, and in homogeneous neighborhoods such as suburban housing developments, where names like Homewood, Pleasantdale, and Community Heights imply commonality and identity.

Commodities

In advanced capitalism, the economic sphere has been largely secularized. Economic life develops unguided by any particular religious ideology. This differentiation of economic life is characteristic of modern institutions. The fragmentation of consciousness, complexity of communication, and disintegration of community make an integration of life around economics seem viable. Richard Fenn (1974, 41–42) argues that religion has not served to integrate modern society and that uniformity or consensus will most likely be limited to political and economic issues. Remaining unanswered is the question whether a society based solely on economic and political consensus can maintain itself.

Economic principles do dominate modern social life. Jacques Ellul (1964) notes that the principle of technique or rational efficiency has moved from the economic realm to all other areas of life, including the political, the educational, and the interpersonal. As the principles and values associated with economic life enter other areas, we see a pattern of the "commodification" of social life developing.

Karl Marx maintained that the capitalist emphasis on commodities results in the alienation of the worker. The intrinsic meaning of work is lost. Work becomes only a means to the end of making money. Consequently, workers define themselves and others in terms of their ability to make money. Money has become a spiritual force in society as well as a moral criterion for judging people and their activities (Ellul 1964). Social interaction and the creative process are subservient to the goals of efficiency and production. The twin phenomena of careerism and consumerism, two evidences of these trends, are found at the center of economic, church, and family life.

The Impact of Modernity on the Family

With this basic understanding of modernity, we can now examine the dilemmas it poses for the family, as well as the false hopes it has generated (see table 9).

The Fragmentation of Consciousness

The problem. The fragmentation of consciousness has produced a crisis in the areas of morality and authority within the family. Each family must construct its own value system, usually without the support of the extended family. Difficulties are especially likely to arise when children reach their teenage years and begin to compare their family's system of morality with that of their friends. Parents are placed in the position of having to defend their view of morality against the view of their children's peers. The crisis in authority brought about by the fragmentation of consciousness also includes questions of the authority of the extended family over the nuclear family and of the husband over the wife. The current redefinition of sex roles comes into play here.

The fragmentation of consciousness has also led to a dichotomy between public and private life. In traditional societies, there tends to be little separation between the two; the primary social unit in both work and private life is one and the same—the family, the clan, or the tribe. In contrast, the recent separation of work and private life has led to two levels of social functioning. While working, individuals experience others as relatively impersonal beings and themselves as anonymous functionaries (Berger, Berger, and Kellner 1973, 34). This anonymity precludes any involvement on a plane higher than what might be described as pseudointimacy. People attempt to find genuine intimacy, meaning, and fulfillment in their private lives. But we suspect that modernity may have so weakened the private institution of the family that even here intimacy and fulfillment are not possible.

False hopes. As the Christian community has felt the crisis created by the fragmentation of consciousness, a major response by conservatives has been traditionalism—an attempt to restore the family to what it was in the past. With the confusion created by modernity, many Christians are quick to hold up the nineteenth-century American version of the family as the biblical ideal. We believe that this is a false hope because it is less the biblical perspective on the family in modern society than a defense of what the family has been in the past. Christians commonly fall into the trap of assuming that the particular family form existing in their culture is God's ideal. They read their own cultural standards into Scripture and accept all biblical accounts of family life as if they were normative. But some of the accounts of how the family was organized during biblical times were never intended to dictate how it should be organized in all cultures at all times.

A second response to the fragmentation of family consciousness is to rely on expert opinion, another false hope. Parents often experience a crisis in confidence and are unwilling to trust their common sense out of fear that they may be doing something wrong in rearing their children. Such self-doubt frequently occurs in the Christian community, where many parents hold to a deterministic view of parenting: they wrongly believe that correct parenting is a guarantee of God-fearing children. Unfortunately, this view is reinforced by a variety of self-proclaimed experts, who attract large numbers of parents eager to be relieved of the agonizingly difficult task of parenting in modern society.

Another false hope is the privatization of family life, an offshoot of the dichotomy between private and public life. In the words of J. A. Walter (1979, 49–50):

> In modern society, marriage and the family enable me to construct a home world in which I am known as the self I would like to be and in which I, in turn, confirm the self of my spouse. Or at least this is the hope. Marriage and the family provide a whole universe of meanings which is for the family members real reality as opposed to the artificial reality of the public world out there. Marriage provides a do-it-yourself reality kit.

To the extent that the do-it-yourself family creates a consciousness that is out of touch with external reality, it can be described as a false hope. Also the privatization of family life can easily lead to an amoral familism, where the family is so preoccupied with its own concerns that it fails to serve far needier people. The amoral privatized family dishonors the biblical concept of family life.

Table 9

The Impact of Modernity on the Family:
Dilemmas and False Hopes

Impact of Modernity	Dilemmas for the Family	False Hopes
Fragmentation of Consciousness		

Fragmentation of thought
Religious and moral
  pluralism
Disjunction between faith
  and life
Subjectivization
	Crisis in morality and
	  authority
	Dichotomy between private
	  and public life
		Traditionalism: restoring the
		  family of the past
		Cult of the expert
		Privitization

Complexity of Communication		

Decline of significant
  symbols
Mystifying technical
  language
Impoverished conversation
	Diverse backgrounds and
	  linguistic styles
	Generation gap
		Overreliance on techniques
		  of communication
		Isolation of communication
		  from regular activities

Disintegration of Community		

Disintegration of traditional
  community life
Lack of social control
Individuals confronted by
  bureaucracy and mass
  society
Government encroachment
  into private matters
	Isolated nuclear family
	Lack of community support
	  and control
	Increased family
	  dependence on mass
	  institutions
	Development of a youth
	  culture
	Little parental stake in
	  children's marriages
	Lack of ties between
	  extended families
	Diminished parental
	  authority
	Equalization of power within
	  the family
		The family as a self-
		  contained unit
		Extrafamilial care of children,
		  the elderly, and
		  handicapped
		Alternative family forms

Dominance of Commodities		

Integration of society around
  economic values
Separation of economic from
  church life
"Commodification" of social
  life
Dominance of technical
  means
	The family as the unit of
	  consumption instead of
	  production
	Separation of work and
	  family life
	Individual and family worth
	  determined by economics
		Assessment of the fair
		  market value of
		  housework
		Community through
		  consumption
		The family as the center of
		  cottage industry
		Full employment for both
		  husband and wife
		  (careerism)

Complexity of Communication

The problem. The complexity of communication in modern society saps vitality from family life. That there is no exact universal understanding of words such as *family, love, parenting, intimacy,* and *sharing* complicates communication and relations. To the extent that a husband and a wife come from diverse backgrounds or experience differing patterns of growth, they will encounter difficulty in communication. It may very well be that the seemingly unending search for intimacy in contemporary society is an attempt to fill a void resulting from a lack of shared experiences.

Parents with teenage children are quick to realize that a good part of what is referred to as the generation gap is in large measure a gap in communication. With the emergence of the adolescent subculture come not only new meanings for old words (*cool, hot, tight, bad, square*) but also new words (*punk, new wave, mod, rad, oye*). To appreciate the complexity of communication among adolescents, one must realize that there is no monolithic adolescent subculture; rather, there are adolescent subcultures (preppies, mods, stoners, rockers, new wavers, surfers, and straights), each developing its own style of communication (much of it nonverbal).

False hopes. Overreliance on the techniques of communication is a common response to the complexity of communication in the family. One need only glance at the many how-to books written on marital and family communication to realize the heavy emphasis placed on technique. But a focus on technique can actually reduce communication. Spouses may find themselves talking about talking rather than engaging in genuine dialogue. The overreliance on technique has spread even into the area of sexual communication; manuals promise a couple complete sexual fulfillment if they will only follow the suggested step-by-step procedure.

Another response to the complexity of communication is to isolate communication from our customary activities. Many parents, realizing the need to explain to their children the reasons for family rules and values, set aside time for discussion rather than having such conversations as a natural part of life together. Essentially, then, family communication is removed from the normal course of activity and becomes one more task for the modern family. It is better to explain family rules and values whenever a suitable occasion presents itself. Communication will be greatly improved if it is embedded in the common experiences of developing family relationships.

Disintegration of Community

The problem. The extended family has been replaced by the nuclear family in most modern societies. With the uprooting of the nuclear family from its extended family, clan, or tribal base comes the loss of community support and control of family life. The isolated nuclear family in modern society is a very fragile system. Gone is the day-to-day support provided by the extended family. The young married couple must go it alone. With no one else to share in the task of child care, the absence of either husband or wife (or of both) from the home can be severely disruptive.

It has been argued that the isolated nuclear family is the most functional social unit for modern industrial society. At a time when others were announcing the decline of the American family, Talcott Parsons and Robert Bales (1955, 9) made the optimistic assessment that the family is not in a state of decline but is instead becoming more specialized:

> The family has become *a more specialized agency than before*, probably more specialized than it has been in any previously known society. This represents a decline of *certain* features which traditionally have been associated with families, but whether it represents a "decline of the family" in a more general sense is another matter; we think not. We think the trend of the evidence points to the beginning of the relative stabilization of a new type of family structure, in a new relation to a general social structure, one in which the family is more specialized than before, but not in any general sense less important, because the society is dependent *more* exclusively on it for the performance of its vital functions.

Parsons and Bales envisioned small community-based organizations such as churches, neighborhood schools, clubs, and voluntary associations assuming the traditional family functions. The family in modern society, however, has become increasingly dependent on mass economic and governmental institutions. Gone are the smaller community-based mediating structures between the nuclear family and the impersonal, centralized, bureaucratic structures of modern mass society.

The lack of community moorings has freed family members to become part of social networks over which the family has very little control. As mentioned previously, teenagers have become part of adolescent subcultures. The trend in society is for family members to participate as individuals in a variety of specialized interest groups. Although most groups are not likely to foster intimate relationships, those that do will further disintegrate the family as a community.

William Goode (1963) identifies three components of modern ideology that set the individual above the traditional community: (1) the primacy of industrial growth over tradition and custom; (2) equality between the sexes; and (3) the primacy of the conjugal relationship over extended-family relationships. Goode sees the emergence of these emphases as serving to free the individual from the domination of the extended family and from the bonds of traditional ways of doing things.

One of the major strengths of Goode's work is the historical and cross-cultural support he garners for his thesis. On the basis of this evidence, Goode concludes that modern societies are moving toward a family system centering on the conjugal relationship. Among the characteristics of this system are (1) a bilateral method of reckoning kinship ties, that is, since husband and wife come from different families, they will recognize a somewhat different set of kindred; (2) little parental stake in children's marriages; (3) mate selection on the basis of romantic love; (4) absence of customs such as the dowry and the bride price, which traditionally served to unite extended families; (5) the diminishing of parents' authority over children and husbands' authority over wives; and (6) the equalization of power within the family and the emergence of negotiation as a means of decision making (1963, 7–10). Goode is right in his observation that these changes have served to free the individual from the dominance of the extended family. However, modern ultra-individualism, with its lack of accountability to the community, causes us to wonder if too large a price is being paid for this freedom.

False hopes. At least three responses to the disintegration of community prove to be false hopes. First, some families become self-contained units. They attempt to meet their every need internally. They develop their own ideology, strive for economic self-sufficiency, and become deeply enmeshed. The self-contained family is an unrealistic ideal that is doomed to fail in modern society. It is also inconsistent with Jesus's definition of family (Mark 3:31–35).

Out of necessity, other families in modern society are turning to extra-familial institutions for the care of dependent members. Many of these families are fractured units that do not have the resources needed to provide adequate care for children, the elderly, or the disabled. In other instances, the stress on individualism and personal self-fulfillment prevents family members from actively assuming caretaking responsibilities. They ignore the fact that the quality of care that large institutions can give needy people rarely measures up to the New Testament standard of *koinōnia* (fellowship, community).

The third response has been the development of alternative family forms. It is true that family forms must change in response to modernity; to think otherwise is to accept the traditional American family as the biblical ideal, instead of merely one among several equally justifiable cultural alternatives. Christians must be aware, however, that, as a result of modernity's secularizing influence, among the alternatives currently being promoted are homosexual marriage, group marriage, planned single parenthood, and nonmarital cohabitation. That is to say, there currently exists a relativistic predisposition to re-create the family in any form that might suit the demands of individual self-fulfillment and modern society. Adoption of such alternative forms ignores not only scriptural authority but also the possibility that the demands of the individual and modern society might well need to be changed for the sake of the family rather than the other way around.

The emergence of genetic technologies such as artificial insemination, in vitro fertilization, surrogate motherhood, external gestation, and cloning makes it possible for one person or any combination of persons to form a family for a newborn child. Ted Peters (1996) gives a Christian response to these issues, arguing that any use of genetic technology must be based on a covenant commitment to have children. The continued development and application of genetic technology in reproductive efforts must also be assessed vis-à-vis their effect on the communal aspects of family life.

Dominance of Commodities

The problem. A major effect of the dominance of commodities has been to change the family from the basic unit of production to the basic unit of consumption. It is rare to find family members together for the purpose of producing; it is equally rare to find family members together for any purpose other than consuming. The world of work and family life are separated; this is, as we have seen, one of the symptoms of the fragmentation of consciousness.

Another effect of the dominance of commodities is that the ability to acquire them is the chief determinant of the worth of individuals and families. Others gauge us by our success in the marketplace, and we gauge ourselves by how much money we earn relative to others. In many instances, a raise is needed more for the purpose of building self-esteem than for meeting financial obligations.

False hopes. There have been various attempts to respond to the dominance of commodities in modern society. Some feminists have argued that true equality for housewives can be achieved only by the state paying them a wage for their work. A less radical suggestion is to assess the market value of their housework in terms of the money earned by their husbands. Home economists estimate that the work of the average American housewife would presently have a fair market value of $32,000 per year. Armed with these figures, housewives would be in a strong position to bargain for more power in the marriage relationship. Although we do not negate marital equality as a biblical ideal, we believe that even this less radical suggestion is a compromise with the view that marriage is based on social exchange, both partners seeking to gain more from the relationship than they give up. We do not deny that this is the basis for many modern marriages; we believe, however, that it flies in the face of the biblical ideal of mutual submissiveness.

Some families wrongly believe that they can create a sense of community solely through consumption, for example, by watching television or going to a movie together. We do not deny that some activities of this nature can play a small role in producing a sense of community; we do deny, however, the naive assumption that the family that consumes together blooms together.

Alvin Toffler (1979) sees a bright future for the family in the technological society. He predicts that large segments of the work now being done outside the home will revert to the home. In view of the computer revolution, he thinks it is simply a matter of time before homes will be turned into electronic cottage industries. Reminded of the medieval guild, Toffler regards the home as a place where work will be done, where children will learn what work entails, and where apprentices will acquire a trade. While this delightful image has become a partial reality and a blessing for some families, given the multitude of unsolved social problems engendered by modernity, it is a false hope for most people.

A final false hope is the phenomenon of careerism. Over 50 percent of all married women in the United States work outside the home. It is unfortunate that some Christians take issue with the wife's working outside the home. We believe that the chief concern ought not to be her working but the adequacy of parental (both paternal and maternal) nurturing of and bonding with dependent children. We applaud the structural changes that many economic institutions are making by providing child care and/or adjusting work schedules for both men and women who have young families.

The phenomenon of careerism needs to be addressed as an identity problem for all adults. Careerism, whether only one or both spouses are involved, promotes the false equation of individual worth with career success. Careers, like money, can detract from the establishment and maintenance of intimate relationships within the family and society as a whole.

This modern age has brought about important changes that have made life easier for most people, yet consciousness is fragmented, communication is overly complex, the traditional community has broken down, and there is an obsession with commodities. The family is in a wretched predicament, since most attempts made to ameliorate the situation have proved to be false hopes. In the next chapter, we consider the impact of postmodernity and the further erosion of biblical family values. What is called for is radical change built on biblical principles.

20

CREATING A FAMILY-FRIENDLY SOCIETY

In the previous chapter, we considered the social environment of the contemporary family. By examining the effect of modernity on the family, we gained an understanding of why it is difficult to live according to biblical ideals. What is needed is a positive environment that strengthens family life.

In this chapter, we propose ideas for creating a healthy environment for family life. Fundamental changes must be made in two general areas: (1) families must make a radical response to modernity; and (2) community and societal structures must incorporate the biblical ideals of *koinōnia* and *shalom*.

Inadequate Responses to Modernity

The family has been greatly challenged and changed by modernity. We cannot simply succumb to the march of progress by adjusting the family lifestyle in accordance with innovations introduced into society. Rather, the challenges—fragmentation of consciousness, complexity of communication, disintegration of community, and dominance of commodities—make it imperative that we develop fresh insights into creating a positive environment in which the family can give glory to God and through their relationships show evidence of the salvation and freedom offered in Christ Jesus. This redemption, which enables us to meet the challenges of modernity, was purchased at a great cost and demands of us in turn a radical response.

It is important to keep in mind that redemption is an unfolding creative work of God in the lives of individuals, families, and societies. We need release from our bondage to commodities, which in turn will make reconstruction of community possible, which will provide an arena for revitalization of communication, which will eventually lead to reintegration of consciousness.

In contemplating the restoration of the family, we must have a general acquaintance with previous attempts that have proven to be false hopes. One general category consists of reactionary endeavors to return the family to an idealized past. These efforts are based on twin fallacies: (1) that the nineteenth and early twentieth centuries were a golden age of family life; and (2) that the traditional patriarchal family represents the biblical ideal for society today. This approach ignores the complexity of the issues. Its attempts to reconstitute the past overlook the dominance of commodities, disintegration of community, complexity of communication, and fragmentation of consciousness. Instead of stumbling into the pitfall of idealizing a particular cultural and temporal form of the family, we must recognize the forces of modernity and respond in a creative manner. As the subtitle of Rodney Clapp's influential book *Families at the Crossroads* (1993) profoundly reminds us, we must move "beyond traditional and modern options."

Postmodern thinking represents a second category of response. Rejecting both a return to the family of an idealized past and the certainty of modernist thinking, this approach embraces the potential good and usefulness of a variety of alternative family forms. Postmodernity represents a radical response to the excessive emphasis on rationalism found in modernity and sees truth as what is in the eye of the beholder, that is, what one experiences. Postmodernity can be a useful corrective to the certainties of modernity, which promote human reason as the basis for a universal human morality. However, in its extreme form, postmodernity also has the potential to undermine family values and structures because it takes an all-inclusive point of view.

Postmodernists do not regard the general laws of nature as grounds for accepting or rejecting ideas. Viewing reality as multilayered, they believe there are many ways of knowing, many flavors of truth. Although the Christian perspective is acknowledged as one possible view, many others are considered equally acceptable. Postmodernism sees danger in accepting one truth or morality over the myriad of other options; to do so is regarded as restrictive and intolerant.

A strict postmodernist view leaves little ground on which to evaluate the morality of one family form or process over against another since all alternatives are equally acceptable. The problem, of course, is that postmodernism cannot adequately respond to the number of abusive and harmful family systems that we know exist. We must stand for a morality that keeps the best interests of all family members in mind and recognizes the potential for evil as well as good in the various systems.

While modernity seeks to assess family life on the basis of scientific and naturalistic assumptions, postmodernity embraces every cultural form of family life. To avoid the modernist pitfall of idealizing a particular cultural and temporal form of the family, postmodernity goes to another extreme and dashes any hopes of finding criteria to assess family morality.

There is a reality that we as Christians uphold. We must, then, have a good understanding of both modern and postmodern thinking so that we can rightly evaluate their benefits and hazards. To embrace modernity or postmodernity uncritically leaves one in the position of choosing human perspectives over God's perspective. We believe that Christians must recognize the positive and the negative forces of both modernity and postmodernity and then formulate a biblically based response.

Toward a Radical Response to Modernity

Release from Bondage to Commodities

The first step toward a healthy environment is to free ourselves from the dominance of commodities (see table 10). One need not be a Marxist to acknowledge that capitalism dominates all of modern life. We are a people for whom the term *productivity* automatically connotes commodities. Clearly, the restoration of family life cannot be accomplished without liberation from the pervasive influence of our economic system.

Without a revolution to free us from our bondage to commodities, we will inevitably be pulled toward conformity to the system that promotes it. Technology, money, careers, and material growth have been spiritual forces in society. We cannot count on society to change by adopting our Christian values; rather, we must be willing to sacrifice and risk appearing foolish in resisting the power of worldly values.

Christian employers can take the lead. They can, for example, establish policies that provide ways for their employees to give priority to family relationships. One option is to offer flexible schedules for both mothers and fathers who desire to be with young children. A strategy that reverses the two-hundred-year-old trend of giving economic institutions priority over parenting would make a significant contribution. Such a program could involve concessions for difficult pregnancies, maternity/paternity leave, and child care on the premises. Excellent health care and disabil-

Table 10

Creating a Positive Family Environment

Challenges of Modernity	Christian Responses

Dominance of Commodities	Release from Bondage to Commodities
	    Employment programs that give priority to relationships
	    Family sacrifice of socioeconomic goals
	    Church support
	    Mutual empowerment (rather than social exchange) as the basis of
	        family relations

Disintegration of Community	Reconstruction of Community
	    Effective boundaries around the family
	    Emphasis on the inclusiveness of the family

Complexity of Communication	Revitalization of Communication
	    Family communication during shared activities
	    Development of family rituals

Fragmentation of Consciousness	Reintegration of Consciousness
	    Dependence on the beliefs and values provided by the church
	    Openness to people who are different
	    Service and witness to Christ

ity coverage as well as good retirement programs go a long way to help families at all stages. Such measures would inevitably cost the company in monetary profits, but gains would be realized in the strengthening of family relationships, in the employees' personal well-being, and in their loyalty to the company. Employees would benefit from the commitment, care, and empowering provided by their employers.

Similarly, Christian employers could make advancement opportunities available to employees who elect not to move their families to a new community. The average young American family moves every three years. It is inconceivable that the community support system that families need, especially during periods of stress and crisis, can develop within such a mobile society.

Commitments from employers to the welfare of their employees need corresponding commitments from employees to produce high-quality work. The present economic system, which makes the profit motive the major consideration, works directly against the development of any sense of loyalty or pride in the quality of work performed. A philosophy of productivity that pressures employees to put in long hours away from home also hurts family life. Christian employers must provide, in addition to salary, a context in which employees are given incentives and rewards for creative service and quality in this work rather than quantity.

Within the family itself, consumerism and careerism must be replaced by a focus on relationships and a sharing of resources with others. This would require, in addition to an attitude of mutual submissiveness, empowering, and servanthood, a willingness to forgo the socioeconomic status and security that we have been conditioned to achieve for ourselves and our families. A basic assumption of middle-class American society is that we are obligated to hand down to our children a certain social status and economic security. Family life is oriented toward this goal. A decision to sacrifice socioeconomic status in order to live more simply will be perceived as a threat to the existing order. The children involved, other family members, and friends may criticize someone who takes a low-paying job in order to spend more time with the family or to serve the community.

It is not an easy task to buck the system and make personal relationships and serving others higher priorities than making money. Our society respects people with high-paying jobs but seldom prizes those who choose relationships as their supreme goal. A typical case in point is parents who choose to stay home with their children out of dedication to the parenting role. These parents are often judged negatively for not being employed outside the home. A single parent who makes such a decision has the additional stigma of living at the poverty level. Our friend Lloyd, a father who was very proud of the fact that he stayed home to raise his three children, constantly faced the disdain of people who made comments such as, "Is that all you do?" and "Why don't you work?" The insinuation was that something had to be radically wrong with him for making such a choice. Needless to say, his rewards for committing himself to family goals had to come from his inner strength rather than from the reactions of the community.

The church must offer its blessing to any individual willing to make sacrifices. Such support and backing will minimize the impact of these sacrifices and protect the individual from the brute economic forces of modern society. Churches can offer sustenance to families that commit themselves to relational goals. They can also provide quality day care for parents who need to be employed outside the home. Further, the church should be sensitive to the special needs of families that have added emotional or financial burdens. The resources provided by a caring community can be of enormous benefit to families who are mentally and/or physically challenged, to those suffering from chronic mental and /or physical health problems, and to the elderly coping with frailty and death. Release from the bondage of commodities can also be achieved by refusing to think of marriage and family relationships in terms of social exchange. Unfortunately, what began as a theory to explain family power has become reified and is now reflected in daily life. Family members maneuver to ensure they gain more from a relationship than they give to it. Indeed, educational materials now advocate that family members consciously engage in a process of self-centered bargaining with one another. This model of family life, with its emphasis on commodities, needs to be replaced by the biblical model of mutual empowering and servanthood.

Reconstruction of Community

The typical nuclear family in the United States is a partial community at best. It is plundered on one side by the demands and intrusions of mass society and on the other by an individualism that has become increasingly self-centered. What is needed most is a recapturing of the biblical perspective of what it means to be a family. In this regard, two points that may at first appear to be paradoxical need to be made.

First, the reconstruction of family life needs to take place in a secure environment with effective boundaries. The family needs protection from the intrusion of a multitude of forces that are currently encroaching on it and sapping its vitality. We have already mentioned the necessity of protecting the family from economic institutions. A similar appeal could be made regarding governmental, educational, and even religious institutions. In trying to meet all the demands with which these institutions bombard it, the family is fractured. Family members need a central place where they can gather together and be nurtured in an environment of acceptance, intimacy, and mutual concern.

In the intimacy of the family community, we have a place where we can be naked and not ashamed (Gen. 2:25), a place where we can be who we are, free from all the demanding requirements of the outside world. Here is a place where family members can relax and be comfortable in a supportive and encouraging atmosphere. Here they do not have to hide but can be honest and real before the other members of the family.

Family life based on contract, law, and conditional love will not provide the refuge needed by weary individuals who have been out battling in the competitive world. However, family life based on covenant, grace, empowering, and intimacy provides a haven and place of refreshment. It embodies the New Testament concept of *koinōnia*. Indeed, any family grounded in the principle of mutual servanthood exemplifies the spirit of Christian community.

Second, the reconstruction of community can take place only when the concept of family is regarded as inclusive rather than exclusive. Whereas servanthood and commitment are meant to begin in the family, the Bible presents a moral imperative that will not permit us to be content with any form of amoral familism. Much in the teaching of Jesus suggests that loyalty is misplaced if it resides in the family only. In fact, on occasion Jesus speaks of leaving, dividing, and even hating one's family.

A case could be made that Jesus actually undermined the family. First, he chose the single life instead of marriage, and second, he taught a radical discipleship that sets people at odds with their family: "From now on five in one household will be divided, three against two and two against three; they will be divided: father against son and son against father, mother against daughter and daughter against mother, mother-in-law against her daughter-in-law and daughter-in-law against mother-in-law" (Luke 12:52–53).

In the wider context of Jesus's teaching, it would, of course, be a mistake to think that Jesus was against strong family life. The point that contemporary Christians should heed is that loyalty must transcend family and extend to the Christian community as a whole. Although Jesus did not dissolve the natural order of the family, he desired that we expand our circle of caring relationships beyond the family. His redefinition of the family bears repeating.

In response to being told that his mother and brothers were outside, Jesus responds, "Who are my mother and my brothers?" And looking around at those who sat around him, he said, "Here are my mother and my brothers. Whoever does the will of God is my brother and sister and mother" (Mark 3:34–35). Membership in the body of Christ binds all believers to one another as family.

Inclusiveness and strong family boundaries are paradoxical only in appearance. For only an internally strong family can adequately empower the Christian community, and it is in ministry to the Christian community that the family fulfills its mission. Likewise, only an internally strong church can empower the wider community of which it is a part, and it is in ministry to the wider community that the Christian community fulfills its mission.

Revitalization of Communication

Communication is vital in reconstructing our community life and reintegrating our consciousness. It should reflect both our individual uniqueness and our shared values and activities. Family communication must be liberated from overreliance on techniques and obsession with words. We suggest two ways in which this can be accomplished. First, communication must be contextualized rather than being a separate activity unto itself. Family members liberated from commodities and living in community will engage in many activities together. These activities provide a natural context in which to share and compare experiences and learn about one another's uniqueness.

Second, families can develop other ways of communicating. Creating or rediscovering family rituals for special occasions is an excellent way to break down barriers between people and symbolize family values. At

ARE YOU SURE THIS IS THE BEST WAY FOR US TO
RECONSTRUCT A SENSE OF COMMUNITY, ALBERT?

Christmastime, for example, it is important that the family de-emphasize commodities. Celebrating through symbolic acts, art, plays, song, and dance can create a solidarity in which all members participate. This intimate time of togetherness is also an opportunity for each family member to express personal uniqueness. Worshiping together as a family in a multigenerational Advent service is just one example.

Reintegration of Consciousness

Individuals are able to integrate their experiences only if a plausible system of beliefs and values is available to them. The isolated nuclear family is incapable of developing and maintaining such a system. The church can help here by providing a coherent structure of beliefs and values so that the family can achieve a reintegration of consciousness. Spiritual formation can also take place in the context of the worshiping community.

Another means of achieving reintegration is for the church and the family to be open rather than closed systems. They should have an expanded awareness of and concern for others who might be different in a variety of ways. The nuclear family can develop fictive kin—people who, though they are not blood relatives, are taken in as extended-family members. Church members should seize the opportunity to become world Christians rather than focusing only on the plight of their own group. The church should learn about Christians around the world and respond to them as brothers and sisters in Christ. Wherever there are poor and oppressed people, the Christian community should reach out with acts of compassion as well as with monetary and political support right in their own community. Also embracing those from different cultures and races and using their gifts and leadership enriches the worshiping community of faith.

The family and the church must strive together to manifest a love that is patient, kind, hopeful, and enduring. Only as witnesses to and exemplars of God's love can church and family enable their members to resist the alternatives presented by the world. The beliefs and value systems of the world are firmly entrenched, ready at all times to oppose the Word of God. This has always been the case; the postmodern situation is unique only in its specific challenges and the temptations of our particular time in history.

Through service and witness to Christ, we have a great hope of reintegrating our lives. We must keep in mind, however, that the disintegrating effects of modernity will be overcome only in part in the present world. Perfection will come in the future. "For we know only in part, and we prophesy only in part; but when the complete comes, the partial will come to an end. . . . For now we see in a mirror, dimly, but then we will see face to face. Now I know only in part; then I will know fully, even as I have been fully known" (1 Cor. 13:9–12).

The fact that change will be only partial and imperfect in our human social systems is no excuse for retreat from giving a radical response to modernity. It is essential that Christians neither deny nor be paralyzed by the serious disruptive effects of postmodernity. They must be both realistic and optimistic. Contemporary society is currently staggering from the blows of modernity and postmodernity. Within this context, the people of God must call for and serve as salt and light effecting the transformation of American culture. Nothing short of such a radical response will do.

Support Structures

Our focus in this chapter has been on how a biblical family structure can be created in the face of modern/postmodern society. But more is needed, for the family does not exist in a vacuum. It is vitally connected,

FIGURE 20 **Support Structures**

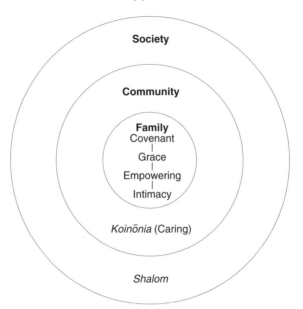

for better or for worse, with community and society. In chapter 1, we cited Rogerson's idea that the Old Testament Scriptures called for "structures of grace" in support of family life. "These 'structures of grace' transcended family ties, but were not intended to abolish the family; rather to support and sustain it. If the Old Testament says anything to us today, it is that we need to devise theologically driven 'structures of grace' appropriate to our situation that will sustain those aspects of family life which, from a Christian perspective, we deem to be most valuable, and which may be most under threat from the state and powerful interests" (1996, 42).

The family, the community, and society are interrelated support structures (see figure 20). We have suggested that a trinitarian theology and the four biblical relationship principles of covenant, grace, empowering, and intimacy are biblical themes on which family life should be patterned. We believe that the corresponding biblical ideals for community and society are *koinōnia* and *shalom*.

Extended Families

Families need caring communities in which they can find a sense of identity and social support. Wherever the extended family is the basic social unit, nuclear families have a built-in supportive community. The basic social unit is in large measure determined by the level of societal complexity (see figure 21). In hunting and gathering societies, where the level of societal complexity is low, the basic unit is the nuclear family. The nomadic lifestyle with its subsistence economy simply cannot support social units larger than nuclear families. Agriculture-based societies can support larger concentrations of people. In addition, ownership of land, tools, and animals fosters the development of larger family units. The extended family is the dominant social unit in virtually all agricultural economies.

The Industrial Revolution, which began in the eighteenth century, required that people concentrate in large cities. The high social and geographical mobility involved caused a decline in the extended-family system. The dominant social unit in highly industrial economies is the isolated nuclear family.

What about the future of family life in postindustrial societies? There are two lines of thought. The pessimistic view is that the fragile, isolated, nuclear-family system will become even weaker. Those making this prediction suggest alternatives such as nonmarital cohabitation and temporary marriages, which would provide the flexibility needed in contemporary society. The optimistic, utopian view is that the emerging electronic revolution will serve to reunite work and family life. As

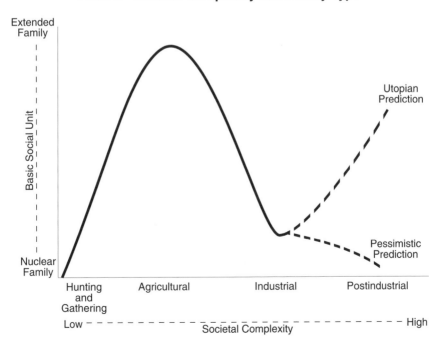

FIGURE 21 **Societal Complexity and Family Type**

parents work at home on computers and teach their children, they will develop closer relationships. Apprentices learning the work will come to live within the home for a while, and nonrelated extended families will emerge. Although some of these developments are occurring today, only a minority of families benefit.

Koinōnia in Communities

Great emphasis is placed on community today. There is little evidence, however, that most of what we call community is providing the care and support that members of isolated nuclear families require. We believe that the New Testament concept of *koinōnia* is an ideal solution. *Koinōnia* refers to a community in which Christians are united in identity and purpose. In the New Testament prototype, members of the church voluntarily shared all their possessions. They joined together in both *politeia* (civic life) and *oikonomia* (family life). *Koinōnia* came to represent a new type of community between the all-inclusive, impersonal state and the exclusive, blood-based household.

Robert Banks (1980, 42) argues that since the first Christian churches met in the houses of believers, the size of any one fellowship was limited to about twenty or thirty people. Significantly, recent social-science research has found that a typical individual is able to maintain intimate relationships with a maximum of twenty-five to thirty people. Those attempting to develop a larger network of intimate friendships find that they lack the time, the capacity, and the energy to keep each relationship growing and vital.

We believe that families need the support of *koinōnia*. Traditional societies are more successful in fostering communities of this type. Mass societies, which are characterized by impersonalization, urbanization, industrialization, rationalization, dehumanization, relativism, bureaucratization, and secularization, make *koinōnia* difficult. Churches that practice *koinōnia* emphasize small groups and the relational themes of covenant, grace, empowering, and intimacy. The members of these groups take time to know one another and care for one another in a variety of ways. They also reach out to the greater community and general society.

The Church

The primary locus of *koinōnia* is the church. In form the church should resemble a family; its members, after all, are described as the children of God and brothers and sisters in Christ. Paul writes, "And I will be your father, and you shall be my sons and daughters, says the Lord Almighty"

(2 Cor. 6:18); and "So then you are no longer strangers and aliens, but you are citizens with saints and also members of the household of God" (Eph. 2:19).

Peter Selby (1996, 164–65) points out that this

> understanding of the church as a "family" has its origin in the determination of the New Testament to speak of the human situation in terms of relationship, and of the transformation of that situation by the grace of Christ in terms of transformed relationship. . . . [We must] recognize that the language of family and kinship is there in relation to church not for the purpose of encouraging some of the attributes which we have seen to be associated with the concept of family in our time. Rather, it is there to emphasize the character of the transformation which has taken place in the relationships which human beings have to each other and to God in the light of God's grace.

The church, then, is to be a family to families and a source of identity and support for isolated nuclear families. Cameron Lee (1998, 13) argues that "rather than emphasize the effort to win the culture war over family values, the church should direct its attention to its primary function of embodying the reign of Christ in its corporate life [by addressing] the classical theological virtues of faith, hope, and love and their relationship to the identity of the church." The church needs to become a community of faith. In seeking to become a community of faith, the church must avoid the pitfall of exclusivity and the tendency to accept only certain types of people. It must welcome the widowed, the orphaned, the handicapped, the poor, the single person, and broken families.

The church can become a family to families if it follows several principles: (1) The church must be a place of diversity, including people of various social classes, races, ages, backgrounds, and religious experiences. It must avoid a unity based on similar images or subjective experiences, for true unity is based only in Jesus Christ. (2) The church needs to be a place where people can get to know one another intimately. Opportunities need to be provided for people to share their burdens and joys in small groups. (3) The church must create (or re-create) roles for all its members. Working together as multigenerational teams (young and old) to focus on spiritual formation, worship, hospitality, peace, justice, and so on is a good example of using a diversity of gifts (differentiation) to serve the whole body.

What can the church do to ensure that everyone feels at home? Single people need to be integrated into the body as mature equals who give of their talents to serve the church community. Married and adult singles should view one another as rich resources as they form relationships to deepen faith through fellowship and service. Mentor or spiritual friendships can be established to encourage and empower others in their growing faith. Women must be encouraged to freely exercise their gifts in the church. The gap between clergy and laity must be minimized so that the pastorate is not viewed as just another career. Thus clergy need to be willing to share the ministry, and parishioners need to accept responsibility and opportunities for ministry.

In short, the empowering process must be practiced in the church. Participatory Bible studies and sermons can focus on communal church life and ways in which to love, forgive, serve, and know one another. Further, individuals should be given the freedom to express their faith creatively. The decline in traditional symbols and language is an opportunity to explore and experiment with new worship expressions. We must be liberated from our fixation on words or the old ways of doing things, which has impoverished communication, and be more open to diverse ways of expressing God's love. As an inclusive family of families, the church should welcome worship and the arts, including the contributions of artists, poets, dramatists, and dancers.

Shalom in Society

Society is larger, more abstract, and more distant from the family than is community. It encompasses political, economic, educational, and religious institutions, each of which entails a complex hierarchy and roles regulated by an integrated set of norms. While it might be easy to picture how communities can be vital sources of support for family life, it is more difficult to imagine ways in which mass society and its institutions can be sources of support.

As noted in the previous chapter, modern society has had a severe negative impact on family life. There is, then, a desperate need to build a society in which institutions promote the well-being of the family. Perhaps more than anything else we need a fresh understanding of the role of society in family life as depicted in the Old Testament. In contrast to our modern individualistic emphasis, family members in ancient Israel held a strong sense of corporate solidarity and identity with the wider community. The family household was not separate from but was formed, shaped, and sustained by society. The Israelites learned to look at their "social world and the world of creation as a household, or a village of households, in which members took up residence and dwelt, nurtured and protected one another, and provided care for the poor person, who was the 'sibling' or the 'neighbor' to be loved as the self" (Perdue et al. 1997, 254).

The Old Testament concept of *shalom* characterized Israelite society. *Shalom* is usually translated "peace." However, this peace is to be understood not merely as absence of conflict but as the promotion of human welfare in both material and spiritual ways. *Shalom* denotes a culture characterized by justice and righteousness as well as peace. Such a society is poignantly described in Isaiah 11:6–8:

> The wolf shall live with the lamb,
>   the leopard shall lie down with
>   the kid,
> the calf and the lion and the
>   fatling together,
> and a little child shall lead
>   them.
> The cow and the bear shall graze,
>   their young shall lie down
>   together;
> and the lion shall eat straw like
>   the ox.
> The nursing child shall play over
>   the hole of the asp,
> and the weaned child shall put
>   its hand on the
>   adder's den.

Shalom is present when both peace and justice exist. Thus, chronic unemployment and oppression of the poor must be eliminated before *shalom* is present. One way to deal with poverty is to provide the poor with food, shelter, and clothing. Although this is all well and good, if the underlying causes of poverty are not dealt with, *shalom* is still not achieved. For *shalom* entails giving the poor a means of helping themselves. A society characterized by *shalom* does not treat people unjustly, nor does it disempower or patronize them. It takes action in terms of housing and work opportunities.

We shall know that *shalom* is present when social structures empower the family. When economic institutions demand time at the expense of one's family, *shalom* is not present. When corporations demand that their junior executives move every two years, making it impossible for the family to establish roots in a community, *shalom* is not present. When the unemployed are simply maintained and not afforded the opportunity to earn a living, *shalom* is not present. Where oppression and discrimination prevent minorities from gaining access to jobs, *shalom* is not present. When churches plan activities for every evening of the week, leaving no time for the family to be together, *shalom* is not present. Where the elderly are denied sufficient resources and health benefits, *shalom* is not present. When divorced women and their children live at poverty levels, while the standard of living of divorced men increases, *shalom* is not present. Where laws make it difficult for divorced fathers to maintain close relationships with their children, *shalom* is not present. Where a single mother must leave her children unattended while she works outside the home, *shalom* is not present. In these and a multitude of other ways, societal structures are damaging family life.

Hope for the Family and Society

Stable and strong family life can be achieved by recapturing and practicing the biblical concept of the family, which entails covenant love and manifestation of that love through grace, empowering, and intimacy. Although God intends for covenant love to be supremely experienced and exemplified in the context of the family, he also intends for it to be the basis for moral authority in society (M. Stackhouse 1997; Witte and Ellison 2005).

Moral authority is considered effective to the extent that a society is controlled by internal rather than external means. Our own society has of necessity come to depend increasingly on coercive political and economic means of control. The truth of this statement is demonstrated by the fact that social relationships are characterized more by contract than covenant, more by law than grace, by coercion than empowering, and by alienation than intimacy.

In this regard, it has been pointed out that the family is the cornerstone of the moral order of society. Therefore, any crisis we are currently experiencing in the moral order of society may well be due to the breakdown of the family. It is hardly an overstatement, then, to argue that the hope of society must begin with a recapturing of the biblical concept of family life. Covenant love, which is the basis of family life and manifests itself in sacrificial acts for others, is also necessary for the proper ordering of society. In fact, Jesus himself taught that we must be prepared to extend covenant love to our neighbor (Luke 10:25–37).

As we strive for covenant love first in our families and then in society, we would do well to keep in mind a powerful incident in the life of our Lord: "When Jesus saw his mother and the disciple whom he loved standing beside her, he said to his mother, 'Woman, here is your son.' Then he said to the disciple, 'Here is your mother.' And from that hour the disciple took her into his own home" (John 19:26–27). Our goal in relationships should be to so forgive, empower, and intimately know one another that Jesus would want to send his mother to be part of our family (Anderson 1985b, 23).

BIBLIOGRAPHY

Adams, B. 2004. Families and family study in international perspective. *Journal of Marriage and Family* 66:1076–88.

Adler-Baeder, F., and B. Higginbotham. 2004. Implications of remarriage and stepfamily formation for marriage education. *Family Relations: Interdisciplinary Journal of Applied Family Studies* 53:448–58.

Ahrons, C. 2004. *We're still family: What grown children have to say about their parents' divorce*. San Francisco: HarperCollins.

Ahrons, C., and R. Rodgers. 1987. *Divorced families: A multidisciplinary developmental view*. New York: Norton.

Airhart, P., and M. Bendroth. 1996. *Faith traditions and the family*. Louisville: Westminster John Knox.

Allen, E., D. Baucom, D. C. Burnett, N. Epstein, and L. Rankin-Esquer. 2001. Decision-making power, autonomy, and communication in remarried spouses compared with first-married spouses. *Family Relations* 50:326–34.

Amato, P. 2004. Tension between institutional and individual views of marriage. *Journal of Marriage and Family* 66:959–65.

Amato, P., and T. Afifi. 2006. Feeling caught between parents: Adult children's relations with parents and subjective well-being. *Journal of Marriage and Family* 68:222–35.

Amato, P., and J. Cheadle. 2005. The long reach of divorce: Divorce and child well-being across three generations. *Journal of Marriage and Family* 67:191–206.

Anderson, R. 1982. *On being human: Essays in theological anthropology*. Grand Rapids: Eerdmans.

Anderson, R. 1985a. Theology of the family. Fuller Theological Seminary. Unpublished manuscript.

Anderson, R. 1985b. The gospel of the family. Fuller Theological Seminary. Unpublished manuscript.

Anderson, R. 1990. *Christians who counsel: The vocation of holistic therapy.* Grand Rapids: Zondervan.

Anderson, R., and D. Guernsey. 1985. *On being family: Essays on a social theology of the family.* Grand Rapids: Eerdmans.

Armor, D. 2003. *Maximizing Intelligence.* New Brunswick, NJ: Transaction Publishers.

Arnett, J. 2000. Emerging adulthood: A theory of development from the late teens through the twenties. *American Psychologist* 55:469–80.

Aronson, S. 2004. The mother-infant relationship in single, cohabiting, and married families: A case for marriage? *Journal of Family Psychology* 18:5–18.

Astley, J. 1996. The role of the family in the formation and criticism of faith. In *The family in theological perspective*, ed. S. Barton, 187–202. Edinburgh: T&T Clark.

Aunola, K., and N. Jari-Erik. 2005. The role of parenting styles in children's problem behavior. *Child Development* 76:1144–59.

Bach, G., and P. Wyden. 1968. *The intimate enemy: How to fight fair in love and marriage.* New York: Morrow.

Balswick, J. K., et al. 1991. *The gift of gender.* Wheaton: Scripture.

Balswick, J. K., J. O. Balswick, B. Piper, and D. Piper. 2003. *Relationship-empowerment parenting: Building formative and fulfilling relationships with your children.* Grand Rapids: Baker.

Balswick, J. K., and B. Piper. 1995. *Life ties: Cultivating relationships that make life worth living.* Downers Grove, IL: InterVarsity.

Balswick, J. O. 1988. *The inexpressive male.* Lexington, MA: Lexington Books.

Balswick, J. O. 1992. *Men at the crossroads: Beyond traditional roles and modern options.* Downers Grove, IL: InterVarsity.

Balswick, J. O., and J. K. Balswick. 1987. A theological basis for family relationships. *Journal of Psychology and Christianity* 6.3:37–49.

Balswick, J. O., and J. K. Balswick. 1994. *Raging hormones: What to do when you suspect your teen might be sexually active.* Grand Rapids: Zondervan.

Balswick, J. O., and J. K. Balswick. 1995. *The dual-earner marriage: The elaborate balancing act.* Grand Rapids: Revell.

Balswick, J. O., and J. K. Balswick. 1997. *Families in pain: Working through the hurts.* Grand Rapids: Revell.

Balswick, J. O., and J. K. Balswick. 1999. *Authentic sexuality.* Downers Grove, IL: InterVarsity.

Balswick, J. O., and J. K. Balswick. 2006. *A model for marriage: Covenant, grace, empowering, and intimacy.* Downers Grove, IL: InterVarsity.

Balswick, J. O., P. King, and K. Reimer. 2005. *The reciprocating self: Human development in theological perspective.* Downers Grove, IL: InterVarsity.

Balswick, J. O., and C. Macrides. 1975. Parental stimulus for adolescent rebellion. *Adolescence* 10:253–66.

Bandura, A. 1977. *Social learning theory.* Englewood Cliffs, NJ: Prentice Hall.

Banks, R. 1980. *Paul's idea of community*. Grand Rapids: Eerdmans.

Barber, B., H. Stolz, and J. Olsen. 2005. Parental support, psychological control, and behavioral control: Assessing relevance across time, culture, and method. *Monographs of the Society for Research in Child Development* 70:1–137.

Barnhill, C. 2004. *The myth of the perfect mother: Rethinking the spirituality of women*. Grand Rapids: Baker.

Barton, S. 1996. Biblical hermeneutics and the family. In *The family in theological perspective*, ed. S. Barton, 3–23. Edinburgh: T&T Clark.

Baumrind, D. 1996. The discipline controversy revisited. *Family Relations* 45:405–14.

Baumrind, D. 2005. Taking a stand in a morally pluralistic society: Constructive obedience and responsible dissent in moral/character education. In *Conflict, contradiction, and contrarian elements in moral development and education*, ed. L. Nucci, 21–50. Mahwah, NJ: Erlbaum.

Baumrind, D., R. Larzelere, and P. Cowan. 2005. Ordinary physical punishment: Is it harmful? Comment of Gershoff (2002). *Psychological Bulletin* 128:580–89.

Beck-Gersheim, E. 2002. *Reinventing the family: In search of new lifestyles*. Malden, MA: Blackwell.

Bell, R. 1974. Contribution of human infants to caregiving and social interaction. In *The effect of the infant on its caregiver*, ed. M. Lewish and L. Rosenblum, 1–19. New York: Wiley.

Bell, S., and M. Ainsworth. 1972. Infant crying and maternal responsiveness. *Child Development* 43:1171–90.

Bellah, R., et al. 1985. *Habits of the heart: Individualism and commitment in American life*. Berkeley: University of California Press.

Ben, D. 1996. Exotic becomes erotic: A developmental theory of sexual orientation. *Psychological Review* 10:320–35.

Bengtson, V., R. Giarrusso, J. Mabry, and M. Silverstein. 2002. Solidarity, conflict, and ambivalence: Complimentary or competing perspectives on intergenerational relationships? *Journal of Marriage and the Family* 64:568–76.

Berger, B., and P. Berger. 1983. *The war over the family*. Garden City, NY: Doubleday.

Berger, P. 1983. From the crisis of religion to the crisis of secularity. In *Religion and America: Spiritual life in a secular age*, ed. M. Douglas and S. Tipton, 14–24. Boston: Beacon.

Berger, P., B. Berger, and H. Kellner. 1973. *The homeless mind: Modernization and consciousness*. New York: Random.

Bernhardt, P., J. Dabbs, J. Fielden, and C. Lutter. 1998. Testosterone changes during vicarious experiences of winning and losing among fans at sport events. *Physiology and Behavior* 65:59–62.

Billings, M. 1982. *Ideology and social psychology: Extremism, moderation and contradiction*. London: Blackwell.

Blalock, L., V. Tiller, and P. Monroe. 2004. "They get you out of courage": Persistent deep poverty among former welfare-reliant women. *Family Relations* 53:127–37.

Blankenhorn, D. 1995. *Fatherless America: Confronting our most urgent social problem*. New York: Basic Books.

Blanton, P. 2001. Marital therapy and marital power: Constructing narratives of sharing relational and positional power. *Contemporary Family Therapy: An International Journal* 23:295–308.

Blumberg, R. 1991. *Gender, family, and economy: The triple overlap*. Newbury Park, CA: Sage.

Bohannon, P., and H. Yahraes. 1979. Stepfathers as parents. In *Families today: A research sample on families and children*, ed. E. Corfman, 347–62. NIMH science monograph. Washington, DC: US Government Printing Office.

Borland, D. 1975. An alternative model of the wheel theory. *Family Coordinator* 24:289–92.

Borrowdale, A. 1996. Right relations: Forgiveness and family life. In *The family in theological perspective*, ed. S. Barton, 203–17. Edinburgh: T&T Clark.

Boss, P. 1987. Family stress. In *Handbook of marriage and the family*, ed. M. Sussman and S. Steinmetz, 695–723. New York: Plenum.

Boss, P. 2000. *Ambiguous loss: Learning to live with unresolved grief*. Cambridge, MA: Harvard University Press.

Bramlett, M., and W. D. Mosher. 2001. *First marriage dissolution, divorce, and remarriage. United States: Advanced data from vital and health statistics* (No. 323). Hyattsville, MD: National Center for Health Services.

Bray, J., and J. Kelly. 1998. *Stepfamilies*. New York: Broadway Books.

Bronfenbrenner, U. 1979. *The ecology of human development: Experiments by nature and by design*. Cambridge, MA: Harvard University Press.

Browning, D., M. Green, and J. Witte Jr. 2006. *Sex, marriage, and family in world religions*. New York: Columbia University Press.

Browning, D., B. Miller-McLemore, P. Couture, B. Lyon, and R. Franklin. 1997. *From culture wars to common ground: Religion and the American family debate*. Louisville: Westminster John Knox.

Browning, S. 1994. Treating stepfamilies: Alternatives to traditional family therapy. In *Stepparenting: Issues in theory, research, and practice*, ed. K. Pasley and M. Ihinger-Tallman, 175–98. Westport, CT: Greenwood.

Brubaker, T. 1985. *Later life families*. Newbury Park, CA: Sage.

Buehler, C. 2006. Parents and peers in relation to early adolescent problem behavior. *Journal of Marriage and Family* 68:109–24.

Bumpass, L., R. Raley, and J. Sweet. 1995. The changing character of stepfamilies: Implications of cohabitation and nonmarital childbearing. *Demography* 32:425–36.

Buss, D., ed. 2005. *The handbook of evolutionary psychology*. New York: Wiley.

Buunk, B., and W. Matsaers. 1999. The nature of the relationship between married individuals and former spouses and its impact on marital satisfaction. *Journal of Family Psychology* 13:165–74.

Canfield, K. 1996. *The heart of a father: How dads can shape the destiny of America.* Chicago: Northfield.

Carlson, M. 2006. Family structure, father involvement, and adolescent behavioral outcome. *Journal of Marriage and Family* 68:137–54.

Carr, D. 2004. Gender, preloss marital dependence, and older adults' adjustment to widowhood. *Journal of Marriage and Family* 66:220–35.

Carr, D. 2005. The psychological consequences of midlife men's social comparisons with their young adult sons. *Journal of Marriage and Family* 67:240–50.

Catherall, D. 2004. *Handbook of stress, trauma and the family.* Hove, East Sussex, UK: Brunner-Routledge.

Catherall, D. 2005. *Family stress: interventions for stress and trauma.* Hove, East Sussex, UK: Brunner-Routledge.

Chao, R. 1994. Beyond parental control and authoritarian parenting style: Understanding Chinese parenting through the cultural notion of training. *Child Development* 65:1111–19.

Chartier, M. 1978. Parenting: A theological model. *Journal of Psychology and Theology* 6:54–61.

Cherlin, A. 2004. The deinstitutionalization of American marriage. *Journal of Marriage and the Family* 66:848–61.

Chodorow, N. 1999. *The reproduction of mothering: Psychoanalysis and the sociology of gender.* Updated edition. Berkeley: University of California Press.

Clapp, R. 1993. *Families at the crossroads: Beyond traditional and modern options.* Downers Grove, IL: InterVarsity.

Clingempeel, W., E. Brand-Clingempeel. 2004. Pathogenic-conflict families and children: What we know, what we need to know. In *Handbook of contemporary families: Considering the past, contemplating the future,* ed. M. Coleman and L. Ganong, 244–61. Thousand Oaks, CA: Sage.

Cobb, N., J. Larson, and W. Watson. 2003. Development of the attitudes about romance and mate selection scale. *Family Relations* 52:222–31.

Colby, A., and W. Damon. 1995. The development of extraordinary moral commitment. In *Morality in everyday life: Developmental perspectives,* ed. M. Killen and D. Hart. 342–70. New York: Cambridge University Press.

Coltrane, S. 2004. Fathering: Paradoxes, contradictions, and dilemmas. In *Handbook of contemporary families: Considering the past, contemplating the future,* ed. M. Coleman and L. Ganong, 224–43. Thousand Oaks, CA: Sage.

Comiskey, A. 2003. *Strength in weakness: Overcoming sexual and relational brokenness.* Downers Grove, IL: InterVarsity.

Connidis, I. 2001. *Family ties and aging.* Thousand Oaks, CA: Sage.

Connidis, I., and J. McMullin. 2002. Sociological ambivalence and family ties: A critical perspective. *Journal of Marriage and the Family* 64:558–67.

Cooney, T., and K. Dunne. 2004. Intimate relationships in later life: Current realities, future prospects. In *Handbook of contemporary families: Considering the past, contemplating the future*, ed. M. Coleman and L. Ganong, 136–52. Thousand Oaks, CA: Sage.

Cooper, S. 1999. Historical analysis of the family. In *Handbook of marriage and family*, ed. M. Sussman, S. Steinmetz, and G. Peterson, 13–38. New York: Plenum.

Coontz, S. 2004. The world historical formation of marriage. *Journal of Marriage and the Family* 66:974–79.

Cordova, J., C. Gee, and L. Warren. 2005. Emotional skillfulness in marriage: Intimacy as a mediator of the relationship between emotional skillfulness and marital satisfaction. *Journal of Social and Clinical Psychology* 24:218–35.

Cowdery, R., and C. Knudson-Martin. 2005. The construction of motherhood: Tasks, relational connection, and gender equality. *Family Relations* 54:335–45.

Cox, H. 1984. *Religion in the secular city: Toward a postmodern theology.* New York: Simon and Schuster.

Crano, W., and J. Aronoff. 1978. A cross-cultural study of expressive and instrumental role complementarity in the family. *American Sociological Review* 43:463–71.

Crowder, C. 1996. The family reunion: Reflections on the eschatological imagination. In *The family in theological perspective*, ed. S. Barton, 329–44. Edinburgh: T&T Clark.

Damon, W. 2004. What is positive youth development? *The Annals of the American Academy of Political and Social Science* 59:13–24.

Danziger, S., E. Ananat, and K. Browning. 2004. Child care subsidies and the transition from welfare to work. *Family Relations* 56:635–54.

Davies, J. 1996. A preferential option for the family. In *The family in theological perspective*, ed. S. Barton, 219–36. Edinburgh: T&T Clark.

Deal, R. 2002. *The smart step-family: Seven steps to a healthy family.* Bloomington, MN: Bethany.

Deddo, G. 1999. *Karl Barth's theology of relationships: Trinitarian, christological, and human. Towards an ethic of the family.* New York: P. Lang.

DeGraff, P., and M. Kalmijn. 2006. Divorce motives in a period of rising divorce: Evidence from a Dutch life-history survey. *Journal of Family Issues* 27:483–505.

Demo, D. 1991. A sociological perspective on parent-adolescent disagreements. *New Directions for Child Development* 51:111–18.

Denton, M. 2004. Gender and marital decision making: Negotiating religious ideology and practice. *Social Forces* 82:1151–80.

Dodson, L., and J. Dickert. 2004. Girls' family labor in low-income households: A decade of qualitative research. *Journal of Marriage and Family* 66:318–32.

Doherty, W. 1997. *The intentional family.* Reading, MA: Addison-Wesley.

Dollahite, D., L. Marks, and M. Goodman. 2004. Families and religious beliefs, practices, and communities: Linkages in a diverse and dynamic cultural context. In *Handbook of contemporary families: Considering the past, contemplating the future*, ed. M. Coleman and L. Ganong, 411–31. Thousand Oaks, CA: Sage.

Doriani, D. 1996. The Puritans, sex, and pleasure. In *Christian perspectives on sexuality and gender*, ed. A. Thatcher and E. Stuart, 33–51. Grand Rapids: Eerdmans.

Douglas, S., and M. Michaels. 2004. *The mommy myth: The idealization of motherhood and how it has undermined all women*. New York: Free Press.

Dreikurs, R. 1991. *Children, the challenge: The classic work on improving parent-child relations*. Reprinted edition. New York: Plume.

Dunn, J. 1996. The household rules in the New Testament. In *The family in theological perspective*, ed. S. Barton, 43–63. Edinburgh: T&T Clark.

Eccles, J., and J. Gootman, 2002. *Community programs to promote youth development*. Washington, DC: National Academy Press.

Echlin, E. 1996. Ecology and the family. In *The family in theological perspective*, ed. S. Barton, 291–305. Edinburgh: T&T Clark.

Ehrensaft, D. 1990. *Parenting together: Men and women sharing the care of their children*. Champaign: University of Illinois Press.

Elkind, D. 1994. *Ties that stress: The new family imbalance*. Cambridge, MA: Harvard University Press.

Ellul, J. 1964. *The technological society*. New York: Random.

Ellul, J. 1976. *The ethics of freedom*. Grand Rapids: Eerdmans.

Erikson, E. 1963. *Childhood and society*. New York: Norton.

Erikson, E. 1968. *Identity: Youth and crisis*. New York: Norton.

Erikson, E. 1985. *The life cycle completed*. New York: Norton.

Fee, G. 2005. Male and female in the new creation: Galatians 3:26–29. In *Discovering biblical equality: Complementarity without hierarchy*, eds. R. Pierce, R. Groothus, and G. Fee, 172–85. Downers Grove, IL: InterVarsity.

Fenn, R. 1974. Toward a new sociology of religion. In *Religion American style*, ed. P. McNamara, 41–52. New York: Harper & Row.

Figley, C., and H. McCubbin. 1983. *Coping with catastrophe*. Vol. 2 of *Stress and the family*. New York: Brunner/Mazel.

Fisher, H. 1996. The origin of romantic love and human family life. *National Forum* 76:31–34.

Fisher, H. 2002. Lust, attraction, and attachment in mammalian reproduction. *Human Nature* 9:23–52.

Fisher, H., A. Aron, D. Mashek, H. Li, and L. Brown. 2002. Defining the brain systems of lust, romantic attraction, and attachment. *Achives of Sexual Behavior* 31:413–19.

Flavell, J. 1963. *The developmental psychology of Jean Piaget*. Princeton, NJ: Van Nostrand.

Flavell, J. 1985. *Cognitive development*. 2nd ed. Englewood Cliffs, NJ: Prentice Hall.

Fletcher, A. 1996. The family, marriage and the upbringing of children in Protestant England. In *The family in theological perspective*, ed. S. Barton, 107–28. Edinburgh: T&T Clark.

Flora, J., and C. Segrin. 2003. Relational well-being and perceptions of relational history in married and dating couples. *Journal of Social and Personal Relationships* 20:515–36.

Flurry, L., and A. Burns. 2005. Children's influence in purchase decisions: A social power theory approach. *Journal of Business Research* 58:593–601.

Ford, D., and R. Lerner. 1992. *Developmental systems theory: An integrative approach*. Newbury Park, CA: Sage.

Forward, S., and J. Torres. 1986. *Men who hate women and the women who love them*. New York: Bantam.

Fowers, B. J., K. H. Montel, and D. H. Olson. 1996. Predicting marital success for premarital couple types based on Prepare. *Journal of Marital and Family Therapy* 22:103–19.

Fowers, B. J., and D. Olson. 1992. Four types of premarital couples based on Prepare. *Journal of Family Psychology* 6:10–21.

Fowler, J. 1981. *Stages of faith*. New York: Harper & Row.

Fowler, J. 1992. Perspectives on the family from the standpoint of faith development theory. In *Christian perspectives on faith development*, ed. J. Astley and L. Francis, 320–26. Grand Rapids: Eerdmans.

Francis, J. 1996. Children and childhood in the New Testament. In *The family in theological perspective*, ed. S. Barton, 65–85. Edinburgh: T&T Clark.

Freud, S. 1949. *An outline of psychoanalysis*. New York: Norton.

Freud, S. 1954. *The origins of psychoanalysis: Sigmund Freud's letters*. New York: Basic.

Friedman, R., and J. Downey, eds. 2002. *Sexual orientation and psychoanalysis: Sexual science and clinical practice*. New York: Columbia University Press.

Fromm, E. 1956. *The art of loving*. New York: Harper & Row.

Furstenberg, F., and A. Cherlin. 1991. *Divided families: What happens to children when parents part*. Cambridge, MA: Harvard University Press.

Galambos, N., E. Barker, and D. Almeida. 2003. Parents do matter: Trajectories of change in externalizing and internalizing problems in early adolescence. *Child Development* 74:578–94.

Gallagher, S. 2003. *Evangelical identity and gendered family life*. New Brunswick, NJ: Rutgers University Press.

Galvin, K., C. Bylund, and B. Brommel. 2003. *Family communication: Cohesion and change*. 6th ed. Needham Heights, MA: Allyn & Bacon.

Gangel, K. 1977. Toward a biblical theology of marriage and family. *Journal of Psychology and Theology* 5:55–69, 150–62, 247–59, 318–31.

Ganong, L., and M. Coleman. 2004. *Stepfamily Relationships*. New York: Kluwer Academic/Plenum.

Garland, D., S. Richmond, and D. E. Garland. 1986. *Beyond companionship: Christians in marriage*. Philadelphia: Westminster.

Gershoff, E. 2002. Corporal punishment by parents and associated child behaviors and experiences: A meta-analytic and theoretical review. *Psychological Bulletin* 128:539–79.

Ghate, D., and N. Hazel. 2002. *Parenting in poor environments: Stress, support and coping*. London: Jessica Kingsley Publishers.

Gilley, S. 1996. Chesterton, Catholicism and the family. In *The family in theological perspective*, ed. S. Barton, 129–47. Edinburgh: T&T Clark.

Gilligan, C. 1982. *In a different voice: Psychological theory and women's development*. Cambridge, MA: Harvard University Press.

Gillis, J. 2004. Marriages of the mind. *Journal of Marriage and Family* 66:988–91.

Goode, W. 1963. *World revolution and family patterns*. New York: Free Press.

Gordon, R. 2005. The doom and gloom of divorce research: Comment on Wallerstein and Lewis (2004). *Psychoanalytic Psychology* 22:450–51.

Gottman, J. 1994. *What predicts divorce? The relationship between marital processes and marital outcomes*. Hillsdale, NJ: Erlbaum.

Gottman, J. 1995. *Why marriages succeed or fail*. New York: Simon and Schuster.

Gottman, J. 1999. *The marriages clinic: A scientifically based marital therapy*. New York: Norton.

Gottman, J., and J. DeClaire. 2001. *The relationship cure*. New York: Crown.

Greeff, A. P., and H. L. Malherbe. 2001. Intimacy and marital satisfaction in spouses. *Journal of Sex and Marital Therapy* 27:247–57.

Grenz, S. 2001. *The social God and the relational self: A trinitarian theology of the imago Dei*. Louisville: Westminster John Knox.

Grolnick, W. 2003. *The psychology of parental control: How well-meant parenting backfires*. Mahwah, NJ: Erlbaum.

Group for the Advancement of Psychiatry, Committee on Preventive Psychiatry. 1989. *Psychiatric prevention and the family life cycle*. New York: Brunner/Mazel.

Grunebaum, H. 1997. On romantic/erotic love. *Journal of Marital and Family Therapy* 23:295–307.

Hall, D., and F. Hall. 1980. Stress and the two career copule. In *Current concerns in occupational stress*, ed. C. Cooper and R. Payne, 243–66. New York: Wiley.

Hamner, T., and P. Turner. 1990. *Parenting in contemporary society*. Needham Heights, MA: Allyn and Bacon.

Hargrave, T., and S. Hanna. 1997. *The aging family: New visions in theory, practice and reality*. New York: Brunner/Mazel.

Harknett, K. 2006. The relationship between private safety nets and economic outcomes among single mothers. *Journal of Marriage and Family* 68:172–91.

Harrison, C. 1996. The silent majority: The family in patristic thought. In *The family in theological perspective*, ed. S. Barton, 87–105. Edinburgh: T&T Clark.

Hart, C., L. Newell, and S. Olsen. 2003. Parenting skills and social-communicative competence in childhood. In *Handbook of communication and social interaction skills*, ed. J. Greene and B. Burleson, 753–800. Mahwah, NJ: Erlbaum.

Harter, S. 1999. *The construction of self: A developmental perspective*. New York: Guilford.

Hauerwas, S. 1981. *A community of character: Toward a constructive Christian social ethic*. Notre Dame, IN: University of Notre Dame Press.

Hays, S. 2003. *Flat broke with children: Women in the age of welfare reform*. New York: Oxford University Press.

Hersey, P., and K. Blanchard. 1988. *Management of organizational behavior*. 4th ed. Englewood Cliffs, NJ: Prentice Hall.

Hetherington, E., M. Cox, and R. Cox. 1982. Effects of divorce on parents and children. In *Nontraditional families: Parenting and child development*, ed. M. Lamb, 233–88. Hillsdale, NJ: Erlbaum.

Hetherington, E. M., and J. Kelly. 2002. *For better or for worse: Divorce reconsidered*. New York: Norton.

Hiebert, P. 1978. Conversion, culture and cognitive categories. *Gospel in Context* 1:4.

Hill, R. 1949. *Families under stress*. New York: Harper & Row.

Ho, M., J. Rasheed, and M. Rasheed. 2004. *Family therapy with ethnic minorities*. 2nd ed. Thousand Oaks, CA: Sage.

Hobart, C. 1987. Parent-child relations in remarried families. *Journal of Family Issues* 8:259–77.

Hochschild, A. 1989. *The second shift*. New York: Viking.

Hocker, J., and W. Wilmot. 1985. *Interpersonal conflict*. Dubuque, IA: William C. Brown.

Hodgson, L. 1995. Adult grandchildren and their grandparents: The enduring bond. In *The ties of later life*, ed. J. Hendricks, 155–70. Amityville, NY: Baywood.

Holden, W., and G. Banez. 1996. Child-abuse potential and parenting stress within maltreating families. *Journal of Family Violence* 11:1–12.

Holman, T., J. Larson, and S. Harmer. 1994. The development and predictive validity of a new premarital assessment instrument: The preparation for marriage questionnaire. *Family Relations* 43:46–52.

Holman, T., et al. 2001. *Premarital predictions of marital quality or breakup*. New York: Plenum.

Holmes, T., and R. Rahe. 1967. The social readjustment rating scale. *Journal of Psychosomatic Research* 2:213–18.

Hsiung, R., and R. Bagozzi. 2003. Validating the relationship qualities of influence and persuasion with the family social relations model. *Human Communication Research* 29:81–110.

Hsu, A. 1997. *Singles at the crossroads*. Downers Grove, IL: InterVarsity.

Hughes, K. 2005. The adult children of divorce: Pure relationships and family values? *Journal of Sociology* 41:69–86.

Hunter, J. 1982. Subjectivization and the new evangelical theodicy. *Journal for the Scientific Study of Religion* 21:39–47.

Hunter, J. 1983. *American evangelicalism: Conservative religion and the quandary of modernity*. New Brunswick, NJ: Rutgers University Press.

Hynes, K., and M. Clarkberg. 2005. Women's employment patterns during early parenthood: A group-based trajectory analysis. *Journal of Marriage and Family* 67:222–39.

Jarrett, R., and S. Jefferson. 2004. Women's danger management strategies in an inner-city housing project. *Family Relations* 53:138–47.

Kaplan, L., C. Hennon, and L. Ade-Ridder. 1993. Splitting custody of children between parents: Impact on the sibling system. *Families in Society* 74:131–43.

Kerckhoff, A., and K. Davis. 1962. Value consensus and need complementarity in mate selection. *American Sociological Review* 27:295–303.

Kerr, J. 2005. Poverty rate continues to rise. *Pasadena Star-News*. August 31, sec. B.

Kettler, C., and T. Speidell, eds. 1990. *Incarnational ministry: The presence of Christ in church, society, and family*. Colorado Springs: Helmers and Howard.

Killen, M., and D. Hart, eds. 1999. *Morality in everyday life: Developmental perspectives*. New York: Cambridge University Press.

Kimball, G. 1997. Empowering parents: How to create family-friendly workplaces, schools, and governments. Unpublished manuscript.

King, P., and J. Furrow, 2004. Religion as a resource for positive youth development: Religion, social capital, and moral outcomes. *Developmental Psychology* 40:703–13.

King, P. E., and R. A. Mueller. 2004. Parents' influence on adolescent religiousness: Spiritual modeling and spiritual capital. *Marriage and Family: A Christian Journal* 6:413–25.

King, V. 2003. The legacy of a grandparent's divorce: Consequences for ties between grandparents and grandchildren. *Journal of Marriage and Family* 65:170–83.

Kinsey, A. 1948. *Sexual behavior in the human male*. Philadelphia: Saunders.

Kinsey, A. 1952. *Sexual behavior in the human female*. Philadelphia: Saunders.

Klein, M. 1932. *The psychoanalysis of childhood*. London: Hogarth.

Knower, S. 2003. "Acquiescence and adolescence": An unstable combination consideration of the good parent/bad parent phenomenon in stepfamilies. *Marriage and Family: A Christian Journal* 6:305–16.

Knox, D., and M. E. Zusman. 2001. Marrying a man with "baggage": Implications for second wives. *Journal of Divorce and Remarriage* 35:67–80.

Kohlberg, L. 1963. Moral development and identification. In *Child psychology: Sixty-second yearbook of the National Society for the Study of Education*, 277–332. Chicago: University of Chicago Press.

Kornhaber, A. 1996. *Contemporary grandparenting*. Thousand Oaks, CA: Sage.

Kübler-Ross, E. 1970. *On death and dying*. New York: Macmillan.

Lamb, M. 1997. *The role of the father in child development*. New York: Wiley.

Lamb, M., A. Frodi, C. Hwang, M. Frodi, and J. Steinberg. 1982. Mother- and father-infant interaction involving play and holding in traditional and nontraditional Swedish families. *Developmental Psychology* 18:215–21.

Larson, J., and R. Hickman. 2004. Are college marriage textbooks teaching students the premarital predictors of marital quality? *Family Relations* 53:385–92.

Larson, J., and T. Holman. 1994. Premarital predictors of marital quality and stability. *Family Relations* 43:228–37.

Larson, J., K. Newell, G. Topham, and S. Nichols. 2002. A review of three comprehensive premarital assessment questionnaires. *Journal of Marital and Family Therapy* 28:233–39.

Larzelere, R., and J. Merenda. 1994. The effectiveness of parental discipline for toddler misbehavior at different levels of child distress. *Family Relations* 43:480–88.

Laueau, A. 2003. *Unequal childhoods: Class, race, and family life*. Berkeley: University of California Press.

Lauer, R., J. Lauer, and S. Kerr. 1995. The long-term marriage: Perceptions of stability and satisfaction. In *The ties of later life*, ed. J. Hendricks, 35–41. Amityville, NY: Baywood.

Lee, C. 1998. *Beyond family values: A call to Christian virtue*. Downers Grove, IL: InterVarsity.

Leman, P. 2005. Authority and moral reason: Parenting style and children's perceptions of adult rule justifications. *International Journal of Behavioral Development* 29:165–270.

Lerner, R. 2002. *Concepts and theories of human development*. 3rd ed. Mahwah, NJ: Erlbaum.

Levine, J. 1997. *Working fathers: New strategies for balancing work and family*. Reading, MA: Addison-Wesley.

Levine, T., and F. Boster. 2001. The effects of power and message variables on compliance. *Communication Monographs* 68:28–46.

Levinson, D. 1978. *The seasons of a man's life*. New York: Knopf.

Levinson, D. 1996. *The seasons of a woman's life*. New York: Knopf.

Levy, M. 1966. *Modernization and the structure of societies*. Princeton, NJ: Princeton University Press.

Lewin, E. 2004. Does marriage have a future? *Journal of Marriage and Family* 66:1000–1006.

Lewis, C. S. 1958. *The allegory of love: A study of medieval tradition*. New York: Oxford University Press.

Lewis, C. S. 1960a. *The four loves*. New York: Harcourt Brace.

Lewis, C. S. 1960b. *Mere Christianity*. New York: Macmillan.

Lewis, R. 1972. A developmental framework for the analysis of premarital dyadic formation. *Family Process* 11:17–48.

Lewis, R., and G. Spanier. 1979. Theorizing about the quality and stability of marriage. In *Contemporary theories about the family*, ed. W. Burr et al., 269–94. New York: Free Press.

Lindsey, E., Y. Caldera, and M. Colwell. 2005. Correlates of coparenting during infancy. *Family Relations* 54:346–59.

Lindsey, L. 2005. *Gender roles: A sociological perspective*. 4th ed. Upper Saddle River, NJ: Prentice Hall.

Loades, A. 1996. Dympna revisited: Thinking about the sexual abuse of children. In *The family in theological perspective*, ed. S. Barton, 253–72. Edinburgh: T&T Clark.

Loder, J. 1998. *The logic of the Spirit: Human development in a theological perspective*. San Francisco: Jossey-Bass.

London, A., E. Scott, K. Edin, and V. Hunter. 2004. Welfare reform, work-family tradeoffs, and child well-being. *Family Relations* 53:148–58.

Long, J., and J. Mancini. 1990. Aging couples and the family system. In *Family relationships in later life*, ed. T. Brubaker, 2nd ed., 29–47. Newbury Park, CA: Sage.

Loughlin, G. 1996. The want of family in postmodernity. In *The family in theological perspective*, ed. S. Barton, 307–27. Edinburgh: T&T Clark.

Loving, T., K. Heffner, J. Keicolt-Glaser, R. Glaser, and W. Malarkey. 2004. Stress hormone changes and marital conflict: Spouses' relative power makes a difference. *Journal of Marriage and Family* 66:595–612.

Lucas, R. 2005. Time does not heal all wounds: A longitudinal study of reaction and adaptation to divorce. *Psychological Science* 16:945–50.

Maccoby, E. 1999. *The two sexes: growing up apart, coming together*. Cambridge, MA: Belknap Press.

MacKay, D. 1974. *The clockwork image*. Downers Grove, IL: InterVarsity.

Macklin, E. 1987. Nontraditional family forms. In *Handbook of marriage and the family*, ed. M. Sussman and S. Steinmetz, 317–53. New York: Plenum.

Manning, W. 2004. Children and the stability of cohabiting couples. *Journal of Marriage and the Family* 62:674–87.

Manning, W., and P. Smock. 2000. Swapping families? Serial parenting and economic support for children. *Journal of Marriage and the Family* 62:112–22.

Marcia, J. 1980. Identity in adolescence. In *Handbook of adolescent psychology*, ed. J. Adelson, 159–87. New York: Wiley.

Markman, H., S. Stanley, and S. Blumberg. 1994. *Fighting for your marriage*. San Francisco: Jossey-Bass.

Marquardt, E. 2005. *Between two worlds: The inner lives of children of divorce.* New York: Crown.

Marsiglio, W. 2004. When stepfathers claim stepchildren: A conceptual analysis. *Journal of Marriage and Family* 66:22–39.

Matson, F. 1966. *The broken image.* New York: Braziller.

Matthews, A. 2005. Toward reconciliation: Healing the schism. In *Discovering biblical equality: Complementarity without hierarchy*, ed. R. Pierce, R. Groothuis, and G. Fee, 494–507. Downers Grove, IL: InterVarsity Press.

Mauldon, J. 1992. Children's risks of experiencing divorce and remarriage: Do disabled children destabilize marriages? *Population Studies* 46:349–62.

May, R. 1969. *Love and will.* New York: Norton.

McBride, B., G. Brown, K. Bost, N. Shin, B. Vaughn, and B. Korth. 2005. Paternal identity, material gatekeeping, and father involvement. *Family Relations* 54:360–72.

McCullough, P., and S. Rutenberg. 1989. Launching children and moving on. In *The changing family life cycle: A framework for family therapy*, ed. E. Carter and M. McGoldrick, 287–309. Needham Heights, MA: Allyn & Bacon.

McHale, J., T. Khazan, and P. Erera. 2002. Coparenting in diverse family systems. In *Being and becoming a parent.* Vol. 3 of *Handbook of parenting*, ed. M. Dornstein, 75–107. Mahwah, NJ: Erlbaum.

McLain, R., and A. Weigert. 1979. Toward a phenomenological sociology of the family: A programmatic essay. In *Contemporary theories about the family*, ed. W. Burr et al., 2:160–205. New York: Free Press.

McLean, S. 1984. The language of covenant and a theology of the family. Paper presented at the Consultation on a Theology of the Family, Fuller Theological Seminary.

McLoyd, V., and J. Smith. 2002. Physical discipline and behavior problems in African American, European American, and Hispanic children: Emotional support as a moderator. *Journal of Marriage and Family* 64:40–53.

Mead, G. H. 1934. *Mind, self and society.* Chicago: University of Chicago Press.

Mead, M. 1928. *Coming of age in Samoa.* New York: Mentor.

Mead, M. 1935. *Growing up in New Guinea.* New York: New American Library.

Mintz, S. 2004. *Huck's raft: A history of American childhood.* Cambridge, MA: Harvard University Press.

Mott, S. 1982. *Biblical ethics and social change.* New York: Oxford University Press.

Mueller, M., B. Wilhelm, and G. Elder. 2002. Variations in grandparenting. *Research on Aging* 23:380–88.

Munsch, R. 1986. *Love you forever.* Scarborough, ON: Firefly.

Murray, C. 1995. *Losing ground: American social policy, 1950–1980.* New York: Basic Books.

Murstein, B. 1980. Mate selection in the 1970s. *Journal of Marriage and the Family* 42:777–92.

Nair, H., and A. Murray. 2005. Predictors of attachment security in preschool children from intact and divorced families. *Journal of Genetic Psychology* 16:245–63.

Ngee Sim, T., and L. Ping Ong. 2005. Parent physical punishment and child agression in a Singapore Chinese preschool sample. *Journal of Marriage and Family* 67:85–99.

The NICHD Early Child Care Research Network, ed. 2005. *Child care and family development: Results from the NICHD study of early child care and youth development.* New York: Guilford.

Nicolosi, J. 1997. *Reparative therapy of male homosexuality: A new clinical approach.* Northvale, NJ: Aronson.

Niebuhr, R. 1987. *The essential Reinhold Niebuhr: Selected essays and addresses.* Ed. McAfee Brown. New Haven: Yale University Press.

Nock, S. 1998. *Marriage in men's lives.* New York: Oxford University Press.

Noller, P., and J. Feeney. 2002. Communication, relationship concerns, and satisfaction in early marriage. In *Stability and change in relationships*, ed. A. Vangelisti, H. Reis, and M. Fitzpatrick, 129–55. New York: Cambridge University Press.

Nomaguchi, K., and M. Milkie. 2003. Costs and rewards of children: The effects of becoming a parent on adults' lives. *Journal of Marriage and Family* 65:356–74.

Norwood, R. 1985. *Women who love too much: When you keep wishing and hoping he'll change.* Los Angeles: J. P. Tarcher.

Oetzel, J., and S. Ting-Toomey. 2006. *The Sage handbook of conflict communication: Integrating theory, research, and practice.* Thousand Oaks, CA: Sage.

O'Hare, W. 1996. A new look at poverty in America. *Population Bulletin.* September.

Olson, D. 1988. Family types, family stress and family satisfaction: A family development perspective. In *Family transitions*, ed. C. Falicov, 55–80. New York: Guilford.

Olson, D. 1998. *Prepare/Enrich counselor's manual, version 2000.* Minneapolis: Life Innovations.

Olson, D., D. Sprenkle, and C. Russell. 1979. Circumplex model of marital and family systems: Cohesion and adaptability dimensions, family types, and clinical applications. *Family Process* 18:3–28.

Olthuis, J. 1975. *I pledge you my troth: A Christian view of marriage, family, friendship.* New York: Harper and Row.

Omoto, A., and H. Kurtzman, eds. 2005. *Sexual orientation and mental health: Examining identity and development in lesbian, gay, and bisexual people.* Washington, DC: American Psychological Association.

Orthner, D., H. Jones-Sampei, and S. Williamson. 2004. The resilience and strengths of low-income families. *Family Relations* 53:159–67.

Oshman, H., and M. Manosevitz. 1976. Father absence: Effects of step-fathers upon psychosocial development in males. *Developmental Psychology* 12:479–80.

Palisi, B. J., M. Orleans, D. Caddell, and B. Korn. 1991. Adjustment to stepfatherhood: The effects of marital history and relations with children. *Journal of Divorce and Remarriage* 14:89–106.

Papernow, P. 1993. *Becoming a stepfamily: Patterns of development in remarried families*. San Francisco: Jossey-Bass.

Parott, T., R. Giarrusso, and V. Bengtsen. 1994. What predicts conflict in parent-adult child relationships? Paper presented to the American Sociological Association, Los Angeles.

Parrott, L., and L. Parrott. 1996. *Saving your marriage before it starts: Seven questions to ask before (and after) you marry*. Grand Rapids: Zondervan.

Parsons, S. 1996. Feminism and the family. In *The family in theological perspective*, ed. S. Barton, 273–90. Edinburgh: T&T Clark.

Parsons, T., and R. Bales. 1955. *Family, socialization and interaction process*. Glencoe, IL: Free Press.

Patton, J., and B. Childs. 1988. *Christian marriage and family: Caring for our generations*. Nashville: Abingdon.

Payne, L. 1996. *The broken image: Restoring wholeness through healing prayer*. Grand Rapids: Baker.

Pellerin, L. 2005. Applying Baumrind's parenting typology to high schools: Toward a middle-range theory of authoritative socialization. *Social Science Research* 34:283–303.

Perdue, L., J. Blenkinsopp, J. Collins, and C. Meyers. 1997. *Families in ancient Israel*. Louisville: Westminster John Knox.

Peters, T., ed. 1996. *For the love of children: Genetic technology and the future of the family*. Louisville: Westminster John Knox.

Peterson, E. 2005. *Christ plays in ten thousand places: A conversation in spiritual theology*. Grand Rapids: Eerdmans.

Peterson, G., and B. Rollins. 1987. Parent-child socialization. In *Handbook of marriage and the family*, ed. M. Sussman and S. Steinmetz, 471–507. New York: Plenum.

Piaget, J. 1932. *The moral judgment of the child*. London: Kegan Paul, Trench, Trubner.

Pierce, R., R. Groothius, and G. Fee. 2005. *Discovering biblical equality: Complementarity without hierarchy*. Downers Grove, IL: InterVarsity.

Pillemer, K., and K. Luscher, eds. 2004. *Intergenerational ambivalences: New perspectives on parent-child relations in later life*. Amsterdam: Elsevier.

Piper, B., and J. K. Balswick. 1997. *Then they leave home: Parenting after the kids grow up*. Downers Grove, IL: InterVarsity.

Pipher, M. 1994. *Reviving Ophelia*. New York: Ballantine.

Pittman, F. 1997. Just in love. *Journal of Marital and Family Therapy* 23:309–12.

Plaskow, J. 1980. *Sex, sin and grace: Women's experience and the theologies of Reinhold Niebuhr and Paul Tillich*. Lanham, MD: University Press of America.

Ponzetti, J., and A. Folkrod. 1989. Grandchildren's perceptions of their relationships with their grandparents. *Child Study Journal* 19:41–50.

Popenoe, D., and B. Whitehead. 2003. *The state of our unions: The social health of marriage in America, 2003*. New Brunswick, NJ: National Marriage Project at Rutgers University.

Popenoe, D., and B. Whitehead. 2004. *The state of our unions: The social health of marriage in America, 2004*. New Brunswick, NJ: National Marriage Project at Rutgers University.

Popenoe, D., and B. Whitehead. 2005. *The state of our unions: The social health of marriage in America, 2005*. New Brunswick, NJ: National Marriage Project at Rutgers University.

Post, S. 1994. *Spheres of love: Toward a new ethics of the family*. Dallas: Southern Methodist University Press.

Pryor, J., and B. Rodgers. 2001. *Children in changing families: Life after parental separation*. Cambridge, MA: Blackwell.

Rabin, C. 1996. *Equal partners, good friends*. New York: Routledge.

Raley, S., M. Mattingly, and S. Bianchi. 2006. How dual are dual-income couples? Documenting change from 1970 to 2001. *Journal of Marriage and Family* 68:11–28.

Raschick, M., and B. Ingersoll-Dayton. 2004. The costs and rewards of caregiving among aging spouses and adult children. *Family Relations* 53:317–25.

Reaves, J. 2001. Do preschoolers and nannies turn kids into bullies? *Time* April 19.

Reimer, K. 2003. Committed to caring: Transformation in adolescent moral identity. *Applied Developmental Science* 7:129–37.

Reiss, I. 1960. Toward a sociology of the heterosexual love relationship. *Marriage and Family Living* 22:139–45.

Reiss, I. 1986. *Journey into sexuality: An exploratory voyage*. Englewood Cliffs, NJ: Prentice Hall.

Reynolds, J. 2005. In the face of conflict: Work-life conflict and desired work hour adjustment. *Journal of Marriage and Family* 68:109–24.

Riesman, D. 1950. *The lonely crowd*. New Haven: Yale University Press.

Roberts, M., and S. Powers. 1990. Adjusting chair timeout enforcement procedures for oppositional children. *Behavior Therapy* 21:257–71.

Roehilkepartain, E., P. King, L. Wagener, and P. Benson. 2005. *The handbook of spiritual development in childhood and adolescence*. Newbury Park, CA: Sage.

Rogerson, J. 1996. The family and structures of grace in the Old Testament. In *The family in theological perspective*, ed. S. Barton, 25–42. Edinburgh: T&T Clark.

Rogge, R., and T. Bradbury. 2002. Developing a multifaceted view of change in relationships. In *Stability and change in relationships*, ed. A. Vangelisti, H. Reis, and M. Fitzpatrick, 229–53. New York: Cambridge University Press.

Rollins, B., and D. Thomas. 1979. Parental support, power, and control techniques in the socialization of children. In *Contemporary theories about the family*, ed. W. Burr et al., 1:317–64. New York: Free Press.

Rosenfield, S. 1992. The costs of sharing: Wives' employment and husbands' mental health. *Journal of Health and Social Behavior* 33:213–25.

Rossi, A. 1984. Gender and parenthood. *American Sociological Review* 49:1–19.

Sabatelli, R., and S. Bartle-Haring. 2003. Family-of-origin experiences and adjustment in married couples. *Journal of Marriage and Family* 65:159–69.

Sanik, M., and T. Mauldin. 1986. Single versus two parent families: A comparison of mothers' time. *Family Relations* 35:53–56.

Santrock, J., R. Warshak, and G. Elliott. 1982. Social development and parent-child interaction in father-custody and stepmother families. In *Nontraditional families: Parenting and child development*, ed. M. Lamb, 289–314. Hillsdale, NJ: Erlbaum.

Sarkisian, N., and N. Gerstel. 2004. Explaining the gender gap in help to parents: The importance of employment. *Journal of Marriage and Family* 66:431–51.

Satir, V. 1983. *Conjoint family therapy*. 3rd ed. Palo Alto, CA: Science and Behavior Books.

Scheirer, M. 1983. Household structure among welfare families: Correlates and consequences. *Journal of Marriage and the Family* 45:761–71.

Schwartz, S., and G. Finley. 2005. Fathering in intact and divorced families: Ethic differences in retrospective reports. *Journal of Marriage and Family* 67:207–15.

Schwarz, P. 1994. *Peer marriage: How love between equals really works*. New York: Free Press.

Seeman, M. 1957. On the meaning of alienation. In *Sociological theory*, ed. L. Coser and B. Rosenberg, 401–14. New York: Macmillan.

Segrin, C., and J. Flora. 2005. *Family communication*. Mahwah, NJ: Erlbaum.

Segrin, C., M. Taylor, and J. Altman. 2005. Social cognitive mediators and relational outcomes associated with parental divorce. *Journal of Social and Personal Relationships* 22:361–77.

Seigler, A. 2005. Home is where the hurt is: Developmental consequences of domestic conflict and violence on children and adolescents. In *A handbook of divorce and custody: Forensic, developmental, and clinical perspectives*, ed. L. Gunsberg and P. Hymowitz, 61–80. Hillsdale, NJ: Analytic Press.

Selby, P. 1996. Is the church a family? In *The family in theological perspective*, ed. S. Barton, 151–68. Edinburgh: T&T Clark.

Shucksmith, J., L. Hendry, and A. Glendinning. 1995. Models of parenting: Implications for adolescent well-being within different types of family contexts. *Journal of Adolescence* 18:253–70.

Shulman, S., I. Seiffge-Krenke, F. Levy-Shiff, B. Fabian, and S. Rotenberg. 1995. Peer group and family relationships in early adolescence. *International Journal of Psychiatry* 30:573–90.

Shults, F. L. 2003. *Reforming theological anthropology: After the philosophical turn to relationality*. Grand Rapids: Eerdmans.

Sider, R. 2005. *Scandal of the evangelical conscience: Why are Christians living just like the rest of the world?* Grand Rapids: Baker.

Sillars, A., D. Canary, and M. Tafoya. 2004. Communication, conflict, and the quality of family relationships. In *Handbook of family communication*, ed. A. Vangelisti, 413–46. Mahwah, NJ: Erlbaum.

Skinner, B. F. 1953. *Science and human behavior*. New York: Macmillan.

Small, D. 1977. *Dwight Small talks about . . . divorce*. Glendale, CA: Regal.

Smedes, L. 1994. *Sex for Christians*. Revised ed. Grand Rapids: Eerdmans.

Smelser, N. 1973. Processes of social change. In *Sociology: An introduction*, ed. N. Smelser, 2nd ed., 671–728. New York: Wiley.

Smock, P. 2004. The wax and wane of marriage: Prospects for marriage in the 21st century. *Journal of Marriage and Family* 66:966–73.

Sobolewski, J., and V. King. 2005. The importance of the coparental relationship for nonresident father. *Journal of Marriage and Family* 67:1196–1212.

Stackhouse, J. 2005. *Finally feminist: A pragmatic Christian understanding of gender*. Grand Rapids: Baker.

Stackhouse, M. 1997. *Covenant and commitments: Faith, family, and economic life*. Louisville: Westminster John Knox.

Stassen, G., and D. Gushee. 2003. *Kingdom ethics: Following Jesus in contemporary context*. Downers Grove, IL: InterVarsity.

Steinberg, L., I. Blatt-Eisengard, and E. Cauffman. 2006. Patterns of competence and adjustment among adolescents from authoritative, authoritarian, indulgent, and neglectful homes. *Journal of Research on Adolescence* 16:47–58.

Stephen, T. 1994. Communication in the shifting context of intimacy: Marriage, meaning, and modernity. *Communication Theory* 4:191–218.

Stephens, L. 1996. Will Johnny see daddy this week? An empirical test of three theoretical perspectives of postdivorce contact. *Journal of Family Issues* 17:466–94.

Sternberg, R. 1986. A triangular theory of love. *Psychological Review* 93:119–35.

Storksen, I., E. Roysamb, T. Holmen, and K. Tambs. 2006. Adolescent adjustment and well-being: Effects of parental divorce and distress. *Scandinavian Journal of Psychology* 47:75–84.

Stright, A., and S. Bales. 2003. Coparenting quality: Contributions of child and parent characteristics. *Family Relations* 52:232–40.

Strohschein, L. 2005. Parental divorce and child mental health trajectories. *Journal of Marriage and Family* 67:1286–1300.

Struening, K. 2002. *New family values: Liberty, equality, diversity*. Lanham, MD: Rowman and Littlefield.

Suggate, A. 1996. Ideology, power and the family. In *The family in theological perspective*, ed. S. Barton, 237–52. Edinburgh: T&T Clark.

Swensen, C. 1994. Older individuals in the family. In *Handbook of developmental family psychology and psychopathology*, ed. L. L'Abate, 202–17. New York: Wiley.

Swisher, R., S. Sweet, and P. Moen. 2004. The family-friendly community and its life course fit for dual-earner couples. *Journal of Marriage and Family* 66:281–92.

Szinovacz, M. 1987. Family power. In *Handbook of marriage and the family*, ed. M. Sussman and S. Steinmetz, 651–93. New York: Plenum.

Tallman, I., and L. Gray. 1987. A theory of problem solving applied to families. Paper presented at the Theory-Methodological Workshop. National Council on Family Relations, Atlanta.

Thatcher, A. 1999. *Marriage after modernity: Christian marriage in postmodern times*. New York: New York University Press.

Thompson, M. J. 1996. *Family: The forming center. A vision of the role of family in spiritual direction*. Nashville: Upper Room.

Tipton, S., and J. Witte Jr. 2005. *Family transformed: Religion, values, and society in American life*. Washington, DC: Georgetown University Press.

Toffler, A. 1979. *The third wave*. New York: Morrow.

Townsend, L. L. 2000. *Pastoral care with stepfamilies: Mapping the wilderness*. St. Louis: Chalice.

Turner, L., and R. West. 2002. *Perspectives on family communication*. 2nd ed. Boston: McGraw-Hill.

Twenge, J., W. Campbell, and C. Foster. 2003. Parenthood and marital satisfaction: A meta-analytic review. *Journal of Marriage and Family* 65:574–83.

Udry, J. R. 1988. Biological predispositions and social control in adolescent sexual behavior. *American Sociological Review* 53:709–22.

Umberson, D., K. Williams, D. Powers, H. Liu, and B. Nedham. 2005. Stress in childhood and adulthood: Effects on marital quality over time. *Journal of Marriage and Family* 67:1332–47.

US Bureau of Labor Statistics. 2001, 2002. Washington, DC: US Department of Commerce, Economics, and Statistics Administration.

VanderValk, I., M. DeGoode, C. Maas, and W. Meeus. 2005. Family structure and problem behavior of adolescents and young adults: A growth-curve study. *Journal of Youth and Adolescence* 34:533–46.

Van Laningham, J., D. Johnson, and P. Amato. 2001. Marital happiness, marital duration, and the U-shaped curve: Evidence from a five-wave panel study. *Social Forces* 79:1313–41.

Van Leeuwen, M. 1990. *Gender and grace: Love, work and parenting in a changing world*. Downers Grove, IL: InterVarsity.

Van Leeuwen, M. 2002. *My brother's keeper: What the social sciences do (and don't) tell us about masculinity*. Downers Grove, IL: InterVarsity.

Van Leeuwen, M., A. Knoppers, M. Koch, D. Schuurman, and H. Sterk. 1993. *After Eden: Facing the challenge of gender reconciliation*. Grand Rapids: Eerdmans.

Vasey, M. 1996. The family and the liturgy. In *The family in theological perspective*, ed. S. Barton, 169–85. Edinburgh: T&T Clark.

Visher, E., and J. Visher. 1996. *How to win as a stepfamily*. New York: Brunner/Mazel.

Visher, E., and J. Visher. 1997. *Stepping together: Creating strong stepfamilies*. New York: Brunner/Mazel.

Volf, M. 1996. *Exclusion and embrace*. Nashville: Abingdon.

Volf, M. 1998. *After our likeness: The church as the image of the Trinity*. Grand Rapids: Eerdmans.

Vygotsky, L. 1986. *Thought and language*. Ed. and trans. E. Hafmann and G. Vakar. Cambridge, MA: MIT Press. Originally published in 1937.

Waite, L., and M. Gallagher. 2000. *The case for marriage: Why married people are happier, healthier and better off financially*. New York: Doubleday.

Waite, L., D. Browning, W. Doherty, M. Gallagher, Y. Law, and S. Stanley. 2002. *Does divorce make one happy? Findings from a study of unhappy marriages*. New York: Institute for American Values.

Walker, K., C. Pratt, and L. Eddy. 1995. Informal caregiving to aging family members. *Family Relations* 44:402–11.

Wallerstein, J. 1986. Women after divorce: Preliminary report from a ten-year follow-up. *American Journal of Orthopsychiatry* 56:65–76.

Wallerstein, J. 2005. Growing up in the divorced family. *Clinical Social Work Journal* 33:401–18.

Wallerstein, J., and S. Blakeslee. 1989. *Second chances: Men, women, and children a decade after divorce*. New York: Ticknor and Fields.

Wallerstein, J., and S. Blakeslee. 1995. *The good marriage: How and why love lasts*. New York: Houghton Mifflin.

Wallerstein, J., and S. Blakeslee. 2003. *What about the kids? Raising your children before, during, and after divorce*. New York: Hyperion.

Wallerstein, J., and J. Kelly. 1980. *Surviving the breakup: How children and parents cope with divorce*. New York: Basic Books.

Walter, J. 1979. *Sacred cows: Exploring contemporary idolatry*. Grand Rapids: Zondervan.

Warner, J. 2005. *Perfect madness: Motherhood in the age of anxiety*. New York: Penguin.

Watters, E., et al. 2003. *Urban tribes: A generation redefines friendship, family, and commitment*. New York: Bloomsbury.

Weitzman, I. 1986. *The divorce revolution: The unexpected social and economic consequences for women and children in America*. New York: Free Press.

Wilcox, B. 2004. *Soft patriarchs, new men: How Christianity shapes fathers and husbands*. Chicago: University of Chicago Press.

Wilcox, B., and S. Nock. 2006. What wives want. http://www.virginia.edu/insideuva/2006/04/happiness.html.

Willson, A., M. Kim, and G. Elder. 2003. Ambivalence in the relationship of adult children to aging parents and in-laws. *Journal of Marriage and Family* 65:1055–72.

Winner, L. 2005. *Real sex: The naked truth about chastity*. Grand Rapids: Brazos.

Winnicott, D. 1971. *Playing and reality*. London: Tavistock.

Witte, J., Jr. 1997. *From sacrament to contract: Marriage, religion, and law in the western tradition*. Louisville: Westminster John Knox.

Witte, J. Jr., and E. Ellison, eds. 2005. *Covenant marriage in comparative perspective*. Grand Rapids: Eerdmans.

Wolterstorff, N. 1980. *Education for responsible action*. Grand Rapids: Eerdmans.

Woo, H., and R. Raley. 2005. A small extension to "Costs and rewards of children: The effects of becoming a parent on adults' lives." *Journal of Marriage and Family* 67:216–21.

Yodanis, C. 2005. Divorce culture and marital gender equality: A cross-national study. *Gender and Society* 19:644–59.

Youngmin, S. 2003. The well-being of adolescents in households with no biological parents. *Journal of Marriage and Family* 65:894–909.

Yount, K. 2005. Women's family power and gender preference in Minya, Egypt. *Journal of Marriage and Family* 67:410–28.

Zipp, J., A. Prohaska, and M. Bemiller. 2004. Wives, husbands, and hidden power in marriage. *Journal of Family Issues* 25:933–58.

INDEX